Oil Crises of the 1970s and the Transformation of International Order

Oil Crises of the 1970s and the Transformation of International Order

Economy, Development, and Aid in Asia and Africa

Edited by Shigeru Akita

BLOOMSBURY ACADEMIC
LONDON • NEW YORK • OXFORD • NEW DELHI • SYDNEY

BLOOMSBURY ACADEMIC
Bloomsbury Publishing Plc
50 Bedford Square, London, WC1B 3DP, UK
1385 Broadway, New York, NY 10018, USA
29 Earlsfort Terrace, Dublin 2, Ireland

BLOOMSBURY, BLOOMSBURY ACADEMIC and the Diana logo are trademarks of
Bloomsbury Publishing Plc

First published in Great Britain 2024

A catalogue record for this book is available from the British Library.

A catalog record for this book is available from the Library of Congress.

ISBN:	HB:	978-1-3504-1380-1
	ePDF:	978-1-3504-1381-8
	eBook:	978-1-3504-1382-5

Typeset by RefineCatch Limited, Bungay, Suffolk

To find out more about our authors and books visit www.bloomsbury.com
and sign up for our newsletters.

Contents

Figures

Tables

Acknowledgments

This volume is the result of six international conferences: (1) the Workshop on "The International Order of Asia in the 1970s," held at National Chengchi University, Taipei, Taiwan (Republic of China) in December 2017; (2) the 12th Indo Japanese Dialogue on "The Transformation of International Economic Order of Asia in the 1970s," at the Centre for Historical Studies, Jawaharlal Nehru University, New Delhi, India in March 2019; (3) Zoom Workshop on "The Oil Crises and Transformation of International Economic Order of Asia in the 1970s," Osaka University, Japan, in September 2020; (4) the Workshop on the same topic at Center for Transcultural Studies, University of Heidelberg, Germany in November 2021; (5) the Workshop on the same topic at Cigur Center for Asian Studies, the Elliot School of International Affairs, George Washington University, Washington, DC, USA, in March 2022; and (6) a session of the 19th World Economic History Congress (WEHC) on the same topic at Campus Condorcet, Paris, France in July 2022.

These six Workshops/Conferences received financial support from research funds of the Japan Society for the Promotion of Sciences (JSPS): Scientific Research (A: 17H00933) to Osaka University, Japan for five years (2017–21), and from the Institute of Open and Transdisciplinary Research Initiative (OTRI), Osaka University. Due to the COVID-19 pandemic, we had to change the joint-research schedule in 2019–21 and extended it by one year to 2022. Fortunately, even during the pandemic, we could organize two international face-to-face workshops in Heidelberg and Washington, DC in 2021 and 2022. I would like to express special appreciation for the collaboration and the warm support of local hosts, Professor Harald Fuess (Heidelberg) and Professor Dane Kennedy (George Washington). In addition, I also thank the co-organizers of initial two workshops, Dr. Lee Weichen (Taipei), Professor Aditya Mukherjee (JNU), and a brilliant commentator (discussant) at WEHC Paris Panel, Professor Gopalan Balachandran, Graduate Institute of International and Development Studies (Geneva).

Shigeru Akita, Osaka, February 2023

Abbreviations

ADB	Asian Development Bank
API	American Petroleum Institute
Aramco	Arabian American Oil Company
BIS	Bank for International Settlements
BP	British Petroleum
BPC	Basrah Petroleum Company
bpd	barrels per day
CIA	Central Intelligence Agency (US)
CIEC	Conference on International Economic Cooperation
CMEA	Council for Mutual Economic Assistance (Comecon)
DAC	Development Assistance Committee (OECD)
ENSO	El Niño—Southern Oscillation
FRUS	*Foreign Relations of the United States*
GATT	General Agreement on Tariffs and Trade
IBRD	International Bank for Reconstruction and Development
IDA	International Development Association
IEA	International Energy Agency
IMF	International Monetary Fund
LDCs	Less Developed Countries
NATO	North Atlantic Treaty Organization
NIEO	New International Economic Order
NSC	National Security Council (US)
OAPEC	Organization of Arab Petroleum Exporting Countries
OAU	Organization of African Unity
OECD	Organization for Economic Cooperation and Development
OPEC	Organization of the Petroleum Exporting Countries
RDJTF	Rapid Deployment Joint Task Force
SALT	Strategic Arms Limitation Talks
SAMA	Saudi Arabian Monetary Agency
Shell	Royal Dutch/Shell
Tapline	Trans-Arabian Pipeline
UAE	United Arab Emirates
UNCTAD	UN Conference on Trade and Development
WB	World Bank

Introduction

Oil Crises of the 1970s and the Transformation of International Order: Economy, Development, and Aid in Asia and Africa

Shigeru Akita

This volume reconsiders the global significance of the 1970s by focusing on the impact of the energy crises on the international order during that decisive decade. It gives particular attention to the transformative effects of the oil crises of 1973–4 and 1979 on developing countries in Asia and Africa. Scholarship on the oil crises has focused on their effects on the advanced Western economies, but their impact on the non-Western world was in many respects even more profound. As contributors to this volume will show, the oil crises of the 1970s laid the groundwork for the restructuring of the international economic order and the so-called economic miracle in Asia.

1. The Cold War, Energy Crises, and Development in the 1970s

The 1970s have been interpreted as a turning point in the world economy, "a crucial transformative phase in the history of Western industrialized countries and, perhaps, even the world as a whole"[1] and as "a phase of transformative crisis" or "a transitional pivot."[2] Several crises and turning points occurred in the world economy during this decade. The "Bretton Woods system" in international finance collapsed in the early 1970s and the world shifted to a floating-rate currency system. Almost at the same time, high worldwide food prices led to a food crisis in developing countries. The fourth Arab-Israeli war in October 1973 triggered a quadrupling of oil prices and caused the first oil crisis of 1973/74. Several excellent works examine the impacts of the worldwide oil crises on the industrialized advanced countries.[3] One of the unique

---

[1] *Historical Social Research*, Special Issue: The Energy Crises of the 1970s. Anticipations and Reactions in the Industrialized World, No. 39 (2014) 4: 7–10.
[2] Daniel Sargent, "The Cold War and the international political economy in the 1970s," *Cold War History* 13(3) (2013): 394–5.
[3] Daniel Yergin, *The Prize: The Epic Quest for Oil, Money, and Power* (New York: Free Press, 1993); Fiona Venn, *The Oil Crisis* (London: Taylor & Francis, 2002); Elisabetta Bini, Giuliano Garavini, and Federico Romero (eds.), *Oil Shock: The 1973 Crisis and its Economic Legacy* (London: I.B. Tauris, 2016).

features of this volume is that it analyzes the divergent responses of non-European countries, particularly in Asia and Africa.

General histories of the second half of the twentieth century often center around the Cold War or the "East-West Divide."[4] As Daniel Sargent pointed out, "while the Cold War ought not to be reduced to a contest between productive systems, its economic dimensions remain, in general, understated in the historiography."[5] However, economic development in the developing countries did attract keen attention.[6] The United Nations declared the 1960s "the Decade of Development" in 1961 and established the United Nations Conference on Trade and Development (UNCTAD) in 1964. The problems of economic development were emerging as a "South-North Divide" following decolonization (political independence and the formation of nation-states) in the 1950s–60s. During these days, the United States and the Soviet Union competed for influence in the Third World by offering developmental aid.[7] In this post-colonial context, the Cold War was also about economic development. The two superpowers' global rivalry and their relations with developing countries are critical to a reconsideration of world history in the second half of the twentieth century.

The oil crises of the 1970s had a serious economic impact on the advanced Organisation for Economic Cooperation and Development (OECD) countries as well as the developing countries. With high inflation, rising commodity prices, and slowing economic growth (stagflation), the prospects for the Third World tended to arouse new fears and new hopes. In April 1974, at the initiative of the Group of 77 developing countries (G-77) and the Non-Aligned Movement, the UN General Assembly passed its resolution for a New International Economic Order (NIEO), which "included the creation of a world commodity system to bolster the prices of LDCs (Less Developed Countries) exports and the establishment of a 'special fund' to support the incomes of the poorest countries."[8] The NIEO symbolized a claim of economic decolonization mixed with development and drew inspiration from the recent show of unity and resolve by the Organization of the Petroleum Exporting Countries (OPEC).

Although they experienced the oil crises in the 1970s, some maritime Asian countries such as Taiwan, Korea, Hong Kong and Singapore, following on the Japanese experience, achieved high economic growth from the late 1970s. The World Bank (WB) called these regional economic developments the "East Asian Miracle"[9] in 1993. How did such a "miracle" of economic resurgence by East Asian countries occur,

---

[4] Melvyn Leffler and Odd Arne Westad (eds.), *The Cambridge History of the Cold War*, 3 vols (New York: Cambridge University Press, 2010).

[5] Sargent, "The Cold War and the international political economy in the 1970s," 393.

[6] Sara Lorenzini, *Global Development: A Cold War History* (Princeton: Princeton University Press, 2019).

[7] Nick Cullather, *The Hungry World: America's Cold War Battle against Poverty in India* (Cambridge, MA: Harvard University Press, 2010); David C. Engerman, *The Price of Aid: The Economic Cold War in India* (Cambridge, MA: Harvard University Press, 2018).

[8] Sargent, "The Cold War and the international political economy in the 1970s," 406; Dane Kennedy, chapter 3 of this book.

[9] The World Bank, *The East Asian Miracle: Economic Growth and Public Policy: A World Bank Policy Research Report* (New York: Oxford University Press, 1993).

despite the oil crises? This volume explores the causes and consequences of the so-called "East Asian Miracle" or the resurgence of East Asian economies in the 1970s.

2. The Cold War and Industrialization in East Asia—Two Sides of the Same Coin

Understanding the historical background of the "East Asian Miracle" requires an introduction to the recent historiography of Asian economic history, especially the transformation and resurgence of "intra-Asian trade" and its implication for the formation of an Asia-Pacific economy in the 1960s–70s.

Recent scholarship in Asian economic history offered a new perspective on an integrated Asian regional economy. The relationship between regional economy and the economies of the two hegemons (the British Empire and the United States) was shifting within a context of modern and post-colonial globalization. A prominent Japanese economic historian, Kaoru Sugihara, has revealed the formation and development of "intra-Asian trade" from the late nineteenth century to the 1970s, using trade statistics from various national archives.[10] Asian merchants played important roles in the formation of "intra-Asian trade," while East Asia occupied a unique and autonomous position within the world economy before the Second World War.

Notwithstanding the vast turmoil of the Second World War in Asia and the Pacific, as well as "political decolonization" and the spread of the Cold War in postwar South and East Asia, these elements of the international economic order survived into the 1950s, helping to explain the pattern of rapid economic growth in East and Southeast Asia in particular.[11]

Japan's high economic growth—the "Japanese miracle"—from the late 1950s drew on two interrelated international economic links or "divisions of labor," one with the United States, the other with Asian countries. The links with the US relied on different types of industrialization. The US concentrated on "capital and energy intensive industrialization," such as petrochemicals, the military (weapons) and aircraft industries, whereas Japan turned mainly to "labor intensive and resource-saving industrialization," like consumer goods, civilian electronics, and, eventually, automobiles and industrial machinery. Under the Cold War regime, the US became a fiscal-military state, increasing its military budget through the "military-industrial complex" while importing consumer goods from newly industrialized East Asian countries (Asian Newly Industrializing Economies, NIEs) including Japan. Dramatic expansion of the trans-Pacific export of industrial goods to the US was made possible by the containerization of Pacific-shipping routes (the so-called second transport revolution).

---

[10] Kaoru Sugihara, *Ajakan-Boueki no Keisei to Kouzo* [*The Formation and Sturcture of Intra-Asian Trade*] (Kyoto: Mineruva-shobo, 1991).
[11] Shigeru Akita and Nicholas J. White (eds.), *The International Order of Asia in the 1930s and 1950s*, (Farnham and Burlington: Ashgate, 2010).

At the same time, the Japanese miracle depended heavily on the revival and expansion of export markets in Asian countries. Under the Cold War regime, newly independent Southeast Asian countries became a crucial export market for Japanese labor-intensive consumer goods—first cotton goods and sundries, and then electronics. For postwar Japan, the Colombo Plan, the Commonwealth-centered regional cooperation network, offered the first opportunity to re-enter the international arena as a liberal economic power.[12] From the 1960s, Japan changed and upgraded industrial production to high-grade, capital-intensive industrial goods as it faced increasing competition from other East Asian industrializing countries. This process produced so-called "intra-Asian competition" among Asian developing countries. Japan frequently shifted some industrial sectors to neighboring East Asian countries. This "flying geese pattern economic development" in East Asia[13] accelerated and strengthened regional economic links in the western part of the Pacific-rim. These regional economic developments were closely related and supported by the "second energy revolution" or the shift of energy from coal to oil and natural gas as huge quantities of oil began to be imported from oil producing countries in the Middle East.

These two economic linkages, one with the United States, the other with Asian NIEs and Southeast Asian countries, resulted in an integrated trans-Pacific trading network, which evolved into the Asia-Pacific economy after the oil crises in the 1970s. The Cold War regime guaranteed the free trade trading order, especially the opening of US markets to Asian industrial goods. The rapid growth of East Asian industrial economies became a symbol of the superiority of the liberal capitalistic world, and it encouraged the United States to specialize in capital-energy intensive military-related industries. In this context, industrialization in East Asia and US militarization under the Cold War regime were complementary and looked like "two sides of the same coin."[14]

3. Emergence of the "Privatized International Currency System" and the "Oil Triangle"

In the realm of international finance, the early 1970s was the great turning point as the Bretton Woods system was replaced by a floating-rate currency system. By 1973, nearly all major currencies had begun to float, and the entire fixed-exchange system ended. A Japanese scholar, Masayuki Tadokoro, has called this financial transformation the

[12] S. Hatano, "Sengo-Ajia Gaiko no Rinen-keisei—'Chiikishugi' to 'Touzai no Kakehashi'" ("The formation of ideals for Japanese diplomacy in postwar Asia: 'regional order' and the 'bridge between East and West')", *Kokusai Mondai* 546, 2005; Shigeru Akita, Gerold Krozewski, and Shoichi Watanabe (eds.), *The Transformation of the International Order of Asia: Decolonization, the Cold War, and the Colombo Plan* (London and New York: Routledge, 2015).
[13] K. Akamatsu, "A historical pattern of economic growth in developing countries," *Developing Economies*, Preliminary Issue No. 1 (1962): 3–25.
[14] Kaoru Sugihara, *Sekaishi no nakano Higashi-Ajia no Kiseki* [*The East Asian Miracle in Global History*] (Nagoya: Nagoya University Press, 2020), 460.

creation of the "Privatized International Currency System."[15] This transformation greatly increased the role of private capital (investment) in development financing. The drastic increase of oil money, around $55 billion US dollars in 1974, was recycled not only through the Eurodollar market ($22.7 billion) but also as investments to the US ($12 billion) and the UK ($7.2 billion). The oil embargo strategy by the Organization of Arab Petroleum Exporting Countries (OAPEC) temporarily contributed to a rise in the relative price of primary products of developing countries against manufactured goods, which led to the "commodity boom" and seemed to pave a new way of development for the Global South.

However, most developing countries were suffering from balance of payments deficits, due to the combined effects of surging oil prices, the stagnation of the industrialized economies and heavy fluctuations of their commodity prices. Under these difficult circumstances, many developing countries grew more dependent on external assistance. Bilateral assistance (official development assistance, ODA) from the advanced countries failed to keep pace, leaving international institutions such as the WB group (International Development Association, IDA), the International Monetary Fund (IMF) and the Asian Development Bank (ADB) with a larger role in development financing. However, the bulk of the external lending to developing countries took place in the form of private-sector loans. Between 1973 and 1979, the share of private international lending allocated to developing countries increased from 6.3 percent to 23.3 percent.[16] The oil crises accelerated the shift from economic aid/ODA to private (non-official) investment.

On the other hand, Japan managed to continue to import a huge amount of oil from the Middle East even at very high prices from 1973 to the middle of the 1980s. How did Japan escape stagflation caused by the spike of oil price? Kaoru Sugihara explained the formation of an "oil triangle" as a macro-level feature of Japan's unique position in the world economy:

Between 1974 and 1985 the Japanese trade deficit with the Middle East amounted to 50,000 billion yen or an annual average of 4,133 billion yen ($17.3 billion at the 1985 exchange rate of 238.54 yen per dollar), while her trade surplus with the main western economies reached 53,000 billion yen or an annual average of 4,435 billion yen. Each of these bilateral trade imbalances was large enough to create concern. Both had to be settled in some way for the smooth running of global trade. The simplest way was to create a mechanism for the transfer of the Middle Eastern surplus to the advanced western economies. This was achieved in several ways. First, the Arab money flowed into the EC and the United States in large quantities.

---

[15] Masayuki Tadokoro, *Amerika wo koeta Doru* [*The Dollar that Transcended "US National Currency": Financial Globalization and International Currency Diplomacy*] Tokyo: Chuokoron-shinsha, 2002; Ikuto Yamaguchi, "Bretton Woods Taisei houkai go no Kokusai-Tuukaseido no Saihensei [Reconsidering the restructuring of the international financial system in the 1970s and early 80s," *Kokusai Seiji* [*International Relations*] 183 (March 2016): 73–86.
[16] Scott Newton, *The Global Economy 1944-2000* (London: Arnold, 2004), 118–19.

A source of a large proportion of this flow was the money the Japanese paid for the purchase of oil.[17]

The distinctive feature of the "oil triangle" is the relationship between trade (of oil and manufactured goods) and finance (money transfers), which connects financial history to the transnational movement of commodity goods. It resembles Asian triangular trade in the nineteenth century and highlights a distinctive pattern of industrialization in East Asian countries.

4. Developmentalism and Export-Oriented Industrialization

Under the Cold War regime, a unique and distinctive state-led economic development strategy was formed in non-communist East and Southeast Asia from the late 1950s to the middle of the 1980s. So-called developmentalism in these late-starter industrializing countries combined with the establishment of a political regime for crisis management under the Cold War.

Cold War developmentalism in East and Southeast Asia shared four main features: (1) the establishment of state institutions for economic development, administered by an American-style educated bureaucracy; (2) a fixed monetary exchange rate with the US dollars (dollar-pegged currency); (3) strong state intervention in capital-labor relations; and (4) enforcement of social policies for improving the standards of living of ordinary people. It aimed to create "nationalism" from above, under the strong leadership of newly formed nation-states.[18] The competition between the US and the Soviet Union (East-West Divide] from the late 1950s and early 1960s and the Cold War in East and Southeast Asia accelerated the diffusion of developmentalism in Asian countries.

In the 1960s, when an import-substitution industrialization (ISI) was heavily discussed at the UNCTAD, a completely different type of economic strategy for export-oriented industrialization (EOI) appeared and was being pursued intensively in East Asia. The pioneer of EOI had been Japan from the late 1950s, with strong support of the US under the Cold War regime. Over the next two decades, the NIEs in East Asia, such as Taiwan, South Korea, and Hong Kong, and Southeast Asian countries (the Association of Southeast Asian Nations, ASEAN) adopted export-oriented developmental policies that focused on consumer goods, modelled on the Japanese model of high-economic growth. This EOI might be classified into two types: a government-led Type I by utilizing ODA, and a private investment-induced Type II.

---

[17] Kaoru Sugihara, "Japan, the Middle East and world economy: a note on the oil triangle," Kaoru Sugihara and J. A. Allan (eds.), *Japan in the Contemporary Middle East* (London: Routledge, 1993), chapter 1, 8; Kaoru Sugihara, *Sekaishi no nakano Higashi-Ajia no Kiseki* [*The East Asian Miracle in Global History*], chapter 10, 513–37.

[18] For "developmentalism," see Akira Suehiro, "Kaihatu-Taisei ron" ["On developmentalism"], in Satoshi Nakano (ed.), *Iwanami-Kouza Tounan-Ajia Kin-Gendai shi 8: Betonamu-Senso no Jidai 1960–1975* [*Iwanami Lectures of Modern Southeast Asian History 8: The Age of Vietnamese War 1960–1975*] (Tokyo: Iwanami-publisher, 2011), 71–96.

The typical examples of Type I are Taiwan and South Korea, both of which received military and economic aid from the US. On the other hand, the models of Type II are Hong Kong (based more on local capital) and Singapore, based on the introduction of foreign capital.

Under the Cold War regime, Taiwan and South Korea adopted EOI policies at an earlier stage, by fully utilizing US military/economic aid for the purpose of economic development. As front-line countries of the Cold War in East Asia, both countries received a ripple effect from US military aid in the private sector, and their governments made intensive investment in infrastructure, such as the construction of power plants and transport networks. In Taiwan, US aid consisting of surplus raw cotton and wheat through Public Law 480 (PL480), offered as gifts, gave an indirect boost to the development of the textile industry and the sugar-refining industry. Taiwan could earn foreign currency through the export of its competitive primary sugar and rice products. The earned foreign currency was invested in labor-intensive consumer goods industries, which led to the development of export-oriented industries, thereby overcoming the limitation of the narrow domestic Taiwanese market.

Similarly in South Korea in the 1960s, President Park Chung-Hee, who had assumed dictatorial power by a military coup d'état in 1961, pursued economic development policies that stressed the export of consumer goods and formed an industrial foundation for further capital goods production. Both countries had labor-intensive EOI in common, under the strong leadership of national governments that took advantage of loans from the US and Japan (and later, ODA).

Hong Kong and Singapore adopted a different export-oriented industrialization strategy (Type II). In Hong Kong, the labor-intensive industrial production of consumer goods had started in the 1950s. This was made possible by combining the flight capital and technology from Shanghai with abundant cheap skilled labor. A distinguishing feature of Hong Kong's industrialization was the frequent change of leading industrial sectors, and the independent roles of private small and medium-sized businesses. The uniqueness of Hong Kong's economy lies in the laissez-faire free port and a "small government." The colonial government of Hong Kong, which avoided decolonization, adopted "positive non-interventionism" in executing economic policies.[19] In the 1960s, Hong Kong achieved dynamic industrial development as one of the Asian NIEs by means of small and medium-sized private businesses.

In contrast to Hong Kong, Southeast Asia's leading free trade port, Singapore, adopted government-supported EOI, inviting powerful foreign multinationals from the US, Europe (the Netherlands, Germany), and Japan, under the strong leadership of Lee Kuan Yew. The Singaporean government preferred overseas private investment to bilateral government-to-government aid or public money from international institutions like the WB. It exerted strong political leadership as a "big government" economy and created favorable investment conditions for foreign multinationals.

---

[19] Hideo Ohashi, "Hong Kong no Koukyo-Seisaku [Public policies in Hong Kong]", in Yukari Sawada (ed.), *Shokuminchi Hong Kong no Kouzou-henka* [*The Structural Transformation of Colonial Hong Kong*], (Tokyo: Institute of Asian Economies, 1997), chap.4.

The EOI developmental strategy was closely linked to external economic aid (developmental assistance) during the Cold War as the US and the Soviet Union competed to provide financial aid and technical assistance to the UNCTAD nations. In addition, international organizations such as the WB and the ADB offered multilateral aid to the developing countries.

How far did these industrial policies of the Asian NIEs complement the external economic aid offered by the US, Japan and international institutions? By utilizing both economic aid (ODA) and the inflow of private capital (oil money) through the international money markets, East Asian countries overcame the economic problems brought about by the energy crises in the 1970s. In order to consider how East Asian countries (Northeast and Southeast Asia) overcame the oil crises and began export-oriented industrialization (EOI) in the 1970s, we focus on the transformation of international development financing and the roles of economic aid and oil diplomacy.

In contrast to East Asia, the Indian case is a typical example of state-sponsored import-substitution industrialization (ISI) as an economic development strategy. After the exhaustion of its sterling balances in 1958, India, which was a leader of the Non-Aligned countries, acquired extensive economic aid from the multilateral Aid-India Consortium, including the US. By skillfully utilizing the Cold War regime for its own purposes, India received imported capital goods and technical assistance, both from Western capitalist countries and from Eastern socialist ones, which it used for its Five-Year Plans for economic development. India's industrialization under consecutive Five-Year Plans slowed down in the 1970s, but it was able to achieve self-sufficiency in food production through the "Green Revolution." We reconsider the background of India's agricultural development and the active role played by the WB group for the promotion of worldwide agricultural development in the 1970s. We thus analyze two fields of development of the Global South: industrialization and agricultural development or the "Green Revolution."

5. Bilateral Comparison and the Perspective of the 1980s

The original countries that the WB identified with the "East Asian Miracle" included four East Asian countries (Japan, Taiwan, Korea, and Hong Kong) and four Southeast Asian countries (Singapore, Thailand, Malaysia, and Indonesia). It excluded mainland China (the People's Republic of China, PRC) and India from its analysis. However, nowadays, the term commonly refers to the dynamic economic transformation across the Asia-Pacific region or even the Indo-Pacific.[20] This volume uses the term "East Asian Miracle" in this context to describe economic transformation across the region of Northeast and Southeast Asia. To evaluate the experiences of these Asian countries, we draw bilateral comparisons[21] between several Asian countries and two African case

[20] "Reinventing the Indo-Pacific," *The Economist*, January 7, 2023, 1–20.
[21] As for the methodology of bilateral comparison by the Californian School, see Roy Bin Wong, *China Transformed: Historical Change and the Limits of European Experience* (Ithaca: Cornell University Press, 1957).

studies (West Africa's Ghana, and East Africa's Kenya) and analyze the different development paths of East Asia, South Asia (India), and Africa under the impact of the two oil crises. The WB group, especially the International Development Association (IDA), greatly increased its commitments to Asian and African countries, by offering "social loans" for community development under the presidency of Robert McNamara.[22] To understand the linkages between the Cold War regime and the oil crises, it is also necessary to consider the socialist countries (the Eastern bloc), especially the second largest oil producer, the Soviet Union, and the potential oil-producing country of the PRC. This volume accordingly gives attention to the oil diplomacy of the United States and the Soviet Union toward their allied and satellite countries.

In 1979, high prices of oil doubled again due to the Iranian Islamic Revolution, causing the second oil crisis. Ikuto Yamaguchi points out that from the end of the 1970s to the early 1980s, three revolutionary changes occurred: the emergence of neoliberal political regimes in the UK with the Thatcher administration in 1979 and the US with the Reagan administration in 1981; the "Volcker Shock" in the US, which produced high interest rates that altered international financial policies in October 1979; and the second oil crisis following the Iranian Islamic Revolution in early 1979. These three upheavals sent the world economy into a tailspin and triggered debt crises in developing countries, especially in Latin America countries (Mexico and Brazil) after 1982. As Mark Metzler makes clear, these interlocking events led to a "Great Depression" comparable to what happened in the early 1930s. In a future project, we would like to explore the impact of the oil shock and "reverse" oil shock through the 1980s.

6. Structure of the Volume

This volume consists of three Parts: Part One, "Oil Diplomacy and the Cold War"; Part Two, "Transformation of International Development Financing"; and Part Three, "The Cold War, Development and Aid—Asia and Africa." As the titles of each part show, this book is an interdisciplinary collaborative work, involving international relations, diplomatic history, financial history, development economics, and Asian/African area studies, framed within the more recently emerging field of global history. The purpose of this book is to present new perspectives on the 1970s and to accelerate academic dialogues across disciplinary borders.

Part One, "Oil Diplomacy and the Cold War" examines geopolitics and oil diplomacy under the Cold War regime and their implications for the Third World project. The oil crises were closely related to American hegemonic geopolitics (Pax Americana) and its Cold War regime, which led to the entanglement of oil diplomacy. The Third World countries (the Global South) were involved in this oil diplomacy as active agents as well as passive recipients. Their reactions to the oil crises brought about the demise of the Third World and the transformation of the Third World project.

---

[22] Patrick Allan Sharma, *Robert McNamara's Other War: The World Bank and International Development*, (Philadelphia: University of Pennsylvania Press, 2017).

Chapter 1 (David Painter) is the foundational chapter of this volume. The oil crises coincided with the US withdrawal from Vietnam, a wave of revolutions in the Third World (Global South), the Soviet Union's achievement of nuclear parity with the United States, and the decline of US manufacturing due to increased competition from Western Europe and Japan. This convergence of events raised questions about US leadership of the Western alliance and heightened concerns about the dangers of Western dependence on resources in the Third World. It led some analysts to argue that the Soviet Union was winning the Cold War. Ironically, the oil crises also set in motion changes in the world energy economy that played an important and generally unappreciated role in the collapse of communism, the reassertion of US hegemony, and the end of the Cold War. Understanding the origins of the crises, their course, and their consequences is crucial to understanding the transformation of the international order in the late twentieth century.

Chapter 2 (Dane Kennedy) examines the intersection between the oil crises and the Third World project. What distinguished the Third World project was its pursuit of a shared set of political and economic objectives, including a determination to wrest control over natural resources from foreign interests, restructure the international economy on behalf of poorer developing countries, and avoid involvement in the Cold War struggle between the United States and the Soviet Union. The central thesis of this chapter is that the two oil crises were simultaneously a major manifestation of the Third World's efforts to achieve these ends and a set of events that undermined these aspirations and brought about the disintegration of the Third World project as a distinct and coherent force in international affairs. The actions taken by the OAPEC and OPEC during the 1973–4 oil crisis seemed at first to supply a case study of how the Third World could overcome a straitjacket of a Western-dominated international economic system. However, it also weakened the economies of many non-oil producing countries in Africa, Latin America, and elsewhere, exposing tensions between them and oil-producing countries. The oil crisis of 1979 accentuated these divisions and precipitated the great debt crisis that afflicted many developing countries in the 1980s. In the end, the two oil crises were instrumental in undermining the Third World project itself.

Chapter 3 (Hideki Kan) analyzes the role of the Asian Development Bank (ADB) in Asian economic development and its involvement in the Cold War regime during the first oil crisis. The ADB was established in November 1966. The United States and Japan played a central role in its establishment, and it symbolized "Japan–US cooperation." The growing need for concessional funds in the early 1970s led to the subsequent establishment of the Asian Development Fund (ADF) in June 1974, by integrating the two existing special funds. In protracted negotiations, the ADB leadership managed to attain the replenishment target ($2.15 billion) of the ADF, by adjusting to the differing interests between the US position and that of the other donor countries. Japan acted as an intermediary between the US and the other donors in favor of the ADB's position. The ADB leadership responded to the challenges of the oil shocks by establishing the concessional ADF and rapidly increasing agricultural loans to Southeast Asia. Between 1968 and 1976, the ADB approved $3.3 billion of loans, of which 52 percent went to the region and 19 percent ($646 million) went to the agricultural sector. Of this total, more than a quarter was on concessional terms to the poorest borrowing members. More than half of ADF lending went to the region and it was more heavily concentrated in agriculture at 34 percent. The Bank made significant contributions to laying the foundation of the development of Southeast Asia in the 1970s and thereafter.

Part Two, "Transformation of International Development Financing," deals with the impact of the oil crises on international finance and its transformation in the 1970s and the early 1980s. The end of the "Bretton Woods era" of international monetary history was closely connected to the oil crises. Vast quantities of oil money suddenly earned by oil-producing countries had to be channeled into, or recycled, in international money markets in order to stabilize the financial world. One result was the rapid expansion of the offshore markets, especially the Eurodollar market centered on the City of London, and the emergence of an Asian dollar-market in Singapore. The recycling of petrodollars was directly connected to the formation of the "oil triangle." Petrodollars also financed developing countries in the Global South, mainly in Latin America, through private Euro/American banks, which supplied capital for the credit booms of the late 1970s and early 1980s. In the aftermath of the second oil crisis, easy lending to Latin American developing countries collapsed and led to a succession of defaults by major countries such as Mexico, Brazil, and Argentina in the 1980s. We will consider the impact of these debt crises on the different policies pursued in East Asia and Latin America in future research.

Chapter 4 (Ikuto Yamaguchi) examines the transformation of international development finance during the 1970s in the context of the international economic disorder brought by the oil shocks and the emergence of the "privatized international currency system." Seeing oil price hikes, developing countries called for a New International Economic Order, insisting that oil surpluses should flow into public international finance to meet their development requirements. However, the bulk of oil surpluses was recycled through Western private financial markets, especially the Eurodollar market. High- and middle-income developing economies increasingly resorted to private capital flows, mainly through Eurodollar borrowing, to meet their external financing needs. The first oil shock thus opened the way toward "privatized" international development finance. The second oil shock changed the international development finance scene even further. Latin American countries fell into debt and default, whereas East Asian countries showed stable economic growth. In the 1970s, both depended on the Eurodollar borrowing for "bank debt-financed, government-led industrialization." South Korea's escape from the debt crisis showed that the Asia-Pacific economy was emerging, with capital flows and industrial markets of Japan and the US connected to East Asian export-oriented economies. The emergence of the Asia-Pacific economy showed how the international financial system began to be based on the "offshore US dollar system" under the financialization of US hegemony.

Malaysia and Singapore are among the countries in broader context of East Asia known to have achieved high economic growth. Chapter 5 (Shigeru Sato) focuses on the neglected role that oil has played in the economic development of both countries. Although the "oil curse" hypothesis posits a relationship between dependence on oil and low economic performance, the high state capacity of both countries enabled them to benefit economically from oil. In addition, the countries of East Asia did not achieve rapid economic growth solely on the strength of one country. "The East Asian oil triangle" is important in this regard, as it provided opportunities for complementary economic development. The East Asian oil triangle enabled intra-regional trade in oil and industrial goods, which supported the economic growth of both countries after the oil crises. The East Asia oil triangle also increased the financial capacity of countries in the region and provided opportunities for further development. As discussed above, this chapter seeks to identify the impact of oil on economic development in terms of both domestic and external factors.

Chapter 6 (Mark Metzler) focuses on credit/debt cycles and argues that the oil shocks were not exogenous to the international economic order. First, each oil shock was preceded by a US dollar shock. The "Nixon Shock" of August 1971 and the shift to floating rates in early 1973 ended the Bretton Woods system. Simultaneously, an era of low, stable international grain prices also ended with the inflationary food crisis of 1972–4. International commodity prices were therefore surging already before the October 1973 oil shock. These three shocks—dollar shock, food shock, oil shock— ended the postwar "petro-Fordist-Keynesian" system, and the period from 1973 to the beginning of the 1980s was accordingly a kind of in-between era. The imbalances caused by the first oil shock were temporarily "fixed" by a surge of Eurodollar lending to developing countries—the launching of the "offshore US dollar system" that continues to this day. In late 1978, a second dollar crisis created the monetary context of the second oil shock. Again international grain prices surged, but this time, instead of a credit "fix," severe monetary contraction in the United States triggered a wave of debt defaults. This was the beginning of the "Third World debt crisis" of the 1980s. In a macrohistorical view, the international lending boom of the 1970s resembles previous international lending booms such as that of the 1920s. The 1970s lending boom was in fact the fourth historic wave of international lending to developing countries and was followed by the fourth great international debt crisis.

Part Three, "The Cold War, Development and Aid—Asia and Africa," analyzes regional case studies of oil crises—East Asia (China), South Asia (India), and Africa (a bilateral comparison of Ghana and Kenya). China's position in the 1970s was unique in several ways. China had some features of a socialist Eastern-bloc country, others of a developing country (the Third World); it was an oil-producing country and an oil-consuming country; it had a state-controlled economy, but Deng Xioping was introducing market reforms by the end of the 1970s. China's responses to the oil crises confirms a unique feature of Asian NIEs in the 1970s. India is another example of how an Asian developing country responded to the oil crises. From the mid-1960s, India received a huge amount of economic aid from abroad, especially the US, to assist in its economic development. By the 1970s, the WB group and other international institutions supplanted the US as major donors. India's response to the oil crises highlights the changing role and relationship of donors and recipients in development aid. The contrasting responses of two African countries (Ghana and Kenya) to the oil crises provide further grounds for comparison. Compared to East Asian countries where the "East Asian Miracle" was starting to materialize, the record of economic development in Africa was modest and in most cases stagnant. What a comparison of the political economy of these two ex-British colonies in Africa reveals is an entanglement of exogenous and endogenous factors in their economic development and deterioration.

Chapter 7 (Kazushi Minami) analyzes how the oil crises of the 1970s and 1980s reshaped China's economic statecraft. It argues that the opportunity and the threat posed by the crises facilitated China's economic and political opening to the capitalist bloc through technological cooperation, which evolved from equipment trade to joint ventures. This cooperation, carried out in the spirit of "self-reliance," helped China avert a major economic crisis in the early 1980s and undergirded "Reform and Opening-Up." The worldwide euphoria about Chinese oil in the wake of the first oil shock soon dissipated, and Beijing's imports of oil equipment, initiated by Mao Zedong and accelerated by his successors, formed the economic basis for the new US–China relationship in the late 1970s. Then the energy crisis threatened China at the advent of the reform era. The remedy that Beijing prescribed after extensive internal debate was joint offshore ventures, which helped its economy hobble along despite the deteriorating energy balance.

Chapter 8 (Shigeru Akita) reconsiders the progress of the "Green Revolution" or agricultural development in India in the 1970s and its relation to the oil crises. How did India achieve de facto self-sufficiency in food production in the 1970s given the critical constraints of the oil crises? What factors contributed to the progress of agricultural development in the 1970s? In the middle of the 1960s, India managed to overcome a serious "food crisis" through international aid, especially US food-aid under PL480. During this crisis, the Indian government changed policy priorities regarding economic development, turning from heavy industrialization to agricultural development. However, in 1973–4, India faced another critical economic situation, which led to the shortage of the most basic requisite for agricultural development: chemical fertilizers, a major product of the petrochemical industries. How could the Indian government overcome this shortage given the global economic crisis? Akita pays attention to external economic aid to India, especially from the WB group (the IBRD and the IDA), led by its President Robert McNamara (1968–81). After the first oil crisis, India quickly overcame a critical economic situation by expanding exports and invisible income. India recorded an exceptionally favorable trade balance between 1974–5 and 1976–7. This steady growth was suddenly reversed in 1979 at the time of the second oil crisis. At this critical juncture, the Indian government skillfully took advantage of lending by the IMF and maintained a unique independent stance against the larger turn to "structural adjustment" policies.

Lastly, Chapter 9 (Gareth Austin) presents the contrasting experiences of two African countries, Ghana (West Africa) and Kenya (East Africa). The 1970s, especially 1973–5, saw a transition in the economic growth of post-independence sub-Saharan Africa from slow growth in the 1960s to stagnation and actual decline in the 1980s and early 1990s. There is a strong case for seeing this transition as accelerated, and in part caused, by the oil-price shock of 1973–4, consolidated by that of 1979. This chapter, however, is not about the oil shocks themselves. Taking them as "global" phenomena, it offers a comparative analysis of two African countries that possessed similar characteristics in several important respects, yet experienced contrasting economic outcomes. Ghana and Kenya were both beverage-crop exporters: the former began the period as the world's largest cocoa exporter; the latter was a major producer of coffee and tea. Neither (in this period) produced oil. Both therefore suffered from the oil price shocks, but had the countervailing advantage of the global boom in the prices of beverage crops, especially cocoa and coffee, of 1976–8. Over the decade as a whole, both countries saw net improvement in their net barter terms of trade. If differences between the terms of trade shifts cannot account for the contrast in outcomes, is it attributable to divergent policies, and if so, why were policies different? It is argued here that the proximate explanation for the divergence in economic performance is the difference in economic policies. The ultimate explanation for why the Kenyan economy weathered the storms of the 1970s whereas the Ghanaian economy succumbed to them resides in policy differences. The contrast in economic performance was mirrored by a contrast in (at least formal) political stability. Austin considers two major political economy explanations that were offered at the time, Colin Leys' (1978) dependency theory, and Robert Bates' (1981) rational-choice analysis. The general proposition is that national responses were more important than the global commodity price shocks themselves in determining the economic histories of African beverage-crop producers in the 1970s.

7. Implications for Current Energy Crises in the Twenty-First Century

Internationally, we are now seeing the highest inflation since the 1970s. The long continuation of quantitative easing and near-zero interest rates—a policy package that originated in Japan—was combined in the early 2020s with fiscal stimulus and supply shocks related to trade tensions and pandemic disruptions. Then came a war that has driven up energy and fertilizer prices four-fold or more. Central banks have begun to shift from easing to tightening, and comparisons with the 1970s economy abound in popular media. It is a timely moment for detailed historical investigation into that era.

The Russian invasion of Ukraine (leading to the Russo-Ukraine War) in February 2022 brought a full "world energy crisis" in global markets due to economic and financial sanctions against Russia by Western countries, the Russian response, and the destruction of the Nord Stream gas pipeline.[23] The 2020s thus bear uncanny resemblances to the 1970s (as well as dangerous differences). One notable resemblance is the drastic spike of fertilizer prices and disruption of Ukraine wheat and corn exports, exposing the poorest developing countries in the Global South to a new "food crisis." The World Bank's top official warned against such a crisis and made strong humanitarian appeals for international cooperation.[24] The present volume indeed seems timely, and we have much to learn from historical perspectives.

---

[23] See *The Economist*, March 26, 2022 (volume 442, number 9289), "Power play: the new age of energy and security."

[24] Juergen Voegele, Vice President for Sustainable Development at the World Bank, "Voices: How to manage the world's fertilizers to avoid a prolonged food crisis", July 22, 2022, http://blogs.worldbank.org/how-manage-worlds-fertilizera-avoid-prolonged-food-crisis?=cidECR_E_NewsletterWeekly_EN/EXT&deliveryName=DM149953 (accessed July 28, 2022); see also "Briefing the food crisis—after the pestilence, after the war…," *The Economist*, May 21, 2022.

Part One

Oil Diplomacy and the Cold War

1

The Oil Crises of the 1970s and the Global Cold War[1]

David S. Painter

The oil crises of the 1970s transformed the international order. Disruptions in oil production and distribution in 1973–4 and again in 1978–80 led to sharp increases in oil prices that affected economies around the world. The crises were also intricately intertwined with the Cold War and significantly shaped, and were shaped by, geopolitics in the 1970s and 1980s.[2] Coinciding with US withdrawal from Vietnam, a wave of revolutions in the Global South, the Soviet Union's achievement of nuclear parity with the United States, and the decline of US manufacturing as a result of increased competition from Western Europe and Japan, the oil crises raised questions about US leadership of the Western alliance, heightened concerns about the dangers of Western dependence on resources in the Global South, and led some analysts to argue that the Soviet Union was winning the Cold War.[3] Ironically, the crises also set in motion changes in the world economy that played important and generally unappreciated roles in the collapse of communism and the reassertion of US hegemony in the 1980s. Understanding the origins of the oil crises, their course, and their consequences is crucial to understanding the transformation of the international order in the late twentieth century.

1. Oil and the Cold War

Although Henry Kissinger wrote in his memoirs that the energy crisis "altered irrevocably the world as it has grown up in the postwar period," neither Kissinger nor most scholarly studies of the 1970s examine the interaction of the decade's oil crises

---

[1] I want to thank Shigeru Akita for his leadership of this project and my fellow participants. I am also grateful to Dane Kennedy, Victor McFarland, Duccio Basosi, Michael De Groot, Gregory Brew, and Marino Auffant for their comments on earlier versions of the chapter.
[2] David S. Painter, "Oil and geopolitics: the oil crises of the 1970s and the Cold War," *Historical Social Research* 39 (2014): 186–208.
[3] "Global South" is a social, economic, and political term used to refer to the less-developed countries of Asia, Africa, and Latin America. It is not a geographical concept; most countries included in the concept are located above the equator.

and the course of the Cold War.[4] Raymond Garthoff's *Détente and Confrontation* mentions oil only twice in 1,180 pages and there is surprisingly little on oil in Odd Arne Westad's *Global Cold War*, despite its focus on the Cold War in the Global South.[5] Edited works on Richard Nixon's foreign policy and the "global shock" of the 1970s lack essays on the oil crises, as do volumes 2 and 3 of the *Cambridge History of the Cold War*, which overlap the decade.[6] Daniel Sargent includes the oil crises as one of three factors leading to a transformation of US foreign policy during the decade, but he does not examine oil's role in the Cold War before the 1970s, arguing instead that the oil crises led to a shift away from Cold War concerns.[7]

Similarly, most studies of the decade's oil crises largely ignore the Cold War. Daniel Yergin's popular survey, Raymond Vernon's classic edited volume on the first oil shock, Steven A. Schneider's detailed study, and Fiona Venn's overview fail to place the crises in the larger geopolitical context of the Cold War.[8] Recent volumes on the 1973 oil shock and the "counter-shock" of the 1980s also largely neglect the Cold War, as do the chapters on the 1970s in Giuliano Garavini's magisterial history of the Organization of the Petroleum Exporting Countries (OPEC).[9] Recently, however, Michael De Groot and Fritz Bartel have argued that the oil crises had a direct and significant impact on the Cold War by raising the costs to the Soviet Union of maintaining a sphere of influence in Eastern Europe.[10]

---

[4] Henry Kissinger, *Years of Upheaval* (Boston, MA: Little, Brown and Company, 1982), 854. Kissinger discusses the oil crisis, the October War, and Cold War issues in separate chapters.

[5] Raymond Garthoff, *Détente and Confrontation: American-Soviet Relations from Nixon to Reagan*, rev. ed. (Washington, DC: Brookings Institution, 1994); Odd Arne Westad, *The Global Cold War: Third World Interventions and the Making of Our Times* (Cambridge: Cambridge University Press, 2005).

[6] Fredrik Logevall and Andrew Preston, eds., *Nixon in the World: American Foreign Relations, 1969–1977* (New York: Oxford University Press, 2008); Melvyn P. Leffler and Odd Arne Westad, eds., *The Cambridge History of the Cold War* (Cambridge: Cambridge University Press, 2010); Niall Ferguson, Charles S. Maier, Erez Manela, and Daniel J. Sargent, eds., *The Shock of the Global: The 1970s in Perspective* (Cambridge, MA: Harvard University Press, 2010). Although most of the chapters in *The Shock of the Global* mention the 1973–4 oil crisis and a few the second oil shock of 1978–80, there is no analysis of the origins or course of the crises, and discussion of their consequences is scattered throughout the volume.

[7] Daniel J. Sargent, *A Superpower Transformed: The Remaking of American Foreign Relations in the 1970s* (New York: Oxford University Press, 2015).

[8] Daniel Yergin, *The Prize: The Epic Quest for Oil, Money, and Power* (New York: Simon & Schuster, 1991); Raymond Vernon, ed., *The Oil Crisis* (New York: W.W. Norton, 1976); Steven A. Schneider, *The Oil Price Revolution* (Baltimore: Johns Hopkins University Press, 1983); Fiona Venn, *The Oil Crisis* (London: Longman, 2002).

[9] Elisabetta Bini, Giuliano Garavini, and Federico Romero, eds., *Oil Shock: The 1973 Crisis and Its Economic Legacy* (London: I.B. Tauris, 2016); Giuliano Garavini, *The Rise and Fall of OPEC in the Twentieth Century* (New York: Oxford University Press, 2019); Duccio Basosi, Giuliano Garavini, and Massimiliano Trentin, eds., *Counter-Shock: The Oil Counter-Revolution of the 1980s* (London: I.B. Tauris, 2018).

[10] Michael De Groot, "The Soviet Union, CMEA, and the Energy Crisis of the 1970s," *Journal of Cold War Studies* 22 (Fall 2020): 4–30; De Groot, "Global Reaganomics: Budget Deficits, Capital Flows, and the International Economy," in *The Reagan Moment: America and the World in the 1980s*, ed. Jonathan R. Hunt and Simon Miles (Ithaca, NY: Cornell University Press, 2021), 84–102; Fritz Bartel, *The Triumph of Broken Promises: The End of the Cold War and the Rise of Neoliberalism* (Cambridge, MA: Harvard University Press, 2022.

2. Oil and World Power

One of the main features of the geopolitics of oil in the twentieth century was that, with two exceptions—the United States and the Soviet Union—none of the great powers possessed significant oil reserves within their borders. The uneven distribution of world oil resources had a significant impact on the balance of power.[11] Oil-powered platforms emerged during World War I, became central to military power during World War II, and remained important in the postwar era despite the development of nuclear weapons and ballistic missiles. Nuclear-powered warships (mainly aircraft carriers and submarines) were developed in the 1950s, but most of the world's warships still relied on oil, as did aircraft, armor, and mechanized transport, and each new generation of weapons consumed more oil than its predecessors used.[12]

In addition to being essential to military power, oil played an increasingly important role in the economies of the industrial countries during the twentieth century. Oil became the main fuel used in land and sea transport as well as the only fuel for air transport, challenged coal as the main source of energy for industry, and played an important role in heating and electricity generation. Oil-powered machinery became crucial to modern agriculture, and oil and natural gas became important feedstocks for fertilizers and pesticides. Already almost one-fifth of US energy consumption by 1925, oil accounted for around one-third of US energy use by World War II. Outside the United States, oil was reserved mainly for the military and accounted for around 10 percent of energy consumption in Western Europe and Japan before World War II.[13]

Oil's economic importance increased after World War II as the United States intensified its embrace of patterns of socioeconomic organization premised on high levels of oil use, and Western Europe and Japan made the transition from coal to oil as their main source of energy. Between 1950 and 1972, total world energy consumption more than tripled. Oil accounted for a large share of this increase, rising from 29 percent of world energy consumption in 1950 to 46 percent in 1972. By 1972, oil accounted for 45.6 percent of US energy consumption, 59.6 percent of west European energy consumption, and 73 percent of Japanese energy consumption. Almost all the oil used by Western Europe and Japan was imported. The Soviet Union moved more slowly, but by 1973, oil supplied around 39 percent of Soviet energy consumption.[14]

[11] Anand Toprani, "Hydrocarbons and Hegemony," *Joint Forces Quarterly* 102 (3rd Quarter 2021), 29–36; Toprani, "A Primer on the Geopolitics of Oil," *War on the Rocks*, January 17, 2019, https://warontherocks.com/2019/01/a-primer-on-the-geopolitics-of-oil.

[12] W. G. Jensen, "The Importance of Energy in the First and Second World Wars," *Historical Journal* 11 (1968), 538–54; Anand Toprani, *Oil and the Great Powers: Britain and Germany, 1914–1945* (New York: Oxford University Press, 2019).

[13] J.R. McNeill, *Something New Under the Sun: An Environmental History of the Twentieth-Century World* (New York: W.W. Norton, 2000), 297–31; Schneider, *Oil Price Revolution*, 520–2.

[14] Joel Darmstadter and Hans H. Landsberg, "The Economic Background," in *The Oil Crisis*, ed. Raymond Vernon, 16–22; Schneider, *Oil Price Revolution*, 49–75; Marshall I. Goldman, *The Enigma of Soviet Petroleum: Half-Empty or Half-Full?* (London: George Allen & Unwin, 1980), 52–4. Oil did not displace coal. Coal production and consumption continued to increase, but oil production grew faster and its share of global energy consumption increased.

Oil fueled American power and prosperity during the twentieth century, and possession of ample domestic oil supplies and control over access to foreign oil reserves were significant, but often overlooked, elements in the power position of the United States.[15] The United States was the world's leading oil producer for the first three-quarters of the twentieth century and remained in the top three for the rest of the century. US oil fields accounted for slightly less than two-thirds of world oil production in 1920, around two-thirds in 1945, 23.5 percent in 1970, and 18.7 percent in 1973.[16] In addition to a thriving domestic oil industry, five of the seven great oil corporations (the so-called Seven Sisters) that dominated the international oil industry from the 1920s to the 1970s were US companies.[17]

US domestic reserves and the ability to ensure access to foreign supplies helped the United States and its allies win two world wars. During the Cold War, US policy focused on containing the Soviet Union, ending destructive political, economic, and military competition among the core capitalist states, mitigating class conflict within the capitalist core by promoting economic growth, and retaining access to the raw materials, markets, and labor of the Global South in an era of decolonization and national liberation. Control of oil was central to these efforts. To maintain access to oil in the Middle East, Latin America, and elsewhere in the Global South the United States sought to contain Soviet influence and opposed economic nationalism.[18]

Oil was also an important and often overlooked element in the power position of the Soviet Union. The Russian Empire was the world's leading oil producer for a few years around the turn of the century, and despite some setbacks, the Soviet Union was among the top three producers until its demise. Years of revolution and war between 1905 and 1921 caused a dramatic decline in production, but by 1930 production recovered and Soviet oil re-entered export markets for a few years. Oil helped fuel industrialization in the 1930s, and production was sufficient for wartime needs, though lack of refinery capacity and advanced technology left the Soviets dependent on US lend-lease aid for specialty products. Overproduction, competing demands for manpower and materials, and wartime damage caused a sharp drop in production, but

---

[15] David S. Painter, "Oil and the American Century," *Journal of American History* 99 (June 2012), 24–39.

[16] DeGolyer and MacNaughton, *Twentieth Century Petroleum Statistics: Historical Data* (Dallas, TX: DeGolyer and MacNaughton, n.d.), 3; *BP Statistical Review of World Energy*, 2022, bp-stats-review-2022-all-data.xlsx.

[17] Known as the "Seven Sisters" because of their close ties and multiple joint ventures, they included Standard Oil of New Jersey (Exxon); Socony (Mobil); Standard Oil of California (Chevron); the Texas Company (Texaco); Gulf Oil; the British-owned Anglo-Iranian Oil Company (after 1954 British Petroleum); and the Royal Dutch/Shell group, a 60 percent Dutch and 40 percent British partnership. See Anthony Sampson, *The Seven Sisters: The Great Oil Companies and the World They Shaped* (New York: Viking, 1975); Edith T. Penrose, *The Large International Firm in the Developing World: The International Petroleum Industry* (London: Allen & Unwin 1968).

[18] Charles Bright and Michael Geyer, "For a Unified History of the World in the Twentieth Century," *Radical History Review* 39 (1987), 82–4; Simon Bromley, *American Hegemony and World Oil: The Industry, the State System, and the World Economy* (University Park: Pennsylvania State University Press, 1991); David S. Painter, *Oil and the American Century: The Political Economy of U.S. Foreign Oil Policy, 1951–1954* (Baltimore: Johns Hopkins University Press, 1986), David S. Painter, "Oil, Resources, and the Cold War," in *Cambridge History of the Cold War*, vol. 1: *Origins*, ed. Leffler and Westad, 486–507.

Soviet oil production recovered in the 1950s as the prolific Volga-Ural fields entered production. A surge in Soviet oil exports in the late 1950s put pressure on oil prices and caused some divisions in the Western alliance, but the West was able to contain the Soviet "oil offensive."[19]

Oil was an important element in Soviet control of Eastern Europe. Except for Romania, Eastern Europe lacked significant indigenous oil reserves and depended on the Soviets for almost all its oil needs. Although the countries in the region drew mainly on their own resources in the 1950s and 1960s, coal consumption declined in every country except Romania in the 1960s, and by 1970 oil imports from the Soviet Union accounted for 11.3 percent of the region's total energy consumption.[20] Although Soviet oil supplies rescued the Cuban Revolution after the United States imposed an embargo, the Chinese, ironically with Soviet assistance, discovered the vast Daqing oil field in 1959, just in time to fend off Soviet economic pressure after the Sino-Soviet split.[21] Despite geographical proximity, extensive efforts, and widespread anti-Western sentiment in Iran and the Arab world, the Soviets failed to achieve a secure foothold in the Persian Gulf and, except for Iraq, failed to displace Western oil companies from the region's oil industry.[22]

3. The Hinge Years

During the 1970s, a combination of political turmoil in the Middle East and shifts in the world oil economy threatened US control of world oil. US oil consumption rose sharply after World War II. US oil reserves peaked in 1968 and oil production in 1970, and US oil imports rose from almost 19 percent of total demand in 1970 to over 35 percent in 1973. Alaskan oil, while promising, would not be available until the mid-1970s. The disappearance of spare productive capacity meant that the United States could no longer provide oil to its allies during supply interruptions, ending what had been an important element underpinning US influence in international affairs. Although Venezuelan production increased during the 1960s, Venezuelan reserves declined as the oil companies shifted the focus of their operations to the Middle East.

---

[19] Vagit Alekperov, *Oil of Russia: Past, Present, Future* (Minneapolis: Eastview Press, 2011), 251–89; Jeronim Perović, "The Soviet Union's Rise as an International Energy Power: A Short History," in *Cold War Energy: A Transnational History of Soviet Oil and Gas*, ed. Jeronim Perović (London: Palgrave Macmillan, 2017), 1–14; Bruce Jentleson, *Pipeline Politics: The Complex Political Economy of East-West Energy Trade* (Ithaca, NY: Cornell University Press, 1986), 76–131.

[20] U.S. Central Intelligence Agency, *Soviet Energy Policy Toward Eastern Europe: A Research Paper*, June 1980, CIA FOIA Electronic Reading Room (hereafter CIA Documents).

[21] Eric. T. Gettig, "Oil and Revolution: Cuban Nationalism and the U.S. Energy Empire, 1902–1961" (Ph.D. dissertation, Georgetown University, 2017), chaps. 6–8; Arthur Jay Klinghoffer, *The Soviet Union and International Oil Politics* (New York: Columbia University Press, 1977), 196–9.

[22] Fred Halliday, "The Impact of Soviet Policy in the Middle East," in *The Superpowers, Central America, and the Middle East*, ed. Peter Shearman and Phil Williams (London: Brassey's, 1988), 155–65. On Soviet aid to the Iraqi oil industry, see Philippe Tristani, "Iraq and the Cold War: A Superpower Struggle and the End of the Iraq Petroleum Company, 1958–72," in *Oil Shock*, ed. Bini, Garavini, and Romero, 80–4; Brandon Wolfe-Hunnicutt, *The Paranoid Style in American Diplomacy: Oil and Arab Nationalism in Iraq* (Stanford, CA: Stanford University Press, 2021), 204–14.

In the 1970s, Venezuelan production began a gradual decline. Large-scale production of North Sea oil production did not begin until the mid-1970s.[23]

In contrast, oil reserves in the Middle East (including North Africa) increased from 126.2 billion barrels in 1955 to 433.7 billion barrels in 1972, around two-thirds of the world total. Middle East production reached 21.7 million barrels per day (bpd) in 1972, half of non-Communist world production. The region's share of world oil production rose from around 15 percent in 1950 to a little more than 42 percent in 1973, as oil companies concentrated their investments there to take advantage of low production costs. By 1972, Middle East oil accounted for 47 percent of total Western European energy consumption and 57 percent of Japanese energy consumption. Around 80 percent of Western Europe's and 90 percent of Japan's oil imports came from the Middle East and North Africa. Middle East oil constituted a much smaller share of US energy consumption—only 2 percent in 1972—but the high absolute level of US oil consumption and the key role of oil in transportation made even this small amount significant in the face of supply difficulties. US annual per capita oil consumption increased from 19.6 barrels in 1960 to 26.3 barrels in 1970. In addition, 85 percent of the oil used by US forces in Southeast Asia came from the Persian Gulf.[24]

The shift in the geography of world oil provided Middle East oil producers with leverage to gain higher prices.[25] In January 1970, the Libyan government, led by Colonel Muammar Qaddafi, who had led a coup against the monarchy in September 1969, demanded that the oil companies pay higher prices for Libyan oil. Libyan oil was more favorably located in relation to oil markets in Western Europe and the United States and had a higher API gravity and lower sulfur content than most crude oil from the Persian Gulf, which made it less expensive to refine into gasoline and other high value products. The Libyans argued that they, and not the oil companies, should receive the rents resulting from the transportation cost and quality differentials. Qaddafi warned if necessary that his country could afford to live without oil revenues while it trained its own technicians.[26]

Qaddafi made his move at an opportune time. Nigerian oil, which competed with Libyan oil in Western Europe and the United States, was still recovering from the disruption caused by the civil war. Iraqi production, part of which moved to the

[23] George Philip, *Oil and Politics in Latin America: Nationalist Movements and State Companies* (Cambridge: Cambridge University Press, 1982), 294–306; Tyler Priest, "Shifting Sands: The 1973 Oil Shock and the Expansion on Non-OPEC Supplies," in *Oil Shock*, ed. Bini, Garavini, and Romero, 120–5.
[24] Joel Darmstadter and Hans H. Landsberg, "The Economic Background," in *The Oil Crisis*, ed. Raymond Vernon, 15–37; Schneider, *Oil Price Revolution*, 49–75; DeGolyer and MacNaughton, *Twentieth Century Petroleum Statistics, 2012* (Dallas, TX: DeGolyer and MacNaughton, 2012); shares of world oil production calculated from figures in *BP Statistical Review of World Energy*, 2017.
[25] *Foreign Relations of the United States, 1969–1976*, vol. 36, doc. 61, NIE 20/30-70, "Security of Supply to NATO and Japan," November 14, 1970 (hereafter *FRUS*, followed by volume and document number).
[26] Frank C. Waddams, *The Libyan Oil Industry* (Baltimore, MD: Johns Hopkins University Press, 1980), 57–9, 191–212.

Mediterranean by pipeline, was down due to the on-going dispute between the Iraqi government and the Iraq Petroleum Company. In May 1970, an accident in Syria shut down the Trans-Arabian Pipeline (Tapline), which carried around 500,000 bpd of oil from Saudi Arabia to the Mediterranean. In addition, the Suez Canal was still closed because of the 1967 war, forcing tankers to sail around Africa to reach Western Europe. In these circumstances, tanker rates tripled, giving Libyan oil an even greater transportation advantage.[27]

The structure of the Libyan oil industry also proved to be to Qaddafi's advantage. To avoid domination by the major oil companies, the Libyan government in the 1950s had invited many small oil companies as well the majors to seek concessions. The result was that by 1970 independent oil companies accounted for around 55 percent of Libyan production. Determined to carve out markets for their oil and unconcerned about the impact of their actions on prices, the independents cut price to sell their oil. Libyan oil production soared from 180,000 bpd in 1962 to 3.3 million bpd by 1970.[28]

The largest producer in Libya was Occidental Petroleum Company, an independent US oil company totally dependent on Libyan oil to supply its Western European refineries. Charging that the companies had not followed sound conservation policies the Libyan government in spring 1970 ordered Occidental and other companies to cut production. After failing to convince Exxon and Shell to supply his company with oil at cost so he could resist Qaddafi's demands, Occidental head Armand Hammer agreed in early September 1970 to a price increase of 30 cents per barrel and an increase in the tax rate on company profits from 50 to 58 percent. Unable to agree on a common strategy, the other oil companies soon accepted similar price and tax increases.[29]

Realizing their bargaining power, the other OPEC members pressed the oil companies for price and tax increase equal to those won by Libya. The oil companies decided to present a united front to OPEC, and under the guidance of oil company counsel John J. McCloy, and in cooperation with the Departments of State and Justice, the companies informed OPEC that they would only negotiate if the settlement covered all companies and all countries. The Justice Department issued Business Review Letters permitting US companies to take collective action without violating the antitrust laws, and the companies operating in Libya signed an agreement pledging them to support each other in case of cutbacks by Libya. Negotiations were set to begin on January 19, 1971, in Tehran.[30]

[27] *FRUS 1969–1976*, 35, doc. 80, NSSM-114, January 24, 1971; Ian Seymour, *OPEC: Instrument of Change* (London: Macmillan, 1980), 55–62; Waddams, *Libyan Oil Industry*, 267–9; John Vincent Bowlus, "The 1967 Closure of the Suez Canal and Mediterranean Oil Unity," in *Les routes du pétrole/Oil Routes*, ed. Alain Beltran (Paris: P.I.E. Peter Lang, 2016), 125–38.

[28] Waddams, *Libyan Oil Industry*, 191–212.

[29] US Congress, Committee on Foreign Relations, Subcommittee on Multinational Corporations, *Multinational Oil Corporations and U.S. Foreign Policy* (Washington, DC: US Government Printing Office, 1975), 22–5 (hereafter *MNC Report*); Waddams, *Libyan Oil Industry*, 230–6.

[30] *MNC Report*, 125–30: Yergin, *The Prize*, 580–1.

It was not clear if the companies could win a confrontation with the producing countries, and the Nixon administration feared that strongly supporting the companies could harm the Western position in the Middle East. In addition, the United States was a major oil producer so higher prices benefited some sectors of the US economy. Indeed, as far as US companies with production in OPEC countries were concerned, higher oil prices were not a problem if they applied to all companies. Higher oil prices for Western Europe and Japan would also erode the cost advantage over the United States they had enjoyed due to US oil import quotas which kept US prices above world prices. Finally, the companies were not opposed to higher prices if they could pass the increased costs on to consumers.[31]

Taking a strong stand against higher oil prices also risked a disruption in oil supplies. National security adviser Henry A. Kissinger warned President Richard M. Nixon that if the companies held the line against Libyan demands, Libya would probably cut oil exports and could be joined by Iraq and possibly other Arab states. Due to the world tanker shortage, the continued closure of the Suez Canal, and the disruption of Tapline, a Libyan-Iraqi shutdown would cause significant oil shortages in Europe. The United States no longer had the spare capacity to help compensate for a cut-off of oil supplies to Europe and could only free oil for Europe by rationing oil domestically. Disruptions in oil supply could also damage the international economy, lead to the nationalization of US oil company holdings, impair European security, and increase pressure on the United States to change its policies toward Israel. In addition, the Europeans might try to head off shortages by striking government-to-government deals with Libya and other producers, at the expense of US and British companies.[32]

As a result of these concerns, the Nixon administration decided not to confront the producing countries. The shah convinced US envoy John Irwin II, who had gone to Tehran to explain the US position, that negotiations with the Persian Gulf producers should be held separately from those with Mediterranean producers (Libya, Algeria, and the portion of Iraqi and Saudi oil that arrived at the Mediterranean by pipeline). The shah claimed that it would not be possible for Iran and the other Persian Gulf producers to dictate terms to Venezuela or the radical Arab producers.[33]

Negotiations between the companies and the Persian Gulf producers resulted in an agreement that provided for a price increase of 35 cents a barrel, a tax rate of 55 percent,

[31] *FRUS 1969–1976*, 36, doc. 69, Bergsten and Saunders to Kissinger, "The Developing International Oil Crisis," January 14, 1971; doc. 80, "NSSM 114: The World Oil Situation: NSSM," January 24, 1971; for the full study, see NSC Institutional Files, "NSSM-114," Nixon Library (also available from the National Security Archive; Kissinger, *Years of Upheaval*, 863; David S. Painter, "From the Nixon Doctrine to the Carter Doctrine: Iran and the Geopolitics of Oil in the 1970s," in *American Energy Policy in the 1970s*, ed. Robert Lifset (Norman, University of Oklahoma Press, 2013), 69.
[32] *FRUS 1969–1976*, 36, doc. 73, Kissinger, Memorandum for the President, January 18, 1971; doc. 69, Bergsten and Saunders to Kissinger, "The Developing International Oil Crisis," January 14, 1971; Painter, "Nixon Doctrine to Carter Doctrine," 69.
[33] *FRUS 1969–1976*, 36, doc. 74, Irwin to State, January 18, 1971; Robert Stobaugh, "The Evolution of Iranian Oil Policy, 1925–1975" in *Iran Under the Pahlavis*, ed. George Lenczowski (Stanford, CA: Hoover Institution Press, 1978), 238–43; Painter, "Nixon Doctrine to Carter Doctrine," 69–70.

and regular increases in prices during 1971–5 to offset inflation.[34] The Mediterranean producers led by Libya refused to negotiate until after the negotiations with the Persian Gulf producers were concluded, and in April, the Tripoli Agreements raised prices an additional 90 cents per barrel for the Mediterranean producers. A month later, Nigeria, which had joined OPEC during the Tehran Conference, received terms similar to those won by the Mediterranean producers.[35]

Oil prices, which had stagnated at $1.80 a barrel since 1961, rose to $2.25 a barrel in 1971, $2.48 a barrel in 1972, and reached $3.29 a barrel in 1973. The rise in oil prices in combination with increases in the volume of exports greatly enlarged the earnings of OPEC's members. OPEC production increased from 22.2 million bpd in 1970 to 30.9 million bpd in 1973 and revenue from $7.3 billion in 1970 to $22.6 billion in 1973.[36]

In addition to prices and taxes, OPEC countries began to assert themselves on questions of ownership and control. In 1968, OPEC adopted a resolution declaring that producing countries had the right to participate in the ownership of their oil. Shortly after the Tehran and Tripoli Agreements, Venezuela passed a Hydrocarbons Reversion Law, which provided for government takeover of the oil industry when the companies' concessions expired in the 1980s and for an immediate increase in government control of the oil companies. In September 1971, OPEC called for member countries to begin negotiations with the oil companies on the question of participation in the ownership of their oil operations.[37]

The oil companies and the US government viewed participation as little more than negotiated nationalization, but there was little that the United States, Britain, or the oil companies could do to oppose it.[38] Negotiations went slowly until actions by Algeria, Libya, and Iraq provided an indication of what non-negotiated nationalization would entail. Algeria had expropriated some minor US oil and mining companies in 1967 in retaliation for US policy during the Six-Day War, and in February 1971 nationalized 51 percent of French oil and gas holdings. Libya nationalized British Petroleum's holdings in December 1971 in retaliation for Britain's alleged role in permitting Iran to seize islands in the Persian Gulf. In June 1972, after an 11-year dispute, Iraq nationalized the Iraq Petroleum Company, a multinational consortium owned by BP, Shell, CFP, Standard Oil of New Jersey, Mobil, and a small independent company, Partex, in June 1972.[39]

---

[34] *FRUS 1969–1976*, E-4, doc. 115, INR Intelligence Note, "OPEC Oil: Persian Gulf Anchored, Mediterranean Next," February 18, 1971; *FRUS 1969–1976*, 24, doc. 94, CIA, "Some Revenue Implications of the 14 February Oil Settlement with the Persian Gulf States," March 1971.

[35] *FRUS 1969–1976*, 36, doc. 88, State 56087, April 2, 1971; For overviews of the negotiations, see Yergin, *The Prize*, 577–83; and James Bamberg, *British Petroleum and Global Oil, 1950–1975: The Challenge of Nationalism* (Cambridge: Cambridge University Press, 2000), 447–66; *MNC Report*, 130–4; Francesco Petrini, "Eight Squeezed Sisters: The Oil Majors and the Coming of the 1973 Oil Crisis," in *Oil Shock*, ed. Bini, Garavini, and Romero, 60–73.

[36] Ian Skeet, *OPEC: Twenty-Five Years of Prices and Politics* (New York: Cambridge University Press, 1988), 102–3, 244.

[37] Skeet, *OPEC: Twenty-Five Years*, 50–7.

[38] *FRUS 1969–1976*, 36, doc. 98, Eliot to Kissinger, December 13, 1971; doc. 112, Jidda 535, February 16, 1972; David S. Painter, "The End of the Postwar Petroleum Order: A Review of *Foreign Relations of the United States, 1969–1976*, Vol. XXXVI, *Energy Crisis, 1969–1974*," *Passport* 45 (April 2014): 31.

[39] Joe Stork, *Middle East Oil and the Energy Crisis* (New York: Monthly Review Press, 1975), chapter 8; Samir Saul, "Masterly Inactivity as Brinkmanship: The Iraq Petroleum Company's Route to Nationalization, 1958–1972," *International History Review* 29 (December 2007): 746–92; Wolfe-Hunnicutt, *The Paranoid Style in American Diplomacy*, 204–24.

The Iraqi nationalization convinced the companies to reach an agreement. Negotiations between the Arab Gulf states and the oil companies resulted in a General Agreement on Participation in October 1972, which provided for 25 percent government participation to take effect on January 1, 1973, with scheduled increases leading to 51 percent government ownership by the beginning of 1982. The agreements compensated the companies based on updated book value and guaranteed them the right to purchase most of the production of the oil that now belonged to the governments. Iran, which had technically owned its own oil industry since 1951, reached an agreement with the consortium in the spring of 1973, providing for Iranian management and control of the industry with the consortium companies continuing to provide operating services and purchasing the bulk of Iranian production at prices equal to those received by the other Gulf states. Not to be outdone, the Libyan government nationalized 51 percent of all the companies operating in Libya in August and September 1973.[40]

It is not clear what the United States, Britain, or the oil companies could have done to prevent these actions, especially given the constraints imposed by the Cold War. Slowly ceding control over ownership could avoid a cut-off of oil supplies and the use of oil as a political weapon. Accommodating the producing countries would also buy time until alternative sources of oil could be developed, thus lessening OPEC's leverage. There were also benefits to allowing oil prices to rise gradually. Although higher oil prices could feed inflation and slow economic growth, they could also stimulate increased investment and production, especially in such high-cost areas as Alaska, off-shore fields, Canada, Mexico, Venezuela, and the North Sea, making the West less dependent on Middle East oil. Higher oil prices could also encourage conservation and increased efficiency in oil use and increased utilization of alternative sources of energy, in particular coal and nuclear power.[41]

4. Oil and the October War

A National Security Council report warned in July 1972 that the changes in the balance of power between oil producers and oil consumers had the potential to become a security problem. The Arab states were gaining the ability to apply "serious pressure" on US policy toward the Arab-Israeli conflict, and they were building up the financial capacity to sustain a total embargo over a long period.[42] The report recommended giving top priority "to addressing the overall foreign policy ramifications of oil policy."

---

[40] Skeet, *OPEC: Twenty-Five Years*, 71–3, 75–8, 80–2; Yergin, *The Prize*, 583–5; Kenneth A. Rodman, *Sanctity Versus Sovereignty: The United States and the Nationalization of Natural Resource Investments* (New York: Columbia University Press, 1988), 245–65; Seymour, *OPEC: Instrument of Change*, 218–30.

[41] "The U.S. and the Impending Energy Crisis," March 9, 1972, U.S. National Archives, RG 59, Central Files 1970–3, PET 1 US; *FRUS 1969–1976*, 36, doc. 116. Rogers to Nixon, March 10, 1972; James E. Akins, head of the State Department's Office of Fuels and Energy and author of the March paper, made these points in a widely read but often misunderstood article, "The Oil Crisis: This Time the Wolf is Here," *Foreign Affairs* 51 (April 1973): 462–90.

[42] *FRUS 1969–1976*, 36, doc. 127, Hormats, Kennedy, and Walsh to Kissinger, July 11, 1972; doc. 128; NSC Staff Paper, "Analytical Summary," July 1972.

Nixon and Kissinger were preoccupied with other matters such as the Vietnam War, the Strategic Arms Limitation Talks, and the opening to China, and Nixon did not approve a study of the problem until March 1973.[43]

In April 1973, President Nixon announced a package of new energy policies designed to reduce US dependence on imported oil. They included an immediate end to the system of import quotas, the deregulation of natural gas prices, and the expansion of domestic energy production, including the expansion of offshore drilling for oil and gas, and removal of the remaining legal barriers to building the Alaska oil pipeline. Although he called on Americans to embrace a "conservation ethic," the policies he promoted were almost entirely focused on boosting production.[44]

Completed in August, the National Security Council (NSC) study, NSSM 174: "National Security and U.S. Energy Policy," warned that increasing oil imports made the United States increasingly vulnerable to short-term supply interruptions. While the United States could still meet its military needs for oil, a sharp reduction in oil supplies caused by war in the Middle East or "a politically motivated decision" to embargo oil shipments to the United States could cause severe economic problems.[45]

Growing Arab frustration over lack of progress toward an Arab-Israeli settlement, pressure from radical Arab states, or radical takeover of Saudi Arabia or other Gulf states could lead to use of oil as a political weapon to force changes in US policies toward Israel. During 1973, Saudi officials repeatedly warned that unless the United States put pressure on Israel to reach a settlement with the Arab states, Saudi Arabia would be forced to use its oil resources as a political weapon. To avoid this, NSSM-174 argued that the United States had to "show some movement on the Arab-Israeli problem," and try harder to accommodate the security and economic concerns of the "moderate" Arabs. The "overriding concern" should be to prevent Saudi Arabia from becoming radicalized or "falling under the control of a Qaddafi."[46]

There was not much that could be done to lessen US dependence on imports from the Middle East in the short term, but in the longer term, the NSC believed that the United States should seek to diversify away from Middle East sources and, within the Middle East, away from Saudi Arabia toward Iran, and to build up domestic supply alternatives. In addition, if the United States developed voluntary and mandatory rationing plans, enlarged oil stockpiles, and negotiated import sharing plans with its allies, it could probably withstand a total cutoff of oil imports well into the 1980s.[47]

US policymakers believed that they had time to remedy the situation. A CIA National Intelligence Analytical Memorandum in May concluded that while "there probably will be some small interruptions of oil supply during the 1970s ... a major and sustained embargo on oil shipments by the Arab states working in concert is highly

[43] *FRUS 1969–1976*, 36, doc. 171, National Security Study Memorandum 174, March 8, 1973.
[44] Jay Hakes, *Energy Crises: Nixon, Ford, Carter and Hard Choices in the 1970s* (Norman: University of Oklahoma Press, 2021, 66–9.
[45] *FRUS 1969–1976*, 36, doc. 192, Odeen to Kissinger, August 11, 1973; Richard Nixon Library, NSC Institutional Files, NSSM-174, National Security and US Energy Policy, August 1973.
[46] *FRUS 1969–1976*, 36, doc. 192, Odeen to Kissinger, August 11, 1973; doc. 193, Odeen to Kissinger, August 15, 1973; Painter, "End of the Postwar Petroleum Order," 32.
[47] Painter, "Nixon Doctrine to the Carter Doctrine," 73.

unlikely." In addition, neither US nor Israeli intelligence believed that a major war was likely for the next two to three years. The Israelis believed that the Egyptians would not risk war until they had amassed sufficient military resources to give them a chance of prevailing. Until this happened, they did not believe that the Egyptians would attack.[48]

Time ran out, however, when, on October 6, 1973, Egyptian and Syrian forces launched simultaneous attacks on Israeli forces occupying the Sinai and the Golan Heights. The attacks caught the Israelis by surprise, and in the initial fighting Egyptian troops broke through Israeli lines and established positions on the east bank of the Suez Canal, and Syrian forces recaptured much of the Golan Heights. The Palestine Liberation Organization, radical nationalists in the Kuwait national assembly, and the Iraqi Ba'ath Party immediately called for Arab oil producers to wield the oil weapon against Israel and its supporters, and oil workers in Kuwait threatened to stop production completely unless shipments to the United States were cut by at least 50 percent. Iraq nationalized the share of Exxon and Mobil in the Basrah Petroleum Company (BPC) and with Algeria declared an embargo on oil exports to the United States. Both actions were largely symbolic. The Iraqis had nationalized the main foreign oil company in Iraq in 1972, and they offered compensation and allowed Exxon and Mobil continued access to oil from the BPC. Algeria sent very little oil to the United States, so its action also had little impact. In addition, the Saudi government directed the US-owned Arabian American Oil Company (Aramco) to supply crude oil and products to aid the Arab war effort. Fearing retaliation if it refused, Aramco complied with the request.[49]

Discounting warnings from the major oil companies and the Saudi government that Saudi Arabia would respond to US support of Israel with an oil boycott, the United States began an airlift of military supplies to Israel on October 14 to counter Soviet resupply of Egypt and Syria.[50] Despite the war, representatives from the oil companies and the Persian Gulf producers had met as scheduled in Vienna on October 8 to discuss revisions in the 1971 Tehran price agreement. The Gulf states wanted adjustments in the price of oil to compensate them for inflation and to restore the 80/20 profit sharing ratio that had prevailed at the time of the Tehran agreement. They rejected the companies' offer of a 15 percent increase in price, a revised inflation-adjustment rate, and a small premium for low-sulfur crude and demanded a 100 percent increase, an improved inflation adjustment formula, and a mechanism for keeping the posted (tax reference) price 40 percent above the market price as it had been at the time of the Tehran Agreement. With the two sides so far apart, the company representatives left Vienna to consult with their home governments. The representatives

---

[48] *FRUS 1969–1976*, 36, doc. 185, NIAM 3-73: *International Petroleum Prospects*, May 11, 1973; Ahron Bregman, "Ashraf Marwan and Israel's Intelligence Failure," in *The October 1973 War: Politics, Diplomacy, Legacy*, ed. Asaf Siniver (London: Hurst, 2013), 199–200.

[49] David S. Painter, "Oil and the October War," in *The October 1973 War*, ed. Siniver, 173–4; Garavini, *Rise and Fall of OPEC*, 217–18; Schneider, *Oil Price Revolution*, 222; *MNC Report*, 144. Standard Oil Company of California (SOCAL, later Chevron), Texaco, Exxon, and Mobil jointly owned ARAMCO.

[50] Painter, "Oil and the October War," 174–5.

of the Gulf States left Vienna for Kuwait, where on October 16, they unilaterally raised the posted price of oil from $3.01 a barrel to $5.11 a barrel, a 70 percent increase.[51]

The next day, the Organization of Arab Petroleum Exporting Countries (OAPEC), which was holding an emergency meeting in Kuwait, announced cuts in oil production to force Western Europe and Japan to put pressure on the United States to change its policy on the Arab–Israeli dispute. Founded in 1968 by Saudi Arabia, Kuwait, and Libya, OAPEC's membership in 1973 had expanded to include Algeria, Bahrain, Egypt, Iraq, Qatar, Syria, and the United Arab Emirates, and its members accounted for around 31.7 percent of world oil production. Although it was an OAPEC member, Iraq refused to participate in the cutbacks, and increased its overall oil production. Abu Dhabi declared an embargo on exports to the United States on October 18 followed by Libya and Qatar on October 19. Libya also raised the posted price for its oil to $8.925 per barrel.[52]

Despite warnings that further aid to Israel would result in an embargo, President Nixon on October 19 requested from Congress $2.2 billion in grant military assistance for Israel. Cold War concerns were a factor in the US decision. As President Nixon told his advisers on October 17, "We can't allow a Soviet-supported operation to succeed against an American-supported operation. If it does, our credibility everywhere is severely shaken." The next day, Saudi Arabia declared a total embargo of oil shipments to the United States and warned that it would continue as long as Israel occupied Arab territory outside its 1967 borders. On October 21, the Saudis extended the embargo against the United States to include all indirect shipments and deliveries to refineries supplying US military forces in Bahrain, Italy, and Greece. Within a few days, the remaining Arab producers, including Iraq, declared embargoes against the United States. OAPEC extended its embargo to the Netherlands on October 23 in retaliation for Dutch support for Israel. Iraq also nationalized Shell's share in the Basrah Petroleum Company (Shell was 60 percent Dutch owned).[53]

The international oil companies complied with the embargo but undercut it by shifting non-Arab oil to the embargoed countries and distributing the cutbacks so that both embargoed and non-embargoed countries had their oil imports cut by roughly the same amount. In the period, December 1973 to April 1974, the United States received 12 percent less oil (crude and products) than in the same period in 1973; Western Europe received 13.6 percent less oil while Japan received 1 percent more. Although these figures seem to indicate an apparent inequity in the allocation of restricted supplies, they do not consider different growth rates in energy demand. Before October 1973, Japanese energy demand had been growing at an annual rate of

[51] David Wight, *Oil Money: Middle East Petrodollars and the Transformation of US Empire, 1967–1988* (Ithaca: Cornell University Press, 202), 56–7; Yergin, *The Prize*, 582–4.
[52] United Kingdom National Archives (UKNA), PREM 15/1765, Telegram 492 from Jedda to the Foreign Office, October 16, 1973; Telegram 493 from Jedda to the Foreign Office, October 16, 1973; Painter, "Oil and the October War," 176–7; Garavini, *Rise and Fall of OPEC*, 174; *BP Statistical Review of World Energy*, 2022.
[53] *FRUS 1969-1976*, 25, doc. 199, Memorandum of Conversation, October 17, 1973; doc. 223, CIA Memorandum, October 19, 1973; Painter, "Oil and the October War," 177.

approximately 17 percent, compared to a 5 percent growth rate in the United States and Western Europe. When the projected growth in demand is considered, the US shortfall was 17 percent, the Western European, 18.0 percent, and the Japanese, 16.0 percent.[54] Increased exports from Canada, Indonesia, Iran, and the Soviet Union partially offset the decline in Arab supplies, but the price of oil skyrocketed, reaching $17 per barrel on the spot market. On December 22, OPEC raised posted prices to $11.65 per barrel, effective January 1, 1974.[55]

It is important to disentangle the production cuts, the oil embargo, and the oil price increases. Focusing on the embargo against the United States and ignoring the production cuts minimizes the scope and impact of the disruption. Although the production cuts were only in force for a short period, they had a significant impact on production, disrupted supplies, and contributed to a sharp increase of the price of oil. Moreover, although most studies focus on the embargo against the United States, the embargo against the Netherlands had a major impact because around 80 percent of the crude oil imported by the Netherlands was re-exported to other European countries as refined products. As a result, the embargo against the Netherlands also disrupted supplies to Belgium, Luxembourg, and West Germany.[56]

The price increase in October was announced a day before the production cuts, and was made by OPEC, not by OAPEC, for economic reasons—to compensate for the impact of inflation, the decline in the value of the dollar, and the increase in market prices relative to the posted prices on which their revenues were calculated. The price hike at the end of December was an opportunistic reaction by OPEC "price hawks" to the disruptions in production and distribution caused by the production cuts and embargoes which drove spot oil prices upwards. It was not directly related to the political demands of the Arab states, and it was not political in motivation. Even though Iran did not cut production or participate in the embargoes, the shah was a leading proponent of higher prices. In contrast, Saudi Arabia, which played a key role in the production cutbacks and embargo argued unsuccessfully for a smaller increase.[57]

Finally, the embargo was not an "OPEC Embargo," as it is often called in many scholarly studies and popular accounts. OAPEC, which included some countries who were not members of OPEC, initiated the embargo and production cuts. Although a member of OAPEC, Iraq went its own way, joining in the embargo, but not the production cuts. Non-Arab OPEC members, including Iran, Venezuela, Nigeria, and

[54] Robert B. Stobaugh, "The Oil Companies in the Crisis," in *The Oil Crisis*, ed. Raymond Vernon, 179–202; Painter, "Oil and the October War," 178–81; M.A. Adelman, *The Genie Out of the Bottle: World Oil Since 1970* (Cambridge, MA: The MIT Press, 1995), 139.

[55] Yergin, *The Prize*, 583–626. Bamberg, *British Petroleum and Global Oil*, 474–89.

[56] Painter, "Oil and the October War," 179; see the table in Adelman, *Genie Out of the Bottle*, 111; Romano Prodi and Alberto Clô, "Europe," in *The Oil Crisis*, ed. Raymond Vernon, 98.

[57] Painter, "Oil and the October War," 174, 184–5; Garavini, *Rise and Fall of OPEC*, 202–3, 221–6; Skeet, *OPEC: Twenty-Five Years*, 87–91, 99–105; Raymond Vernon, ed., *The Oil Crisis*, 290; and Adelman, *Genie Out of the Bottle*, 120, provide tables showing how oil prices were calculated. Robert Vitalis, *Oilcraft: The Myths of Scarcity and Security That Haunt U.S. Energy Policy* (Stanford University Press, 2020), 67; Timothy Mitchell, *Carbon Democracy: Political Power in the Age of Oil* (London: Verso, 2011), 184–6.

Table 1.1 Crude oil production, September 1973 through March 1974 (in millions of barrels per day)

	9/73	10/73	11/73	12/73	1/74	2/74	3/74
Arab	20.8	19.8	15.8	16.1	17.6	17.9	18.5
Non-Arab	38.4	38.9	39.0	39.3	39.6	39.5	39.5
Total	59.2	58.7	54.8	55.4	57.2	57.4	58.0

Source: Federal Energy Administration, *U.S. Oil Companies and the Arab Oil Embargo: The International Allocation of Constricted Supplies* (Washington, DC: U.S. Government Printing Office, 1975, 7).

Indonesia, did not join the embargo or cut back production and exports. They were content to profit from the price increases and even boosted production and exports, as did the Soviets. Labeling the embargo an OPEC embargo obscures the specific political circumstances that led to it and confuses the embargo with the production cuts and the pressure OPEC had been putting on prices since 1971.[58]

5. Ending the Embargo

During the crisis Henry Kissinger, who in September 1973 had become Secretary of State as well as national security advisor, and Secretary of Defense James Schlesinger made public threats of military intervention. Schlesinger also raised the issue with the British Ambassador to the United States and with NATO officials, and both Kissinger and Schlesinger brought up the possibility in many meetings during the crisis.[59]

Kissinger claimed in his memoirs that "these were not empty threats," and that contingency plans were prepared. Schlesinger later told interviewers that the United States planned to make use of already scheduled military exercises in the Persian Gulf as a cover for intervention in Abu Dhabi, which he believed would intimidate the other producers.[60]

---

[58] George Lenczowski, "The Oil-Producing Countries," in *The Oil Crisis*, ed. Raymond Vernon, 60–7; Andrew Scott Cooper, *Oil Kings: How the U.S., Iran, and Saudi Arabia Changed the Balance of Power in the Middle East* (New York: Simon & Schuster, 2011), 143–8; De Groot, "The Soviet Union, CMEA, and the Energy Crisis of the 1970s," 14.

[59] *FRUS 1969–1976*, 36, docs. 229, 244, 247, 251, 253, 255; United Kingdom, Foreign and Commonwealth Office, *Documents on British Policy Overseas*, Series 3, Vol. 4: *The Year of Europe: America, Europe and the Energy Crisis, 1972–1974*, Discussion between the Defence Secretary and the US Secretary of Defense, November 7, 1973; UKNA, PREM 15/1768, Cromer to Douglas-Home, November 15, 1973; Ministry of Defence to the Prime Minister, "Middle East," November 28, 1973; "Note by the Assessments Staff, Middle East: Possible Use of Force by the United States," December 12, 1973.

[60] Kissinger, *Years of Upheaval*, 880; Cooper, *Oil Kings*, 129–30; Jeffrey Robinson, *Yamani: The Inside Story* (London: Simon & Schuster, 1988), 100–2; Victor McFarland, *Oil Powers: A History of the U.S.-Saudi Alliance* (New York: Columbia University Press, 2020), 138–9. On the exercises, see *FRUS 1969–1976*, 27, doc. 42, Washington 217485, November 4, 1973; doc. 46, Tehran 8321, November 26, 1973.

The British government took Schlesinger's statements seriously and commissioned a study on the impact of the United States using force against Arab oil producers. The study concluded that if the United States intervened before exhausting all possibilities of a peaceful settlement, the consequences for Europe would be "disastrous." Schlesinger and Kissinger apparently believed that seizing Abu Dhabi would suffice, but the British study concluded that for military intervention to be successful, all the fields in the region, including those in Saudi Arabia, would have to be seized. This would be a huge task that would take some time, increasing the likelihood of sabotage of the oil fields and related infrastructure.[61]

Rather than reflecting actual plans to intervene, the threats were probably intended to intimidate the Saudis and other Gulf producers.[62] The Saudis and Kuwaitis threatened that if attacked they would destroy their oil facilities, thus denying the West access to their oil for many years. According to the official history of the Saudi Arabian Monetary Agency (SAMA), "King Faysal ordered Prince (later King Abdullah) to reinforce the National Guard's protection of the oilfields with orders to destroy the facilities if the Americans attacked." Similarly, a review of possible contingencies by the Central Intelligence Agency (CIA) concluded that military intervention to gain control of the oil fields would be counterproductive because it would probably result in "destroying the very objective we seek." In addition, the Soviets would most likely have opposed US intervention, possibly by aiding allies such as Iraq. Finally, most European countries opposed the use of force except as the last resort, and the American public, in the wake of Vietnam, probably would not have supported US military intervention in the absence of a clear threat to US security.[63]

The United States sought to use the crisis to reassert its leadership of the Western alliance. The State Department Policy Planning Staff pointed out on December 1 that the United States, as the only major Western country that could not be shut down by an oil embargo, had an opportunity to "revitalize" its alliances. What "revitalize" meant is clear in a National Security Council (NSC) memorandum three days later, which noted that "the unique role of the U.S. in the current oil crisis and in the longer-term oil situation gives us some leverage with the Europeans. We have the power to make their oil situation better or worse."[64] To gain the initiative as well as put pressure on the

---

[61] UKNA, PREM 15/1768, "Note by the Assessments Staff, Middle East: Possible Use of Force by the United States," December 12, 1973; Hunt to the Prime Minister, "Middle East," January 3, 1974. A study by the Congressional Research in summer 1975 came to similar conclusions; Congressional Research Service, *Oil Fields as Military Objectives: A Feasibility Study*, prepared for the Special Subcommittee on Investigations of the House Committee on International Relations (Washington, DC: Government Printing Office, 1975).

[62] On the communicative aspects of the embargo, see the astute analysis by Rüdiger Graf, "Making Use of the 'Oil Weapon': Western Industrialized Countries and Arab Petropolitics in 1973–1974," *Diplomatic History* 36 (January 2012), 185–208.

[63] "Saudi Arabia Warns U.S. Against Oil Countermoves," *New York Times*, November 23, 1973, 1; "Kuwait threatens oil field destruction should the US step in," *New York Times*, January 1, 1974; *FR 1969-1976*, 36, doc. 250, Rousel to Bush, November 27, 1973; doc. 255, Saunders to Kissinger, November 30, 1973, note 2; SAMA history quoted in Duccio Basosi, "Oil, dollars, and US power in the 1970s: re-viewing the connections," *Journal of Energy History/Revue d'Histoire de l'Energie* 3 (June 2020), 31, energyhistory.eu/en/node/192.

[64] Painter, "Oil and Geopolitics," 192; McFarland, *Oil Powers*, 140–1.

Arab states, Kissinger wanted the main oil consuming nations to coordinate their policies. President Nixon, on January 9, 1974, invited the major industrial nations to participate in an energy conference in Washington to develop a consumer group to improve the position of bargaining position of the oil consuming countries.[65]

The main consumer countries met in Washington February 11–13, 1974. Most European nations, including the United Kingdom, desired a more independent role for Europe, but were reluctant to follow the French in openly opposing US policies. Unable to promote alliance cohesion by providing oil to its allies, the United States resorted to threats and warnings to try to gain cooperation. In his toast at the beginning of the conference, Nixon suggested that failure of Europe and Japan to follow US leadership on energy matters encouraged isolationism in the United States. Similarly, Kissinger warned that failure to solve the energy problem cooperatively "would threaten the world with a vicious cycle of competition, autarky, rivalry, and depression such as led to the collapse of world order in the 1930s."[66]

Most US allies blamed US policies for the production cutbacks and embargo. Nevertheless, most also understood the benefits of cooperation with the United States and, with the significant exception of France, went along with US plans to establish a consumer group to balance the power of the producers. The French government later changed course and acquiesced in the formation of the International Energy Agency (IEA) within the framework of the Organization for Economic Cooperation and Development (OECD) in November 1974.[67]

In March, OAPEC decided to end the embargo after the United States helped negotiate ceasefire agreements between Israel and Egypt and Syria. Saudi willingness to end the embargo was influenced by agreements with the United States to strengthen military and economic ties. In addition to providing military equipment, training, and technical assistance, the United States recommitted itself to protecting the Saudi regime against its internal as well as its external enemies. Most Arab states agreed to end the embargo on March 18. The same day the Saudis announced that they would immediately increase oil production by one million barrels a day. Israel and Syria signed a ceasefire agreement on May 31. Libya, however, did not end its embargo until July.[68]

[65] Painter, "Oil and Geopolitics," 192–3; Kissinger, *Years of Upheaval*, 896–7.

[66] *FRUS 1969-1976*, 36, doc. 318, Editorial Note; Kissinger, *Years of Upheaval*, 905–25; Ethan B. Kapstein, *The Insecure Alliance: Energy Crises and Western Politics Since 1944* (New York: Oxford University Press, 1990), 171–5; Henning Türk, 'The Oil Crisis of 1973 as a Challenge to Multilateral Energy Cooperation Among Western Industrialized Countries, *Historical Social Research* 39 (2014): 209–30.

[67] Kissinger, *Years of Upheaval*, 896–7; Skeet, *OPEC: Twenty-Five Years*, 107; Aurélie Elise Gfeller, *Building a European Identity: France, the United States, and the Oil Shock, 1973-1974* (New York: Berghahn Books 2012), 120–2, 127–30, 171–5. France did not join the IEA until 1992.

[68] The U.S.-Saudi agreements were not signed until June. McFarland, *Oil Powers*, 140–51; Wight, *Oil Money*, 71–3; Lenczowski, "The Oil-Producing Countries," 60–7; Telecon, President Nixon/Secretary Kissinger, March 11, 1974, Digital National Security Archive, Kissinger Telephone Conversations, KA 12113. On Kissinger's shuttle diplomacy, see Salim Yaqub, "The Weight of Conquest: Henry Kissinger and the Arab-Israeli Conflict," in *Nixon in the World*, ed. Fredrik Logevall and Andrew Preston, 227–48.

6. The Economic Impact

Between 1970 and 1978, oil prices rose from $1.80 to $14.02 per barrel in nominal dollars; ($11.99 to $55.65 in 2021 dollars).[69] Higher oil prices intensified the economic problems faced by the United States and the other Western industrial countries in the 1970s, especially inflation, which was accompanied by stagnation and unemployment. Industrial output fell and unemployment rates reached postwar highs. The cost of importing large amounts of more expensive oil also harmed the balance of payments of the United States and other importing countries.[70] Japan imported almost all the oil it consumed, and its industries were heavily dependent on oil. Japan's gross national product, which had been growing at around 10 percent a year, stagnated for two years before resuming growth at around 5 percent a year.[71]

The first oil shock coincided with the emergence of China as a major oil producer and oil exporter. Chinese oil production rose from 1,077,000 bpd in 1973 to 2,122,000 bpd in 1980 and 2,508,000 bpd in 1985, and Chinese oil exports increased from around 60,000 bpd in 1973 to 351,639 bpd in 1980 and peaked at 727,779 bpd in 1985. Revenues from oil exports increased from $536,000,000 in 1974 to $4,221,000,000 in 1980 and peaked at $6,712,000,000 in 1985. As Kazushi Minami details in his chapter, domestic oil production allowed China to meet growing demand from domestic sources, and the revenues from oil exports helped finance imports of machinery, equipment, and technology for Chinese industrial development, including modernizing the oil industry, and thus contributed to the transformation of China's economy and its relations with the rest of the world.[72]

Shigeru Sato's chapter analyzes how Malaysia and Singapore navigated the oil crises and highlights the role of oil exports in the economic development of both nations and the emergence of an "East Asian Oil Triangle." Malaysian oil production increased from 18,000 bpd in 1973 to 276,000 bpd in 1980, and 445,000 bpd in 1985, and revenues from oil exports help finance investment in modernizing Malaysia's economy. Although not an oil producer, Singapore also managed to benefit from oil exports. Imports of crude oil, from Malaysia and Indonesia as well as the Persian Gulf, and exports of refined products skyrocketed in the 1970s, and at their peak in 1982 accounted for around 40 percent of Singapore's exports. Singapore became a major refining center in Southeast Asia and the revenue from oil product exports played an important intermediary role in its industrialization.[73]

It is difficult to generalize about impact of oil crises on Latin America due to the diversity of the region. Overall, oil provided about 65 percent of the region's energy

---

[69] *BP Statistical Review of World Energy*, 2022.

[70] Venn, *The Oil Crisis*, 145–72; Schneider, *Oil Price Revolution*, 457–507; Simon Pirani, *Burning Up: A Global History of Fossil Fuel Consumption* (London: Pluto Press, 2018), 96–100.

[71] Kaoru Sugihara, "Japan, the Middle East, and the World Economy: A Note on the Oil Triangle," in *Japan in the Contemporary Middle East*, ed. Kaoru Sugihara and J.A. Allan (London: Routledge, 1993), 3–6; John S. Duffield, *Fuels Paradise: Seeking Energy Security in Europe, Japan, and the United States* (Baltimore, MD: Johns Hopkins University Press, 2015), 198.

[72] *BP Statistical Review of World Energy*, 2022; Larry Chuen-ho Chow, "The Changing Role of Oil in Chinese Exports, 1974–89," *China Quarterly* 131 (September 1992): 751, 753.

[73] *BP Statistical Review of World Energy*, 2022.

requirements, natural gas around 16 percent, hydroelectric power 14 percent, and solid fuels 5 percent, making Latin America the most dependent on oil and natural gas of the major regions of the world. Venezuela produced 1,814,000 bpd in 1973 and 1,173,000 bpd in 1980 and was a leading supplier of oil to the United States and Europe as well as the Caribbean. Mexican oil production rose from 259,000 bpd in 1973 to 1,072,000 bpd in 1980 and Mexican oil exports reentered international oil markets. Although many countries in South America met portions of their oil requirements from domestic production, 45 percent of Latin America's oil requirements were met by imports and as a region Latin America spent almost a quarter of its export revenues to pay for imported oil.[74]

Venezuela's oil revenues tripled from $3 billion in 1973 to $9.3 billion in 1974, declined to $7.3 billion in 1978 and rose again due to the Second Oil Crisis, reaching $16.3 billion in 1981. Most countries in the region faced higher oil import bills. Brazil was dependent on oil for 45 percent of its energy requirements and imports accounted for 80 percent of its oil requirements, 76 percent from Middle East, and 15 percent from Africa. The cost of oil imports increased from $469.4 million in 1972 to $2.89 billion in 1974 and reached $4.06 billion in 1977 and absorbed over a third of Brazil's export revenues. Latin America also suffered indirectly from higher prices for imports as increased energy costs in industrialized countries were passed through in the prices of manufactured goods. As a result, growth rates slowed in many countries and, in many cases, declined on a per capita basis, and external debt increased as countries borrowed abroad to cover their trade deficits and to maintain their development programs.[75]

Unlike South Korea, many Latin American countries relaxed capital controls and a large portion of loans apparently made a quick return to the developed countries in the form of capital flight rather than being invested productively.[76] As Ikuto Yamguchi notes in his chapter, the privatized international currency system that made loans available at low rates in the mid-1970s worked in reverse after 1979 as the United States sought to drive inflation down by raising interest rates. High interest rates in the United States also re-routed capital away from developing countries to finance the growing US budget deficit. The result was a regional debt crisis beginning in 1982 and a "lost decade" as countries struggled to pay off their debts. In contrast, South Korea, which had also borrowed heavily to pay for oil imports and to maintain its development efforts, was able to avoid a debt crisis by expanding its exports. While Brazil's debt service payments consumed 31.9 percent of its export earnings in 1981, South Korea's debt service payments were only 13 percent of its export earnings in 1981.

---

[74] Stephen J. Randall, "The 1970s Arab-OPEC Oil Embargo and Latin America," H-Energy 1973 Energy Crisis Anniversary Discussion, 2014, 3–4, henergy-s-randall-latin-america-and-1973-oil-crisis.pdf; Bernardo F. Grossling, *Latin America's Petroleum Prospects in the Energy Crisis* (Washington, DC: US Government Printing Office, 1975), 9–10.

[75] Skeet, *OPEC: Twenty-Five Years*, 241; James H. Street, "Coping with Energy Shocks in Latin America: Three Responses," *Latin American Research Review* 17 (1982): 130.

[76] Jeremy Adelman, "International Finance and Political Legitimacy: A Latin American View of the Global Shock," in *The Shock of the Global*, ed. Ferguson et al., 124.

As in the case of Latin America, it is difficult to generalize about the impact of the oil crises on Africa due to continent's diversity. Africa produced much more oil than it consumed; production was more than six times consumption in 1973 and over four times consumption in 1980. Algeria, Libya, and Nigeria were the largest producers and exporters, accounting for almost 90 percent of African oil production in 1973 and a little over 80 percent in 1980. Gabon, Congo, Angola, Egypt, and Tunisia also produced some oil and were net exporters. Although the level of oil consumption was low, except for South Africa and Egypt, the oil price increases in 1973–4 and 1979–80 had a negative economic impact on most African countries. The oil exporting countries received higher revenues, but higher oil prices increased oil import costs for oil importing countries. Oil imports accounted for not more than 10 percent of Africa's total imports before the crisis, but the cost of oil imports as a percentage of total imports increased sharply during the 1970s. The cost of goods imported from the industrial world also increased sharply and, with some exceptions, the prices of the region's exports stagnated or declined, wiping out the foreign exchange reserves some countries had built up during the short-lived commodity boom of the early 1970s and forcing many countries to borrow to pay for increased import costs and maintain general consumption levels.[77]

Most African countries were not considered credit worthy by private capital markets and borrowed largely from international financial institutions like the World Bank and the IMF or from foreign governments.[78] Although their debt burdens were small relative to wealthier developing countries in other regions, they were high in relation to size of their economies and export revenues, and the privatization of international development finance, as outlined in Ikuto Yamaguchi's chapter, meant that they faced stricter conditions for the funds they received. In addition, high interest rates in the United States after 1979 increased debt burdens and rerouted private capital away from developing countries.[79]

Aggregate per capita growth rates dropped from about 1.6 percent in the 1960s to less than one percent during the 1970s, and Sub-Saharan Africa's share of world GNP per capital fell from 17 percent in 1970 to 12 percent in 1990. In addition, food production in many countries fell to critically low levels, and external debt burdens increased. Despite facing somewhat similar conditions, different outcomes often depended on government policies and factors such as political stability as Gareth Austin demonstrates in his chapter comparing Ghana and Kenya.[80]

As Mark Metzler's chapter points out, the 1970s saw financial and food shocks as well two oil shocks. Oil was a key feedstock in the production of chemical fertilizer, so oil prices had a direct impact on food production and prices due to the growing use of chemical fertilizers related in part to the Green Revolution. Domestic oil production

---

[77] Willard R. Johnson and Ernest J. Wilson III, "The 'Oil Crises' and African Economies: Oil Wave on a Tidal War of Industrial Price Inflation," *Daedalus* 111 (Spring 1982): 211–41.

[78] David E. Spiro, *The Hidden Hand of American Hegemony: Petrodollar Recycling and International Markets* (Ithaca, NY: Cornell University Press, 1999), 63, 71–4, 129.

[79] Giovanni Arrighi, "The African Crisis: World Systemic and Regional Aspects," *New Left Review* 15 (May/June 2002): 21–4.

[80] Arrighi, "African Crisis," 15; Johnson and Wilson, "The 'Oil Crises' and African Economies," 211–12.

met 31 percent of India's oil needs in 1973 and 30 percent in 1980, and Shigeru Akita's chapter examines how higher prices for imported oil raised the cost of chemical fertilizer, domestically produced as well as imported, and threatened to undermine India's success in meeting the nation's food needs. Although India was able to cope with the first shock by increasing exports and through remittances from Indian workers in the Persian Gulf, the second shock of 1979 renewed the stress on India's balance of payments, underlining the important role of oil in Indian economic development.[81]

The increases in oil prices also had the potential to affect food production in Southeast Asia. Hideki Kan traces the successful efforts of the Asian Development Bank to increase its lending, shift the focus of its assistance to agriculture, and provide a larger percentage of its aid on concessional terms to the poorer countries in the region. These efforts helped mitigate the impact of higher oil prices on the region and laid the foundation for its continued development.

7. Oil and Money

Between 1970 and 1980, OPEC members' revenues increased from $7.3 billion to $275 billion. Some oil exporters, like Iran, spent a large portion of their increased oil revenues by sharply increasing imports, including military equipment. Countries with large oil export revenues but small populations, especially Saudi Arabia, Kuwait, and the UAE, were unable to increase their imports significantly in the short term and deposited large amounts of money in dollar-denominated accounts, particularly but not exclusively in the London Eurodollar market and with US banks. According to statistics compiled by the Bank for International Settlements, OPEC members' investible surplus for the period 1974 to 1982 was $373.7 billion, approximately 21.4 percent of its members' total revenue of $1,744,800,000 for this period.[82]

The sudden and massive transfer of wealth from oil importers to oil exporters threatened economic stability and seemed to portend a shift in political power. US and other Western leaders were concerned that oil exporting countries could use their newly acquired oil wealth for political purposes, especially since so much money was in highly liquid short-term deposits. The solution in the long run would be to encourage them to invest in Western economies, thus giving them a stake in the economic health and stability of the countries where they invested. In the short run, the problem was to ensure that these funds would be recycled by Western and particularly US banks to bolster the financial system and to help finance the balance of payments deficits that the oil price increases had exacerbated.[83]

Under the Bretton Woods system, the International Monetary Fund (IMF) had the task of financing abrupt balance of payments deficits, but in the 1970s the IMF played a marginal role in petrodollar recycling. The IMF established two "oil facilities" to help

---

[81] *BP Statistical Review of World Energy*, 2022.
[82] Skeet, *OPEC: Twenty-Five Years*, 244; Spiro, *Hidden Hand*, 128; Ryan C. Smith, *The Real Oil Shock: Re-examining Petrodollar Recycling's Impact on International Credit Markets* (Ph.D. dissertation, University of Glasgow, 2022), 77. https://theses.gla.ac.uk/82854.
[83] Wight, *Oil Money*, 68–9; Spiro, *Hidden Hand*, 28–9, 33–9, 45–6.

countries experiencing severe balance of payments deficits, but United States preferred that recycling be handled by private banks and limited IMF funding to low levels and tended to view the IMF as a competitor for petrodollars. The United States also hoped that limiting the ability of LDCs to obtain public financing to pay for oil imports would lead to them blaming OPEC for their economic problems and put pressure on OPEC to lower oil prices.[84]

The Saudis were interested in providing funds to the IMF, but only if they could obtain an executive directorship, which the United States opposed because it would undermine US influence in the IMF. Saudi Arabia eventually got an executive directorship in April 1978 with the second amendment to the IMF charter. In addition, the US government removed remaining restrictions on the flow of funds to and from the United States and allowed US banks, in addition to those already active on the London market, to participate in the management of petrodollars. As a result, most petrodollars flowed into the private banking system.[85]

Private banks in London and the United States got a relatively large share of OPEC's investments, around 40 percent (35.5 percent with Eurodollar banks including US banks in the Eurodollar market and 4.5 percent with US banks in the United States). Around 18 percent went to direct bilateral and multilateral aid and loans to developing countries; 11 percent was invested in US government securities; 7 percent in portfolio investments in the United States; 15 percent to direct and equity investments in other industrialized countries; and 6 percent to IMF and World Bank facilities. In addition, OPEC members in the Middle East spent large sums on purchases of military equipment and services, largely but not entirely in the United States and other Western countries.[86]

The US government worked out an arrangement with Saudi Arabia that allowed the Saudi Arabian Monetary Authority to purchase US Treasury bonds outside regular auctions and at preferential rates. The Saudis insisted that their investments in US securities be kept secret, and Treasury designed a special mechanism known as "add-ons" which let Saudi purchases be hidden from the usual published figures of US debt sales. Treasury reports also grouped Saudi holdings with those of other oil exporters rather than publishing figures for each country. Keeping information about Saudi investments secret reduced the chance of public and congressional questioning of Saudi investment in the United States and guarded the Saudi government from criticism for investing in the West instead of Arab countries like Egypt that badly needed capital.[87]

[84] Wight, *Oil Money*, 88–9; Spiro, *Hidden Hand*, 96–101; Sargent, *A Superpower Transformed*, 130, 141, 184; Christopher R.W. Dietrich, *Oil Revolution: Anticolonial Elites, Sovereign Rights, and the Economic Culture of Decolonization* (New York: Cambridge University Press, 2017), 281–301; Dietrich, "Oil Power and Economic Theologies: The United States and the Third World in the Wake of the Oil Crisis," *Diplomatic History* 40 (June 2016), 512–29.
[85] Basosi, "Oil, Dollars, and US Power in the 1970s," 11–13.
[86] Wight, *Oil Money*, 117–21; Basosi, "Oil, Dollars, and US Power in the 1970s," 5; Deborah J. Gerner, "Petro-Dollar Recycling: Imports, Arms, Investment, and Aid," *Arab Studies Quarterly* 7 (Winter 1985): 1–26. Michael T. Klare, *American Arms Supermarket* (Austin: University of Texas Press, 1984), 108–62.
[87] Spiro, *Hidden Hand*, 105–13, 118–21; Andrea Wong, "The Untold Story Behind Saudi Arabia's 41-Year US Debt Secret," *Bloomberg*, May 30, 2016, https://www.bloomberg.com/news/features/2016-05-30/the-untold-story-behind-saudi-arabia-s-41-year-u-s-debt-secret.

At the same time the financial arrangements were finalized in December 1974, the Saudis announced that they would only accept US dollars as payment for their oil. Until 1974, around 75 percent of international oil transactions were in dollars, with around 20 percent in British pounds. After the Saudi decision the use of the pound in international oil transactions declined, leading to a de facto oil-dollar standard.[88] With oil priced and sold mostly in dollars, the United States benefitted from the central position of the dollar in international monetary affairs. The dollar's dual role as the US national currency and the de facto international reserve currency allowed the United States to print dollars to pay not only for oil imports but also for goods and services from other countries that had to pay for oil in dollars but could not print dollars. Because OPEC countries continued to price oil in dollars the US could continue "to tap the resources of the rest of the world virtually without restriction, simply by issuing its own currency."[89] The link between oil and the dollar ensured that the dollar would continue to have a major role in world monetary reserves and trade transactions.

US–Saudi financial arrangements were part of a larger recasting of the informal alliance between the two countries that included strengthened military ties and cooperation in economic development. An unnamed former US ambassador to the Middle East told one scholar that the financial arrangements were linked to an explicit US offer to "provide a security umbrella for the Gulf," a "security for dollars" version of the much-criticized "security for oil" characterization of the US–Saudi relationship. In addition, Duccio Basosi quotes the authors of the official history of SAMA as arguing that working out ways to manage high oil prices was in effect an alternative to US military intervention.[90]

The end of the embargo did not end talk about a possible US military intervention to seize Arab oil fields. On August 12, 1974, Kissinger told newly installed President Gerald Ford that the oil situation was still bad and that if there was another embargo, "we may have to take some oil fields." Kissinger also urged Ford to warn the Egyptian government, who he was sure would pass along the warning to the Saudis, that another oil embargo would have "dire consequences." Kissinger made a similar statement to Ford on September 6, and in early December told Secretary of Defense James Schlesinger that the United States needed plans for seizing Middle East oil fields in case of another war in the region.[91]

In late December, just after US–Saudi financial negotiations concluded, Kissinger gave an interview to *Business Week* that warned that while the United States would not

[88] Basosi, "Oil, Dollars, and US Power in the 1970s," 19. In December 1974, the Saudi government held a 60 percent share in ARAMCO.
[89] Spiro, *Hidden Hand*, 121–2, 132–3; Basosi, "Oil, Dollars, and US Power in the 1970s," 31; Giovanni Arrighi, "The World Economy and the Cold War, 1970–1990," in *Cambridge History of the Cold War*, vol. 3: *Endings*, eds. Melvyn P. Leffler and Odd Arne Westad, 31.
[90] McFarland, *Oil Powers*, 181–234; Spiro, *Hidden Hand*, 116, 148; Vitalis, *Oilcraft*, chapter 4; Basosi, "Oil, Dollars, and US Power in the 1970s," 31.
[91] *FRUS 1969–1976*, E-9, doc. 95, Memorandum of Conversation between Ford and Kissinger, August 12, 1974; *FRUS 1969–1976*, 37, doc. 1, Memorandum of Conversation, August 13, 1974; Gerald R. Ford Library, National Security Adviser, Memoranda of Conversations, 1973–7, Digital File, Memorandum of Conversation between Ford and Kissinger, September 6, 1974; Memorandum of Conversation between Kissinger and Schlesinger, December 7, 1974.

use force against the oil producing nations over the price of oil, force was an option in situations where there was "some actual strangulation of the industrialized world." Although President Ford, Kissinger, and the State Department sought to assure the Saudis that Kissinger's remarks were not intended as a threat to Saudi Arabia and were actually "designed to put a stop to irresponsible talk about reckless military or political action on the price issue," the Saudis interpreted them as a threat.[92] Yamani warned the US ambassador that the fields and oil facilities could be sabotaged easily and any attempt to seize them would result in the loss of Saudi production for years to come. Whatever Kissinger's intent, it seems clear that he and other US officials believed that the threat of US forces occupying Saudi oil fields would help prevent another embargo and, along with economic, military, and financial ties, make it less likely that Saudi Arabia would take actions that harmed US interests.[93]

In early 1975 a pair of articles by conservative writers calling for the United States to occupy Arabian oil fields continued the pressure on Saudi Arabia. Robert W. Tucker, a prominent American political scientist, argued that the oil crisis threatened the breakdown of international order and that the United States should be prepared to use force to restore order and US leadership in the world. In March, *Harper's* published "Seizing Arab Oil", by Miles Ignotus (Unknown Soldier), who the magazine described as the "pseudonym of a Washington-based professor and defense consultant, with intimate links to high-level policymakers." The article argued that the United States should seize Arab oil fields and facilities and run them for ten years. The article provided detailed description of the logistics of such an operation and claimed that it was feasible and would not result in destruction of the oil facilities or Soviet intervention. The article caused an uproar in the United States as well as Saudi Arabia, and the US ambassador to Saudi Arabia stated on television that whoever wrote it was either "a madman, a criminal, or an agent of the Soviet Union." Although neither Tucker nor Miles Ignotus, who some scholars believe was Edward Luttwak, a Washington-based scholar who was working as an adviser to the Department of Defense, were US government officials, both had close ties to policymakers and Luttwak apparently received assistance from the Pentagon's Office of Net Assessment. Both were clearly intended to send a message to Saudi Arabia and other oil producing countries about the dangers of challenging US interests. Ambassador Akins wrote a detailed critique of these and similar articles but was later dismissed from his post by Kissinger for criticizing them and similar statements, some of which turned out to be by Kissinger speaking off the record.[94]

---

[92] *FRUS 1969–1976*, 37, doc. 30, Editorial Note; *FRUS 1969–1976, E-9*, doc. 125, Jidda 138, January 7, 1975; doc. 126, Ford to King Faisal, January 11, 1975.

[93] McFarland, *Oil Powers*, 168–9; Sebastian Herbstreuth, *Oil and American Identity: A Culture of Dependency and US Foreign Policy* (London: I.B. Tauris, 2016), 164–5; Gerald R. Ford Library, National Security Adviser, Memoranda of Conversations, 1973–7, Digital File, Memorandum of Conversation between Kissinger and Ford, January 6, 1975.

[94] Robert W. Tucker, "Oil: The Issue of Intervention", *Commentary* 59 (January 1975): 21–31; Miles Ignotus, "Seizing Arab Oil," *Harper's* (March 1975), 45–8, 50–2, 57–8, 60, 62; *FRUS 1969–1976*, 37, doc. 52, "War for Oil: Armageddon as Fun City," attached to Jidda A-23, April 13, 1975; Herbstreuth, *Oil and American Identity*, 166–8.

8. The Soviet Union and Eastern Europe

Higher oil prices produced windfall earnings for the Soviet Union. Between 1960 and 1973, Soviet oil production increased from around 2,957,118 bpd to 8,569,000 bpd. As production in Volga-Ural region plateaued, rich fields were found in the West Siberian Basin, making Soviet oil reserves the largest in the world outside the Persian Gulf. In the mid-1970s, the Soviet Union overtook the United States as the world's leading oil producer.[95] Soviet oil exports to hard currency markets increased and hard currency earnings from oil exports doubled in 1973 and again in 1974 and continued to increase for the rest of the decade. Hard currency earnings from natural gas exports increased even more sharply. By the early 1980s, oil exports were responsible for around half of the Soviet Union's hard currency earnings and energy exports for almost 80 percent, enabling the Soviets to import large amounts of Western grain and machinery.[96]

The Soviets also earned hard currency through arms sales to oil producing countries. Exports to developing countries of arms, military equipment, and dual-use civilian goods grew after the 1973 Arab-Israeli War as the rise in the revenues of oil exporters increased their purchasing power. Before 1973, Soviet arms transfers were mainly to leftist regimes and national liberation movements. After 1973, more than half of Soviet arms deliveries went to Middle Eastern states with access to oil money. Most of these sales were for hard currencies or barter arrangements in which the Soviets received oil that they re-exported for hard currency. Between 1974 and 1984, the Soviets received around $19 billion in hard currency from arms sales and earned around $23 billion on bilateral or soft currency arms sales.[97]

The Soviet leadership initially hoped to find markets for their oil and gas in the West, including the United States. Energy exports to the West would not only strengthen détente but would also provide access to technical and financial assistance needed to develop their energy resources. Although exports to Western Europe increased, the Soviets were not able to develop markets in the United State for political as well as economic reasons. Nevertheless, higher oil revenues may have made it possible for the Soviets to afford increased involvement in the Third World in the 1970. Conservative critics of détente even claimed that the October War 1973 Arab-Israeli War was an attempt by the Soviets to expand their influence in the Middle East, but scholars have found no evidence that this was the case.[98]

---

[95] Alekperov, *Oil of Russia*, 289–99; Goldman, *Enigma of Soviet Petroleum*, 33–56. Perović, "The Soviet Union's Rise as an International Energy Power," 14–24.

[96] CIA, *Soviet Energy Policy Toward Eastern Europe*, June 1980; CIA, *Soviet Energy Data Resource Handbook: A Reference Aid*, SOV 90–10021, May 1990, 7, both in CIA Documents; Goldman, *Enigma of Soviet Petroleum*, 6–7, 9, 91–2; Thane Gustafson, *Crisis Amid Plenty: The Politics of Soviet Energy under Brezhnev and Gorbachev* (Princeton: Princeton University Press, 1989), 264.

[97] Smith, *Russia and the World Economy*, 88–96. The total sales figures were higher, but many of the countries did not pay their bills, resulting in a lower net gain.

[98] Jeronim Perović and Dunja Krempin, "'The Key is in Our Hands': Soviet Energy Strategy during Détente and the Global Oil Crises of the 1970s," *Historical Social Research* 39 (2014): 116–32; Richard Ned Lebow and Janice Gross Stein, *We All Lost the Cold War* (Princeton, NJ: Princeton University Press, 1994), 149–288; David S. Painter, *The Cold War: An International History* (London: Routledge, 1999), 77–94; John Rosenberg, "The Quest Against Détente: Eugene Rostow, the October War, and the Origins of the Anti-Détente Movement, 1969–1976," *Diplomatic History* 19 (September 2015): 720–44.

Most Soviet oil exports went to Eastern Europe, 42 percent in 1970, 50 percent in 1974, and 47 percent in 1978. Exports to hard currency markets made up 32 percent of Soviet oil exports in 1970, 26 percent in 1974, and 35 percent in 1978.[99] Exports to Asia were limited by the closure of the Suez Canal from 1967 to 1975, though the Soviets made special efforts to supply North Vietnam's needs. Cuba received around 6 percent of Soviet oil exports, while the rest went to a variety of markets.[100]

Energy exports to Eastern Europe, of which oil was the most important by the 1970s, were a key element in Soviet efforts to maintain its sphere in Eastern Europe. Oil imports from the Soviet Union as a percentage of total energy consumption in the region rose from 11.3 percent in 1970 to 15 percent in 1977.[101] The sharp rise in oil prices caused serious problems for the communist governments in Eastern Europe. To deal with a slowdown in economic growth, which had matched that in Western Europe in the 1950s and 1960s, Eastern European governments planned to borrow capital from Western banks to import Western technology, modernize domestic production, and develop industries capable of producing exports competitive on the world market that would earn enough hard currency to pay off the loans. Although coal remained essential to the economies of most countries in the region, their modernization plans were dependent on increased imports of Soviet raw materials, especially oil and natural gas on favorable terms.[102]

The Soviets calculated the "price" they charged Eastern European countries for Soviet oil using the so-called Bucharest formula, which fixed prices for bloc members for five years based on the average of world market prices for the previous five years. In 1970, the Soviets set the reference price for oil for members of the Council for Mutual Economic Assistance (CMEA) at around 14 rubles per ton, which was approximately $2.43 per barrel using an inflated figure for the value of the ruble, compared to $1.80 per barrel on world markets. The dollar price was roughly the same if the value of the ruble was set at market rates. In any event, the ruble price was used for accounting purposes only and trade was conducted on a barter basis with Eastern European countries trading finished products for raw materials including oil. The East Europeans received an additional subsidy because the goods they furnished were uncompetitive on world markets due to outdated technology and inferior quality, while the oil they received could be sold for hard currency.[103]

Providing oil to Eastern Europe at subsidized prices limited the hard currency the Soviets could earn from increasing exports to the West at world market prices, thus highlighting the cost of maintaining a sphere of influence in the region. On the other hand, raising the price of oil supplied to Eastern Europe and not increasing the volume of oil supplied threatened economic growth and political stability in the region. In late

---

[99] CIA, *Soviet Energy Policy Toward Eastern Europe*, CIA Documents.
[100] CIA, *Soviet Energy Policy Toward Eastern Europe*, CIA Documents; Klinghoffer, *The Soviet Union and International Oil Politics*, 97–105.
[101] CIA, *Soviet Energy Policy Toward Eastern Europe*, CIA Documents.
[102] De Groot, "The Soviet Union, CMEA, and the Energy Crisis of the 1970s," 7, 14, 21; De Groot, "Global Reaganomics," 94; Bartel, *Triumph of Broken Promises*, 10, 49.
[103] De Groot, "The Soviet Union, CMEA, and the Energy Crisis of the 1970s," 15; Bartel, *Triumph of Broken Promises*, 36.

1974, the Soviets announced a new pricing system that set the reference price for 1975 based on an average of world prices for 1972, 1973, and 1974. After 1975, the reference price would be based on a rolling average of world market prices for the previous five years. The new system delayed the shock but still resulted in higher prices for Eastern Europe. In addition, the Soviets sought to limit the volume of oil supplied to Eastern Europe, which forced Eastern Europe to buy more oil on world markets for hard currency.[104]

The twin crises—higher prices for Soviet oil and for oil purchased on world markets—led East European governments to increase borrowing from Western banks. Flush with petrodollars from the oil exporting countries, international banks were eager to lend and offered low interest rates. Eastern European governments seemed like a good risk due to the widespread belief among bankers that countries did not go bankrupt. Socialist states also had a good record of timely payment and had never defaulted on their debts. Many bankers believed that authoritarian systems could control investment and consumption and would be able to impose austerity to pay back loans. In addition, many Western bankers subscribed to the so-called "umbrella theory," the idea that if East European states got into financial trouble, the Soviet Union would bail them out. Eurocurrency loans to Eastern European countries more than doubled between 1974 and 1975 and continued to rise through the 1970s.[105]

9. Iran and the Second Oil Shock

From World War II to 1971, the United States looked to Great Britain to play a leading role as guardian of Western access to the oil resources of the Persian Gulf. Over time, the United States assumed greater responsibility for the security and stability of the region, but British forces in the Middle East and the Far East remained an important element in the defense of the Persian Gulf from internal unrest and external pressure. In 1968, however, the British government informed the United States that they planned to withdraw their military forces from positions "East of Suez" by the end of 1971.[106]

Embroiled in an unpopular war in Vietnam, the United States turned to Iran to take over as guardian of the gulf. The shah was eager to accept, hoping to restore the power and prestige of ancient Persia. Iran's oil revenues rose from around $2.4 billion in 1972 to $4.4 billion in 1973, $17.8 billion in 1974, and $21.2 billion in 1977. Iran's military spending increased, from $1.4 billion in 1972 to $9.4 billion in 1977, around 40 percent

---

[104] De Groot, "The Soviet Union, CMEA, and the Energy Crisis of the 1970s," 6, 14, 16, 19; Bartel, *Triumph of Broken Promises*, 37–41.

[105] De Groot, "The Soviet Union, CMEA, and the Energy Crisis of the 1970s," 20–3; Bartel, *Triumph of Broken Promises*, 31–3, 41, 46; Lukas Dovern, "Frankfurt Stories: Narrative Economics and West German Lending to Socialist Poland, 1969–1989," *German Studies Review* 45 (May 2022): 270–2.

[106] Roland Popp, "Subcontracting Security: The United States, Britain, and the Gulf Before the Carter Doctrine," in *European-American Relations in the Middle East from Suez to Iraq*, ed. Daniel Mockli and Victor Mauer (London: Routledge, 2010), 171–86; Toru Onozawa, "The United States and the British Withdrawal from South Arabia, 1962–1967," *Japanese Journal of American Studies* 28 (2017): 83–103.

of Iran's budget. Iran became the largest single purchaser of US military equipment, as the Nixon administration, ignoring warnings from the US military mission in Iran, decided to give the shah a "blank check" to buy any US weapons system short of nuclear weapons. Between 1970 and 1978, the United States sold Iran over $20 billion worth of military equipment and training. Non-military trade also increased. Between January 1973 and September 1974, US companies signed contracts and joint ventures with Iran totaling $11.9 billion, and in March 1975 the United States and Iran signed an economic agreement that committed Iran to spend $15 billion on US goods and services over the following five years.[107]

The massive influx of oil money resulted in extravagant military spending, inflation, massive rural-urban migration, and increases in already sharp inequalities in wealth and income. The weapons systems the shah bought brought thousands of Western technicians and military advisers into Iran, further inflaming conservative fears of corrosive Western influence and swelling the ranks of the shah's opponents. The decline in real oil prices in 1978 led to economic problems in Iran and the outbreak of widespread demonstration against the regime starting in early 1978, ironically shortly after US President Jimmy Carter had visited Iran and had praised the shah for making Iran "an island of stability in one of the more troubled areas of the world."[108]

The unrest escalated during the year, but Carter and his top officials, preoccupied with other important issues including the Strategic Arms Limitation Talks (SALT) II treaty, negotiations with China, the Camp David negotiations, and unrest in Nicaragua, paid little attention. By the time they realized how serious the situation was, it was too late to take action to save the shah's regime. Carter's national security adviser Zbigniew Brzezinski lobbied for military intervention, either by the shah's forces or by the United States. At the end of December Brzezinski warned: "the disintegration of Iran, with Iran repeating the experience of Afghanistan would be the most massive American defeat since the beginning of the Cold War, overshadowing in its *real consequences* the setback in Vietnam."[109]

Brzezinski failed to convince the shah to crush the opposition by force or to organize a military coup, and President Carter refused to intervene directly with US forces. The

---

[107] Painter, "From the Nixon Doctrine to the Carter Doctrine," 74; Roham Alvandi, "Nixon, Kissinger, and the Shah: The Origins of Iranian Primacy in the Persian Gulf," *Diplomatic History* 36 (April 2012): 337–72; David R. Collier, *Democracy and the Nature of American Influence in Iran, 1941–1979* (Syracuse, NY: Syracuse University Press, 2017), 246–59; Skeet, *OPEC: Twenty-Five Years*, 240; James A. Bill, *The Eagle and the Lion: The Tragedy of Iranian-American Relations* (New Haven, CT: Yale University Press, 1988), 201–4; Klare, *American Arms Supermarket*, 108-26. Stephen McGlinchey, *US Arms Policy and the Shah* (New York: Routledge, 2014) provides detailed information about US arms sales to Iran.

[108] On the relationship between uneven economic growth and the emergence of radical opposition to the shah, see Mark J. Gasiorowski, *U.S. Foreign Policy and the Shah: Building a Client State in Iran* (Ithaca: Cornell University Press, 1991), 142–51, 187–222; Fakhreddin Azimi, *The Quest for Democracy in Iran* (Cambridge: Harvard University Press, 2008), 244–7, 297–303. For Carter's remarks, see Michael H. Hunt, *Crises in U.S. Foreign Policy: An International History Reader* (New Haven: Yale University Press, 1996), 400.

[109] CIA Memorandum, November 3, 1978 on PRC Meeting on Iran, November 6, 1979; Stansfield Turner, Memorandum for the Record, December 8, 1978, both in CIA Documents; *FRUS 1977–1980*, 1, doc. 100, Brzezinski to the President, December 2, 1978; Jimmy Carter Library, Brzezinski Collection, Subject File, Weekly Reports, 82–90, Brzezinski to the President, Weekly Report #83, December 28, 1978.

shah left Iran in mid-January 1979, and in February, opposition leader Ayatollah Ruhollah Khomeini returned to Iran from exile and began the long and violent process of establishing a regime controlled by the Shia clergy.[110]

The turmoil surrounding the Iranian Revolution and its aftermath disrupted oil supplies and markets. Iranian exports briefly stopped in November 1978 and again in early 1979, before resuming later in that year at a reduced level. Although increases in production in other countries, in particular Saudi Arabia, partly offset the drop in Iranian exports, fear of spreading turmoil, the disruption of marketing channels, and a build-up of inventories due to fear of further problems resulted in a 6 percent drop in the amount of oil available in international markets. Oil prices jumped from $14.02 a barrel in 1978 to $31.61 in 1979 and reached $36.83 (in nominal dollars) in 1980 after the Saudis began to cut back their production.[111]

10. Guardian of the Gulf

The fall of the shah and fears of internal unrest in Saudi Arabia convinced US policymakers that the previous policy of reliance on regional surrogates to guard Western interests in the Middle East was no longer viable and renewed efforts to build up US military forces in the region. Concerns about Western vulnerabilities in the Middle East had existed since the onset of the Carter administration. Soviet and Cuban involvement in the Horn of Africa, astride the maritime routes to and from the Persian Gulf, raised concern about threat to Western access to the region's oil.[112] Reports about an impending oil shortage in the Soviet Union further fed fears of Soviet designs on the Persian Gulf. In 1977, three CIA studies had predicted that Soviet oil production would peak in 1980 and decline sharply thereafter, forcing the Soviet Union and its East European allies to look outside the Soviet bloc to meet their oil needs.[113] Although

---

[110] Zbigniew Brzezinski, *Power and Principle: Memoirs of the National Security Adviser, 1977–1981* (New York: Farrar, Straus, Giroux, 1983), 358; Cyrus Vance, *Hard Choices: Critical Years in America's Foreign Policy* (New York: Simon and Schuster, 1983), 326; Jimmy Carter, *Keeping Faith: Memoirs of a President* (New York: Bantam Books, 1982), 438–45. The U.S. Ambassador to Iran, William H. Sullivan, chronicles the course of the revolution in *Mission to Iran* (New York, W. W. Norton, 1981). Bill, *The Eagle and the Lion*, chapter 7, and Collier, *Democracy and the Nature of American Influence in Iran*, chapter 8, provide brief, perceptive accounts of the US response to the Iranian revolution.

[111] *BP Statistical Review of World Energy*, 2021; Yergin, *The Prize*, 684–91; Schneider, *Oil Price Revolution*, 422–56. Many accounts play down the impact of the second shock because in percent terms the price increase was less than those in 1973. The absolute amount of the increase was greater, however.

[112] *FRUS 1977–1980*, 18, doc. 1, Quandt and Sick to Brzezinski, February 2, 1977; *FRUS 1977–1980*, 1, doc. 100, Carter to Brzezinski to the President, December 2, 1978; Adam M. Howard and Alexander R. Wieland, "Confronting the Arc of Crisis: The Carter Administration's Approach to Security Building in the 'Greater Gulf' Region, 1977–1980," in *United States Relations with China and Iran*, ed. Osamah F. Khalil (London: Bloomsbury Academic, 2019), 153–69; Brzezinski, *Power and Principle*, 177–81, 203–4.

[113] Brzezinski to the President, NSC Weekly Report #31, October 7, 1977; Military Assistant to Brzezinski, Weekly Report, September 22, 1977; Jimmy Carter Library, Brzezinski Collection, Subject File, Weekly Reports, US Central Intelligence Agency, *The International Energy Situation: Outlook to 1985*, ER 77-10240 U, April 1977; CIA, *Prospects for Soviet Oil Production*, ER 77-10270, April 1977; CIA, *Prospects for Soviet Oil Production: A Supplemental Analysis*, July 1977, CIA Documents; Donald L. Bartlett and James B. Steele, "The Oily Americans," *Time*, May 19, 2003, *Time* Archive, http://www.time.com.

independent experts raised doubts about these predictions, and the CIA later qualified its conclusions, the belief that the Soviets needed to gain control of Persian Gulf oil persisted.[114] Scholars have yet to find convincing evidence that Soviet involvement in the so-called arc of crisis was driven by a desire to gain access to the oil resources of the Persian Gulf or to deny the West access to these resources.

The storming of the US Embassy in Tehran by radical supporters of the Ayatollah Khomeini in November 1979 and the taking of over fifty US diplomats hostage intensified the US determination to secure bases and gain access rights in the region and to develop and deploy the military capacity to ensure access to Persian Gulf oil. In December, an interagency intelligence memorandum warned that US influence in the area had declined, and that "manifestations of anti-American feeling" had increased. Although the changed circumstances were mainly due to internal factors such as the Arab-Israeli conflict, higher oil prices, and "the resurgence of a politicized Islam and a rejection of Western culture," the CIA believed that the Soviets were "abetting the growing instability in the region" to expand their influence there. The greatest potential for substantial Soviet gains in the near term, the report warned, was in Iran, "where continuing serious instability could give way to a leftist regime more sympathetic to the USSR." Even if the government of Ayatollah Khomeini was able to restore order, which the CIA viewed as unlikely, "it may only be the precursor to more determined efforts to export the revolution."[115]

Soviet intervention in Afghanistan in December 1979 revived fears of direct Soviet encroachment in the region.[116] Brzezinski wrote Carter on December 26 that if the Soviets succeeded in Afghanistan and Pakistan acquiesced to Soviet pressure, "the age-long dream of Moscow to have direct access to the Indian Ocean will have been fulfilled."[117] Brzezinski recommended that the United States fashion deeper security arrangements with allies in the Middle East to prevent Soviet influence from spreading from Afghanistan to Pakistan and Iran, which "would place in direct jeopardy our most vital interests in the Middle East." The fate of Western Europe, East Asia, and the United States, he warned, were linked to the Persian Gulf and its oil. Invoking the legacy of the Truman Doctrine for more aggressive policies toward the Soviet Union, he also pushed

---

[114] "CIA Chided on Soviet Oil Predictions," *Washington Post*, May 22, 1978, A1, 7; Roger Stern, "Oil Scarcity Ideology in US Foreign Policy, 1908–1997," *Security Studies* 25 (2016): 241–7. The CIA revised its estimate in late 1983, noting that Soviet proved oil reserves were probably about twice as large as it previously believed and that in late 1977 the Soviets began an intensive, high priority effort to develop West Siberian oil and gas. CIA, *Soviet Energy Prospects into the 1990s*, NIE 11-7-83, December 14, 1983, CIA Records Search Tool (CREST).

[115] McFarland, *Oil Powers*, 226; *FRUS 1977–1980*, 18, doc. 34, Odom to Brzezinski, November 28, 1979; doc. 35, CIA, Intelligence Memorandum, "New Realities in the Middle East," NI IIM 79-10026, December 1979; Olav Njølstad, "Shifting Priorities: The Persian Gulf in US Strategic Planning in the Carter Years," *Cold War History* 4 (April 2004): 26–33, 51, note 19; William E. Odom, "The Cold War Origins of the U.S. Central Command," *Journal of Cold War Studies* 8 (Spring 2005): 57–9.

[116] Jimmy Carter, *White House Diary* (New York: Farrar, Straus and Giroux, 2010), 368, 371, 372, 389; Brzezinski, *Power and Principle*, 177–81, 203–4, 482–5; Soviet intervention in Afghanistan led the United States to shelve plans to take military action against Iran.

[117] *FRUS 1977–1980*, 12, doc. 97, Brzezinski to the President, December 26, 1979.

for sharp increases in military spending and establishing a strategic relationship with China.[118]

The CIA, on the other hand, did not believe that Soviet intervention in Afghanistan constituted the "beginning of a premeditated strategic offensive." Rather the CIA assessed the intervention as a reluctant response to what Soviet leaders feared was the "imminent and otherwise irreversible deterioration" of their position in a neighboring country. The CIA also argued that the Soviet move in Afghanistan did not presage action against Iran.[119] Subsequent research supports the CIA analysis, but President Carter followed Brzezinski's recommendations.

In his State of the Union address on January 23, 1980, President Carter warned that the Soviet invasion of Afghanistan "could pose the most serious threat to the peace since the Second World War." The Persian Gulf contained more than two-thirds of the world's exportable oil, and Soviet control of Afghanistan would put Soviet military forces within 300 miles of the Indian Ocean and close to the Straits of Hormuz, through which most of the region's oil flowed. The Soviets, he concluded, were "attempting to consolidate a strategic position, therefore, that poses a grave threat to the free movement of Middle East oil." To meet this threat, the President announced what became known as the Carter Doctrine: "An attempt by any outside power to gain control of the Persian Gulf region will be regarded as an assault on the vital interests of the United States of America, and such an assault will be repelled by any means necessary, including military force."[120]

To back up his policy, the United States took steps to improve its capability to deploy military forces rapidly in the region. In March, the Defense Department established a Rapid Deployment Joint Task Force (RDJTF) at MacDill Air Force Base in Florida. The United States also began negotiations to secure access to facilities in the region and made preparations to preposition equipment on land and on special ships.[121] Planned from the time of the collapse of the shah's regime, the move reflected US belief that local forces were not sufficient to protect Western interests in the Middle East from either Soviet aggression or internal instability.[122]

---

[118] Brzezinski, *Power and Principle*, 431; National Security Council Meeting, January 2, 1980, in *The Fall of Détente: Soviet-American Relations during the Carter Years*, ed. Odd Arne Westad (Oslo: Scandinavian University Press, 1997), 332–51; *FRUS 1977–1980*, 12, doc. 134, Brzezinski to the President, January 2, 1980; doc. 140, Brzezinski to the President, January 3, 1980; "An Interview with Zbigniew Brzezinski," *Wall Street Journal*, January 15, 1980, 20; for context, see Melvyn P. Leffler, "From the Truman Doctrine to the Carter Doctrine: Lessons and Dilemmas of the Cold War," *Diplomatic History* 7 (Fall 1983): 245–66. On the overall US reaction to the Soviet intervention, see Garthoff, *Détente and Confrontation*, 1046–75.

[119] *FRUS 1977–1980*, 12, doc. 147, CIA Intelligence Assessment, January 1980; doc. 158, CIA Intelligence Assessment, January 1980; doc. 168, "Soviet Union and Southwest Asia," attached to Turner, Memorandum for the President, January 15, 1980; Westad, *Global Cold War*, 316–26; Leffler, *For the Soul of Mankind*, 303–11, 329–34.

[120] Jimmy Carter, *Public Papers of the Presidents, 1980–1981* (Washington, DC: U.S. Government Printing Office, 1980–1), 194–200, quotation on 197; also in *FRUS 1977–1980*, 1, doc. 138.

[121] Brzezinski, *Power and Principle*, 446, 456; Michael A. Palmer, *Guardians of the Gulf: A History of America's Expanding Role in the Persian Gulf, 1833–1992* (New York: Free Press, 1992), 106–11; McFarland, *Oil Powers*, 227–33.

[122] McFarland, *Oil Powers*, 226–7.

Planning continued through the year, and in one of its last official acts, the Carter administration in January 1981 elevated the status of the Persian Gulf in terms of US strategic priorities. In a pair of Presidential Directives signed on January 15, 1981, the Carter administration assigned the Persian Gulf region top priority for resources in the Five-Year Defense Plan and second place, after Western Europe, in terms of planning for wartime operations.[123]

Although the US Naval presence in the Persian Gulf more than doubled, progress in getting Persian Gulf states to sign basing and access agreements moved slowly. In 1983, the RDJTF became the US Central Command (CENTCOM), a regional unified military command with responsibility for protecting US interests in the Middle East, North Africa, and Central Asia. Eventually, the Iran–Iraq War, and especially US involvement in the so-called "tanker war" between Iran and Iraq in 1987–8, convinced regional states to allow the US military greater access to facilities in their territory.[124]

11. Economic Fallout

The decline in the value of the dollar in the late 1970s relative to other world currencies, in part due to concerns that US oil consumption was on the rise, led the Saudi Arabian government to urge the United States to take action to stem the dollar's decline. Saudi investments gave them an interest in the stability and value of the dollar. Oil was priced in dollars as were around 75 percent of Saudi Arabia's financial assets, and a weak dollar reduced the value of Saudi earnings and its overseas investments. Concerned that the Saudis could price their oil in other currencies or withdraw some of their investments in the United States, the Carter administration announced steps on November 1, 1978, to curb inflation and defend the dollar, including a sharp rise in the Federal Reserve's discount rate.[125]

After the Iranian Revolution and cuts in Iranian oil production and exports sent oil prices soaring and inflation continued to worsen, the Federal Reserve Board, under newly appointed chairman Paul Volcker, announced in October 1979 that it would focus on restraining inflation by regulating growth of the money supply. Over the following three years, the Federal Reserve Board raised interest rates to all-time highs. This policy boosted the value of the dollar and eventually tamed inflation, but at the cost of triggering a recession, reducing the competitiveness of US industry, and increasing unemployment.[126]

---

[123] Presidential Directive PD/NSC-62, "Modifications in US National Security Strategy," January 15, 1981, Federation of American Scientists website; *FRUS 1977–1980*, 18, doc. 98, Presidential Directive PD/NSC-63, "Persian Gulf Security Framework," January 15, 1981; Njølstad, "Shifting Priorities," 42–8.

[124] Hal Brands, *Making the Unipolar Moment: US Foreign Policy and the Rise of the Post-Cold War Order* (Ithaca, NY: Cornell University Press, 2016), 235, 238–9; Toby Craig Jones, "After the Pipelines: Energy and the Flow of War in the Persian Gulf," *South Atlantic Quarterly* 116 (April 2017): 417–25.

[125] Spiro, *Hidden Hand*, 122–6, 59–60.

[126] McFarland, *Oil Powers*, 196–200; Smith, *The Real Oil Shock*, 115–24, 268; and Evan A. North, "Saudi Arabia and the US Dollar Crisis of 1978–80" (unpublished paper, Georgetown University, 2008).

Higher interest rates in the United States resulted in a massive flow of foreign capital into the United States, which helped the Reagan administration finance the staggering budget deficits that resulted from sharply increased military spending and massive tax cuts without large-scale reductions in spending on other programs. Western Europe, Japan, and the newly industrializing countries of East Asia benefitted from increased US demand for their exports but developing countries and Eastern Europe suffered as high interest rates drove up the cost of their loans and capital shifted its focus from them to the United States.[127]

Although the oil producers' initial success in increasing their revenues encouraged demands by the nations of the Global South for a new international economic order, higher oil prices hit non-oil-producing developing countries hard because they had to pay higher prices for oil at the same time as demand for their exports dropped due to the impact of high oil prices on the economies of their key customers. Developing countries were also largely left out of the "oil triangle" of trade and financial flows that allowed Japan and other East Asia industrial countries to pay for oil imports from the Middle East by increasing their exports to the United States and Western Europe, which exported military equipment and absorbed petrodollars from Middle East oil exporters into their banking systems.[128]

In contrast, Latin American debt increased from $59 billion in 1975 to $331 billion in 1982 and led to a region wide debt crisis in the 1980s due mostly to massive borrowing by countries which sought to take advantage of low interest rates to finance industrialization but also due to the increase in oil prices after the second oil shock and higher interest rates.[129] Most African countries borrowed smaller sums largely from international financial institutions rather than private banks, but their debts were still large in proportion to the size of their economies and their capacity to increase exports, and they also suffered from higher oil import costs, declining terms of trade, and loss of markets. Increased interest rates and the diversion of capital to the United States in 1980s also worsened their situation.[130]

Eastern Europe's experience paralleled that of Latin America. As noted earlier, many East European countries borrowed from Western banks during the 1970s, and by the end of the decade they held debts they struggled to repay. The second oil price shock made matters worse, and after the United States raised interest rates, the flood of Western credits turned into a drought. High US interest rates diverted capital flows away from the region and higher interest payments made existing loans more costly to service and reduced the ability of the region's governments to receive new loans. When loans were available, interest rates were high, and borrowers had to comply with stringent conditions set by the IMF to ensure repayment. In addition, the United States

[127] De Groot, "Global Reaganomics," 94.
[128] Sugihara, "Oil Triangle," 6–10.
[129] De Groot, "Global Reaganomics," 97; Robert E. Wood, *From the Marshall Plan to the Debt Crisis: Foreign Aid and Development Choices in the World Economy* (Berkeley; University of California Press, 1986), 266–7. For an overview, see Venn, *The Oil Crisis*, 173–200.
[130] De Groot, "Global Reaganomics," 97–8; Arrighi, "The Africa Crisis," 5–36.

used its influence in international financial institutions to insist on political as well financial conditions for receiving aid.[131]

12. The Counter-Shock of the 1980s

To address the economic conditions that had led to the oil shock, the OECD nations in the mid-1970s launched a coordinated campaign to protect themselves from future disruptions in supply. The campaign focused on reducing oil consumption through greater efficiency and conservation, replacing oil with other energy sources, particularly in electricity generation, and reducing oil imports from OPEC producers, especially those in the Middle East, by increasing oil production elsewhere.[132] IEA members also sought to increase their oil stocks, through either working with private companies or, as in the case of the United States, establishing a government-owned Strategic Petroleum Reserve.[133]

Although these efforts lagged due to declining real prices for oil between 1974 and 1979, the second oil shock revived them. Between 1979 and 1985, oil consumption in the non-communist world fell from 51.6 to 46.3 million bpd because of higher prices and recessions in 1973–5 and 1979–82. In addition, coal and natural gas replaced fuel oil in many industrial and utility uses, and total use of nuclear power by the advanced industrial countries more than doubled. Over the same period, non-OPEC oil production in the non-communist world, mainly in Great Britain, Norway, Mexico, and the United States, increased from 17.7 to 22.6 million barrels per day, as higher prices and advances in technology, especially in offshore production, spurred increased output. The result was a 10.2 million bpd drop in demand for OPEC oil. Chinese oil production and exports also increased during this period, further adding to global supply.[134]

Japan accounted for around 20 percent of the decrease in oil consumption. The Japanese government responded to higher oil prices and insecurity of supply by promoting conservation and efficiency in energy use, conversion of electricity generation and industrial processes from oil to other fuel sources, accelerating construction of nuclear power plants, expanding coal and liquefied natural gas (LNG) imports, and seeking oil supplies outside the Middle East. These policies took time to bear fruit, and Japanese oil consumption, which had reached 5.265 million bpd in 1973, fell only slightly in 1974 and increased to 5.491 million bpd in 1979, but over time

[131] De Groot, "Global Reaganomics," 95–6; Stephen Kotkin, "The Kiss of Debt: The East Bloc Goes Borrowing," in *The Shock of the Global*, ed. Ferguson et al., 80–93; Bartel, *Triumph of Broken Promises*, 201–91.
[132] Henning Türk, "Reducing Dependence on OPEC Oil: The IEA's Energy Strategy Between 1976 and the Mid-1980s," in *Counter-Shock*, ed. Basosi, Garavini, and Trentin, 241–58.
[133] Bruce A. Beaubouef, "The US Strategic Petroleum Reserve and Energy Security Lessons of the 1970s," in *American Energy Policy in the 1970s*, ed. Lifset, 163–83; Paul Sabin, "Crisis and Continuity in US Oil Policies, 1965–1980," *Journal of American History* 99 (June 2012), 183–6.
[134] Garavini, *Rise and Fall of OPEC*, 301–26; Edward T. Dowling and Francis G. Hilton, "Oil in the 1980s: An OECD Perspective," in *The Oil Market in the 1980s: A Decade of Decline*, ed. Siamack Shojai and Bernard S. Katz (New York: Praeger, 1992), 75, 77–8; Priest, "Shifting Sands," 122–41.

Japan was able to reduce its oil consumption by over a million barrels per day by 1985.[135]

Despite the disruption caused by the Iran–Iraq War, these changes in supply and demand began to affect oil prices. The oil crises, by providing the producing countries with extra revenues and the confidence to assert their prerogatives, had led to a massive buy-out of the major producing firms and the establishment of national oil companies in the producing countries. In 1970, national oil companies owned less than 10 percent of their oil industries; by 1979, the figure was almost 70 percent (68.7 percent). Full ownership of all aspects of their oil industries gave producing countries greater control over such factors as the pace of development of their reserves, their rate of production, and the destination of their exports.[136] Ironically, the breakup of vertical integration increased competition among producers for markets, a development that the major oil companies promoted and exploited to drive down prices.[137]

The Saudis initially tried to support prices by reducing output, but the Saudi leadership decided in the summer of 1985 to regain their position in world markets by increasing production. Instead of selling oil at a fixed price, oil prices would be based on what refined products sold for in the marketplace minus a fixed margin for the refiner. The new system put a premium on volume rather than price and led to a collapse of world oil prices, which fell to around $17 a barrel in the first quarter of 1986 and $11 in the second quarter.[138]

The price collapse decimated Soviet hard currency earnings. Initially the decline in the price of oil after 1980 was, in part, offset by the rise in the value of the dollar against other major Western currencies, which enhanced the Soviet Union's foreign purchasing power because Soviet oil and gas exports were priced in dollars while most of their hard currency purchases were made in Western Europe and Japan in non-dollar currencies. The depreciation of the dollar beginning in the mid-1980s, on the other hand, eroded the purchasing power of Soviet energy revenues.[139] Hard currency oil export earnings, which had reached approximately $15.6 billion in 1983, fell to around

[135] Duffield, *Fuels Paradise*, 199–200; Yergin, *The Prize*, 654–5: Kaoru Sugihara, *Middle East, East Asia, and the World Economy: Further Notes on the Oil Triangle*, Working Paper Series No. 9 (Kyoto: Afrasian Centre for Peace and Development Studies, 2006), 4–7; *BP Statistical Review of World Energy*, 2018.
[136] Brian Levy, "World Oil Marketing in Transition," *International Organization* 36 (Winter 1982): 113–33; Rodman, *Sanctity Versus Sovereignty*, 232–69, 294–304.
[137] Francesco Petrini, "Counter-shocked? The Oil Majors and the Price Slump of the 1980s," in *Counter-Shock*, ed. Basosi, Garavini, and Trentin, 76–96.
[138] Garavini, *Rise and Fall of OPEC*, 326–60; Ian Skeet, *OPEC: Twenty-Five Years*, 194–212, 241; Majid Al-Moneef, "Saudi Arabia and the Counter-Shock of 1986," in *Counter-Shock*, ed. Basosi, Garavini, and Trentin, 99–116; CIA, "Threat Outlook: Lower Oil Prices: Impact on the Soviet Union," February 13, 1985; CIA, *Saudi Arabia, Kuwait, UAE: Asset Management in Austere Times*, GI 85-10099, April 1985; CIA, *OPEC: Narrowing Options in a Softening Oil Market*, GI 85-10165, June 1985; CIA, *The Saudi Oil Offensive*, GI M 86-20084, March 31, 1986, all in CIA Documents. See also Yergin, *The Prize*, 745–51; Victor McFarland, "The United States and the Oil Price Shock of the 1980s," in *Counter-Shock*, ed. Basosi, Garavini, and Trentin, 259–77.
[139] CIA, "Threat Outlook: Lower Oil Prices: Impact on the Soviet Union," February 13, 1985, CREST; CIA, *Implications of the Decline in Soviet Hard Currency Earnings*, NIE 11-23-86, September 1986, CIA Documents; Smith, *Russia and the World Economy*, 139.

$6.96 billion in 1986, due to a drop in production as well as lower prices. Low oil prices also took a toll on hard currency earnings from gas sales since the price of natural gas was often linked to oil prices. Natural gas earnings fell from almost $4 billion in 1981 to a little over $2.6 billion in 1988 despite an increase in exports from 61.7 billion cubic meters (bcm) in 1981 to an estimated 86 bcm in 1988.[140]

The drop in oil prices also hurt Soviet weapons exports, because many of their best customers were oil exporters. According to a CIA study, around 5 percent of Soviet hard currency earnings and 10 percent of Soviet oil exports were derived from re-exported Middle East oil, obtained mostly in exchange for Soviet arms. Soviet exports of arms and military goods to non-socialist countries denominated in hard currencies fell from $9.18 billion in 1984 to $7.49 billion in 1985.[141]

The sharp decline in export earnings undermined the reform plans of the new Soviet government of Mikhail Gorbachev, who came to power in March 1985. Gorbachev hoped to use oil and gas export earnings to finance a modernization of Soviet industry and to improve living standards, thus easing the transition from a command economy to a market economy and a more democratic society. Instead, declining oil and gas revenues played an important role in the collapse of the Soviet economy.[142] The collapse of oil prices also eroded Soviet willingness and ability to pay the cost of maintaining a sphere of influence in Eastern Europe. Higher interest rates after 1979 exacerbated the debt problems facing Eastern European regimes, making them vulnerable to pressures from international financial institutions, Western governments, and their own populations, but the Soviet Union stood by as the region's governments fell swiftly and, except for Romania, peacefully, in the revolutions of 1989.[143]

13. Conclusion

The oil crises of the 1970s played a central role in the transformation of the international order in the late twentieth century. The oil crises reflected and intensified the larger crisis of US/Western hegemony in the decade, but they also set in motion changes in the global economy that played an important role in collapse of communism and reassertion of Western dominance in the Global South.

---

[140] CIA, *USSR: Facing the Dilemma of Hard Currency Shortages*, SOV 86-10027X, May 1986, CREST; CIA, *Soviet Energy Data Resource Handbook*, May 1990; CIA, *USSR: Coping with the Decline in Hard Currency Revenues*, SOV 88-10014X, April 1988, CIA Documents; Smith, *Russia and the World Economy*, 81, 91, gives slightly different figures.

[141] Smith, *Russia and the World Economy*, 91, 147–8. According to CIA figures, Soviet arms sales were $4.9 billion in 1985 and increased to an average of $7.3 billion in 1986–7, CIA, *USSR: Coping with the Decline in Hard Currency Revenues*, SOV 88-10014X, April 1988, CIA Documents.

[142] David S. Painter, "Energy and the End of the Evil Empire," in *The Reagan Moment*, ed. Hunt and Miles, 43–63; Painter, "From Linkage to Economic Warfare: Energy, Soviet-American Relations, and the End of the Cold War," in *Cold War Energy*, ed. Perović, 298–302; David S. Painter and Thomas S. Blanton, "The End of the Cold War," in *A Companion to Post-1945 America*, ed. Jean-Christophe Agnew and Roy Rosenzweig (Oxford: Blackwell, 2002), 479–500.

[143] De Groot, "Global Reaganomics," 95–6; Bartel, *Triumph of Broken Promises*, 263.

The structure of the world oil economy changed dramatically in the 1970s. US oil reserves peaked in 1968 and oil production in 1970s, and the shift in investment to the Middle East resulted in a decline in excess capacity in the rest of the world making oil importers increasingly vulnerable to political events in the region. The result was the first oil shock that coincided with the 1973–4 Arab-Israeli War. The second price shock at the end of the 1970s was likewise the result of the interaction of structural changes in oil market including the failure of the largest oil consuming countries, especially the United States, to reduce significantly their oil consumption and their dependence on imports, with political instability in the Middle East, in this case the Iranian Revolution. The collapse of oil prices in the 1980s resulted from structural changes in the oil market, in particular a sharp increase in non-OPEC production, primarily from Mexico and the North Sea, but also from Russia, China, and Canada, and changes in consumption patterns—less oil use per unit of GDP and greater use of coal, natural gas, and nuclear power. OPEC's share of world oil production fell from 50.3 percent in 1973 to 40.6 percent in 1980 and 26.9 percent in 1985. In addition, although producing country governments gained full ownership of all aspects of their oil industries and greater control over such factors as the pace of development of their reserves, their rate of production, and the destination of their exports by the end of the 1970s, the breakup of vertical integration increased competition among producers for markets and put downward pressure on prices.[144]

In addition to the limits that structural factors placed on OPEC's ability to achieve its goals, the diversity of the organization's membership often undermined its ability to act cohesively. Although they shared the fundamental interest of sovereign landlords in protecting an international rent deriving from trading a non-renewable resource, OPEC's members did not share cultural identities, inhabited different geographic regions, embraced a range of political orientation, and largely lacked economic ties with each other. This lack of common interests hindered OPEC's ability to function as a cartel, even though Western observers routinely referred to it as a cartel. Its success in raising prices in the 1970s was due to the disruption and uncertainty caused by extraneous political events coupled with momentarily favorable structural factors. When it tried to operate as a cartel in the early 1980s, it failed.[145]

The oil crises of the 1970s had a profound impact on the Global South. As Dane Kennedy points out in his chapter, OPEC's success in gaining control of prices and production levels gave other developing countries hope that collective action could enable them to wrest control over their natural resources from foreign interests and restructure the international economy to take account of the interests of the developing countries of the Global South. Over time, however, increased oil prices presented problems for many African, Asian, and Latin American countries, including higher import costs for oil and manufactured goods and reduced revenues for their exports. The second oil shock caused a sharp rise in oil prices, further declines in the prices of

---

[144] Jochen H. Mohnfeld, "Implications of Structural Change," *Petroleum Economist* 49 (July 1982): 269–72; *BP Statistical Review of World Energy*, 2022.

[145] Garavini, *Rise and Fall of OPEC*, chapter 8.

Table 1.2 Oil prices and production, selected years, 1970–90

	PRICE US$	WORLD	UNITED STATES	SOVIET UNION	OPEC	SAUDI ARABIA
1970	1.80/12.70	48,075	11,297	7,127	22,523	3,851
			23.5%	14.8%	46.8%	8.0%
1973	3.29/19.17	58,552	10,946	8,664	29,439	7,693
			18.7%	14.8%	50.3%	13.1%
1974	11.58/55.47	58,671	10,461	9,270	29,281	8,618
			17.8%	15.8%	49.9%	14.7%
1978	14.02/55.65	63,322	10,274	11,531	28,233	8,554
			16.2%	18.2%	44.6%	13.5%
1980	36.83/115.68	62,942	10,170	12,116	25,569	10,270
			16.2%	19.2%	40.6%	16.3%
1985	27.56/66.29	57,345	10,580	11,870	15,445	3,601
			18.4%	20.7%	26.9%	6.3%
1986	14.43/34.08	60,176	10,231	12,269	17,891	5,208
			17.0%	20.4%	29.7%	8.7%
1990	23.73/46.98	65,022	8,914	11,403	23,195	7,106
			13.7%	17.5%	35.7%	10.9%

Source: *BP Statistical Review of World Energy*, 2022. Prices are dollars of the day/2021 dollars. Production in thousands of barrels per day.

their exports, and increases in interest rates that led to a Third World debt crisis and reduced economic growth in the 1980s. The impact of these events, reinforced by Western and especially US policies, shattered Third World unity, largely ending the Global South's challenge to Western dominance of the international order.

The oil crises also interacted with changes in the international financial order that reinforced Western, and especially US, influence in the global economy. As Mark Metzler points out in his chapter, the oil crises were preceded by financial, and especially dollar, crises. The huge influx of petrodollars following the first oil shock provided liquidity that facilitated the development of a new privatized international financial order based on the dollar as Western political leaders and bankers were able to devise non-disruptive ways for oil exporters to spend or invest their earnings that complemented the interests of the capitalist West. The dominant position of the United States in the world economy allowed it to garner the bulk of petrodollars and to recycle them on its own terms, thus reestablishing its hegemony in the international system. The losers were "poor countries that had nothing substantial to exchange as the price of oil and food and industrial goods all shot upwards."[146]

The impact of the oil crises of the 1970s on the environment is an extremely important but very complex topic. Political scientist Michael Ross argues that that energy conservation and investment policies enacted after the 1973 oil shock, though mostly motivated by the false fear of an imminent depletion of global oil and gas reserves, brought about a "deceleration of total carbon emissions." Global carbon

---

[146] Spiro, *Hidden Hand*, 152; William Glenn Gray, "Learning to 'Recycle': Petrodollars and the West, 1973–5," in *Oil Shock*, ed. Bini, Garavini, and Romero, 191.

emissions from energy increased from 16,335.4 million tonnes (mt) of carbon dioxide in 1973 to 18,564.2 mt in 1979, 19,217.3 mt in 1985, and 21,306.3 mt in 1990. Global growth in carbon emissions, however, fell from just under 5 percent annually in the decade before 1973 to less than 2 percent annually in next four decades. Although total emissions continue to increase, Ross concludes that they would have increased much faster without the changes induced by the oil shocks.[147]

Other scholars interpret the data differently and point out, among other things, that while the oil crises led to some efforts to reduce oil consumption, the main response in most countries was to expand production and consumption of other sources of energy. One of the most important impacts of the oil crises was an expansion of coal production and consumption, especially in China and India, which had a significant negative impact on the environment. Global coal consumption, 1,519.6 million tonnes of oil equivalent (mtoe) in 1973, increased to 1,793.3 mtoe in 1980, 2,055.6 mtoe in 1985 and 2,219.9 mtoe in 1990. In addition, the decline in energy intensity in the industrialized countries resulted in part from the transfer of energy-intensive industries to the Global South, which did nothing to reduce global energy use.[148]

At first glance, it appears that the oil crises of the 1970s weakened the United States and its allies and strengthened the Soviet Union. The sharp increase in oil prices exacerbated the economic problems faced by the United States and the other Western industrial countries in the 1970s, raised questions about US leadership of the Western Alliance and its ability to ensure access to Middle East oil, heightened concerns about the dangers of Western dependence on Third World resources and fed fears that the Soviet Union was winning the Cold War. In contrast, the Soviet Union overtook the United States as the world's leading oil producer in the 1970s, and higher oil prices increased Soviet oil export revenues.

After a difficult decade, the United States was able to reassert its influence in global oil through a combination of military power, government policies, and market forces. Higher oil prices led to the development of alternative sources of oil supply, alternative sources of energy, and to a reduction in oil consumption. These factors in combination led to a steep decrease in oil prices in the 1980s that not only sharply reduced OPEC's revenues and influence and but also played an important role in the end of the Cold War and the collapse of the Soviet Union.

---

[147] Michael L. Ross, "How the 1973 Oil Embargo Saved the Planet," *Foreign Affairs*, October 15, 2013. The article was published as an online posting (Snapshot) rather than in the print edition.
[148] Pirani, *Burning Up*, 94–100; *BP Statistical Review of World Energy*, 2019.

2

The Oil Crises as Fulcrum for the Rise and Fall of the Third World Project[1]

Dane Kennedy

The oil crises of 1973–4 and 1979 take on very different meanings depending on the vantage points from which they are viewed. Historians of the United States, for example, tend to cast them in the context of the systemic shift in that country's role in the world in the 1970s, placing the oil crises alongside the collapse of the postwar Bretton Woods economic order, the Watergate scandal that drove President Richard Nixon from office, the American military defeat in Vietnam, the onset of stagflation, and the transition to a market-driven, neoliberal system of international trade and finance as contributors to that shift.[2] The oil shocks impacted other countries in other, often widely varied ways. Even within the non-oil producing developing world, the economic and political consequences of 1973–4 and 1979 differed from country to country, as several contributors to the present volume demonstrate. The oil crises also can be viewed from a regional perspective, and here again they generated a range of repercussions. While the most obvious impact occurred in the Middle East, which assumed a new and outsized influence on world affairs, the present project shows that much of Asia underwent an important transformation in response to the oil shocks as well. Finally, the events of 1973–4 and 1979 cannot be divorced from the global forces that did so much to shape the decade. David Painter details the close connections between the oil crises and the changing contours of the Cold War in his contribution to the present volume. The purpose of my chapter is to examine how the oil crises intersected with another major aspect of global affairs in the 1970s—the rise and fall of the Third World project.

---

[1] I want to thank Shigeru Akita for inviting me to take part in the study project that has resulted in this volume. I also am grateful to David Painter for his advice, insight, and informed comments on several drafts of this paper and to the other participants in the Osaka, Heidelberg, and Washington D.C. workshops for their helpful suggestions.
[2] Daniel Sargent, *A Superpower Transformed: The Remaking of American Foreign Relations in the 1970s* (New York: Oxford University Press, 2015); Thomas Borstelman, *The 1970s: A New Global History from Civil Rights to Economic Inequality* (Princeton: Princeton University Press, 2012). For an American-centered introduction to the 1973–4 oil crisis, see Karen R. Merrill, *The Oil Crisis of 1973–1974: A Brief History with Documents* (Boston: Bedford/St. Martin's, 2007).

"The Third World was not a place," Vijay Prashad reminds us: "It was a project."[3] It drew together poorer, largely postcolonial countries in Africa, Asia, the Middle East, Latin America, and elsewhere, insisting that they shared a collective identity and sense of purpose. The objectives that informed the Third World as a political and economic project included a determination to wrest control over natural resources from foreign interests, restructure the international economy on behalf of developing countries, and avoid involvement in the Cold War struggle between the United States and the Soviet Union. The central thesis of this chapter is that the two oil crises were simultaneously a major manifestation of the Third World's efforts to achieve these ends and a set of events that undermined its aspirations and brought about its disintegration as a distinct and coherent force in international affairs.

1. The Rise of the Postcolonial International Order

The decades immediately following World War II saw the collapse of the European colonial empires and the creation of a whole host of new nation-states in their place. The size and significance of this transformation is evident in the dramatic increase in the United Nations' member states. When it was formed in 1945, the United Nations had fifty-one founding members, including countries like Britain and France, which still retained overseas colonial empires. By 1970, the United Nations had grown to 127 states, and a decade later it numbered 154. Of the 104 states admitted to the UN between its founding and 1980, the vast majority were postcolonial states, the products of European decolonization.[4]

By the early 1970s, Britain, France, and the Netherlands had relinquished all but a few of their overseas possessions, and Belgium had lost its African colonies. The Portuguese empire and the renegade Rhodesian white settler regime would collapse before the decade was over. Colonialism had lost legitimacy in the eyes of the international community. This is not to say that imperialism had ended. Britain and France continued to intervene politically and militarily in the affairs of some of their ex-colonies, especially in sub-Saharan Africa. Though South Africa and Israel were classified as nation-states, their discriminatory racial/ethnic policies toward the indigenous peoples within their borders resembled colonial practices. And both the United States and the Soviet Union possessed immense empires of their own, though they wielded power in most instances through less direct means than the now-discredited colonial mode of governance.

---

[3] Vijay Prashad, *The Darker Nations: A People's History of the Third World* (New York: The New Press, 2007), xv.
[4] Recent surveys of the process of decolonization include Jan C. Jansen and Jürgen Osterhammel, *Decolonization: A Short History* (Princeton: Princeton University Press, 2017) and Dane Kennedy, *Decolonization: A Very Short Introduction* (New York: Oxford University Press, 2016). The best introduction to current scholarship on the subject is Martin Thomas and Andrew S. Thompson, eds., *The Oxford Handbook of the Ends of Empire* (Oxford: Oxford University Press, 2018).

Above all, however, the postcolonial states of Africa, Asia, and other ex-colonial territories remained subject to an international economic order that privileged the interests of the ex-imperial powers and the developed industrial world more generally. The newly empowered political and intellectual elites of postcolonial states attributed the structural inequalities of global trade to the enduring effects of imperialism and colonialism. They coined terms like unequal exchange, underdevelopment, dependency, and neocolonialism to describe the economic constraints that throttled their countries' growth. As Christopher Dietrich has so convincingly shown, these postcolonial critics shared the conviction that the assertion of national sovereignty over natural resources was essential to overcoming the economic disparities between the developed and the developing world. This premise was foundational to the project that helped inspire the oil boycott and price hikes of 1973–4.[5]

The Third World, a term coined in the early 1950s by a French academic to echo and evoke the Third Estate's key role in the French Revolution, soon gained traction as a catch-all category for the poorer countries, many of them new and politically fragile, of Asia, Africa, and the Middle East, as well as the Caribbean, Latin America, and the South Pacific. This appellation held particular appeal for those who believed that these countries had shared interests that set them apart from the US-centered First World and the Soviet-centered Second World. Unlike the First and Second Worlds, the Third World had no center: it was a loosely affiliated network of countries brought together by the conviction that the international system was structured to ensure their economic and political subordination to the great powers, and that the only way to escape this subordination was through some sort of transnational partnership of postcolonial states. This was what made the pan-African, pan-Asian, pan-Arab, and pan-Islamic movements so appealing to so many nationalist leaders—while, at the same time, making them so difficult to bring to fruition. The Organization of African Unity (OAU), founded in 1963, was inspired by such sentiments. Even more ambitious was the effort to forge an Afro-Asian alliance at the Indonesian-sponsored Bandung Conference (1955), which brought together representatives from 29 African and Asian states. One year later Josip Tito of Yugoslavia, Jawaharlal Nehru of India, Kwame Nkrumah of Ghana, Sukarno of Indonesia, and Gamal Abdul Nasser of Egypt launched the Non-Aligned Movement (NAM), which aimed to voice the shared concerns of developing countries across the globe. In his speech as host of the movement's sixth summit in 1979, Fidel Castro summarized its purpose as a struggle to resist "all forms of foreign aggression, occupation, domination, interference or hegemony as well as against great power and bloc politics."[6]

Third World countries also began to exert their collective influence over major international organizations, even those that had originated as imperial projects. The British Commonwealth had come into existence in the interwar years as an imperial association between Britain and its so-called "white dominions" (Canada, Australia,

---

[5]   Christopher R. W. Dietrich, *Oil Revolution: Anticolonial Elites, Sovereign Rights, and the Economic Culture of Decolonization* (Cambridge: Cambridge University Press, 2017).

[6]   Fidel Castro, Speech to Sixth Summit of Non-Aligned Countries, September 3, 1979. (https://web.archive.org/web/20120702093914/http://lanic.utexas.edu/project/castro/db/1979/19790903.html).

New Zealand, South Africa, and, for a time, Ireland), but after the war it expanded membership beyond that racially exclusive club, granting entry to India, Pakistan, and other ex-colonies in a bid to retain some influence over their foreign affairs. As more and more of these new, postcolonial countries joined the Commonwealth, its power dynamics increasingly shifted in their favor. Member states pressured the Commonwealth to take a stand against South Africa's policy of apartheid, provoking that country's withdrawal from the organization in 1960. They also condemned white-ruled Rhodesia and prevented the British government from recognizing the "internal settlement" that the Rhodesian government of Ian Smith had engineered to forestall black majority rule in 1978.[7]

The United Nations underwent a similar transformation. The creators of the UN, as Mark Mazower and others have shown, originally envisioned it as an instrument of global hegemony by the great powers, whose permanent seats on the Security Council (held by United States, the Soviet Union, Britain, France, and republican China) were intended to ensure their control over the organization.[8] But as increasing numbers of newly independent states entered the UN, the General Assembly was transformed into a far more active and influential forum for their concerns than its founders had envisioned. An "Afro-Asian Bloc" of nations joined together to press their members' interests, often with the assistance of Latin American states.[9] In 1960, they succeeded in passing Resolution 1514, which denounced colonialism "as a serious abuse of human rights" and declared that self-determination was "legally binding."[10] In 1964, these new states formed the Group of 77 (G-77) to highlight the economic plight of developing countries. A year later, when Rhodesia's white minority regime issued its Unilateral Declaration of Independence, intended to forestall black majority rule, the UN imposed international economic sanctions. The General Assembly continued into the 1970s to pass resolutions that targeted states engaged in colonial-style racism and oppression. South Africa's policy of apartheid was the subject of 12 percent of all General Assembly resolutions in this period.[11] A 1971 resolution condemned South Africa for shunting much of its black population into so-called "bantustans." A resolution to expel South Africa from the UN passed the General Assembly in 1974, but was vetoed by Britain, France, and the United States in the Security Council. The General Assembly also objected to Israeli treatment of Palestinians. In 1974, the Palestine Liberation Organization (PLO) was granted "observer status" by the General Assembly, and in 1975, a controversial resolution denounced Zionism as a form of

---

[7]   Philip Murphy, *The Empire's New Clothes: The Myth of the Commonwealth* (London: Hurst, 2018).

[8]   Mark Mazower, *No Enchanted Palace: The End of Empire and the Ideological Origins of the United Nations* (Princeton: Princeton University Press, 2009); Saul Dubow, "Smuts, the United Nations and the rhetoric of race and rights," *Journal of Contemporary History*, 43, 1 (2008): 45–74.

[9]   See, for example, Nicole Eggers, Jessica Lynn Pearson, and Aurora Amada e Santos, eds., *The United Nations and Decolonization* (New York: Routledge, 2020).

[10]   "Declaration on the granting of independence to colonial countries and peoples" (1960) at https://www.ohchr.org/en/instruments-mechanisms/instruments/declaration-granting-independence-colonial-countries-and-peoples.

[11]   Glenda Sluga, "The transformation of international institutions: global shock as cultural shock," in Niall Ferguson et al., eds., *The Shock of the Global: The 1970s in Perspective* (Cambridge, MA: Belknap Press, 2010), 230.

racism. President Gerald Ford responded to these actions by protesting what he called the "tyranny of the majority" at the UN.[12] His peevish outburst reflected the Western powers' growing frustration with a General Assembly that had clearly escaped their control.

Underlying these expressions of solidarity by postcolonial states in the General Assembly and other international and transnational organizations was their shared conviction that Western imperialism remained a clear and present danger to the Third World.[13] Even as it retreated from earlier colonial practices, imperialism persisted through informal economic means, employing various trade, credit, and treaty mechanisms to ensure the First World's continued control over the Third World. The cradle of this critique was Latin America, where it arose to explain the persistent underperformance of the region's economies. Raul Prebisch, an Argentinean economist who directed the UN Economic Commission for Latin America and the Caribbean (and later the UN Conference on Trade and Development), laid the foundations for the theory of unequal exchange with his argument that the terms of international trade favored Western countries, creating a structural imbalance between what he termed the core and the periphery.[14]

The attitudes and actions of First World powers did little to diminish the suspicions of Third World critics that the game was rigged against them. President Nixon reportedly pronounced Latin America to be fifty years away from mattering in international relations and dismissed Africa as at least 500 years away. His foreign affairs advisor, Henry Kissinger, concurred, smugly asserting that "nothing of importance can come from the South."[15] The leaders of Europe's post-imperial states were hardly more enlightened: they viewed much of the developing world relevant to international affairs only insofar as it provided a steady supply of natural resources to the industrialized world. For a time, European integration itself was premised on continued exploitation of Africa's natural resources, an agenda labeled as "Eurafrica."[16]

Moreover, colonialism was still alive, especially in southern Africa, though it was hardly healthy. Portugal, the last remaining European imperial state to resist "the winds of change" that had been sweeping across the continent since the mid-1950s, had encouraged hundreds of thousands of Portuguese settlers to immigrate to Angola and Mozambique in the decades after World War II, a clear sign of its determination to keep its African colonies. By the early 1970s, however, the Portuguese military was bogged down in increasingly costly and deadly counterinsurgency campaigns against liberation movements in Mozambique, Guinea-Bissau, and, above all, Angola. Like the

---

[12] Mark Mazower, *Governing the World: The History of an Idea, 1815 to the Present* (New York: Penguin Books, 2012), 309.

[13] Adom Getachew, *Worldmaking after Empire: The Rise and Fall of Self-Determination* (Princeton: Princeton University Press, 2019).

[14] See Joseph Love, "Raul Prebisch and the origins of the doctrine of unequal exchange," *Latin American Research Preview* 15(3) (1980): 45–72; Dietrich, *Oil Revolution*, 41–54.

[15] Mark Atwood Lawrence, "Containing globalism: the United States and the developing world in the 1970s," in Ferguson et al., *Shock of the Global*, 208.

[16] Peo Hansen and Stefan Jonsson, "Building Eurafrica: reviving colonialism through European integration, 1920–60," in Kalypso Nicolaidis, Berny Sebe, and Gabrielle Maas, eds., *Echoes of Empire: Memory, Identity and Colonial Legacies* (London: I. B. Tauris, 2015), 227–50.

campaigns that the French, the British, and the Dutch had conducted in their colonial wars of the 1950s and 1960s, and like the one the United States was concurrently conducting in Vietnam, the Portuguese campaigns involved detentions without trial, summary executions, forcible resettlement of civilians, and indiscriminate bombing raids (made more deadly with the introduction of napalm). Yet these tactics failed to suppress the insurgencies, and in 1974, a group of despairing young Portuguese military officers carried out a coup against their government, which resulted in Portugal's precipitant retreat from empire.[17]

Rather than draw Africans' campaigns for independence to an end, the collapse of Portuguese colonial rule simply internationalized the struggle, especially in Angola, which became a pawn in the Cold War conflict between the United States and the Soviet Union. Three rival nationalist groups, each representing a different ethnic group and each backed by a different set of foreign powers, fought for supremacy. The MPLA was backed by the Soviet Union, which provided material assistance and military training, and Cuba, which eventually sent 12,000 troops to Angola. The FNLA's patrons were the United States, which funneled aid through the CIA, and, in an example of the curious bedfellows that sometimes arose during the Cold War, China, which provided weapons and military advisors. UNITA, too, received supported from the US and China, and in 1975 South African forces invaded southern Angola in a bid to boost UNITA and defeat the MPLA. Intervention by these outside powers simply prolonged and intensified Angola's civil war.[18]

The collapse of Portuguese colonial rule had wider ramifications for the region. The white settler regime in Rhodesia now faced rebel incursions not only from Zambia on its northern border, but from Mozambique to its east, making its strategic position increasingly untenable. Britain sponsored peace negotiations that eventually brought black majority rule to Zimbabwe, as it was rechristened, in 1979. The political situation in South West Africa/Namibia also became unstable. It had been granted to South Africa as a mandated territory by the League of Nations after World War I and had remained under South African control ever since, despite a UN resolution in the late 1960s that called for its end. With the collapse of Portuguese rule in Angola, the pressure to grant Namibia independence intensified. But efforts to resolve the issue became entangled in the Cold War struggle in neighboring Angola, delaying the transition to independence by more than a decade. By this point, white minority rule in South Africa itself had become unstable, causing the continent's last quasi-colonial society to collapse in 1994.[19]

Southern Africa wasn't the only site of anti-imperial struggles in the 1970s. The Vietnam War was arguably the most important of those struggles. When the United States withdrew from Vietnam in 1975, conceding victory to North Vietnam and the

---

[17] See Elizabeth Schmidt, *Foreign Intervention in Africa: From the Cold War to the War on Terror* (Cambridge: Cambridge University Press, 2013), ch. 4.

[18] Schmidt, *Foreign Intervention*, chapter 4; Odd Arne Westad, *The Global Cold War: Third World Interventions and the Making of Our Times* (Cambridge: Cambridge University Press, 2007), chapter 6.

[19] Schmidt, *Foreign Intervention*, chapter 5.

Vietcong, it paved the way for what the historian Lien-Hang Nguyen has termed "a new wave of decolonization struggles."[20] More than any event of the decade, it encouraged liberation organizations like South Africa's African National Congress, the Palestine Liberation Organization, and the Sandinistas of Nicaragua to pursue revolutionary strategies to gain independence. It also expanded the conceptual parameters of decolonization to include among its goals the overthrow of those ostensibly independent countries (e.g., South Vietnam) that acted as puppets of Western powers and/or oppressed much of their own population. Some of those who contributed to the overthrow of monarchical regimes in Ethiopia, Afghanistan, and Iran in the late 1970s framed their actions in precisely these terms. At the same time, the outcome of the Vietnam War exposed tensions within the communist world itself. Vietnam became embroiled in conflicts with its communist neighbors, Cambodia and China, and the rivalry between the Soviet Union and China in Africa and elsewhere was exacerbated by their troubled relationship over Vietnam.

2. Oil as Agent of the New International Economic Order

It is important to set the oil crises of 1973–4 and 1979 in the context of the struggles detailed above. These crises bracketed the events of this era, punctuating the prolonged campaign by developing countries to escape the straitjacket of an international economic system that still favored the developed world. Indeed, the two oil crises were instrumental in shaping that campaign's rise and fall. Its leaders were inspired and enabled by the first oil crisis to work collectively on behalf of a project—the Third World project—to achieve economic independence from neocolonial institutions that favored ex-imperial powers and reconstitute the terms of international trade to benefit poorer, weaker countries. This project would fragment and fail in the aftermath of the second oil crisis.

At the Bandung Conference in 1955, Sukarno had warned his audience against colonialism in "its modern dress, in the form of economic control, intellectual control, actual physical control by a small but alien community within the nation."[21] It proved difficult, however, for developing countries to escape these forms of control when their own fragile economies, which relied mainly on the export of raw materials, were so dependent on the developed world's markets, capital, and technology. The oil industry was a perfect example; most of its extraction, processing, pricing, and distribution was still in the hands of Western companies. But all of this changed in the 1970s as Third World oil producers gained control over their oil resources and acted as a commodity cartel to turn the terms of international trade upside down. The result was economic upheaval in the First World. At the same time, the oil crises were at least as damaging to the economies of many non-oil producing countries in the developing world, and its

---

[20] Lien-Hang T. Nguyen, "The Vietnam decade: the global shock of the war," in Ferguson et al., *Shock of the Global*, 172.
[21] Quoted in Bradley R. Simpson, "Southeast Asia in the Cold War," in Robert J. McMahon, ed., *The Cold War in the Third World* (New York: Oxford University Press, 2013), 48.

most lasting political repercussion may have been the destruction of the Third World as a distinct, if only loosely connected, entity with shared goals.

The Organization of Petroleum Exporting Countries (OPEC) was founded by Iran, Iraq, Kuwait, Saudi Arabia, the United Arab Emirates, and Venezuela in 1960.[22] At this time, Western-owned multinational companies set oil production and price levels, and one of the purposes of the new organization was to shift some of that control to the countries that harbored these oil reserves. Most of the Gulf member states also resented the fifty-fifty profit sharing agreements that the oil companies had instituted in the aftermath of World War II. OPEC's efforts to strengthen its members' bargaining position was part of a broader campaign by developing countries to gain greater leverage in the international economy by claiming control over the production and pricing of their export commodities. The 1962 Cairo meeting of the Non-Aligned Movement declared that "'complete decolonization' would not be possible without the exercise of 'sovereign rights over national resources.'"[23] This position was endorsed by the UN General Assembly later that year when it passed a resolution titled "Permanent Sovereignty over Natural Resources."[24] In 1964, widespread frustration among developing countries with GATT's policies found expression in the formation of the UN Conference for Trade and Development (UNCTAD) and, under its egis, the G-77, which declared the establishment of "a new and just world economic order" as its goal.[25] These developments "confirmed the arrival of the Global South" on the world economic stage.[26]

Over the next decade, the Third World used these and other international organizations to press for a restructuring of economic relations between poor and rich countries. They made little headway until the early 1970s, when, as Mark Metzler details in this volume, a commodity boom brought what the Bank of England described as "unprecedentedly large" increases in prices for a range of products from developing countries.[27] Copper, zinc, tin, lead, phosphates, rubber, cotton, coffee, wood, grains, and other goods became more costly, giving Third World producers greater leverage in the global marketplace. But the key development occurred in the oil sector. The nationalization of oil production by Iran in 1951 and Algeria, Libya, and Iraq in the late 1960s and early 1970s laid the groundwork for what has been called "the oil decolonization" of the region.[28]

---

[22] See Guiliano Garavini, *The Rise and Fall of OPEC in the Twentieth Century* (New York: Oxford University Press, 2019).

[23] Dietrich, *Oil Revolution*, 100.

[24] General Assembly Resolution 1803(XVII) of 14 December 1962, in https://www.ohchr.org/Documents/ProfessionalInterest/resources.pdf.

[25] Joint Declaration of the Seventy-Seven Developing Countries, June 15, 1964, at https://www.g77.org/doc/Joint%20Declaration.html.

[26] Giuliano Garavini, *After Empires: European Integration, Decolonization, and the Challenge from the Global South, 1957–1986* (Cambridge: Cambridge University Press, 2012), 2.

[27] C. A. Enoch and M. Panic, "Commodity prices in the 1970s," *Bank of England Quarterly Bulletin* (March 1981): 44.

[28] Philippe Tristani, "Iraq and the oil Cold War: a superpower struggle and the end of the Iraq Petroleum Company, 1958–72," in Elizabetta Bini, Giuliano Garavini, and Frederico Romero, eds., *Oil Shocks: The 1973 Crisis and its Economic Legacy* (London: I. B. Tauris, 2016), 69.

In April 1973, a US State Department official who studied the oil market warned that a growing shortage of petroleum made its use as a political weapon by producer states a real possibility.[29] Even so, the US intelligence community's assessment of the situation a month later concluded that it was "highly unlikely" that Arab producers would use an oil embargo as "a potential source of leverage over the industrialized West." It did, however, offer a caveat: "renewed or imminent Arab-Israeli hostilities" could precipitate such a move.[30]

The Yom Kippur War between Israel and its Arab neighbors broke out in October 1973. When the Arab combatants learned that the United States was covertly supplying arms to Israeli, the Organization of Arab Petroleum Exporting Countries (OAPEC) imposed an oil embargo on the US, along with its co-conspirators, the Netherlands and Portugal. At the same time, it reduced oil production to hinder efforts to evade the embargo. But the more serious blow to the international economy was OPEC's decision to take advantage of the crisis by dramatically hiking oil prices. The industrial world suddenly discovered that the multinational oil companies no longer called the shots. Nor could the Western powers rely on military intervention to rectify the problem. Henry Kissinger, for one, lamented the loss of this imperial option:

> I know what would have happened in the nineteenth century. But we can't do it. The idea that a Bedouin kingdom would hold up Western Europe and the United States would have been absolutely inconceivable. They would have landed, they would have divided up the oil fields, and they would have solved the problem.... That would have been done. And I am not even sure that this is so insane. But that obviously we cannot do.[31]

OPEC's oil price hike and its ramifying repercussions in the West were a dramatic demonstration of the fact that the Third World had come into its own as a force to be reckoned with in the international arena.[32]

The person who did more than anyone else to turn the oil crisis into a weapon wielded on behalf of the Third World project was Algeria's leader, Houari Boumediene. Algeria had established a reputation in the 1960s as the "mecca of revolution," forging close links with revolutionary regimes like Castro's Cuba and liberation movements

[29] James E. Akins, "The oil crisis: this time the wolf is here," *Foreign Affairs* 51(3) (April 1973): 464–9; Garavini, *OPEC*, 201.

[30] "National intelligence analytical memorandum, May 11, 1973," in *Foreign Relations of the United States, 1969–1976, Volume XXXVI, Energy Crisis, 1969–1974*, 482–3.

[31] "Minutes of the Secretary of State's staff meeting," in *FRUS, Vol. XXXVI*, 643. Still, the US gave serious consideration to military intervention, as David Painter demonstrates in his chapter.

[32] A good summary account of the 1973 oil crisis and its aftermath is Christopher R. W. Dietrich, "'First class brouhaha': Henry Kissinger and oil power in the 1970s," in Bini, *Oil Shock*, 36–62. For a contrarian assessment that argues the United States and the oil companies colluded in the 1973 oil crisis, see Timothy Mitchell, *Carbon Democracy: Political Power in the Age of Oil* (London: Verso, 2011), chapter 7.

like the PLO.[33] It had also been an active player in the various international organizations that had arisen to advance the interests of developing countries, with intersecting memberships in OPEC, NAM, the OAU, the Arab League, and the G-77. Boumediene himself was viewed by the US State Department as a "major figure of the Third World." In 1973, he was both president of NAM and secretary-general of OPEC. In the former role, he persuaded the NAM delegates who met in Algiers to endorse his call for a "new international economic order," and in his latter capacity, he convinced non-Arab members of OPEC to demonstrate their support for OAPEC's boycott by agreeing to hike oil prices.[34]

Boumediene followed up on these successes by urging the UN General Assembly to hold a special session on the oil crisis and the broader issue of commodity prices and economic development. The special session was duly set for April 1974, with Boumediene giving the keynote speech. The election of Algeria's foreign minister, Abdelaziz Bouteflika, as president of the General Assembly served as a further indication that Boumediene was the man of the hour. Boumediene saw the special session as an opportunity to make his case on the world stage for a reworking of the international economic system to better meet the needs of the Third World. The case he laid out at the General Assembly would come to be known as "Boumedienomics."[35] In his speech and the memorandum that accompanied it, Boumediene declared that the "OPEC action is really the first illustration, of the importance of raw material prices for our countries, [and] the vital need for the producing countries to operate the levers of price control" through the nationalization of their export commodities. Such action, he proclaimed, demonstrated "the great possibilities of a union of raw material-producing countries," working collectively to increase prices for their copper, iron, bauxite, rubber, coffee, and other products.[36]

At the heart of Boumediene's argument was the conviction that the only way Third World countries could overcome the structural disadvantages that colonialism and neocolonialism had imposed on them was to restructure the international economic order itself. As Boumediene and many of his contemporaries across the Third World saw it, the main constraints on development came not from domestic deficiencies, but from the neocolonial terms of international trade, which privileged the post-imperial countries and prevented their ex-colonies from acquiring capital and technology, in part by artificially underpricing the primary resources they exported.[37]

---

[33] Jeffrey James Byrne, *Mecca of Revolution: Algeria, Decolonization, and the Third World Order* (New York: Oxford University Press, 2016). Byrne, who ends his book with the 1965 coup that brought Boumediene to power, argues that it produced "a surprisingly homogeneous, constrictive, and even conservative postcolonial order" (p. 287). My analysis challenges that view.

[34] Jürgen Dinkel, *The Non-Aligned Movement: Genesis, Organization and Politics (1927–1992)* (Leiden: Brill, 2019), 150–64, quoting a State Department assessment of Boumediene on p. 152.

[35] Giuliano Garavini, "From Boumedienomics to Reaganomics: Algeria, OPEC, and the international struggle for economic equality," *Humanity,* 6,1 (Spring 2015): 79–92; Garavini, *OPEC,* 236–47.

[36] H. E. Houari Boumediene, *Petroleum, Raw Materials and Development* (Algiers: Democratic and Popular Republic of Algeria, 1974), x, passim.

[37] For a fascinating analysis of the intellectual roots of these ideas, see Johanna Bockman, "Socialist globalization against capitalist neocolonialism: the economic ideas behind the New International Economic Order," *Humanity,* 6, 1 (Spring 2015): 109–28.

The UN General Assembly endorsed Boumediene's call for change, passing a UNCTAD-drafted document at its special session titled "Declaration for the Establishment of a New International Economic Order."[38] This declaration was perhaps the single most important expression of the grievances and ambitions that gave Third World states a shared sense of purpose. It identified the most pressing international problem they faced as the ongoing threat to their national sovereignty and economic development by imperial and post-imperial states. What inspired the declaration, in other words, was the conviction that decolonization remained incomplete and required a new economic order to fulfill its promise.

Given the relevance of the Declaration to the concerns of the oil producing countries that had precipitated the oil crisis with their embargo and price hike, its stated objectives demand attention.[39] The Declaration began by affirming that the "greatest and most significant achievement during the last decades has been the independence from colonial and alien domination of a large number of peoples and nations." Even so, "the remaining vestiges of alien and colonial domination, foreign occupation, racial discrimination, apartheid and neo-colonialism in all its forms continue to be among the greatest obstacles to the full emancipation and progress of the developing countries." Although 70 percent of the world's population lived in developing countries, they accounted for only 30 percent of the world's income, making it "impossible to achieve an even and balanced development of the international community under the existing international economic order." This, then, was why the world needed a New International Economic Order (NIEO).

What should this new order look like? Tellingly, the first requirement identified by the Declaration was respect for the "sovereign equality of States, self-determination of all peoples, inadmissibility of the acquisition of territories by force, territorial integrity and non-interference in the internal affairs of other States." Imperialism, colonialism, and neocolonialism would have no place in this new world order. Instead, it would encourage the "broadest co-operation of all States" and "special measures in favour of the least developed" countries. Paramount importance was placed on the sovereign rights of countries to control their own economic affairs, expanding on OPEC's achievement. This should include the "right of every country to adopt the economic and social system that it deems most appropriate for its own development," the "full permanent sovereignty of every State over its natural resources," "the right to nationalization" of those resources, the right "to restitution and full compensation for the exploitation and depletion of... natural resources," and the right to regulate and supervise "the activities of transnational corporations." In order to rectify the

---

[38] Resolution 3201 (S-VI), "Declaration on the establishment of a New International Economic Order," General Assembly, United Nations, May 1, 1974 (http://www.un-documents.net/s6r3201.htm). The quotations in the paragraphs that follow come from this document.

[39] The New International Economic Order has begun to receive increased scholarly attention. See "Toward a history of the New International Economic Order," a special issue of *Humanity: An International Journal of Human Rights, Humanitarianism, and Development*, 6, 1 (Spring 2015), as well as Vanessa Ogle, "State rights against private capital: the 'New International Economic Order' and the struggle over aid, trade, and foreign investment, 1962–1981," *Humanity*, 5, 2 (Summer 2014): 211–34, and Getachew, *Worldmaking after Empire*, chapter 5.

inequalities imbedded in the existing economic order, the declaration called for "active assistance to developing countries by the whole international community" and "preferential and non-reciprocal treatment for developing countries," especially in terms of access to markets, capital, and new technologies.

The overall aim of the declaration, it affirmed, was the creation of a "New International Economic Order based on equity, sovereign equality, interdependence, common interest and cooperation among all States, irrespective of their economic and social systems which shall correct inequalities and redress existing injustices, make it possible to eliminate the widening gap between the developed and the developing countries and ensure steadily accelerating economic and social development and peace and justice."

With the endorsement of the New International Economic Order by the UN General Assembly, the Third World arguably reached its peak as a coherent, collective enterprise.[40] OAPEC and OPEC's success in wrestling oil production and pricing from the control of multinational corporations and mobilizing their member states to work together to set the terms of trade with the developed world during the 1973-4 crisis inspired hopes for a much broader restructuring of the political and economic relationship between the Third World and the First and Second Worlds. At the 1976 meeting of the UNCTAD, representatives from Third World countries "stopped differentiating ideologically between the socialist and capitalist states of the northern hemisphere," thereby highlighting how their own economic interests differed from those of First and Second World countries.[41] Third World commodity producer organizations started looking to OPEC as a model for strengthening their position in the global economy. Flush with cash and a sense of pan-Arab pride, OAPEC began to commit substantial sums in financial aid to oil-poor neighbors like Egypt, Jordan, and Syria. OPEC as a whole affirmed its intention to provide economic assistance to other Third World countries, establishing an OPEC Fund for International Development that dispersed billions of dollars to African, Asian, and Latin American countries that had seen their economies suffer from the oil crisis.[42]

The European Economic Community (EEC) responded to this challenge by negotiating the 1975 Lomé Convention with 71 African, Caribbean, and Pacific countries. This economic agreement granted duty free access to European markets for agricultural and mineral exports from the non-European signatories and promised them substantial aid and investment commitments. The Convention also recognized the "right of each state to determine its own policies," an affirmation of the sovereignty of all parties to the agreement.[43] It was possible to see the harbingers of a new economic order in these transnational initiatives.

---

[40] At the same time, as Bret Benjamin argues in "Bookend to Bandung: the New International Economic Order and the antinomies of the Bandung era," *Humanity*, 6. 1 (Spring 2015): 22–46, some of the NIEO's aspirations were already evident in embryo in the Bandung conference.

[41] Eva-Maria Muschik, "Special issue introduction: towards a global history of international organizations and decolonization," *Journal of Global History* (2022): 10.

[42] Keisuke Iida, "Third World solidarity: the Group of 77 in the UN General Assembly," *International Organization* 42(2) (Spring 1988): 385.

[43] European Commission: Development and Relations with African, Caribbean, and Pacific States, "The Conotau Agreement" (http://ec.europa.eu/development/body/cotonou/lome_history_en.htm).

Giuliano Garavini has argued that decolonization and the challenge posed by the Third World helped drive the policy decisions of the EEC more broadly.[44] It is worth noting in this context that Britain abandoned its empire-centered Sterling Zone in 1972 and gained admission to the EEC in 1973, a decade after it originally applied for entry and the very year that OAPEC instituted its oil embargo. By this point, Britain retained only a few scattered colonial possessions. It had come to see the EEC as an economic refuge from the uncertainties of a post-imperial world. At the same time, Britain's entry into the EEC was indicative of a broader post-imperial trend among industrial countries: a shift from trade with ex-colonies toward trade with one another. Despite the Lomé Convention and similar initiatives, this trend would contribute over time to the weakening of the economies of primary producing countries.[45]

3. The Erosion of Third World Solidarity

While the 1973–4 oil crisis was a triumph for the Third World project in the short term, over the longer term it led to the erosion of Third World nations' commitment to a common agenda. The sharp increase in the price of oil "will hit developing countries very hard," an American official warned in 1973.[46] Its effects varied from country to country, as contributors to this volume show, but its overall impact on non-oil-producing African, Asian, and Latin American nations was demonstrably adverse. Even those countries that received financial assistance from OPEC or other international organizations had trouble coping with the increased cost of fuel, fertilizer, and other petroleum products.[47] Its challenging impact on India's agricultural sector is detailed in this volume by Shigeru Akita. While OPEC members' share of global exports grew from 5.6 percent in 1970 to 15 percent in 1974, other Third World countries saw their share shrink.[48]

These economic difficulties led in turn to the political destabilization of some developing countries and growing strains within the Third World project. The oil crisis is seen as a contributing factor in the overthrow of Emperor Haile Selassie in Ethiopia in 1974.[49] It heightened political instability in Thailand, Ghana, and elsewhere. In India, it may have contributed to Indira Gandhi's decision to institute a state of emergency in 1975.[50] The CIA reported in 1976 on "tensions among developing states about representation in CIEC [Conference on International Economic Co-Operation]" that had arisen from "fear [that] the temptation may exist to sacrifice group objectives to narrow interests," especially given "the disproportionate representation of OPEC states." The report continued:

---

[44] Garavini, *After Empires*.
[45] I am grateful to Andrew Thompson for reminding me of these developments.
[46] "Minutes of the Secretary of State's staff meeting," in *FRUS, Vol. XXXVI*, 641.
[47] See, for example, Morten Jerven, *Economic Growth and Measurement Reconsidered in Botswana, Kenya, Tanzania, and Zambia, 1965–1995* (Oxford: Oxford University Press, 2014), and, more generally, Dietrich, *Oil Revolution*, chapter 8.
[48] Iida, "Third World solidarity," 381.
[49] Schmidt, *Foreign Intervention*, 146.
[50] Dietrich, *Oil Revolution*, 296–7.

There have already been debates among the developing countries in Paris over agenda items which the OPEC states do not wish to consider. Brazil and Jamaica, for example, have pushed for a full conference airing of the balance of payments problems of developing countries. OPEC states are strongly opposed to any such discussion because it would point up how much the four-fold OPEC oil price increase contributed to these difficulties. The developing states are almost paranoid about perceived efforts to split their ranks.[51]

Despite the promises made by OPEC, especially its increasingly wealthy Arab members, development aid for non-oil producing Third World countries never amounted to more than a small fraction of oil revenues. The gush of petrodollars flowed instead into Western financial markets, which were seen as stable and profitable. Even before Arab producers had imposed the oil embargo, American policymakers had anticipated that "the large and flexible markets of the US [would] prove very attractive" to them as places to park their profits.[52] Now the United States "became the largest single destination of Arab capital," partly because of an active lobbying campaign carried out by the State and Treasury Departments.[53] With monetary decisions that would lay the foundations for the neoliberal world order, the United States, along with other leading western countries, freed up capital markets to attract petrodollars, laying the groundwork, as Ikuto Yamaguchi and Mark Metzler demonstrate in their contributions to this volume, for the rise of "stateless" Eurodollars, much of which was funneled into loans to the developing countries whose energy needs had become so costly. As one historian observes, "the oil exporters found ways to spend or invest their vast earnings in non-disruptive ways that complemented the interests of the capitalist West. The losers... were poor countries that had nothing substantial to exchange."[54]

4. The Second Oil Crisis and the Collapse of the Third World Project

The circumstances that precipitated the second oil crisis of 1979 can be viewed in the context of the Third World project as well. The Shah of Iran was seen by many of his subjects as a puppet of the United States. He had been installed in power by an American-engineered coup in 1953, itself the result to Prime Minister Musaddiq's bid to nationalize the Iranian oil industry. The Shah's increasingly repressive regime became heavily dependent on American arms and advisors. When a popular revolution drove him from power in early 1979, most Iranians celebrated his fall as a defeat for US imperialism and an assertion of national independence.

[51] CIA, "Intelligence memorandum: the preparations of the developing countries for UNCTAD IV, April 2, 1976," in cia.gov/library/readingroom/docs/CIA-RDP85T00353R000100270002-5.pdf.
[52] "National intelligence analytical memorandum, May 11, 1973," *FRUS, Volume XXXVI*, 482.
[53] Salim Yaqub, *Imperfect Strangers: Americans, Arabs, and U.S.-Middle East Relations in the 1970s* (Ithaca: Cornell University Press, 2016), 279.
[54] William Glenn Gray, "Learning to 'recycle': petrodollars and the West, 1973–5," in Bini et al., *Oil Shock*, 191.

While the Iranian revolution seemed to affirm the widespread view in developing countries that the struggle against imperialism and neocolonialism was far from over, it also precipitated an oil crisis that would shatter any remaining hopes for a New International Economic Order and become the death knell for the Third World as a coherent political project. The 1979 oil crisis, unlike its predecessor in 1973–4, had little if anything to do with OPEC states' insistence on their sovereign rights to the natural resources in their possession. Instead, it was a consequence of the shock waves that spread through international oil markets when the Iranian revolution disrupted its oil industry. Although other oil exporting countries soon increased their production to offset much of the shortfall from Iran, panic buying caused oil prices to spike and shortages to break out in the United States and elsewhere.

For many developing countries, especially those that relied on oil imports, the 1979 crisis was economically disastrous, contributing to a sharp drop in prices for their export commodities.[55] They had already suffered a serious blow from the first oil crisis; the second one brought economic growth to a screeching halt across much of sub-Saharan Africa and other parts of the Third World. Hideki Kan notes that the debt held by less developed countries increased six-fold—from $69 billion to $494 billion—in the 1970s.[56] Moreover, a growing proportion of that new debt was held by banks and other private investors, flush with Eurodollars and insistent on profits. Countries seeking assistance from the IMF and World Bank were subject to increasingly harsh terms, commonly known as structural adjustment. The rise to power of Margaret Thatcher in 1979 and Ronald Reagan in 1981 marked a decided shift in favor of neoliberal, monetarist policies by the West.[57] The rejection of the redistributionist economic proposals made at the North-South Summit in Cancun in 1981 was a turning point, Ikuto Yamaguchi tells us. The United States and other "developed countries stood firm" in the face of developing countries' demands, insisting instead that "economic development is best achieved through...the private sector and free market programs."[58] This meant policies that undermined the ability of developing states to protect their domestic producers from foreign competition or cushion their populations against price gouging, job losses, and other threats to their livelihoods. The entire premise of the New International Economic Policy was undermined by the economic disturbances that surrounded the oil crisis of 1979.

This crisis also marked a political and ideological turning point for the Third World itself. Marxist-inspired leftist movements had led the way in the struggle against colonialism, neocolonialism, and imperialism through much of the 1970s. They had triumphed in Vietnam, Cambodia, Angola, Mozambique, Nicaragua, Ethiopia, Yemen, and, at least briefly, in Afghanistan and Grenada. The two superpowers expected the Iranian revolution to produce a similar outcome—the United States with foreboding, the Soviet Union with anticipation. Instead, Islamists under the leadership of the

---

[55] Priya Lal, "African socialism and the limits of global familyhood: Tanzania and the New International Order in sub-Saharan Africa," *Humanity* 6(1) (Spring 2015): 26.
[56] Hideki Kan, "The Cold War, the 1970s, and the role of the ADB in Southeast and Northeast Asia," working paper for Taiwan workshop, December 20, 2017, p. 6.
[57] Ogle, "State rights against private capital," 224–6.
[58] CIA, "Briefing paper: North/South issues, July 29, 1983," in cia.gov/library/readingroom/docs/CIA-RDP85M00364R000400510025-8.pdf.

Ayatollah Khomeini came to power, crushing the Iranian communist party and rejecting both the American and Soviet models of development. Inspired in part by the Iranian revolution, Afghan Islamists organized to overthrow that country's Marxist regime, provoking the Soviet invasion of Afghanistan in 1979. Other Islamist movements sprang up elsewhere across the Muslim world. Like the original leaders of the Non-Aligned Movement, the Islamists offered a "third way" that rejected the Soviet and American options, but unlike those leaders, they also refused to make common cause with anyone outside their strictly patrolled circle of faith. The outbreak of the long and bloody Iraq-Iran war, which began in 1980, prolonging the oil crisis, was an early indicator of the increasing fragmentation of the Middle East along secular vs. religious and Sunni vs. Shia lines, a fissure that persists to the present day.[59]

This process of fragmentation reached well beyond the Middle East. Perhaps the most significant development for the future of the global economy was China's stunning move from a command to a market-based economy, which began when Deng Xiaoping came to power in 1978. A year later China went to war with its fellow communist regime of Vietnam, shattered any remaining illusions that a shared Marxist ideology would supersede nationalist self-interest.[60] In a further blow to leftists, their expectation that liberation struggles would naturally and inevitably embrace Marxist doctrines was tested and found wanting in Afghanistan, where the Soviets conducted an increasingly brutal counter-insurgency campaign against Islamist rebels. Any pretense that the countries that identified with the Third World shared a common ideological or economic purpose was no longer sustainable. The 1979 NAM summit exposed a stark rift between more conservative member states, such as India, Egypt, and Indonesia, and the more radical ones, including Cuba, Libya, and Vietnam.[61] Julius Nyerere, Tanzania's founding president, frankly acknowledged the problems that faced the G-77, and the Third World more broadly:

> I want to reiterate that it was our nationalism that brought us together, because we must first understand ourselves in order to pursue progress. The Group of 77 does not have an ideology in common. Some of us are for a socialism that claims to be "scientific," others simply socialists, others capitalists, others theocracies, and still others fascists! And we are not necessarily all friendly with one another: Several countries are today at war with each other. Our per capita income varies from $100 to $2,000 dollars per year. Some of us have minerals, others do not; some of us have no access to the sea, while others are surrounded by enormous oceans. The immediate interests and negotiating priorities of the G77 countries are thus quite different. There is OPEC, the poorest countries, the Least Developed, the Newly Industrialized, the landlocked, and so on; some of these classifications are our own

---

[59] See Ayesha Jalal, "An uncertain trajectory: Islam's contemporary globalization 1971–1979," in Ferguson et al., *Shock of the Global*, 319–36; Westad, *Global Cold War*, chapter 8.

[60] The war also provided the impetus for Benedict Anderson's seminal study of nationalism, *Imagined Communities: Reflections on the Origin and Spread of Nationalism* (London: Verso, 1983).

[61] Sara Lorenzini, *Global Development: A Cold War History* (Princeton: Princeton University Press, 2019), 159.

doing, others have been created by others for their own purposes. This type of subdivision of the G77 can be useful... But it is also very dangerous.[62]

5. Conclusion

The oil crises of the 1970s are integral to understanding how the Third World project peaked and collapsed so quickly. These two great global upheavals were driven to a large degree by economic and political problems that the formal process of decolonization—the international recognition of ex-colonies and dependencies as independent sovereign states—had failed to resolve. The first crisis marked the culmination of the decades-long struggle by OPEC's member states to assert their sovereign rights over the oil reserves that lay beneath their soil, including the production and pricing of this increasingly valuable commodity. OPEC's stunning success gave other developing countries a new sense of hope that their collective action as agents of the Third World project could overcome the various international institutions and organizations that seemed designed to maintain neocolonial control over their natural resources and access to global markets. The shared sense of purpose that inspired the developing world in the aftermath of the 1973–4 oil crisis was enunciated most clearly and powerfully in the "Declaration on the Establishment of a New International Economic Order."

The unfinished business of decolonization also made its mark on the event that precipitated the oil crisis of 1979, the Iranian revolution. By portraying the Shah as the puppet of the United States, which was condemned as the "great Satan," the revolutionaries presented their cause as a nationalist struggle to free their country from imperial subjugation. The oil crisis that followed, however, confirmed a problem that had already begun to reveal itself in the aftermath of the 1973–4 crisis: national self-interest all too often superseded any commitment to shared economic interests and common political and ideological enemies on the part of developing countries. Not only did the end of the 1970s bring the era of decolonization to a close, but it also shattered hopes of unity among the countries of the developing world. As a result, the Third World would cease to be a meaningful geopolitical category even before the Cold War rivalry between the First and Second Worlds reached its conclusion with the collapse of the Soviet Union.

---

[62] Quoted in Garavini, *After Empires*, 243–4.

3

The Cold War, the 1970s, and the Role of the Asian Development Bank in Southeast Asia

Hideki Kan

1. Introduction

The Asian Development Bank (ADB) was established in 1966 while the United States was escalating the war in Vietnam. Consequently, Washington policymakers expected the institution to play an important role not only in the field of finance and economy but also in strengthening the regional solidarity of Asian non-Communist countries to contain Communism in Asia.[1] Johnson administration officials viewed security and economic development in the Asian region as inseparably linked with each other.[2] They hoped, therefore, that the ADB would contribute to the political stability in Asia through economic and social development of Asian non-Communist countries.

Another key player deeply involved in the establishment of the Bank was Japan. Washington's expectations matched the rising nationalism among the Japanese who desired to play a larger role in the region against the background of high economic growth. When President Johnson, in the Baltimore speech in 1965, announced his intention to promote cooperative efforts in Asia for economic and social development in a regional framework, Prime Minister Eisaku Sato welcomed it with enthusiasm. He responded to the Baltimore speech by agreeing to contribute $200 million to the ADB fund, the amount equal in capital contribution to that of the United States.

David Painter points out in this volume that "few examine the close connections between the oil crises and the Cold War." This is also true of the past research on the ADB which almost exclusively concentrated on negotiations leading to the establishment of the ADB, management, loan operations, organizational features, and aid purposes without taking into considerations the influences of the Cold War. Given the political origin of the establishment of the ADB in the context of the Cold War and the emergent regionalism in Asia, however, it is relevant to view, as Sanford observes, in

---

[1] For a more detailed analysis, see Hideki Kan, "U.S.-Japan relations in the 1960s and U.S. policy toward the Emerging Regionalism in Asia: nationalism, regionalism, and collective security," *Hosei Kenkyu* 66(2) (July, 1989): 41–59.

[2] *Administrative History of the Department of State*, Vol. 1, chapter 7, Lyndon B. Johnson Library (hereafter referred to as LBJ Library), Austin, Texas.

his study of US foreign policy and multilateral development banks (MDBs), that the MDBs are "political institutions whose activities are directly relevant to U.S. foreign policy."[3] In line with Sanford's view, this chapter focuses on the political and economic aspects of the activities of the ADB in the context of the Cold War and "Japan–US cooperation."

Section 1 will analyze the interactions between the ADB and the two key donor countries (the US and Japan) during the 1970s in the Cold War context, and show that the ADB leadership tried to depoliticize its activities as much as possible and made efforts to keep a distance from the political interventions of the US which tended to prioritize the Cold War imperatives, while Japan maintained a low profile and behaved as an intermediary between the ADB and Washington. Section 2 will examine the growing need for concessional funds in the early 1970s and the subsequent establishment of the Asian Development Fund (ADF) by integrating the existing two special funds, the Agricultural Special Fund (ASF) and the Multi-Purpose Special Fund (MPSF), while retaining the Technical Special Fund (TSF) as it was. Section 3 will analyze the subsequent interactions among the donors, focusing on prolonged negotiations over the replenishments of the newly established ADF, due to Washington's responses arising from the complicated interactions between the administrations and the Congress. In these protracted negotiations, the ADB leadership managed to attain the replenishment target ($2.15 billion) of the ADF by adjusting to the differing interests between the US position and that of the other donor countries. Section 4 will discuss how the ADB leadership managed to navigate the mounting pressures caused by the first oil shock and the protectionist tendencies of donor countries in the 1970s. Noting the timely publication of the Second Asian Agricultural Survey of 1976, this chapter will argue that the ADB responded to these challenges by successfully carrying out the replenishments of the concessionary ADF and rapidly increasing agricultural loans to Southeast Asia along the lines recommended by the 1976 agricultural survey. The chapter will summarize the points of arguments and conclude that the Bank made a significant contribution to laying the foundation of the development of Southeast Asia in the 1970s and thereafter.

2. The "Japan–US Cooperation" and the Role of the Asian Development Bank in Southeast Asia in the Context of the Cold War

The "Japan–US cooperation" was framed in such a way that postwar Japanese diplomacy was constrained by twin-pillars, namely, "Japan–US security treaty system" based upon the Japan–US security treaty of 1952 and its dependence on the US for security, on the one hand, and a deepening economic interdependence between the two countries, closely linked with the promotion of the triangular trade relationships

---

[3]   Jonathan E. Sanford, *U.S. Foreign Policy and Multilateral Development Banks* (Boulder, Colorado: Westview Press, 1982), 19, 23.

among Japan, the US, and Southeast Asian countries, on the other.[4] Given that the Japan–US security treaty was signed in the midst of the Cold War, Japan acted on the assumption that its national interests would be best served by working closely with the US as a collaborator, complementing Washington's Cold War policy to contain Communism in Asia.

Due to the limitations that Article 9 (the so-called "war-renunciation clause") of the postwar Japanese Constitution imposes upon Japan's potential military power, its major foreign policy instrument has been technical and economic aid (Official Development Assistance, ODA) throughout the postwar years. Another important instrument for advancing Japan's political as well as economic and commercial interests in Asia was Japan's financial contributions to International Financial Institutions (IFIs) such as the World Bank, the IMF, and the ADB.

In multilateral aid, Japan gave high priority to the ADB. From the start of the ADB operations until the end of the 1970s, Japan assumed a leading role in mobilizing resources for the Bank's special funds which were concessional. Starting in 1968, Japan made regular annual contributions to the special funds, increasing from $20 million in 1968 to $45.4 million in 1973.[5] When there were increasing calls among ADB members for the establishment of a unified mechanism for various special funds, the Japanese government announced in 1972 that Japan would be prepared to contribute one third of an increase in special funds.[6] In 1974, Japan contributed one third of the initial funds for the ADF. In the following year, Japan announced it would continue to contribute a third of ADF funds. In 1978, due to cutbacks in US commitments to the ADF, again Japan and other donors had to make up for the shortfall to achieve the targeted replenishment of $2,141 million (ADF III 1979–82). At this juncture, the Japanese contribution reached 37 percent of the replenishments.[7]

Japan's concentration on pursuing economic and commercial interests in Southeast Asia obliged the Japanese government to maintain its low political profile so as not to remind its peoples of the wartime atrocities. Moreover, the emergence of a close tie between the Ministry of Finance (MOF) and its reserved posts in the ADB also made a low-key posture possible. Since the successive ADB presidents were Japanese nationals, the Japanese government could assume that the policies taken by the president would usually reflect Japan's interests.[8] Besides, the MOF in Tokyo provided successive Directors of the Budget, Personnel and Management Systems Department

---

[4] For a detailed analysis of Washington's effort to promote the triangular relationships, see Hideki Kan, "Amerika no Sengo-chitsujo Koso to Ajia no Chiiki Togo, 1945–1950," *Kokusai Seiji*, 80 (October, 1988): 109–25.

[5] "Comments of Governors at the Third Annual Meeting," Seoul, April 9–11, 1970. RG 286 Entry UD-WW756, Acc # 286-73A-0976, Box 1. National Archives, College Park (hereafter referred to as NACP).

[6] Sixth Annual Meeting-Comments of Governors, April 26–8, Sec. M 70-73, June 11, 1973, confidential (excerpts from Statements). RG 286, AID, USAID Mission to Korea/Executive Office, Entry # P 583: Central Subject Files, 1963–79. EFCI IBRD, ADB, Vol. 1 thru EFCI ADB, vol. 5. Container # 61. NACP.

[7] Peter McCawley, *Banking on the Future of Asia and the Pacific: 50 Years of the Asian Development Bank* (Manila: Asian Development Bank, 2017), see Table A2.15 and Table A2.17, 443–7.

[8] Dick Wilson, *A Bank for Half the World: The Story of the Asian Development Bank 1966–1986* (Manila: Asian Development Bank, 1987), 281.

and other important posts in the administrative machinery of the ADB. By the early 1970s, Japan's institutional ties with the ADB were routinized. With the exception of the second ADB President Shiro Inoue, who was from the Bank of Japan, all the ADB presidents made their careers at the MOF. The MOF sent their officials to the ADB for two or three years on "temporary leave of absence." This practice contributed to the emergence of a close tie between the MOF and its reserved posts in the ADB.[9]

Compared with Japan's low-key political profile, Washington's participation in the ADB was more often motivated by the political and strategic importance of Asia to US interests in the Cold War struggle. Washington policymakers' Cold War imperatives, together with Tokyo's cooperation, impacted the Bank's lending policy in such a way that it tended to favor the US, Japan, and their friends and allies in Asia. In the years from 1967 to 1977, twenty-three out of twenty-six developing member countries (DMCs) (except India, the Maldives, and the Cook Islands) were the major recipients of the total ADB loans including both capital loans and special fund loans: South Korea 16.1 percent, the Philippines 14.3 percent, Pakistan 13.4 percent, Indonesia 12.0 percent, Thailand 8.4 percent, Malaysia 7.9 percent, Bangladeshi 6.4 percent, Burma 3.2 percent, Singapore 3.05 percent, Nepal 2.9 percent, and Taiwan 2.3 percent.[10] South Korea, the Philippines, Taiwan, Thailand, and Pakistan (1954–65) were important as US allies, while aid to Indonesia and Burma as non-alignment members was considered necessary by the US in its fight against Communism. Japan had crucial trading ties with Indonesia, Thailand, Malaysia, South Korea, and the Philippines. Others such as Singapore, Malaysia, Pakistan, and Bangladesh (1972) were members of the Commonwealth.

Some member countries grew critical of such allocation of the ADB's loans. The American Embassy in Helsinki reported to the State Department that the government of Finland would raise this question during the ADB Vice President C.S. Krishna-Moorthy's visit to Finland on April 11–12, 1972. The Finnish view of the ADB operations was that there was a "tendency of loans to go to areas such as Taiwan, South Korea and South Vietnam, which might be described as areas of particular interest to U.S. and Japan."[11] On the other hand, US officials reasoned that the government supported the Bank because the nations of Asia looked to the US for "assurance that our determination to defend freedom in Southeast Asia is matched by our determination to assist the cause of economic and social progress among Asia's peoples." In Washington's view, the growth of regional cooperation in Asia would complement the US effort "to make Communist aggression unprofitable in Vietnam."[12]

[9] Ibid., 282. Ming Wan, "Japan and the Asian Development Bank," *Pacific Affairs* 68(4) (Winter, 1995–6): 516, 519.
[10] Koji Nakagawa, *Ajia Kaihatsu Ginko* (Tokyo: Kyoiku Sha, 1979), 101. For statistical data, see also Appendixes in McCawley, *Banking on the Future of Asia and the Pacific*, 433–5.
[11] Amembassy Helsinki to SOS, Telegram 00434, "5th Meeting of Board of Governors of ADB, April 20–22, 1972," RG 286, AID, Entry No. P 514, IDFs, 1969–84, ADB Annual Meeting, 1971–1972 thru 1971–1972 [sic], Box 3. NACP.
[12] The Statement of Eugene Black, Special Advisor to President Johnson on Asian Economic and Social Development, Testimony before the House Subcommittee on International Finance of the Committee on Banking and Currency, February 27, 1968. 90th Congress, 2nd session on H.R. 13217, February 27, 1968, 39, 45. NACP.

According to Schoultz, who studied the relationship between the US government and Congress, the latter's influence over US policy toward the Multilateral Development Banks (MDBs) "was relatively insignificant" in comparison with its impact on bilateral aid programs.[13] However, things began to change in the wake of the impending Communist victories in Vietnam in the mid-1970s. In December 1974, the U.S. Congress passed the Foreign Assistance Act which prohibited the US government from providing security assistance to countries that engaged in a persistent pattern of human rights violations.

When Jimmy Carter came to the White House in 1977, he gave first priority to the human rights issue in his foreign policy agenda. For the Carter administration, the human rights issue was regarded as a political and ideological weapon to highlight the repressive nature of the Soviet system in the Cold War struggle. It was also considered to serve as a strategy that appealed to both liberals and conservatives of the Democratic Party and a wider audience. During the Carter administration's negotiations with Congress over the Foreign Assistance Appropriations Bill for FY 1978, however, members of the Senate and House Appropriations Subcommittee introduced the restrictive amendments to prohibit International Development Banks (IDBs) including the ADB from using US subscriptions and contributions for lending loans to seven countries and/ or for the production of certain commodities where such production was for export and would damage producers in the United States. Such restrictive subscriptions and contributions would have been rejected by all IFIs. Therefore, in order to prevent the House from adopting such restrictive amendments, President Carter pledged that he would instruct the US Executive Directors to the IDBs, during FY 1978, to oppose and vote against any loans to recipient countries with gross human rights violations.[14]

Consequently, between 1968 and 1980, Lester Edmond, the US Executive Director at the ADB, voted against or abstained on approximately 40 loan or technical assistance proposals mainly during the Carter administration, which included the targeting of ideological rivals of the United States.[15] After FY 1977, the Carter administration continued to oppose loans to Laos and Vietnam for human rights reasons. Between January 1977 and July 1979, the US opposed, through "no" votes or abstentions, eighteen out of nineteen MDB loans to five Asian countries where the human rights situation was considered severe.[16]

[13] Lars Schoultz, "Politics, economics, and U.S. participation in multilateral development banks," *International Organization* 36(3) (Summer, 1982): 544.

[14] The Appropriations Subcommittee Testimony on the Witteveen Facility and the FY 79 Appropriations Request for the International Development Banks, February 27, 1978, General Briefing Book, Regional Banks Briefing Book (IDB, ADB, AFDF), ADB (hereafter referred to as Testimony on the Witteveen Facility). RG 56, General Records of the Department of the Treasury, Office of Assistant Secretary for International Affairs, Office of the Deputy Assistant Secretary for Developing Nations, Office of International Development Banks (hereafter referred to as RG 56, GRDOT), Subject Files Related to IDBs, 1978–9, BCOP-3, Subcommittee on Multilateral Aid Working Group to BP-5-1, Senate Appropriations Sub-Committee, Box 1. NACP.

[15] Robert Wihtol, *The Asian Development Bank and Rural Development: Policy and Practice* (London: The Macmillan Press, 1988), 46–7.

[16] Arnold Nachmanoff, Acting Ass. Sec., the Department of the Treasury to Ms. Paula R. Newberg, Project Director, Policy Studies, UN Association, regarding "Human Rights and U.S. Voting Record on MDB Loans to Asia." RG 56, GRDOT, Subject Files Related to MDBs, 1978–9, RP-4-4 Correspondence- Government Agencies to Trav-5 Travel Vouchers, Box 15. NACP.

The Carter administration's abstentions or no votes on ADB loans for human rights reasons caused a tense atmosphere at the Bank. A State Department official reported in December 1977 after his recent orientation trip to the ADB headquarter in Manila that Board members had warned "their countries' patience is running out" and that they "would soon have to counter U.S. 'attacks.'" Koreans were especially "dismayed over being singled out for overt action." Bong Hyok Kay, the Executive Director of South Korea, made the following points to the State Department official: "this type of visible, confrontational approach was counter-productive," and US abstentions for non-economic reasons violated the Bank's charter, which restricted Bank matters to purely economic matters. Bong also complained that the US was being selective and discriminatory in the application of its human rights policy because many other ADB loan recipients also had "tarnished human rights records." The Korean representative added that the two Executive Directors were considering the Board to adopt a "motion of regret" regarding the US abstentions. Ambassador Edmond described the situation on the Board as "tense" and regarded a motion of regret to be "a real possibility." Nevertheless, the Ambassador recommended a strong US rebuttal "should a motion be introduced."[17]

The ADB leadership was also concerned about Washington's human rights/IFI "linkage." At a Geneva meeting on February 14, 1978, Deputy Assistant Secretary of the Treasury Department Arnold Nachmanoff and the third ADB President Taroichi Yoshida (1976.11~1981.11) exchanged opinions about the human rights issues in the ADB. Nachmanoff expressed his belief that a larger share of the Bank's resources should be directed to countries with good human rights records. Yoshida responded that we could agree on human rights in principle but "differ as to the proper method of implementation." Given that there was no established view of what human rights meant, he insisted, classification "remains very political." "Banks can work well," the ADB President believed, "if a common recognition is available—if not, they won't." He tried to depoliticize the issue so that ADB member countries could approach this question in a cooperative, mutually supporting way. He also felt it necessary for the Bank "to avoid appearing as a U.S. puppet advancing a specific U.S. concept."[18] As expected, at the Vienna meeting of the ADB in April 1978, representatives of France, South Korea, and Vietnam criticized US officials. South Korean Finance Minister Kim Yon Hnam stated that as the Bank's purpose was economic development, "no other considerations should be allowed to influence its operating activities."[19]

Washington policymakers' ADB policy toward Indochina was characterized by a marked difference before and after the collapse of the Saigon regime in the mid-1970s.

---

[17] DOS memorandum (confidential), December 29, 1977, from EA/EP-W. Robert Warne to EA-Mr. Gleysteen, SA-Mar. Oakley, EA-Mr. Heiginbottom. Subject: "Human Rights Issues in EA—Comments." RG 56, GRDOT, 1978–9, DA-7-2 IDB to DA-7-3 ADB (2 of 2), Box 5. NACP.

[18] Memorandum of conversation (hereafter referred to as MOC), February 14, 1978, Geneva, Switzerland. Participants: President Taroichi Yoshida, Nachmanoff, US Executive Director Les Edmund, Mr. Shigemitsu Sugisaki of ADB, Donald Sherk, Reporting Officer. Subject: "Human Rights in the ADB." RG 56, GRDOT, Subject Files Related to MDBs, 1978–9 DA-7-2 IDB to DA-7-3 ADB (2 of 2), Box 5. NACP.

[19] Schoultz, "Politics, economics, and U.S. participation," 564–5.

Until then, the ADB had made sixteen loans to Indochina countries. All had been made prior to 1975, and to the previous government in Saigon "with strong U.S. support."[20] In April 1975, the ADB suspended all loan operations to Vietnam and Cambodia due to "the unsettled circumstances" in the wake of the US retreat from Indochina. Since the suspension, the Bank had no communication with Cambodia and its membership remained inactive. The Bank continued its activities in Laos. The Socialist Republic of Vietnam (SRV) took up the former South Vietnamese seat in the ADB in the summer of 1976. The new Communist regime agreed with the Bank that the reactivation of the previously suspended loans should come before any new projects should be undertaken.

In the meantime, the Bank management had been under considerable pressure from a number of its European members, France in particular, to resume activities in the SRV. On the other hand, the US had privately urged "extreme caution" upon the Bank. Between these two opposing pressures, the Bank management, sensitive to Washington's concerns, had followed "a very deliberate course" with regards to the reactivation of the suspended loans to the SRV.[21] In a discussion of April 26, 1977 with President Yoshida, Assistant Secretary of the Treasury Fred Bergsten stressed that the Indochina lending issue "remained highly sensitive" in the U. S. and insisted that Vietnam was a member in good standing and in full compliance before resumption. Yoshida replied he would keep a close watch on the political climate, and added that under the ADB charter he could not keep the suspension in effect much longer. He stated "the unsettled circumstances" had been the justification for the length of the suspension but this was no longer an adequate justification.[22]

Congressional hostility toward Vietnam remained strong. When Ambassador Edmund called on Congressmen (Long, Young, Schweiker, Inouye) in March 1978, they all advocated for extreme caution with regard to the reactivation of loans to Vietnam.[23] Concerning the Vietnam loan reactivation, Bergsten reiterated his hope during a meeting of September 25, 1978 with President Yoshida that no action would be taken before the appropriation bill would be finished by the end of next week in Congress. Yoshida remained unmoved. He responded that it was important to avoid giving the impression that the "ADB is commanded by the U.S." Bergsten also agreed.[24]

---

[20] ADB, Table of Contents, 6. ADB Lending to Indochina, prepared in response to questions on the ADB from Congressman Stokes. Testimony on the Witteveen Facility. RG 56, GRDOT, Subject Files Related to IDBs, 1978–9, BCOP-3, Subcommittee on Multilateral Aid Working Group to BP-5-1, Senate Appropriations Sub-Committee, Box 1. NACP.

[21] Ibid.

[22] MOC, April 26, 1978, Hotel Intercontinental, Vienna, Australia. Participants: ADB Taroichi Yoshida, President, Ashok Bambawale, Vice President, Stanley Katz, Vice President, and Graham Race, General Counsel; U.S.-C. F. Bergsten, Ass. Sec. of the Treasury, William Jordan, Congressional Staff, Alexander Watson, EB, DOS, and Donald Sherk, OIDB, Recording Officer. Ibid.

[23] Memorandum from Donald Sherk to Ass. Sec. Bergsten, March 2, 1978. Subject: "U.S. Executive Director Edmund's Consultations on the Hill." MOC, September 26, 1978. Subject: "President Yoshida's Call on Senator Inouye," ibid.

[24] MOC, September 25, 1978. Subject: "General ADB Issues." Participants: Treasury-Blumenthal, Bergsten, Richard Fisher, and Donald Sherk, ADB-Yoshida, Kazumi, and Sugisaki, ibid.

During these years, the ADB tried to seal off the influences of the Cold War, taking a "non-political" position so far as its lending operations were concerned. President Shiro Inoue (1972.11-1976.11), Watanabe's successor, took the same stance. Welcoming the Vietnamese delegation of the transitional revolutionary government of South Vietnam at the ADB annual meeting held in Jakarta, April 1976, he noted that the Bank "is a non-political entity."[25] The ADB President's remarks show that the ADB tried to maintain its own independent position with the new socialist government in Vietnam. On the other hand, the US tended to bring ideological and strategic factors into the ADB lending operations. Due to US objections, Cambodia received only one loan in 1971. Laos also got a low level of lending. Vietnam received no loans after 1974. These cases were a result of Washington's opposition to lending to a socialist Indochina.[26]

Criticism was voiced toward Washington's attitude. At the ADB annual meeting in April, 1978, the French delegate expressed regret that Vietnam and Laos had not received loans from the ADB in 1977. He especially noted the Bank's failure to reactivate the suspended loans that had been made earlier to the former Vietnamese government. The Swedish Governor also reminded the participants of his country's calls for support by the Bank for Vietnam development.[27]

Yoshida, Inoue's successor, was of the opinion that Vietnam should receive no special treatment once it had met its obligations to pay back $50, 000 in arrears. US Assistant Secretary of the Treasury Bergsten noted, however, that the issue remained very sensitive in the US and could affect the level of Congressional support. In an attempt to find a way out, both the Japanese and Australian governments raised the issue in bilateral meetings with Bergsten at the Bank's annual meeting in April 1978. Both supported the view that reactivation of the suspended loans should not take place until Vietnam had met all its obligations. Like President Yoshida, however, they contended that once the obligations had been met, the ADB should treat Vietnam as any other member.[28]

In September 1978, Secretary of the Treasury Blumenthal told President Yoshida that he "was particularly appreciative" of his handling of the Vietnam issue.[29] Nevertheless, the Treasury Department continued to insist that no new loans should be extended to Vietnam. Deputy Secretary Robert Carswell and Nachmanoff were briefed for the coming 12th ADB's annual meeting scheduled on May 2–4, 1979. They were advised President Yoshida should be told that the U.S. Congress was particularly sensitive about loans to Vietnam and that if any new loan "should come forward between now and November," the results could be "severe budget cuts and/or restrictive

[25] Jakarta to DOS, telegram 05402, April 26, 1976, "Summary of Issues at ADB Annual Meeting," RG 286, AID, Entry No. P 514, IDFs, 1969–84, ADB Annual Meeting, 1971–1972 thru 1971–1972 [sic], Box 3. NACP.

[26] Wihtol, *The Asian Development Bank and Rural Development*, 102.

[27] Vienna to DOS, telegram 83985, April 27, 1978, "ADB Annual Meeting," RG 286, AID, Entry No. P 514, IDFs, 1969–84, ADB Annual Meeting, 1971–1972 thru 1971–1972 [sic], Box 3. NACP.

[28] Ibid.

[29] MOC, September 25, 1978. Subject: "General ADB Issues." Participants: Treasury-Secretary Blumenthal, Ass. Sec. Bergsten, Richard Fischer, and Donald Sherk, Recording Officer, ADB-President Taroichi Yoshida, Mr. Kazumi, and Mr. Sugisaki. RG 56, GRDOT, Subject Files Related to MDBs, 1978–9 DA-7-2 IDB to DA-7-3 ADB (2 of 2), Box 5.

amendments" on this year's requests for the ADB.[30] Bergsten was also briefed that any new loans would expose the US politically. Subsequently, Bergsten brought this question up in his meeting with the President. Yoshida meekly responded that he had a problem with the Vietnamese who were pressing for new lending, while the US had a problem with Congress. The ADB leadership was more cautious about new loans to Vietnam. Nevertheless, they managed to reactivate the past loans to Vietnam in the face of Washington's delaying actions.

3. The Increasing Need for Concessional Funds and the Establishment of the Asian Development Fund

"Because the bulk of aid flows consists of loans," pointed out Robert E. Wood, "aid itself creates debt." Debt service as percentage of gross disbursements (both loans and grants) began to increase steadily since the late 1960s. It was 23.1 percent in 1968, 28.2 percent in 1969, 30.9 percent in 1970, and came to 34.0 percent in 1971. The proportion increased constantly until 1980 at 39.0 percent. These figures indicate that a debt problem was a growing concern in borrowing countries in the late 1960s and early 1970s.[31] Beginning with publication of the report[32] by the Pearson Commission in 1969, the problem was receiving increasing attention by the UN Conference on Trade and Development (UNCTAD) and the Development Assistance Committee of the Organisation for Economic Co-operation and Development (DAC-OECD). In May, 1972, a special subsidiary body to tackle the debt problem was established within the UNCTAD.[33] Such a trend also reflected upon the discussions in the ADB loan operations.

"Sound banking principles" advocated by President Watanabe were becoming a burden for less developing countries. As early as June 1969, at the second annual meeting of the ADB Board of Governors, borrowing countries had ardently expressed their desire for an increase in concessional funds. The Governor of Nepal remarked that "one of the basic difficulties" of making use of the Bank's ordinary capital resources (OCRs) was "the interest rate at which we have to borrow." Pointing out that the debt service problems of most of less developed countries (LDCs) were severe, the Governor for Ceylon also stated that the OCRs of the Bank, "at the rate of interest which sound banking principles require," must be improved "by a high mix of Special Funds on concessionary terms." "Otherwise," added the Ceylonese Governor, "we might approach a point where some countries would not find it possible to utilize the ordinary

[30] To Deputy Sec Carswell and Acting Ass. Sec. Nachmanoff, "Scope Memorandum for the 12th ADB Annual Meeting, Manila, May 2–4, 1979," April 13, 1979, ibid.

[31] Robert E. Wood, *From Marshall Plan to Debt Crisis Foreign Aid and Development Choices in the World Economy* (Berkeley: University of California Press, 1986), 234–6.

[32] Lester Pearson, *Partners in Development Report of the Commission on International Development* (Liverpool: Pall Mall Press, 1969).

[33] Kazuhiko Yago, "Ruiseki Saimu Mondai no Hakken," *Keizai Kenkyu* 230 (December 2020): 15–18, 20.

resources of the Bank."[34] Two years later, at the fourth annual meeting of the ADB held in Singapore, April 15–17, 1971, the participants reached a consensus that, in addition to the need for an increase in the Bank's OCRs, the proportion of Special Funds to ordinary capital loans should be increased.[35] At the fifth annual meeting of Governors held in Vienna, April 20–2, 1972, a Governor for Australia commented that developing members had to borrow from the Bank "at going rates of interest in the capital markets of the world," but in many cases they could not afford it.[36]

The need for increasing "soft loan" funds had been building up for several years due to the following reasons. First, the average grant element in the Bank's loan did not compare very favorably either with the recommendations of the DAC-OECD or with the average grant elements in lending by the IBRD/USAID and the Inter-American Development Bank (IDB). Improvement could only be achieved by a considerable increase in the proportion of concessional loans in the Bank's overall lending.[37]

Second, the past few years witnessed a significant increase in the debt service burden of a number of DMCs, as well as decline in grants in ODA and in some cases a reduction in the grant element in loans. The breakdown of the Bretton Woods system and the subsequent poor economic performances of industrialized countries had an adverse impact upon the economies of developing countries. *The Economic Survey of Asia and the Far East 1971* prepared by the Secretariat of the Economic Commission for Asia and the Far East (ECAFE) referred to the adverse effects on international trade and foreign exchange earnings by recent international monetary problems, the decline in the total of concessionary aid flows, the decline in the prices of some important export commodities coupled with the continued rise in import prices, and the pressing need for transfer of appropriate technology adapted to the conditions of the ECAFE region.[38] Both Ikuto Yamaguchi and Mark Metzler, in particular, note in this volume that the marked increase in the share of private capital inflows to less developed countries through the Eurodollar market after the first oil crisis of 1973, seriously aggravating their debts service.

[34] From USADB Manila to SOS, June 4, 1969, "2nd Annual Meeting of the ADB Board of Governors," Airgram A-176, RG 286, AID, Entry No. P 514, IOFs, 1969–84, ADB Annual Meetings, 1971–2, Box 3. NACP.
[35] Amembassy Singapore to Manila for USADB, "Fourth Annual Meeting of ADB, Singapore, Apr 15–17," telegram 01004, April 17, 1971, ibid.
[36] "Fifth Annual Meeting—Comments of Governors," held in Vienna, April 20–2, 1972, Board of Governors Meeting, confidential, RG 286, AID, Entry No. P 664, Records Relating to the ADB, 1972–1972, Sec. M46-72, August 18, 1972, Box 2. NACP. For example, the Bank's OCRs' interest rate was 7.7 percent in 1978. Inter-office memorandum, William R. Thomson for Nachmanoff, July 14, 1978. Subject: "ADB Lending Rate Proposal." RG 56, GRDOT, Subject Files Related to MDBs, 1978–9, BCOP-3, Subcommittee on Multilateral Aid working Group to BP-5-1, Senate Appropriations Subcommittee, Box 1. NACP.
[37] "Review of Special Funds Resources of the ADB," confidential, R 43-72, July 10, 1972. RG 286, AID, USAID/B/S/t, O/Reg Dev, Entry No. P 664, Records Relating to the ADB, 1972–1972, PR M 7-2, ADB Docs Misc Papers thru ADB Working Papers, '72, Box 3. NACP.
[38] "A report by the Secretary D. C. Gunesekera and K. Nakasawa on the 28th session of the ECAFE," confidential, IN 21-72, April 25, 1972, RG 286, AID, USAID/B/SA O/Reg Dev, Entry No. P 664, Records Relating to the ADB, 1972–1972, PRM 7-2 ADB Docs Info 1972 thru PRM 7-2, ADB Docs Minutes, Box 1. NACP.

Third, there was a growing awareness of the importance of social aspects of development such as housing, education, water supply and sewage, and population control. At the fifth annual meeting of the Board of Governors held in Vienna, April 20–2, 1972, the Governor for Sweden noted the 1970 UN Report on the World Social Situation and emphasized the need to base development strategies upon the objectives of equality and social justice and not those of growth alone. The Governor for Pakistan also stated that pursuit of economic growth was not enough and that it must be "blended with social justice."[39] A report on the twenty-second meeting of the Consultative Committee on the Colombo Plan held in New Delhi in November 1972 encapsulated "a qualitative shift in development perspective." The report stressed the need to view development in wider perspectives "by defining it not merely in terms of the attainment of increases in levels of per capita income but also in terms of satisfying the basic human needs."[40]

Added to the urgency for increasing Special Fund resources was the inadequacy of the aggregate resource requirements, given the Bank would reach the ceiling for loan commitments set by existing resources in the last quarter of 1973.[41] About $980 million in Special Fund resources was needed to cover the Bank's existing concessional loan commitments and to finance further commitments to the end of 1975. Given the availability of existing resources of $317 million and set-aside resources of $39 million, President Watanabe estimated that the Bank would need $625 million in additional resources to achieve the operational target by 1975. Thus it was proposed that the amount of $625 million would be mobilized during the 1973–5 period.[42]

President Watanabe himself clearly recognized the Bank's lending problem. At the ADB meeting in Vienna held in April, 1972, Watanabe called for "the consolidation of all concessionary money into a single fund of maximum flexibility, contributed on standard terms."[43] "The Bank had been criticized," remarked Watanabe at the meeting of representatives of developing member countries of the Bank held in Washington, DC in September, 1972, "for concentrating its operations on the more advanced developing countries and not doing enough for the least developed countries." But in order to change this lending pattern, he pointed out, the Bank "needed substantial

---

[39] "Fifth Annual Meeting—Comments of Governors," (Vienna, April 20–2, 1972, Board of Governors Meeting), confidential, Sec. M 46-72, August 18, 1972, RG 286, AID, Entry No. P 664, Records Relating to the ADB, 1972–1972, PRM72 ADB DCS Secretary Minutes thru PRM 12 ADB DOCs, Secretary Minutes, Box 2. NACP.

[40] "Report on the 22nd Meeting of the Consultative Committee on the Colombo Plan Held in New Delhi," November 6–8, 1972, IN. 48-72, December 5, 1972, confidential, RG 286, AID, USAID/B/SA O/Reg Dev, Entry No. P 664, Records Relating to the ADB, 1972–1972, PRM 7-2 ADB Docs Info 1972 thru PRM 7-2, ADB Docs Minutes, Box 1. NACP.

[41] "Review of Special Funds: Report on Meeting of Representatives of Developed Member Countries of the Bank," Washington, DC, September 30, 1972, confidential, Sec. M 66-72, October 23, 1972, RG 286, AID, Entry No. P 664, Records Relating to the ADB, 1972–1972, Box 2. NACP.

[42] "Review of Special Funds resources of the ADB," confidential, R 43-72, July 10, 1972, RG 286, AID, USAID/B/S/T, O/Reg Dev, Entry No. P 664, Records Relating to the ADB, 1972–1972, PR M 7-2 ADB Docs Misc Papers thru ADB Working Papers, '72, Box 3. NACP.

[43] Kenneth Rabin to Roderic O'Connor, "ADB Meeting, Vienna, Apr 20–22, 1972," May 3, 1972, RG 286, AID, Entry No. P 514, IDFs, 1969–84, ADB Annual Meeting, 1971–72, thru ADB Annual Meetings, 1971–2, Box 3. NACP.

Special Fund resources" that were concessional.[44] Accordingly, Watanabe proposed that, of the three Special Funds currently being administered,[45] the TAF should be retained as a separate and independent Fund and that the ASF and the MPSF should be replaced with a single unified Fund, i.e., an Asian Development Fund. In April, 1973, the meeting of ADB governors adopted a resolution looking toward establishment of a new Asian Development Fund for concessional lending.[46]

The ADF was finally authorized by the Board of Governors in 1973. It became operational on June 28, 1974 when ten developed countries pledged contributions totaling $225 million. With a total of $525 million agreed at the Donor's Meeting, an initial amount of $487 (ADF I) was mobilized among fourteen regional and non-regional developed countries in 1974. The US share of $150 million or 29 percent was the second only to the Japanese share of $320 million or 54 percent.[47] By the end of 1974, total ADB lending was approaching two billion dollars. Of these, 124 loans were from OCRs totaling $1,431 million. The remaining 87 loans were from Special Fund resources totaling $493 million.[48] Given that the first oil shock had precipitated the need for further loans, it was apposite for the ADF to be operational at this juncture.

4. The Politics of Negotiating the ADF Replenishments (ADF II~III)

In the early 1970s, however, the relationship between the US administrations and Congress had become increasingly strained due to the imminent debacle in Vietnam. Both President Johnson and his successor Nixon had earlier pledged US contributions of up to $200 million to Special Funds for soft loans and technical assistance. But administration officials had difficulty obtaining Congressional appropriations. In light of Congressional opposition, the US proposal to the Special Funds was subsequently

---

[44] "Review of Special Funds: Report on Meeting of Representatives of Developed Member Countries of the Bank," Washington DC, September 30, 1972, confidential, RG 286, AID, Entry No. P 664, Records Relating to the ADB, 1972–1972, Sec. M66-72, Box 2. NACP.

[45] On September 17, 1968, the Board of Directors adopted Special Funds Rules and Regulations establishing three separate Special Funds for concessional lending operations: The TASF, the ASF and the MPSF. The ASF received contributions totaling $23.1 million from Denmark, Japan, and the Netherlands. The MPSF received $152.5 million from eight countries (Australia, Belgium, Canada, Denmark, Japan, Germany, the Netherlands and the US), plus indications of the intention to contribute from Italy, New Zealand, Norway, Switzerland, and the US. In addition, the Board of Governors authorized the setting-aside of some $24.5 million from the Bank's ordinary capital for the MPSF.

[46] "Review of Special Funds: Report on Meeting of Representatives of Developed Member Countries of the Bank," Washington, D.C., 30 Sept. 1972," confidential, Sec. M66-72, October 23, 1972, RG 286, AID, Entry No. P 664, Records Relating to the ADB, 1972–1972, Sec M 66-72, Box 2. NACP. Amembassy Manila to SOS, April 29, 1973, telegram 04893, "Sixth Annual Meeting of ADB," RG 286, AID, Entry No. P 514, IDFs, 1969–84, ADB Annual Meeting, 1971–1972 thru 1971–1972 [sic], Box 3.

[47] McCawley, *Banking on the Future of Asia and the Pacific*, 443–7.

[48] Robert Watson, Secretary of the National Advisory Council (NAC) to NAC, Subject: "ADB Annual Meeting—U.S. Position Papers, attachment," April 23, 1975, RG 286, AID, Entry No. P 514, IDFs, 1969–84, ADB Annual Meeting, 1971–1972, thru ADB Annual Meetings, 1971–1972 [sic], Box 3. NACP.

scaled down to $100 million. Consequently, during these critical years of the ADB, the US tended to lag behind in contributions to the ADF. At the sixth annual ADB meeting of April 1973, the delay caused "concern over [the] future of [the] U.S. role" in the ADB. Some of the participants wondered whether the US government was "dissatisfied with [the] Bank's operations."[49]

In the ADF II replenishment (1976–8), Washington continued to delay in payments of contribution. Accordingly, the Board of Governors had to adjust to the delay each time. On December 3, 1975, the Board of Governors adopted Resolution No. 92, authorizing the Bank to receive contributions from developed member countries to be the first replenishment of the ADF II. Under the Resolution, the member committed itself to paying the amount of its contribution in three equal annual instalments. When it became apparent that no budgetary appropriations for a US contribution could occur as expected, the Board of Governors on September 10, 1976 adopted Resolution No. 103 to facilitate the receipt of ADF II contributions from New Zealand and the US. In the case of the US, it permitted the Bank to receive a contribution of $180 million from the US, payable in three consecutive instalments of unequal amounts, with the first instalment in the year commencing October 1, 1976.[50] However, the US government again did not find itself in a position to pay its first instalment in the year commencing October 1, 1976.[51] It became apparent that the US was not yet able to make any payment prior to October 1, 1977 at the earliest. In such circumstance, the Board of Governors adopted Resolution No. 107 on April 14, 1977 so as to authorize the Bank to accept payment from the US of its ADF II contribution in unequal installments over the three years commencing October 1977.[52] The long procrastination in US payments placed strains on the US relationship with the Bank and other Bank donors. Donors including Germany indicated at the annual ADB meeting held in Jakarta in April 1976 that they would reconsider their pledges to the ADF if the US decided on a reduced amount.[53]

In 1977, the Bank proposed a second replenishment of the ADF III (1979~1982) of $2.15 billion to finance lending over the four-year period 1979–82. An initial round of negotiations was held in October 1977 in Kyoto. It was intended to raise the ratio of

[49] Amembassy Manila to SOS, April 29, 1973, telegram 04893. Subject: "Sixth Annual Meeting of ADB," RG 286, AID, Entry No. P 514, IDFs, 1969–84, ADB Annual Meeting, 1971–1972 thru 1971–1972 [sic], Box 3. NACP.
[50] Letter from Taroichi Yoshida to Michael Blumenthal, Governor, the Department of the Treasury, ADB, January 27, 1978, regarding "Further Measures to Facilitate Commitment and Payment of United States' Contribution to First ADF Replenishment: Amendment of Resolution No. 103," RG 56, GRDOT, Subject Files Related to MDBs, 1978–9, AD-7-2 IDB to DA-7-3 ADB (2 of 2), Box 5.
[51] Amembassy Kuala Lumpur to SOS, Airgram A-62. Subject: "ADB Seventh Annual Meeting Statement by George P. Schults, May 3, 1974" (held in Kuala Lumpur, Malaysia, April 25–7, 1974), RG 286, AID, Entry No. P 514, IDFs, 1969–84, ADB Annual Meeting, 1971–1972 thru 1971–1972 [sic], Box 3. NACP.
[52] See footnote 50.
[53] Glenn A. Lehman to Arthur Z. Gardner, memorandum, May 11, 1976, "ADB Annual Meeting, Jakarta, April 22–24, 1976," RG 286, AID, Entry No. P 514, IDFs, 1969–84, ADB Annual Meeting, 1971–1972 thru 1971–1972 [sic], Box 3. NACP.

concessional loans to total loans including the OCRs, to 40 percent by 1982. The replenishment target of $2.15 billion was set by the Bank without official Board approval. Consequently, the US government regarded the target ratio as quite arbitrary and high. Nevertheless, the ADB management indicated at the Kyoto meeting that a continuation of the U.S percentage share of 22.24 percent in ADF II was unwarranted and that the share should be raised for ADF III, "possibly up to the 26~27 percentage range." However, the US delegate took the position that its share would not exceed 22.24 percent, down from the original US share of 28.57 percent. As for the target of $2.15 billion, the US continued to insist that the figure was too high and asked for additional justification.[54]

At the second meeting of the donor countries held in Geneva, Switzerland, in mid-February, 1978, with the exception of three countries (the US, Canada, and Belgium), all other countries supported the $2.15 billion figure. Deputy Assistant Secretary Nachmanoff, however, replied that it was "extremely unlikely" for the US to commit to a 22.24 percent share of a $2.15 billion replenishment. The Administration thought the $1.8~$2.0 billion range to be a more proper figure.[55]

A round of negotiations over the replenishment target of $2.15 billion were closely linked with an ongoing review of the lending criteria for ADF loans. The criteria of ADF borrowing were established in 1974 in terms of per capita GNP, repayment capacity, and absorption capacity. It was agreed at the time that "Fully Eligible Countries" were those with a per capita GNP of less than $200 in 1972; "Marginally Eligible Countries" were those with a per capita GNP of from $200~$300; Countries with a per capita GNP of greater than $300 in 1972 were "Not Eligible."[56] In 1974, the Bank classified Indonesia, mainly at US insistence. as a marginally eligible country and agreed that the two concessional loans in late 1974 would be the last such loans for Indonesia. But the US voted against both of these loans on the ground that the country's status as a major oil exporter and member of the Organization of the Petroleum Export Countries (OPEC) disqualified Jakarta as an ADF borrower.[57] Given the oil price hikes in the wake of the October 1973 Arab-Israeli War, Indonesia's classification seemed reasonable at that time. It soon became apparent, however, that initial forecasts of Indonesia's repayment capacity were excessively optimistic due to the plateauing petroleum exports.

In February 1975, Pertamina, Indonesia's largest oil and natural gas company, found itself in a financial crisis. The company's debt problems ($10 billion in debts, equivalent to approximately 30 percent of Indonesia's GNP) were eventually solved through a large government bailout, which nearly doubled Indonesia's foreign debt. The Pertamina

---

[54] Statement of C. Fred Bergsten before the Subcommittee on International Development Institution and Finance of the House Committee on Banking, Finance and Urban Affairs, April 5, 1978, RG 56, GRDOT, Subject Files Related to MDBs, 1978–9, BCOP-3, Subcommittee on Multinational Aid Working Group to BP-5-1, Senate Appropriations Sub-Committee, Box 1.

[55] MOC, undated. Subject: "Second ADF Meeting," Geneva, Switzerland, February 13–14, 1978, ibid.

[56] Memorandum, Donald R. Sherk to Deputy Ass. Sec. Nachmanoff, September 2, 1978, RG 56, GRDOT, Subject Files Related to MDBs, 1978–9, BCOP-3, Subcommittee on Multilateral Aid Working Group to BP-5-1, Senate Appropriations Sub-Committee, Box 1. NACP.

[57] Donald R. Sherk for Bergsten, June 26, 1978. Subject: "Indonesia's Status as an ADF Borrower." Ibid.

crisis and accelerated development borrowings by the Indonesian government raised the debt service ratio from around 9 percent to 16 percent in 1977.[58] Worried that Indonesia, a strategically located country in the Cold War context, would face a serious financial situation in the years ahead, the US government began to insist that Jakarta be reclassified as "Fully Eligible."

There was another reason for Washington's insistence on review of the ADF lending criteria. During its three years of existence (1974–6), the ADF made forty-nine loans to fifteen DMCs for a total volume of $575 million. However, the lending was extremely concentrated. Six South Asian countries (Bangladesh, Pakistan, Burma, Nepal, Afghanistan, and Sri Lanka) accounted for more than 85 percent.[59] From Washington's viewpoint, other advantages to reducing the heavy South Asia bias of the ADF included the increase in ADB resources for East and Southeast Asian countries by reducing ordinary capital lending that Indonesia had hitherto received.[60]

The Bank's position, however, was to keep the criteria of 1974. The Bank management argued that the present resource constraint in the ADF precluded any loan to the "Marginally Eligible" DMCs and that considerably more resources were required under ADF III. The US government did not accept this logic, arguing that some additional lending to the "Marginally Eligible" countries such as Indonesia, Thailand, and the Philippines could occur in 1978. The U.S called for a full-scale review of the lending criteria.[61]

In early July, 1978, Assistant Secretary Bergsten authorized the US delegate Lester Edmond to participate in a joint US–Australian initiative to propose that Indonesia be reclassified as a fully eligible ADF borrower. ADB President Yoshida, however, asked Edmond and the Australian Executive Director not to raise the issue in the Board of Directors' Meeting. Yoshida feared the proposal would be divisive in the Board. He felt that the poorer ADF borrowers would resent Indonesia reducing the concessional resources available to them. After further discussions, a tentative compromise was worked out. Yoshida accepted the conclusion that Indonesia had a greater claim to ADF funds than did Thailand and the Philippine, and agreed to using language in the paper to that effect. Thus, Washington decided to go along with the compromise package arrived at with Yoshida at the Board of Directors meeting on September 12, 1978.[62]

---

[58] Ibid.
[59] Memorandum, Donald Sherk to Nacmanoff, September 2, 1978. Subject: "Review of the Lending Criteria for Lending from the ADF," ibid.
[60] Donald Sherk for Bergsten, June 26, 1978. Subject: "Indonesia's Status as an ADF Borrower." Ibid.
[61] Memorandum from Rea Brazeal, Executive Secretariat for Karen Anderson, March 10, 1978. Subject: "IFIs" regarding Meeting on March 15 with Vice President Mondale, Mr. McNamara, and Senators and Congressmen to discuss IFI's. "Talking Points." RG 56, GRDOT, Subject Files Related to MDBs, 1978–1979, BCOP-3, Sub-Committee on Multilateral Aid Working Group to BP-5-1, Senate Appropriations Sub-Committee, Box 1. NACP.
[62] Donald Sherk for Bergsten, June 26, 1978. Subject: "Indonesia's Status as an ADF Borrower"; inter-office memorandum, Donald Sherk for Nachmanoff, July 24, 1978. Subject: "Increased ADF Lending to Indonesia; memorandum from Donald Sherk to Nachmanoff, September 2, 1978. RG 56, GRDOT, Subject Files Related to MDBs,1978-9, BCOP-3, Sub-Committee on Multilateral Aid Working Group to BP-5-1, Senate Appropriations Sub-Committee, Box 1. NACP.

Linked to the above negotiations were two other considerations that influenced US acceptance of the compromise package. Firstly, President Yoshida was "caught between two fairly strong and opposing forces." The developing countries of South Asia, the South Pacific, Laos, and Vietnam were supported by certain European countries that wanted ADF lending to go exclusively to the poorest countries. On the other hand, the Southeast Asian countries backed up by Australia, the US, and Japan wanted a redistribution of ADF lending in favor of the "Marginally Eligible" countries. Under the circumstance, US officials felt it unwise to push Yoshida too far. Secondly, the Treasury Department needed to work out a compromise about the replenishment target discrepancy between the ADB management's $2.15 billion and the US's range of $1.8–2.0 billion. When Bergsten and Sir Chadwick, advisor to ADB President, discussed the issue on April 5, 1978, the Assistant Secretary hinted that he could agree to the $2.0 billion target if "there should be some redistribution of lending" toward the "Marginally Eligible" countries, while Sir John said the Bank planned on a full review of the lending criteria in the coming summer of 1978.[63] At the eleventh annual meeting held in Vienna, Switzerland, on April 24–5, 1978, an agreement was reached by the donors to a four-year $2 billion dollar replenishment to the resources of the ADF III. Bergsten who attended the meeting expressed Washington's desire "to see some of the additional concessional resources directed toward the marginally eligible countries of Indonesia, Thailand and the Philippines for projects meeting basic human needs,"[64] whereby suggesting a strong link between the US replenishment target of $2.0 billion and the eligibility question.[65] The US offer for the amount of $2.0 billion instead of $1.8 billion was in exchange for the eligibility issue on Indonesia.

During the discussions between Washington and the ADB management concerning these issues, the German delegate stated Germany would take its share of a $2.15 billion, but opposed Resolution 103 that would allow the US to contribute an amount less than that agreed to. Japan, in an awkward position, acted as an intermediary between the US and the other donors in favor of the ADB's position. The Japanese delegate, like Germany, supported the figure of $2.15 billion, adding that Japan would take one third as the upper limit. At the same time, in terms of the "Japan–US cooperation," Tokyo was sympathetic to Washington's difficulties with Congress. "A realistic view of U.S. difficulties," said the Japanese delegate, "should be taken account of."[66] Moreover, the Cold War logic moved Japan to lean toward the US and Australia in favor of reclassifying the status of Indonesia from "Marginally Eligible" to "Fully Eligible," though the ADB management believed it unjustified. Understandably, the Japanese "rather timidly" supported the US position on the eligibility question.[67] "With Australia taking lead and with the United States in support," described another memorandum prepared by a Treasury official, Washington could expect Japan's support

[63]   MOC, April 5, 1978. Subject: "ADF II," ibid.
[64]   Remarks by the Honorable C. Fred Bergsten, Ass. Sec. of the Treasury Department for International Affairs, the 11th Annual Meeting, Vienna, Switzerland, April 24–5, 1978, ibid.
[65]   See footnote 76.
[66]   See footnote 66.
[67]   See footnote 76.

for "Indonesia's reclassification as well."[68] Japan was caught between the two conflicting views, with the ADB management sticking to the $2.15 billion proposal and the US insisting on the $1.8–2.0 billion range. In this situation, the logic of the "Japan–US cooperation" had to be reconciled with the ADB management's proposal. In the final analysis, however, the compromise package taking both sides' interests into account was regarded as acceptable to Japan.

5. The Oil Shocks, The Second Asian Agricultural Survey, and the ADB's Increased Lending in Southeast Asia

The developments leading up to the establishment of the ADF coincided with the oil shock of 1973 that caused the first region-wide economic crisis that the Bank faced. Developing countries had to adjust to a sharp rise in energy prices. Higher costs of imports of fuel and fertilizers exacerbated many countries' balance of payments, which forced them to borrow more, leading to alarmingly high levels of international debt.

The Bank responded to the oil shock by increasing lending quickly. In the years leading up to 1976, lending rose from $316 million in 1972 to more than $770 million in 1976.[69] President Shiro Inoue took several steps to increase the Bank resources. He worked toward a second general capital increase. In October 1976, member countries voted to raise the authorized capital of the Bank by 135 percent. All member countries, with the exception of the US, voted in favor of the increase. Inoue looked to further borrowing in international capital markets. Borrowing rose from $310 million in 1974 to almost $530 million in 1976. By the end of 1976, the ADB had issued around $1,100 million in bonds in twelve countries.[70]

Following the first oil crisis, the low-income countries' need for concessional loans dramatically increased. It was of particular importance that the ADF, constituting the "soft loan" window at low rates of interest (approximately 1 percent as of 1973) to meet the needs of the smaller and poorer member countries, had become operational in June 1974.

It should be noted that the mid-1970s, in response to the World Bank's initiative, marked a significant rise in the priority of the agricultural and rural sector in ADB lending. It became clear in the early 1970s that the Green Revolution benefited large-scale farmers and plantation companies as they had the capability to adopt the new technologies and, in the case of agriculture, high-yielding seed varieties (HYVs). However, small-scale farmers could not utilize them to their benefits. The report on the twenty-second meeting of the Colombo Plan Consultative Committee of November 1972 pointed out that as a result of the Green Revolution, there had been a significant breakthrough in agricultural production, but the benefits had been limited to wheat

---

[68] Donald Sherk for Bergsten, June 26, 1978. Subject: "Indonesia's Status as an ADF Borrower," ibid.
[69] McCawley, *Banking on the Future of Asia and the Pacific*, 93–4.
[70] Ibid., 99, 441. See also Dick Wilson, *A Bank for Half the World*, Appendix IV-1.7, 461.

and rice production. Moreover, it noted "the side-effects of the Green Revolution" that had widened economic inequalities in rural areas.[71]

Stagnation in rice production in Asia during 1971–2 and decline in rice production in 1972–3 due to the severe drought of 1972 had contributed to a worldwide food shortage. Metzler mentions in this volume that Thailand, Asia's largest rice exporter restricted its rice export in April 1973 for nine months until its resumption in January 1974. Moreover, the 1973 oil shock sharply increased the prices of fertilizers and caused a decline in their consumption, which necessitated and accelerated the Bank's emphasis on the agricultural sector. Bad weather in 1973 and 1974 brought disasters for major food crops in the region. To counter the situation, the Bank's lending to the agricultural sector increased from 11 percent in 1973 to 24 percent in 1974

In his speech to the Board of Governors in April 1974, President Inoue, aware of the importance of the food production in Asia, stressed the need to increase investment in agriculture to ensure adequate availability of rice. The ADB management and the donors now shared the view that, given the food shortage, greater priority would be given to agricultural production and agro-related industries in developing countries.[72]

The real take-off in agricultural lending came with the introduction of the ADF in June 1974 when agricultural loans almost doubled. Thereafter, it continued to increase. President Inoue noted that several Governors had stressed the importance of agricultural and rural development, and of developing educational skills. Inoue promised that the Bank would "continue to pay full attention to agriculture and expand the role of the ADB in developing educational skills." In response, most delegates complimented the ADB on committing 37 percent of its loans to projects in the agricultural sector and "the endeavor to direct resources to the poorest sectors."[73]

It was timely that the ADB undertook the Second Asian Agricultural Survey in 1976. This survey's recommendations for the rural sector were closely in line with the World Bank's strategy for rural development. President Yoshida's forward of August 1977 to the second survey clearly acknowledged the need for a change in Bank policy. He noted that "the severity of food shortages in many Asian countries during the early 1970s and the continued presence of widespread rural poverty and un(der)employment suggest that the expectations implicit in the AAS [the first survey of 1967] have for various reasons not been realized."[74]

Faced with the threat of rising food shortage, widespread unemployment in rural areas, worsening conditions for the environment after the first oil shock, the agricultural survey of 1976 identified three principal problems (food production, unemployment, and poverty), in contrast to the first survey which had identified food production as

[71] "Report on the 22nd Meeting of the Consultative Committee on the Colombo Plan Held in New Delhi," November 6–8, 1972, IN. 48-72, December 5, 1972, confidential, RG 286, AID, USAID/B/SA O/Reg Dev. Entry No. P 664, Records Relating to the ADB 1972–1972, PRM 7-2, ADB Docs Info 1972 thru PRM 7-2, ADB Docs Minutes, Box 1. NACP.

[72] See footnote 59.

[73] Jakarta to DOS, telegram 05402, April 26, 1976, "Summary of Issues at ADB Annual Meeting."

[74] ADB, *Rural Asia: Challenge and Opportunity* (New York: Praeger, 1978), forward, August 1977. *Asian Agricultural Survey 1976* was first printed by the Bank in 1977 and was later published as ADB, *Rural Asia: Challenge and Opportunity*.

the main problem.[75] In addition to the considerable acceleration of agricultural production, it recommended that participation by a large number of small farmers and employment in agriculture should be greatly expanded to provide income opportunities and purchasing power to the rural poor. The recommendation also noted the importance of land reform that had not been considered essential in the 1967 survey, as well as expansion of agricultural production through utilization of technology suitable for small farms, the provision of support services including credit, and the extensive off-farm employment.

The second survey particularly singled out land reform as the prerequisite for rural improvement.[76] One of the major reasons for the unequal distribution of the benefits of the Green Revolution was that existing credit arrangements were not readily accessible to small farmers. Consequently, the second survey underscored the importance of supportive measures, particularly credit so that small farmers could purchase fertilizer and other chemicals as well as HYVs.[77] The survey also regarded large-scale programs for off-farm employment as essential for alleviation of poverty in the rural area. The assumption was that employment created through expansion of agricultural production would be inadequate to absorb the rapid population growth in the rural area and would need to be supplemented with extensive off-farm employment opportunities. The second survey, therefore, called for massive allocation of public resources to labor-intensive rural works, such as the construction of farm-to-market roads, irrigation works, drainage, and flood control facilities.[78]

Finally, the second survey recommended a substantial increase in ODA for the rural sector, a reduction in the cost of aid to recipients through increased concessional lending, increased local cost financing, the untying of bilateral aid and the improvement of the operational procedures of multilateral aid for DMCs to increase the use of domestic consultants and labor-intensive technology, and the modification of procurement procedures favoring domestic procurement.[79]

At the 1977 annual meeting, President Yoshida had already endorsed the second survey as a basis for modifying ADB policy. At the eleventh annual meeting held in Vienna, April 24–6, 1978, many member countries including the US and Japan, particularly the borrowers and the small donors, also endorsed it. Moreover, by the time of the Vienna meeting, an agreement had been reached by the donor countries to a four-year $2 billion replenishment to the resources of the ADF. The US agreed to a 22.24 percent share ($445 million) of the replenishment.[80] Assistant Secretary of the Treasury Fred Bergsten delivered a speech assuring that the US would strongly support the ADB, viewing it as an important contributor to development in Asia as well as a

---

[75] *Rural Asia*, 1–3. For the first survey, see the ADB, *The Asian Agricultural Survey* (Tokyo: The University of Tokyo Press, 1969).
[76] Ibid., 207–92, 231–41.
[77] Ibid., 256–61.
[78] Ibid., 269–92.
[79] Ibid., 295–317.
[80] Inter-office memorandum, from William R. Thompson to Deputy Ass. Sec. Nachmanoff. Subject: "Investment Guidelines for ADB," May 3, 1978. Item for the Secretary's daily summary, April 27, 1978. RG 56, GRDOT, Subject Files Related to MDBs, 1978–9, BCOP-3, Sub-Committee on Multilateral Aid Working Group to BP-5-1, Senate Appropriations Sub-Committee, Box 1. NACP.

focal point for cooperation in the region.[81] The Vienna meeting was characterized by "a spirit of harmony and general support for the Bank" among donors and recipients alike. The Japanese delegation, the partner of the "Japan–US cooperation," told Bergsten that they "now felt the U.S. was fully behind" the ADB, whereas they had "some doubts before."[82] Moreover, the Bank's increased attention to the agricultural and rural sectors "was widely praised."[83]

The survey's recommendation was approved by the Board of Directors in April 1979. It was agreed that lending to the agricultural and rural sector would be increased by 20 percent a year from 1979 to 1982. The Bank doubled its lending for agriculture during those years to reach $620 million. For the entire second decade (1977~1986), ADB operational approvals reached more than $16 billion, an almost fivefold increase from the previous decade. A third of this was sourced from the ADF. As for operational approvals by sector, loans were largely for agriculture at 31 percent ($5,025 million) and energy at 25 percent ($4,054), accounting for more than half of total lending.[84] As for operational approvals by region for the second decade, more than half of the lending went to Southeast Asia at 52 percent ($8,300 million), followed by East Asia at 10 percent ($1,578 million).[85] During the second decade, technical assistance operations increased fivefold to $125 million, and by sector, 41 percent went to agriculture.[86]

Agricultural production expanded fast in the late 1970s and early 1980s. As a result, Indonesia and the Philippines achieved self-sufficiency in food. In other countries, the dependence on imports of food was considerably reduced, contributing to an improvement of balance of payments.[87] As Shigeru Akita demonstrates in this volume, India, after overcoming a serious "food crisis" in the mid-1960s, also managed to achieve de facto self-sufficiency in food production in the 1970s. India's self-sufficiency was made possible by changing policy priorities regarding economic development from heavy industrialization to agricultural development which, interestingly enough, coincided with the ADB's renewed emphasis on the agricultural sector after the first oil shock. India, however, did not begin to borrow from the ADB until 1986. Instead, the Indian government overcame the first oil shock through aid from the World Bank Group, and the second oil shock by skillfully utilizing the large IMF lending.

It should be recalled at this point that the ADB had undertaken a study of "Southeast Asia's Economy in the 1970s." The study was published in 1971. An Overall Report section was written by Hla Myint, Professor of London School of Economics.[88] First, he

---

[81] Amembassy Vienna to DOS, telegram 03831, April 24, 1978. Subject: "ADB Annual Meeting: US speech before the 11th Annual Meeting," April 25, 1978. RG 286, AID, Entry No. P 514, IDFs, 1969–84, ADB Annual Meeting, 1971–1972 thru ADB Annual Meetings 1971–1972 [sic], Box 2. NACP.

[82] Vienna to DOS, telegram 83985, April 27, 1978, "ADB Annual Meeting" (Vienna, April 24–5, 1978), ibid. Box 3.

[83] Ibid.

[84] See Figure 7.2, McCawley, *Banking on the Future of Asia and the Pacific*, 148.

[85] See Figure 7.3, ibid., 149.

[86] Ibid., 147.

[87] Wilson, *A Bank for Half the World*, 158–9.

[88] For Myint's contribution in the genealogy of development theory, see Kohei Wakimura "'Nanboku Mondai' Saikou—Keizai Kakusa no Guro-baru Histori," *Keizaigaku Zasshi* 118(3–4) (March 31, 2018): 27–47, especially 33–5.

examined the economic policies required to "turn the Green Revolution into a dynamic force for economic development." To that end, he advocated that the Southeast Asian countries should move away from the existing import-substitution policies toward an "export-substitution" policy. The rationale was that the Southeast Asian countries should orient their industrialization strategy towards the export market by taking advantage of both abundant natural resources and an increasing supply of labor. Such an export-oriented industrialization strategy should aim at gradually substituting the existing exports of raw materials by the export of processed and semi-processed materials.[89] Second, he suggested that the region should try to make private foreign investment more attractive by improving their social infrastructure. Investment in social structure "must be directed not only to the improvement of transport and communications but also to improvement in the quality and skills of their labor force." He emphasized the importance of developing human resources to attract private foreign investment into labor-intensive primary export industries.[90]

All these recommendations in Myint's report have proved in accord with some of the major elements noted in the World Bank report of 1993. The report, in referring to "the East Asian Miracle," singled out the following factors: Southeast Asian countries' early switch from import-substitution policies to their export-industrialization strategy (in the report's phrase, "export-push strategy") and the resultant high export performances, openness to foreign technology and "building human capital," and an emphasis on agricultural production and "wide adoption of Green Revolution technology" as well as "high investment in rural infrastructure."[91]

Myint perceptively observed that the demand conditions for Southeast Asia export products were expected to be very favorable during the 1970s, given the prospects for rapid economic growth in Japan, the Republic of China, Korea and Hong Kong. So if Southeast Asia pursued economic policies "to link up her abundant natural resources with the expanding world market demand for their products," the region could expect to enjoy rapid economic growth through export expansion.[92] The Newly Industrializing Economies (NIEs) (Korea, Hong Kong, Singapore, Republic of China), more or less, followed the pattern of development as had been suggested by Mint. They had already been pursuing export-oriented industrial development by the time of the first oil shock. When a world economy began to show a recovery in 1976, the NIEs' export growth resumed, and would remain more than 20 percent per year for the rest of the 1970s, which made these countries the attractive markets for foreign direct investments. The NIEs started out as exporters of low-skilled, labor-intensive goods. However, they were successful in making structural adjustments shifting to skill-and capital-intensive manufactured goods under the adverse circumstance brought about by the oil shocks.[93]

[89] Asian Development Bank, *Southeast Asia's Economy in the 1970s* (London: Longman, 1971), 5, 19–22.
[90] Ibid., 44, 102.
[91] The World Bank, *The East Asian Miracle* (Oxford: Oxford University Press, 1993), 21–3, 32–4, 37–8, 43–6, 351–2.
[92] ADB, *Southeast Asia's Economy in the 1970s*, 101.
[93] McCawley, *Banking on the Future of Asia and the Pacific*, 110–11.

ASEAN-4 countries (Malaysia, Thailand, Indonesia, and the Philippines) would soon follow the NIEs. In the 1970s, Malaysia and Thailand shifted from a strategy of import-substitution industrialization to that of export-oriented labor-intensive industrialization based on unskilled and semi-skilled workers in small and medium-sized industries. Malaysia established several export processing zones where multinational companies, especially from Japan, produced textiles and electronics. Thailand, as an oil importer, was affected by the oil price shocks but pursued pro-market and export-oriented foreign investment policies, thereby achieving around 7 percent growth throughout the late 1970s into the early 1980s. What is striking about ASEAN-4 countries' development policies was that they embarked on policies of adjustment towards development of more competitive labor force, thereby producing relatively competitive human-capital intensive products.[94]

Yamaguchi, in his comparative analysis of Brazil and Korea in this volume, has shown that, despite their heavy borrowing from private banks (Brazil: 66.7 percent, 1976–80, 61.2 percent, 1981–2 and Korea: 60.4 percent and 59.3 percent, respectively), Korea owed its success to its export-oriented strategy as well as to capital flow and industrial markets from Japan and the United States. Debt service as a share of export revenues in 1981, for example, was 13.0 percent in South Korea against 31.9 percent in Brazil. As for Malaysia and Singapore that came to achieve industrialization in the latter half of the 1980s, Shigeru Sato has also located their high economic performances in their export oriented strategy.

6. Conclusion

The 1970s have been variously characterized by contributors to this volume as the emergence of the "privatized international development finance" (Yamaguchi), "the interregnal moment" between the postwar Fordist-Keynesian paradigm of the 1960s and the neoliberal techno-economic paradigm of the 1980s (Meztler), as well as "the transformation of the global system" (Painter) that eventually led to the collapse of the Soviet Union and communism and the reassertion of US hegemony. More relevant to my arguments is Dane Kennedy's characterization of the decade as an era in which the two oil crises brought about the disintegration of the Third World "as a distinct and coherent force in international affairs." What happened to the "Global South" reveals another aspect of the concurrent processes in which Southeast Asian countries, notably the Asian NIEs, subsequently followed by the ASEAN-4 countries, were graduating from the category of the Third World. In this process, the Asian Development Bank played a significant part in promoting Asia's development called "the East Asian Miracle."

---

[94] Rashid Amjad ed., *The Development of Labour Intensive Industry in ASEAN Countries* (Geneva: International Labour Organization, 1981). Kaoru Sugihara, "Tonan Ajia ni okeru Rodoshuyaku-gata Kogyoka-ron no Seiritsu," *Keizai Shirin* 73(4): 163–79.

Starting from the assumption that the ADB, like other multilateral development banks, is a political institution as well as an aid organization, this chapter examined the "Japan–US cooperation" and the activities of the ADB in the context of the Cold War and the oil shocks. It showed that Washington policymakers expected the ADB to contribute to the political stability in Asia through economic and social development of Asian non-Communist countries, thereby promoting the US containment of Communism in the region. Japan's commitment to the ADB activities in terms of financial contributions was also in line with the "Japan–US cooperation" in the Cold War context.

This chapter also tried to show that the ADB, interacting at the crossroads of different goals and interests of donors and recipients, managed to maintain its own lending policy and operations. In this context, the chapter detailed Washington's approach to the ADB, showing that Washington policymakers, compared with their counterparts in Tokyo, were more openly political in their approach to the Bank. US officials were active in using the Bank as an instrument of promoting its Cold War objectives as well as its commercial and financial interests. With the cooperation of the Japanese government, US officials tried to ensure that a high level of lending would go to countries of political and strategic importance to the US and its allies. They supported ADB loans to South Vietnam and Taiwan. After the Saigon regime fell, however, Washington policymakers began to oppose lending to the Socialist Republic of Vietnam.

Japan, on the other hand, generally maintained a low-key profile and was very cautious about politically sensitive issues. In addition to the constraints on Japanese diplomacy imposed by the "Japan–US cooperation," Japanese policymakers were careful not to evoke the past memory of wartime atrocities in Asia. The emergence of a close tie between the MOF and its reserved posts in the ADB also made a low-key posture possible. The ADB presidents being Japanese nationals, the Japanese government could assume that the policies taken by the president would usually reflect Japan's interests.

All in all, it can be said that the ADB played a significant role in laying the foundation of the development of Southeast Asian countries in the 1970s and early 1980s. In spite of politically motivated interventions by the US in the Bank's lending operations, the ADB leadership managed to navigate the mounting pressures caused by the oil shocks and the protectionist tendencies of donor countries. The Bank responded to these challenges by rapidly increasing lending by mobilizing a general capita increase as well as by successfully carrying out the replenishments of the concessionary ADF and quickly increasing agricultural loans. During the prolonged negotiations over the replenishments of the ADF, the ADB leadership managed to attain close to the replenishment target of the ADF by adjusting to the differing interests between the US position and other donor countries. Moreover, the publication of the Second Asian Agricultural Survey in 1976, which identified three principal problems (food production, unemployment, and poverty), had a significant impact on shifting the Bank's policy so as to tackle these problems in the agricultural sector in Southeast Asia.

Greatly increased agricultural production contributed to foreign trade and an improvement of balance of payments in the region in the 1970s. Total agricultural exports more than quadrupled to $24 billion. Southeast Asia recorded surplus in agricultural production during the 1970s, whereas South Asia showed moderate surpluses or deficits. But if we take the years up to 1986, Burma, Pakistan, and Thailand enjoyed being substantial net exporters of rice during the two decades of the Bank's history. India, Indonesia, and the Philippines also changed during those twenty years from net importers to net exporters of rice.[95]

[95]   Wilson, *A Bank for Half the World*, 159, 163.

Part Two

Transformation of International Development Financing

4

Privatization of International Development Finance: Oil-money, the Emerging Eurodollar Market, and Developing Countries in the 1970s

Ikuto Yamaguchi

1. Introduction

The move of the major Western major currencies into a floating currency regime in 1973 promoted the freer movement of money (in terms of both current and capital payments) in the world. Simultaneously, the US dollar retained its position as the world's dominant reserve and clearing currency. The revised International Monetary Fund (IMF) Charter of 1976 accepted the status of this post-Bretton Woods international monetary system. A Japanese scholar, Tadokoro, called this transformed system from around the mid-1970s the "privatized international currency system."[1] This chapter examines the transformation of international development finance during the 1970s in the context of international economic disorder brought by two oil shocks, international monetary expansion, and the emergence of the "privatised international currency system." (Table 4.1).

From the mid-1970s, many so-called "less developed countries'"(LDCs) were suffering from severe losses in their balance of payments because of surging petrol prices, the stagnation of industrialized economies and the instability of commodity prices (other than oil). However, official development assistance (ODA) to LDCs from Western countries was not increased to compensate for these losses. Hence, international multilateral institutions such as the IMF, the World Bank, the International Development Association (IDA), and regional developmental organizations such as the Asian Development Bank (ADB) and EEC's Lome arrangements began to play a larger role. In addition, the growth of international private transfers to LDCs was remarkable. Between 1973 and 1979, the share allocated to developing countries increased from 16.5 percent to 23.3 percent.[2] There were five types of private capital

---

[1] Masayuki Tadokoro, *Amerika wo koeta doru [US Dollar that Transcended "National Currency": Financial Globalisation and International Currency Diplomacy]* (Tokyo: Chuoukouronshinsya, 2001).

[2] Scott Newton, *The Global Economy 1944–2000* (London: Arnold, 2004), 118–19.

Table 4.1 Total foreign exchange (billions of SDR)

	1970	1974	1980
Developed countries	29.6	64.9	164.7
Oil producing countries	3.5	34.9	62.8
Non-oil producing developing countries	11.7	27.0	63.8

Source: IMF, *International Financial Statistics 1984.*

inflows to LDCs: private direct investments; private export credits; bond issuing in developed countries' markets; portfolio investments; and borrowing through the Eurodollar market. Unlike direct private investments and export credits, there was a huge growth in Western countries' banks' lending to LDCs. Between 1971 and 1982, while direct investments increased from $3.3 to $11 billion and export credits from $2.71 to $9 billion, bank lending surged from $3.3 to $29 billion.[3]

The following discussion will focus mainly on the period between 1974 and the early 1980s. In 1974, the first oil shock occurred after the Yom Kippur War in the Middle East, and the New International Economic Order (NIEO) resolution was adopted at the special session of the United Nation. At the end of the decade, the world faced three "revolutions" in 1979/80: the Iranian Islamic revolution with the second major oil price hike; the US tightening monetary policy after the nomination of Paul Volcker as Chairman of the Federal Reserve Board; and the formation of conservative governments in both the UK and the US. The first part of this chapter discusses the impact of the first oil price surge on international development finance in the context of the emerging "privatized international currency system." The oil producers' huge surpluses flowed into the US and UK financial markets, especially into the Eurodollar market in London.[4] The emergence of the oil-money recycling structure based on Western private financial markets directed the discussion of restructuring international development finance; not the enhancement of public development finance structures, but the way toward the "privatized" international development finance was opened.

In the latter half of this chapter, the impact of the second petrol price surge on the international development finance is analyzed. The cases of Brazil and Korea are discussed. Both depended on private capital inflows, especially the Eurodollar finance, for government-led industrialization during the 1970s. However, from the early 1980s, while Latin American countries fell into the debt crisis, East Asian countries showed stable economic growth. The different dynamics to which the impact of the three "revolutions" in 1979/80 on the "privatized" international development finance gave led to the divergence of economic trajectories between Latin America and East Asia.

---

[3] Edwin Allan Brett, *The World Economy since the War: The Politics of Uneven Development* (London: Macmillan, 1985), 216–17.

[4] A Eurodollar refers to a US currency or a deposit account that was denominated in US dollars held in banks outside the US. In this chapter, the Eurodollar market refers to the capital markets conducting Eurodollar or Euro-currencies (other than the US dollar) finance in European countries and offshore markets in the Caribbean, the Far East, and the Middle East.

2. Oil-Money Recycling and the Eurodollar Market

At the end of the 1960s, while ODA was stagnant, private flows began to constitute a larger part of financial flows to developing countries. Apart from the expanding presence of international development institutions such as the World Bank, US private bank lending was increasing. During the 1960s, an estimated 40 percent of the financial resources that flowed to LDCs were private in origin. The proportion rose to 50 percent in the early 1970. By 1974, 60 percent of all LDC financing consisted of private transfers. In 1974, for developing countries, private capital constituted approximately 15 percent of the total capital formation of both domestic and international capital.[5] Even before the oil crisis, "the bond markets as the principal channel for raising international funds" were displaced by "the medium-term euro-credit market." (Table 4.2).[6] A World Bank Staff Working Paper called this change, which started in the mid-1960s, "the bank-oriented phase" of the international flow of funds. This third phase dominated international finance through the 1970s and 1980s.[7]

In December 1973, the Organization for Economic Co-operation and Development (OECD) consulted with private bankers regarding Eurodollar lending to developing countries. This kind of lending was growing rapidly at the beginning of the 1970s ($3 billion in 1971, $8 billion in 1972 and $12 billion in 1973), While ODA stagnated ($8 billion in 1971), the liabilities of LDCs reached around $80 billion. Bankers hinted that the amount of Eurodollar financing to LDCs was underestimated. The share of Eurodollar money from oil producers was estimated to be 10 percent at most (indeed, because the distinction between contributors and mediators in the Eurodollar market was difficult to ascertain, the scale of oil-producing countries' investments was never clear at this time). It was expected that the market would continue to grow with channeling oil procurers' surpluses. A reason for growing the Eurodollar market before the oil crisis was to hedge against inflation and increasing interest rates. Owing to these circumstances, Western private banking sectors were somewhat unsure about private direct investments, private export credits, and bond issuing. Prior to the first oil crisis, major borrowers were the United Kingdom and Italy from developed countries (60 percent) and Mexico, Argentina, Brazil, Colombia, Algeria. Zaire, Zambia, Indonesia, Korea, the Philippines, North Korea, Poland, and the Soviet Union from developing countries/the Eastern bloc (30 percent).[8]

In the last months of 1973, OPEC quadrupled the price of oil. By the end of 1974, the OPEC states oil surplus surged to around $70 billion. Most oil-producing counties sought places to invest excess capital abroad, then the problem of "recycling" oil-money emerged. Consequently, most oil-money flowed into the Eurodollar market as well as the US and the UK bank deposits and government securities in 1974/75 (Table 4.3).

---

[5] "Recent trends of private capital flows to developing countries," CPE/TWP(76)6, Note by the Secretariat of OECD, March 5, 1976, OECD Historical Archives.

[6] "The international capital markets: 1973," Memo by the Overseas Office, Group 4C, January 25, 1974, 8A406/5, Bank of England Archive.

[7] T. M. Rybczynski, *The Internationalization of the Financial System and the Developing Countries: The Evolving Relationship* (World Bank Staff Working Papers Number 788; Series in International Capital and Economic Development Number 4) (1986), 15–20.

[8] "OECD/DAC Secretariat consultations with private bankers on Euro-currency lending to developing countries (Paris, 7th December)," December 13, 1973, 8A406/5; "The international capital markets: 1973," Memo by the Overseas Office, Group 4C, January 25, 1974, 8A406/5, Bank of England Archive.

Table 4.2 Private flows (net) from Development Assistance Committee (DAC) countries and Euro-currency loan commitments (US$ million)

	1964–6 average	1970	1971	1972	1973	1974
Direct investment	2068	3543	3632	4474	6711	6625
Bilateral portfolio	654	716	733	1984	3286	3795
Private export credits	911	2142	2831	1448	1196	2482
Multilateral portfolio	295	474	771	667	250	-70
Euro-currency lending	---	---	1475	3888	9336	9805
Total (private flows from DAC countries)	3928	6875	7966	8573	11450	12832

Source: "Recent trends of private capital flows to developing countries," CPE/TWP(76)6, note by the Secretariat of OECD, March 5, 1976, OECD Historical Archives.

Table 4.3 Disposition of oil exporters' surplus (US$ billion)

		1974	1975	1976	1977
Investments in UK	UK total	21.0	4.3	4.5	4.1
	British government stocks	0.9	0.4	0.2	==
	Treasury bills	2.7	-0.9	-1.2	==
	Sterling deposits	1.7	0.2	-1.4	0.3
	Foreign currency deposits	13.8	4.1	5.6	3.4
	Other [1]	1.9	0.5	1.3	0.4
Investments in US	US total	11.6	10.0	12.0	8.9
	Treasury bonds and notes	0.2	2.0	4.2	4.3
	Treasury bills	5.3	0.5	-1.0	-0.8
	Bank deposit	4.0	0.6	1.6	1.4
	Other [1]	2.1	6.9	7.2	5.0
Other countries: bank deposit		9.0	5.0	7.0	8.5
Other countries: special bilateral facilities and other investments [1][2]		11.9	12.4	10.3	11.2
Loans to international organizations		3.5	4.0	2.0	0.3
Total (of which: bank deposits)		57.0	35.7	35.8	33.0
		(28.5)	(9.9)	(12.8)	(12.6)

Notes: [1] Including holdings of equity, property, etc., and other foreign currency borrowing.
[2] Including loans to LDCs.

Source: "International banking and bond markets: recent developments and prospects for 1978," June 21, 1978, Table 6, SM/78/160, IMF Documents (originally, the Bank of England prepared this table).

The appearance of petrodollars led to the concern that the Eurodollar market could not absorb the huge capital of oil-producing countries. While oil producers sent their money in short-term deposits, the participating banks in the Eurodollar market needed to proceed with money in the medium and long term. This gap between short term and medium/long term raised concerns about the soundness of banks in the market. In September, after the crisis of the German bank, Herstatt Bankhaus, the G10, and Switzerland central bank governors issued a communique which assessed the central banks' responsibility as lenders of last resort on the Eurodollar market.[9]

However, whether the international private financial markets including the Eurodollar market became the nucleus of petrodollar recycling or not depended on the dynamism of international relations as well as international economic diplomacy. In early autumn of 1974, partly because of Britain's own deficit, the UK cabinet proposed the creation of official facilities which involved OPEC countries' surpluses to finance the deficits of both industrialized nations and LDCs. The IMF director, Johannes Witteveen, welcomed the proposal and prepared to organize an official fund of oil facility (the first IMF Oil Facility, Witteveen I, had been established in June). Regarding the Eurodollar market's future role, although the deputy governor of the Bundesbank, Otomar Emminger, admitted its ability of flowing oil-money into the international financial markets without major disruptions, he was skeptical about the long-term prospects. Emminger stressed the importance of guiding oil-money into stable, long-term investments. His proposals were: creating a bilateral governmental credit from oil producers; supporting investments in the deficits of non-oil producing countries' capital markets; and flowing oil-money through international institutions.[10] However, because of the concerns of controlling German companies' shares, importing inflation, and bringing upward pressure on deutsche marks, West Germany hesitated on allowing the direct inflow of oil-money into the German economy rather than Eurodollar deposits.[11]

The September G5 meeting (the United States, the United Kingdom, France, Germany, and Japan) in Washington DC was an important occasion for deciding the future of oil-money recycling.[12] The US Secretary of State, Dr. Henry Kissinger, opposed the British and German approaches above. He emphasized that OPEC countries' new wealth would lead to a change in political power in the world. He was also afraid that the official facilities administrated by the IMF or the UN would give OPEC countries or international organizations greater power and influence in the

[9] Carlo Edoardo Altamura, *European Banks and the Rise of International Finance: The Post-Bretton Woods Era* (Abingdon: Routledge, 2017), 109–10. The issued communique was that they [central bank governors] recognized that it would not be practical to lay down in advance detailed rules and procedures for the provision of temporary liquidity. However, they were satisfied that means were available for that purpose and would be used if and when necessary.

[10] "Recycling of oil funds and Euromarkets," Treasury brief (draft), August 30, 1974, T358/175; "The monetary consequences of the oil price explosions and its implications for the Euro-currency markets," Address of Otomar Emminger on October 14, 1974, T358/175, The National Archives (UK) [hereafter, TNA].

[11] William Glenn Gray, "Learning to 'recycle': petrodollars and the West, 1973–5," in Elisabetta Bini, Giuliano Garavini, and Federico Romero (eds.), *Oil Shock: The 1973 Crisis and its Economic Legacy* (London and New York: I.B. Tauris, 2016), 188.

[12] Record of a Meeting September 28–9, 1974, OV53/81, Bank of England Archive.

world economy, at the expense of Western countries' interests. Kissinger insisted that oil surpluses should flow back to oil-consuming developed countries and Western countries' private financial markets should decide where the oil-money would flow. His idea was to utilize the dollar deposited in the Western countries which had a strong economy as well as a flexible banking system to support Western consuming countries' position against oil producers.[13]

Furthermore, some US policymakers thought Arab investments were not a threat but an opportunity. While the Treasury suggested that OPEC investments [to Western developed countries] would give the oil producers a greater stake in the continued economic growth and stability of the consumers, its memo argued: "the introduction of new competition along with the vast financial wealth of the OPEC states might bring the additional benefit of making capital markets generally more efficient than they currently are."[14] The US administration had abolished some foreign exchange regulations in January 1974. The Treasury Secretary, William Simon, hoped that the liberalizing capital would direct the growing flows of oil-money to American banks and solidify the United States' dominant position in international finance. As US capital barriers were removed, the interest rate gap between the US and the London Eurodollar market was narrowing, and the movement of money between the two was beginning to increase. It is said that the integration of the trans-Atlantic financial markets began at this stage. The *Daily Mail* observed that "the close relationship between US and Eurodollar rates enable the market to take Arab deposits—and lend to countries like Britain—without interest rates jumping about too much."[15]

The US proposed the formation of a Western consumer countries' common trust fund, by which industrialized countries could force "oil producers to put money on the market, depressing the rate of interest against themselves." This kind of fund presupposed that the Western financial markets could absorb vast sums of oil-money. After the G5 meeting and the IMF annual conference in the fall of 1974, there were intensive discussions and negotiations between US proposed common trust fund and the enlargement of the IMF Oil Facility from $3.6 billion (Witteveen I). The Americans saw the common trust as the only new mechanism required for recycling oil producers' surplus funds. Meanwhile, the UK, together with most other members of the G10, saw the trust fund "as something complementary to the central role of IMF where the proposed Witteveen II proposals was a principal feature." The result was a compromised one: The OECD "solidarity" fund, which would be a safety net in accommodating money among the Western developed countries in the case of stagnation of petrodollar

[13] "Petro dollar once more," Varley to Wilson, January 16, 1975, PREM16/359, TNA.
[14] "Financial consequences of OPEC investment funds," Willett to Volcker and Bennett, January 10, 1974, 1/74 vol. 1, box. 1, Action/Briefing Memos 1973–5, OASIA, RG59, National Archives and Record Administration (NARA), quoted in Victor McFarland, *Oil Powers: A History of the US-Saudi Alliance* (New York: Columbia University Press, 2020), 189.
[15] Christopher R.W. Dietrich, *Oil Revolution: Anticolonial Elites, Sovereign Rights, and the Economic Culture of Decolonization* (Cambridge: Cambridge University Press, 2017), 286; Daniel J. Sargent, *A Super Power Transformed: The Remaking of American Foreign Relations in the 1970s* (Oxford: Oxford University Press, 2015), 127–30; "$155 billion Eurodollars!," *Daily Mail*, June 11, 1976.

recycling through private markets, and the new IMF Oil Facility from the spring of 1975, whose size was of $5 billion, were agreed among the Western countries.[16]

Though the Americans finally consented to making several IMF facilities (both for developed and developing countries), their idea reminded the same. In early January, US Treasury's assistant secretary made speech before an investors' gathering in New York. In that speech, he mentioned that Western developed countries proposed a "comprehensive approach to multilateral financing" (i.e., IMF new facilities/funds and OECD solidarity common fund) that would "supplement the private capital markets' role in recycling." Further, he emphasized that the safety net of the proposed OECD common fund would help to "assure the continued openness of the national and international capital markets" and "minimize the amount of official recycling."[17]

In the spring of 1975, US representatives for the OECD Economic Policy Committee expressed their confidence in the ability of the international financial market to withstand the strain that channeling surplus of oil revenue would impose. They observed that these surpluses were concentrated in a small number of oil-producing countries, and that these countries sifted their investments into long-term stable funds.[18] Furthermore, in the October memo, the OECD Temporary Working Party of Economic Policy Committee confirmed that oil-producing countries' investment policies had been reasonably conducted and volatile movements "would tend to be moderated by the regime of floating exchange rates and by the limited range of alternative assets that could absorb very large amounts."[19]

What were the attitudes of oil-producing countries toward the recycling problem? First, the drastic increase of military equipment imports by Saudi Arabia, Iran and other Middle Eastern countries should be noted.[20] The US administration eagerly sought to involve the major oil-producing actor, Saudi Arabia, in the recycling mechanism that Washington saw as an ideal. After the US–Saudi negotiation at the end of 1974, the Joint US–Saudi economic commission was formed. The commission was arranged for "assisting Saudi industrialization and development while recycling petrodollars and facilitating the flow to Saudi Arabia of American goods, services and technology." The joint commission was assigned not to the Department of State or the Department of Commerce to which most joint commissions with other countries attached, but to the Department of the Treasury. The US–Saudi agreement was one of

[16] "Oil and the world economy: Dr Kissinger's 15 November proposals," draft memo for the Ministers, December 1974, T354/411, TNA.
[17] "Remarks of the Honorable Gerald L. Parsky, Assistant Secretary of the Treasury before the Investment Association of New York at the Bankers Club, January 1975," *Department of the Treasury News*, in T354/411, TNA.
[18] "Temporary Working Party of Economic Policy Committee, CPE/TWP (75)3 and 4," Slater (UK delegation to OECD) to Littler (Treasury), May 20, 1975, T317/2471, TNA.
[19] "The Investment of Surpluses by Oil Producers: The Main Financial Repercussions and the Scope for Co-operative Financial Arrangements," Draft report by the Temporary Working Party of the Economic Committee, CPE/TWP(75)10, October 1, 1975, OECD Historical Archives.
[20] As for the UK governments' inter-departmental discussion (Committee on Vast Surplus of Oil Producers: VSOP) on relations between recycling and the imports of military equipment by the Middle Eastern counties, see the Third Report, January 31, 1975, VSOP(75)10, T354/591, TNA. The memo estimated that total OPEC countries' military imports might rise from $1.73 billion in 1973 to $3.56 billion in 1980.

the important factors for the consolidation of US financial position.[21] Indeed, OPEC countries appealed their intension to cooperate with the non-oil producing LDCs for the establishment of the NIEO. Not small funds were supplied to LDCs (but mostly passed to the Arab neighboring states) or international multilateral aid organizations in the form of a grant or concessional lending.[22] However, "OPEC's ad hoc bilateral arrangements offered only sporadic respite for the financial strains faced by the Global South" and "fund managers from the Gulf states were determined to make sound investments, not charitable contributions." For example, it was said that the Saudi finance minister acknowledged privately that "oil revenues reinvested in India would be doubtful and insecure." Brazil received only "a trickle of petrodollars [directly]."[23] OPEC's investment policy was not a kind of altering the recycling structure that was based on US and UK private financial markets.

The UK memorandum prepared for the Commonwealth Finance Ministers conference summed up the outcome of oil-money recycling:[24] The Euro-currency markets have played principal role in recycling, receiving between January 1974 and March 1975, 42 percent of the oil exporters' cash surplus $65 billion. The markets have then lent funds to oil consuming countries, principally developed countries and a few of the more advanced LDCs. On a small scale, the domestic currency banking markets in the US and UK have acted as recycling channels. US dollar deposits accounted for 5 percent and UK sterling deposits for 3 percent of the fifteen months' flow. The US and UK balance of payments have also been assisted by oil exporters' investments in US and UK government securities (11 percent and 7 percent of the flow, respectively). Oil exporters' investments have thus been mostly short-term and liquid—50 percent in bank deposits and 17 percent in liquid government securities. The oil exporters have provided medium-term loans in bilateral deals with developed countries (almost 10 percent of the flow). Although some long-term direct investment deals have attracted wide publicity (e.g., Iranian participants in Krupps), they account for only a small proportion of the recycling flow.

Whereas assistance toward developing countries were in the stage of discussion, the prospect of the Eurodollar market was seen by the UK Treasury as follows: "We do not believe that petro-dollars pose a serious threat to banking stability ... there are signs that oil exporters are investigating at longer term. A number of banks have strengthened their capital base. Official supervisions have been strengthened."

[21] Duccio Basosi, "The US, Western Europe and a changing monetary system, 1969–1979," in Antonio Varsori and Guia Migani (eds.), *Europe in the International Arena during the 1970s: Entering a Different World* (Brussels: P. I. E. Peter Lang, 2011), 108–9; David E. Spiro, *The Hidden Hand of American Hegemony: Petrodollar Recycling and International Markets* (Ithaca and London: Cornell University Press, 1999), 88–91.
[22] Giuliano Garavini, *The Rise and Fall of OPEC in the Twentieth Century* (Oxford: Oxford University Press, 2019), 243–53.
[23] William Glenn Gray, "Learning to 'recycle'," 190.
[24] "Oil: continued recycling of surplus funds," UK Treasury Memo, CFM(75)6, August 1975, T317/2471, TNA.

3. Toward "Privatized" International Development Finance

At the meeting of the IMF Board Directors in March of 1974, Witteveen noted that the problems of oil-money recycling, LDCs financing, and reforming the international monetary system should be tackled as a one-piece problem.[25] However, as mentioned previously, the size of the IMF Oil Facility of 1975 did not amount to the $30 billion that the UK Chancellor of Exchequer, Denis Healy, proposed, but $5 billion. Seeing the lower size of the Facility, Raul Prebisch noted that "there will be a vacuum that has to be filled ... to avoid a very difficult situation for the hardest hit developing countries."[26] The IMF did not play a major role in official recycling. Spiro pointed out that Witteveen saw the relative insignificance of the IMF oil facility because the IMF was in direct competition with the US Treasury for Saudi funds.[27]

The World Bank President, Robert McNamara, facing oil price hikes, began to move swiftly. He thought that some inter-governmental mechanisms for recycling would be necessary. While McNamara expected there was a chance that OPEC countries would lend to the IMF Oil Facility (Witteveen II), he visited some Middle Eastern countries and discussed using oil-producing countries' funds as Bank's capital. In a discussion with Algerian President Boumedienne, McNamara also mentioned the idea of channeling OPEC funds to developing countries by using Banks' services. However, tapping oil funds for Bank's capital soon presented difficulties. Although McNamara succeeded in getting $750 million from Saudi Arabia in December 1974, in the summer of that year the World Bank had stated a new borrowing policy that would avoid borrowing the OPEC's local currencies against Saudi's and Kuwait's demands. There were two reasons for this. First, as a major international borrower, the World Bank was concerned that the borrowing made a "bad precedent" by using currencies other than US dollars. Second, although increasing the role of OPEC countries was seen as "quid pro quo" for a flow of funds to the Bank, this increased voting share of oil producers would alarm the United States, Japan, and West Germany. It was also mentioned that the increased power of OPEC and developing countries might affect investor confidence. Inside the Bank, Japan's fund was expected to meet some of its mid/long-term capital requirements, but it was concluded that, for the time being, the World Bank could use only US financial markets because of costs and several other conditions.[28]

Moreover, based on both free-market ideology and on the desire for steering oil-money toward the United States, the US Treasury argued: "the [World] Bank bonds are

[25] Telegram from UK Director IMF/IBRD, March 21, 1974, FCO59/1234, TNA.
[26] Quoted in Dietrich, *Oil Revolution*, 289.
[27] Spiro, *The Hidden Hand of American Hegemony*, 100.
[28] Telegram from UK Director IBRD/IMF, April 2, 1974; "The Role of Oil Producing States and other LDCs in the World Bank," Memo by the Bank of England, May 7, 1974; "Relations between the IBRD and Oil Producers," Paper prepared by the Ministry of Overseas Development for Working Party on Financial Aspects of the Washington Energy Conference, FAWC(74)14, May 8, 1974; A. K. Rawlinson (UK Treasury and Supply Delegation in Washington DC) to F. R. Barratt, June 17, 1974, FCO59/1234, TNA. See also Patrick Allan Sharma, *Robert McNamara's Other War: The World Bank and International Development* (Philadelphia: University of Pennsylvania Press, 2017), 79–83.

basically directly competitive with Treasury issues" and "the Bank's growing dependence on borrowing from governments is changing its nature of the World Bank—further eroding its support for the private sector in LDCs and for the sound financial policies needed to have full support from private capital markets."[29]

Meanwhile the G77 developing nations, rallying at the United Nations Conference on Trade and Development (UNCTAD), began to see the collapse of the Bretton Woods system and the oil shock as a chance to transform the world economy drastically. As for petrodollar recycling, the LDCs insisted that oil surpluses should be transferred to public international finance to meet the development requirements of developing countries. After the UN's NIEO session in the summer of 1974, the new General Secretary of UNCTAD, Gamani Corea, proposed the establishment of a "Common Fund" to support the stabilization of commodity prices. Corea considered allowing the $6 billion-sized fund to accept foreign investments. In particular, he expected that the surpluses of oil producers would be a major source for the fund. It was natural to think that yet another cartelization of commodities (other than petrol) and this new idea of oil-money recycling, which favored the LDCs, would alarm Kissinger.[30]

In October of 1974, the new arena for discussing international development finance was formed: the Ministerial Committee of the Boards of Governors of the World Bank and the IMF on the Transfer of Real Resources to Developing Countries. The next summer, a working group was formed to discuss ways to stimulate private financial flows to developing countries. Industrialized countries, including Canada, France, Germany, Japan, the Netherlands, the United Kingdom, and the United States, and countries from LDCs, including Malaysia, the Philippines, Mexico, Trinidad and Tobago, and Kuwait, participated in the working group. The group submitted an interim report in February 1976. The report emphasized that middle-income developing nations, Latin American countries and Asian NIEs should obtain money through private capital markets. While there were no proposals for embedding resource transfers to LDCs into the reformed international monetary system, the report's recommendations regarding developing countries were maintaining their creditworthiness and making private capital inflow safer. As for the role of the developed countries, the working group urged for the expansion of foreign investments to allow the Eurodollar market to provide more capital to developing countries. The group also supported the US proposal to form the International Investment Trust (to stimulate portfolio investment) and the International Resources Bank (for stimulating private enterprise investments into developing natural resources).[31]

---

[29] "Guidance to McNamara on borrowing from oil exporters and related issues," Charles Cooper to Simon, August 3, 1974, folder Aug. 74, vol. 1, Action/Briefing Memos & Memcons box 2, OASIA, RG56, NARA, quoted in David M. Wight, *Oil Money: Middle East Petrodollars and the Transformation of US Empire, 1967–1988* (Ithaca and London: Cornell University Press, 2021), 89.

[30] John Toye and Richard Toye, *The UN and Global Political Economy* (Indiana and Bloomington: Indiana University Press, 2004), 242–51.

[31] Report of the Ministerial Committee of the Boards of Governors of the Bank and the Fund on the Transfer of Real Resources to Developing Countries (July 1976–June 1977, third annual report), in M.G. de Vries (ed.), *International Monetary Fund 1972–1978, vol. 3: Documents* (Washington DC, 1985).

The trends toward the "privatized" international development finance could be clearly seen in the mid-1970s. It could be mentioned that US policy played a major role. From December 1975, a North-South dialogue meeting of the Conference on International Economic Cooperation (CIEC) started in Paris. In April 1976, for the session of financial affairs the US delegation submitted the documents that emphasized the major role of private capital in financing LDCs development efforts, referring to the US markets as "one of the freest in the world."[32] The Japanese delegation for the CIEC meeting observed the following:

> The US was very keen to get some positive results in this field [private money inflows]. The US, which had opened its financial markets, was seeking to divide the LDCs nations by gaining support from high-income countries like Brazil or Mexico. These countries are most interested in the expansion of access to developed countries' financial markets.[33]

Just before the ending of CIEC (April 1977), the new Carter administration's Secretary of State, Cyrus Vance, said that "official aid should not ... substitute for the flows of private investment capital to the LDCs." Meanwhile, the director of the United Nations Economic Commission for Latin America, Enrique V. Iglesias, remarked that the final report of the conference signaled "the end of the Prebisch-inspired UN Conference for Trade and Development scheme."[34]

The emergence of the vast surpluses of the oil exporters, the upset in the international monetary system and the growth of the Eurodollar market changed the structure and nature of development finance for LDCs. According to the US estimation, in 1975 the deficits of the non-oil developing countries ($37 billion) were financed partly with official bilateral loans and grants from DAC countries ($9 billion); loans and grants from international and regional institutions ($3 billion); aid from Communist countries ($1 billion); and official export credits ($1 billion). The remaining $23 billion was covered by foreign direct investments ($4 billion); loans and grants from OPEC states ($4 billion); IMF facilities ($2 billion); decline in reserves ($3 billion); and private credit (supplier credit, portfolio investment, bank credits, and Euro-borrowing) ($10 billion).[35]

A US delegation to an OECD meeting claimed that for the highly industrializing, higher-income LDCs (see Table 4.4), relying on the private banking system was a "reasonable strategy." Subsequently, the US delegation made a sample of the developing countries' balance of payments prospects as following table. Differentiation within LDCs was reinforced by a trend toward the "privatized" international development finance that occurred after the oil price hikes and inflow of oil money into the Eurodollar market.[36]

[32] US comments on the question of access to capital markets and concern about developing countries being crowded out of US capital market, April 21, 1976; "Legal aspects of LDC access to US capital market," Summary of Statement of US Delegation in T383/288, TNA.
[33] Report from Ambassador Hirahara (OECD) to the Foreign Minister, November 27, 1976, File number 2016-2435, Diplomatic Archives of the Ministry of Foreign Affairs of Japan.
[34] Dietrich, *Oil Revolution*, 308; Garavini, *The Rise and Fall of OPEC*, 265–6.
[35] "Financing of the deficits of the non-oil developing countries," United States Views, January 19, 1976, CPE/TWP(76)2, OECD Historical Archives.
[36] Ibid.

Table 4.4 A sample of twenty-three LDCs

Group 1	Thailand, Taiwan, Singapore, Malaysia, Columbia, Morocco	These countries were in full control of their balance of payments, were able to attract direct investment on a continuing basis, had low debt-service ratios, were able to borrow in the private capital market, and some had not suffered declines in the terms of trade.
Group 2	Egypt, Israel	These two faced large deficits, but political considerations assured that every effort would be made by DAC or OPEC donors to arrange financing these deficits.
Group 3	Ghana, Bangladesh, India, Pakistan	The growing deficits were a major source of concern. These countries were not considered creditworthy by the private capital markets, so a great deal of attention was being devoted to these countries by aid donors.
Group 4	Brazil, Mexico, South Korea	These countries were distinguished from Group 1 in the size of deficits and the large borrowing from private capital markets. However, they were considered creditworthy by private lending institutions. These countries possessed the most productive and diversified economies among LDCs.
Group 5	Argentina, Bolivia, Chile, Peru, Uruguay, Zaire, Zambia, the Philippines	Some were highly dependent on single-export products. Some confronted internal political problems and suffered from the effects of unwise economic policies.
Residual	Remaining sixty-five non-oil LDCs	Similar situation of Group 3 and 5. These countries would benefit from a series of IMF facilities. To facilitate the adjustment process, any increase in bilateral and multilateral assistance might have to be directed toward these countries.

Source: see note 35, above.

Whereas world and regional multilateral developmental institutions (such as the World Bank, IDA, and ADB) were making larger bond issuing in the international capital markets, foreign lending activities, initially of US banks, then of the Eurodollar market, began to occupy a central position in terms of growing the flow of resources into the developing world (Table 4.5). In the fall of 1976, OECD members agreed to include the figures of Eurodollar flows into DAC's statistical records. The major part of developing countries' transactions on the Eurodollar market and offshore banking centers was the syndicated medium-term (more than three years) credits (with flexible interest rates). In 1978, for example, Brazil and Mexico accounted for about half of the Eurodollar market, while Argentina, Korea, Malaya, and the Philippines also borrowed substantial amounts.[37] As the borrowing by middle-income LDCs grew drastically, for the private banks in the developed countries, lending to developing countries became

[37] "International Banking and Bond Markets: Recent Developments and Near-term Prospects," July 10, 1979, SM/79/185, IMF Documents.

Table 4.5 Borrowing in international capital markets (US$ million)

	1976	1977	1978	1979
Industrial countries	23130.2	22792.2	22565.6	24553.9
	7434.9	11055.1	31343.5	19041.8
Centrally planned	72.0	255.5	30.0	48.1
economies	2371.4	2691.0	3702.1	7451.2
International	8255.8	7160.0	8424.6	8670.0
organizations	377.0	197.0	181.7	310.0
Developing countries	2336.2	4755.9	6090.9	4014.5
	18131.4	20145.2	38247.3	43220.2
Brazil	193.3	855.8	936.1	735.6
	3288.3	2341.1	5110.7	5833.8
Korea	74.2	71.5	56.0	43.6
	979.6	796.0	1699.0	2589.5
World total	34311.1	36094.3	37481.1	37763.9
	28703.3	34185.3	73694.6	70209.4

Note: above: foreign and international bonds (private and public); below: euro-currency credits.

Source: World Bank, *Borrowing in International Capital Markets*, EC-181/801 (First Half 1980).

a cornerstone of their profits, especially after the recession reduced the demand for investment in the richer countries.[38]

Meanwhile, the subject of the countries that lacked sufficient creditworthiness to qualify for private banking financing was raised. For example, LDCs' limited access to developed countries' capital markets led to the idea of using the World Bank or other regional multilateral aid organizations as a co-financer or facilitator of development finance.[39] Furthermore, a UK cabinet memorandum pointed out that "greater use of the conditional [IMF] credit" might enhance these developing countries' creditworthiness and pave the way for the inflow of lending from private banks.[40] Financing LDCs became one of the major tasks for the IMF, because its role in observing the exchange rates relations of developed countries had been eroded since the collapse of the Bretton Woods system. It could be said that the origin of the structural adjustment policy and the conditionality of the IMF and the International Bank for Reconstruction and Development (IBRD) coincided with the emergence of the "privatized" international development finance.[41]

[38] "An analysis of the supply of Euro-currency finance to developing countries," by Ishan Kapur (IMF Exchange and Trade Relations Department), December 9, 1976, IMF Documents. See also Simone Selva, *Before the Neoliberal Turn: The Rise of Energy Finance and the Limits to US Foreign Economic Policy* (London: Palgrave Macmillan, 2018), 226–41; Judith Stein, *Pivotal Decade: How the United States Traded Factories for Finance in the Seventieth* (New Haven and London: Yale University Press, 2010), 94–5.

[39] "Delegations remarks on the 3rd meeting of CIEC Committee 4, 22 April 1976," Report to Tokyo from the Japanese delegation, File number 2016-2430, Diplomatic Archives of the Ministry of Foreign Affairs of Japan.

[40] Brief for Trade and Development Board, 16th session, Geneva, October 5–22, 1976, UNC(76)5, October 5, 1976, T383/288, TNA.

[41] David H. Pollock and Carlos Massad, "The International Monetary Fund in a new international financial constellation: an interpretational commentary," ECLA, *CEPAL Review* (1978).

4. Why Asian Miracle? Three "Revolutions" in 1979/80 and Developing Countries

Although the impact of the first oil shock receded in 1976, the Eurodollar market continued to expand, and its pivotal position in international finance was cemented. The broad structure of the international capital markets at the end of 1970s is introduced.[42]

In 1978, net new bank lending in the world was $110 billion while net new bond lending was $30 billion. At the end of 1978, net international bank claims totaled $540 billion. (This figure excluded estimated redepositing. If including interbank transactions, it rose to $903 billion.) Among $540 billion, non-oil LDCs' outstanding was $126,7 billion, and bank claims against LDCs rose by $25.7 billion in 1978. Of the total gross international bank claims (i.e., $903 billion), 73 percent ($660 billion) was lending in foreign currencies, "commonly referred to as Eurolending." Among $660 billion, the claims of US banks' branches in the Caribbean and the Far East were $106 billion, and the size of European countries' foreign currency lending (IMF report called this as the narrowly defined Eurocurrency market) reached $502 billion.[43] As for direct cross-border lending in "domestic" currencies, it reached $243 billion. Among them, the banks in the US claimed $129 billion ($80.3 billion was of foreign banks' and $48.7 was US banks' claims).[44]

From 1976 to 1978, not oil-producers' surpluses, but rather, the money inflow from developed countries sustained the expansion of the Eurodollar market (Table 4.6). US deficit, stagnation of European economies and the continuing inflation among the developed countries pushed the Western private banks to international businesses, including lending to the LDCs. The IMF report pointed out that "developed countries were the only group which were net providers of funds to the market in 1978," and meanwhile "the oil exporting countries, whose new net deposits had dwindled to about US$3 billion a year in 1976 and 1977, actually became large net borrowers in 1978."

The dollar policy of the Carter presidency showed that the post-Bretton Woods system was becoming the "offshore US dollar system,"[45] which was brought by the huge US deficit and its expanding external investments. During the Carter administration, American banks and corporations almost tripled their foreign investments up to $530 billion.[46] With the downward pressure of the US dollar, unstable international currency

---

[42] "International banking and bond markets: recent developments and near-term prospects," July 10, 1979, SM/79/185, IMF Documents.

[43] London's claims were $203 billion of the European foreign currency lending.

[44] According to the IMF report, the most dynamic element of international banking in 1978 was foreign lending by Japanese banks. External claims of banks located in Japan rose by approximately 55 percent, from $21.7 billion at year-end 1977 to $33.6 billion at year-end 1978. Claims booked at foreign branches of Japanese banks also rose rapidly in 1978. "A large part of the offshore lending of Japanese banks was booked out of London where … loans and advances in currencies other than sterling rose by 36 percent in 1978 to a year-end total of $38.7 billion" (IMF Report, SM/79/185, p. 21).

[45] Steffen Murau, Joe Rini, and Armin Haas, "The evolution of the offshore US-dollar system: past, present and four possible futures," *Journal of Institutional Economics* 16(6) (2020).

[46] Jeffry A. Frieden, *Global Capitalism: Its Fall and Rise in the Twentieth Century* (New York: Norton, 2006), 371.

Table 4.6 External lending and deposit taking, in domestic and foreign currency of, banks in the G10 countries, Switzerland, and of the foreign branches of US banks in the Caribbean Area and the Far East (US$ billion)

	1976	1978	Amounts outstanding, December 1978
Lending to			
BIS reporting area (including the offshore centres) and other developed countries	33.8	54.5	300.5
Eastern Europe	7.4	8.2	45.1
Oil exporting countries	9.4	17.1	54.0
Non-oil developing countries	18.3	25.7	126.7
Unallocated and international organizations	1.1	4.5	13.8
Total	**70.0**	**110.0**	**540.0**
Sources of funds			
BIS reporting area (including the offshore centres) and other developed countries	40.0	83.5	350.6
Eastern Europe	1.4	2.3	10.5
Oil exporting countries	12.3	5.9	83.0
Non-oil developing countries	12.9	16.0	78.8
Unallocated and international organizations	3.4	16.0	17.0
Total	**70.0**	**110.0**	**540.0**

Source: "International banking and bond markets: recent developments and near-term prospects," July 10, 1979, SM/79/185, IMF Documents.

markets, difficulties of European export against weakening dollars (which facilitated the discussion of establishing the European Monetary System), and the oil producers' frustration against depreciation of their dollar assets, which was partly a cause of second oil price increase, the position of the US dollar as an international currency was in doubt. On October 2, 1979, the US representative agreed that the IMF should study a "substitution account" that would gradually shift world reserves from US dollars to SDR. However, on October 6, Paul Volcker, who had been nominated as the Federal Reserve's new Chairman in August, "produced a spectacular change in US monetary policy," starting to push up interest rates to historical highs. The Volcker shock mainly targeted domestic inflation, but it proved "a strategic choice that the US would pursue for years with important consequences across the world." "By opting clearly for high interest rates, the Fed prioritized the consolidation of finance as the US's main source of foreign revenue."[47] Charles Maier pointed out that the United States changed its position from "an empire of production" to "an empire of consumption."[48] The United

[47] Basosi, "The US, Western Europe and a changing monetary system," 109–16.
[48] Charles S. Maier, *Among Empires: American Ascendancy and Its Predecessors* (Cambridge, MA: Harvard University Press, 2006).

States, by ensuring the dollar remained as the world's dominant reserve and clearing currency and using its financial power, began to build the international financial order based on the "offshore US dollar system."

Toward the end of the 1970s, concerns over the situation in depressed countries in Africa and South Asia that depended heavily on borrowing or aid for concessional terms loomed. In addition, the inadequacy of such loans and aid was mounting. Moreover, the increasing demands for private bank lending by Latin America, Turkey, and Eastern European countries also began to raise concerns. In 1979, the Iranian Islamic revolution and the second oil price hike shook the international financial system and development finance once again. Some people expected that OPEC counties' surpluses might flow into international capital markets to sustain LDCs' financing yet again. However, the development finance in the 1980s did not evolve in the same manner as it did after the first oil price increases. The US Reagan administration's high interest rates and "strong dollar policy" further deteriorated LDCs' borrowing conditions. Furthermore, the election of conservative governments in both the United Kingdom and the United States confirmed the overall trends of developed countries' suppressing ODA. The World Bank and the IMF warned that the anti-inflation policy of developed countries and oil-producing countries' lending policies would hinder world monetary expansion. The sluggishness of ODA and other official flows would continue for several years. It was also indicated that private commercial banks were taking a conservative attitude in lending money to developing countries (partly due to some LDCs' nationalization policies and partly due to Western monetary authorities' concerns about the exposure of their banks in the Eurodollar market). Conversely, private direct investments, bond issuing and export credits were likely to expand, but such expansions did not seem to compensate for the shortage in private bank lending for the time being. A World Bank paper argued that the OECD members' slow growth and stagnation as well as the surging price and the mounting burden of debt servicing did not bring good prospects for developing countries' financial prospects. It emphasized, therefore, that capital flows and creditworthiness would be linked. The paper also emphasized that since the latter was dependent on economic performance, so developing countries needed to pursue more effective structural adjustments.[49]

In 1981, the leaders of both developed and developing countries gathered in Cancun, Mexico. The Cancun summit discussed the Brandt Report (commissioned by McNamara in 1977).[50] The report urged that the North-South problem should be solved by pursuing "Global Keynesianism" (namely through economic expansion throughout the world). The report also pointed out that a large-scale transfer of resources to developing countries should be achieved through the establishment of a "World Development Fund," in which both developed and developing countries would participate on equal terms. However, US President Ronald Reagan and UK Prime Minister Margaret Thatcher never compromised on that idea. Rather, referring to the

---

[49] "IBRD staff paper on recycling," IFP(80)25, July 22, 1980, T277/3620, TNA.
[50] *North-South: A Programme for Survival: Report of the Independent Commission in International Development Issues.*

"successes" of the NIEs economy, they emphasized the importance of fighting inflation and enhancing market mechanisms.[51]

In 1979, a UK Treasury memorandum categorized LDCs into three groups: (1) NIEs countries (South Korea, Hong Kong, Brazil, and others) and some Asian countries whose adaptation to the world economic environment had been relatively smooth. The memo pointed out that these countries had been getting plenty of private capital; (2) African nations suffering from severe poverty that had not been able to adapt to the world economic situation; and (3) Latin American and South Asian countries that stood midway between (1) and (2).[52] However, with the three "revolutions" of 1979/80, while Latin American countries fell into the debt crisis, East Asian countries, following Asian NIEs, showed stable economic growth. What made Latin America and East Asia so different in the 1980s? To answer this question, the cases of Korea and Brazil are compared.[53]

Both countries borrowed large sums from the Eurodollar markets to meet external deficits and, therefore, succeeded in sustaining their industrial expansions (Table 4.7). For the Brazilian military government, large investment policies, especially for industrial development, were crucial for their political legitimacy. However, inducing foreign direct investments would cause political difficulties, while small private enterprises were not able to make enough investments. Thus, the government began to depend on the Eurodollar borrowing for the state-led development policy. A significant part of the inward capital movement was financial loans, primarily from the Euro-currency market. The borrowing was mainly done by the Banco de Brazil or BNDES (Banco Nacional de Desenvolvimento Economico e Social), providing roughly three-quarters of all investment capital to the private sector in 1974. For Korea, from the beginning of the 1970s, the inflow of foreign direct investment began to increase. It amounted to 17 percent of Korean manufacturing investment. However, while $0.7 billion in foreign direct investment flowed, Korea net borrowing of foreign loans was $3.7 billion. Similar to Brazil's case, the Korea Development Bank (KDB) had a major role in the borrowing. The KDB provided half of all financing to Korea's capital goods industries.[54]

---

[51] "Cancun Summit, 22–23 October 1981: Economic Prospects for Developing Countries," Brief by HM Treasury, PMVQ(81)4, October 13, 1981; "Cancun Summit, 22–23 October 1981: monetary and financial issues," Brief by HM Treasury, PMVQ(81)9, October 13, 1981, CAB133/519, TNA.

[52] "The world economic prospects and developing country," Brief to the Chancellor of Exchequer by M. Hedley-Miller (draft), August 31, 1979, T385/224, TNA.

[53] The following two paragraphs are mainly based on Jeff Frieden, "Third world indebted industrialization: international finance and state capitalism in Mexico, Brazil, Algeria and South Korea," *International Organization*, vol. 35, no. 3 (1981); Stephan Haggard, "Macroeconomic policy through the first oil shock, 1970–1975," in S. Haggard, R. Cooper et al., *Macroeconomic Policy and Adjustment in Korea 1970–1990* (Cambridge, MA: Harvard Institute for International Development, 1994); Atul Kohli, *Imperialism and the Developing World: How Britain and the United States Shaped the Global Periphery* (Oxford: Oxford University Press, 2020), 342–4; J.D. Sachs and J. Williamson, "External debt and macroeconomic performance in Latin America and East Asia," *Brookings Papers on Economic Activity* 1985(2) (1985).

[54] The role of development banking in Brazil and Korea, see Alice H. Amsden, *The Rise of "The Rest": Challenges to the West from Late-industrializing Economies* (Oxford: Oxford University Press, 2001), 125–9.

Table 4.7 Types of long-term net foreign capital

		Bilateral (public) (%)	Multilateral (public) (%)	Private banks (%)	Foreign direct investment (%)	Average amount (US$ millions)
Brazil	1971–5	5.3	8.1	52.0	34.6	2834.4
	1976–80	3.0	4.4	66.7	25.9	6701.0
	1981–2	5.2	6.1	61.2	27.5	8570.3
Korea	1971–5	34.9	14.9	38.7	11.5	854.1
	1976–80	18.1	16.3	60.4	5.2	2026.2
	1981–2	19.6	18.0	59.3	3.1	2748.0
All developing countries	1980	19.3	15.9	47.7	17.0	59609.0

Source: Barbara Stallings, "The role of foreign capital in economic development," in Gary Gereffi and Donald L. Wyman (eds.), *Manufacturing Miracles: Paths of Industrialization in Latin America and East Asia* (Princeton: Princeton University Press, 1990), Table 3.1.

Both Brazilian and Korean "nationalistic state-capitalist regimes had joined with the internationalist finance-capitalists of Euromarkets." Nevertheless, there were some differences between the two countries' policy. Due to the limits of domestic market scale, intensive export promotion was necessary for Korean industrialization. Facing the first oil price surge, the Korean government, falling into the precarious balance of payments position, had to borrow a $200 million syndicated loan by a group of twenty-eight banks (headed by Citibank) in mid-1975. Oil price rises and world recession seemed to bring negative prospects for Korean economy. However, Korea overcame some pessimistic assessments by embarking on a strategy to push export growth by diversification of its markets and export products. As a result, Korean maintained a relatively high growth rate (8 percent) by recourse to heavy short-term borrowing at commercial rates. "This admittedly risky strategy," IMF saw at that time, succeeded in tiding Korea over the difficult period of adjustment. Seeing the strong recovery in the balance of payments in 1976 and 1977, which was based on the improvement of exports (and the receipts from construction activities in the Middle East), the Korean government sought long-term and better-conditioned foreign bank borrowings. The IMF reported that the major component of longer-term borrowing was related to specific projects such as steel mills, petrochemicals, and cement plants.[55] Against the advice of economists in the Korean Economic Planning Board, the Park Chung Hee regime began to secure large-scale international loans and embarked on a massive industrialization drive. From 1977, the Korean government commenced a further ambitious export promotion program. Regarding the policy of inducing foreign capital, with an improved foreign exchange position and the sophistication of its industry, Korea implemented a more selective policy regarding inward flows which paid more

[55] "Korea: recent economic developments," August 1, 1978, SM/78/206, IMF Documents.

attention to technology transfers.[56] Behind this strong Export-Oriented Industrialization (EOI) policy, there was severe political and military tension with North Korea in the 1970s. Strengthening the Korean economy, especially its industry, was necessary for competing with the North and sustaining Korean military potential.[57]

Brazil had a long history of industrialization as well as a large scale of domestic market. Furthermore, the Brazilian government tended to accept their currency appreciation because it was beneficial for domestic oriented economic sectors. Thus, one could say that Brazil's industrial development was not entirely concentrated in the export-oriented industries. Regarding the problem of external borrowing, even before the second oil crisis, the IMF pointed out that the scale and increase of outstanding foreign debt as well as the burden of debt service was one of the major concerns of the macro-economic situation.[58]

The second oil hike in 1979 and the rise in interest rates hit Brazilian external accounts severely. The inflows of foreign direct investment were recorded at the lowest level in the three years preceding 1980, and market borrowing in the form of financial loans occupied 70 percent of Brazil's outstanding external debt by the end of the year. An IMF report warned that the very high share of debt contracted at adjustable interest rates made Brazil's debt service payments susceptible to fluctuations in international interest rates. Facing the deterioration of their external deficit, the Brazilian authorities responded with devaluation and monetary restraint, and in late 1980, adapted the IMF's proposed substantial adjustment measures. However, apart from the oil price increase and rising interest rates, the weakening in external demand of both industrial countries and the trade partners of developing countries worsened Brazil's external financial situation further by 1982.[59]

Korea also faced economic difficulties caused by oil price surge and the effects of expansionary domestic policies in 1977 and 1978. However, IMF staff found that the maintenance of export levels and increase in government investment led to a resumption in overall economic growth in 1981. Already in 1980, the Korean government took strong adjustment measures that included a depreciation of the won in real terms with tightening financial policies. Although current account deficit widened, "the increase was equivalent to less than one half of price-induced rise in the oil price bill." Then, in 1981 and 1982, Korea succeeded in making external adjustment by gaining export market share, attaining competitiveness, and diversifying exports. These successes were based on the government's further structural reform in

---

[56] See FCO21/1664, TNA (South Korean Economy 1978), especially "The economy of South Korea in the Middle 1978," from the British Embassy to the Secretary of State of FCO, July 28, 1978; "South Korea: inward investment current attitudes and past performance," Memo by Commercial Department of the British Embassy, June 1978; "US Embassy's Briefing Paper on the South Korean Economy," attached to the Despatch from British Commercial Counsellor to the Department of Trade, April 12, 1978.

[57] Korea's defense expenditure still accounted for 35 percent of the budget in 1978, but it represented less than 7 percent of "a growing GNP."

[58] "Brazil: recent economic developments," November 1, 1978, SM/78/266, IMF Documents.

[59] "Brazil: recent economic developments," November 3, 1981, SM/81/207; "Brazil: use of fund resources—compensatory financing facility," the Secretary to the Members of the Executive Board, November 24, 1982, EBS/82/15, IMF Documents.

government-oriented rationalization as well as reviewing industrial and export incentive systems. It should be emphasized that, even in the crisis of 1980–2, Korean government continued foreign borrowing to sustain the investments for heavy and chemical industry. The Korean economy was able to maintain large external earnings while making large foreign borrowing. As for the composition of external borrowing, under the political uncertainty following the assassination of President Park in October 1979, Korean had to rely on short-term trade credits. However, with the stabilization of political situation, "long-term capital flows retuned to the normal pattern in 1981 and provided most of the financing."[60]

According to Adelman, Latin American countries had borrowed heavily to pay for current account deficits as well as public debts. However, from around the mid-1970s, it became difficult for central banks to contain inflation through tight local monetary policy; therefore, the over-valuation of foreign exchange rates became necessary. Toward the end of the decade, especially after the second oil shock, "since currencies were increasingly overvalued and the constraints on capital mobility lifted ... there were more and more inducements and fewer and fewer constraints on shipping money out of the region, back into *global* accounts." Between 1975 and 1985, the cumulative capital flight from Latin America exceeded $100 billion. By contrast, East Asian countries kept strictures on local banking systems. In addition, East Asian "tigers" used foreign money to promote vigorous export diversification and growth.[61] They succeeded in connecting foreign borrowings to sustaining their EOI economies. As a result, debt service as a share of export revenues in 1981 turned out to be 13.0 percent in Korea against 31.9 percent in Brazil, and also Korea's interest payments as a share of export revenues were kept at low levels compared with Brazil's case (Table 4.8).

Table 4.8 Economic performance of Korea and Brazil (US$ millions)

	Korea 1974 1978 1981	Brazil 1974 1978 1981
Total debt service	549.5	1224.7
	1824.5	4476.5
	3597.4	8616.1
Debt service: official creditors	98.0	273.3
	402.7	702.0
	741.0	1039.2
Debt service: private creditors	451.5	951.1
	1421.8	3774.5
	2856.4	7576.9

[60] "Korea: Review of Stand-by Arrangements," The Secretary to the Members of the Executive Board, July 16, 1981, EBS/81/154; "Korea: recent economic developments," April 15, 1982, SM/82/70, IMF Documents. See also Alice H. Amsden, *Asia's Next Giant: South Korea and Late Industrialization* (New York and Oxford: Oxford University Press, 1989), 104–5.

[61] Jeremy Adelman, "International finance and political legitimacy: a Latin American view of the global shock," in Niall Ferguson et al., (eds.), *The Shock of the Global: The 1970s in Perspective* (Cambridge, MA and London: The Belknap Press of Harvard University Press, 2010), 124–5

Suppliers	347.4	204.6
	700.1	406.6
	962.5	402.5
Financial markets	104.0	728.1
	721.7	3336.7
	1893.9	7149.3
Interest payments (total)	196.1	591.0
	656.9	1848.2
	1776.9	4999.3
Interest payments: financial markets	38.1	388.6
	227.7	1389.3
	1117.2	4390.3
Net flows of external credit (total)	825.2	3121.9
	2215.5	6998.4
	4266.5	5514.2
Net flows: private creditors (financial markets)	343.0	2298.2
	895.5	6247.4
	3181.4	5263.7
GNP	18312	108147
	47350	201769
	63368	274214
Exports	5353	9371
	17124	14458
	27577	26993
Imports	7602	16934
	18652	21561
	32550	38920
Total debt service/exports (%)	10.3	13.1
	10.7	31.0
	13.0	31.9
Total debt service/GNP (%)	3.0	1.1
	3.9	2.2
	5.7	3.1
Interest payments/exports (%)	3.7	6.3
	3.8	12.8
	6.4	18.5
Interest payments/GNP (%)	1.1	0.5
	1.4	0.9
	2.8	1.8

Source: World Bank, *World Debt Tables 1982–1983 edition* (1983).

5. Conclusion

This chapter examined the transformation of international development finance in the context of international economic disorder and the emergence of the "privatized international currency system," both of which were caused by the collapse of the Bretton Woods system, the introduction of flexible exchange rates of major Western currencies, huge inflows of petrodollars into international financial markets, and the growth of the Eurodollar market.

Seeing oil price hikes, developing countries, seeking the NIEO, insisted that oil surpluses should flow into public international finance to meet their development requirements. The concept of the NIEO was not confined only to problems regarding the sovereignty of natural resources, but also connected to the reform of the international monetary system (for example, the reorganization of the IMF based on the South's demands, enhancements of SDR or establishing the Common Fund program by UNCTAD). Between 1974 and 1976, the international society saw two alternatives for restructuring international development finance: the "privatized" international development finance or the enhancement of public development financing structures. The outcome of oil-money recycling and the role of the Eurodollar market in the recycling were the key issues in directing the decision. The recycling structure was to be based on Western private financial markets, especially the Eurodollar market. High- and middle-income developing economies began to utilize private capital flows, mainly through Eurodollar borrowings, for financing economic development. The first oil shock opened the way toward the "privatized" international development finance. Private banks' syndicated finance became a particularly important form of finance for these developing countries. Conversely, low-income LDCs were forced to depend on public flows through the IMF or the IBRD, with supervision for structural adjustments.

At the end of the decade, the three "revolutions" in 1979/80 further changed the international development finance scene. Latin American countries fell into the debt crisis, whereas East Asian countries showed stable economic growth. In the 1970s, both depended on the Eurodollar markets finance for "bank debt-financed, government-led industrialization." However, under the impacts of the three "revolutions," the two economies began to develop differently. The Korea's escape of debt crisis showed that the Asia-Pacific economy was emerging, in which both capital flows and industrial markets of Japan and the United States were connected to East Asian EOI economies. Moreover, the emergence of the Asia-Pacific economy was assuming conformity to the process in which international financial system became the "offshore US dollar system" in the financialization of US hegemony.

5

Economic Development through Oil in Malaysia and Singapore: Increased State Capacity and Formation of the East Asian Oil Triangle

Shigeru Sato

1. Introduction

1.1. The Oil Crises and Economic Development in Malaysia and Singapore

Malaysia and Singapore, the two countries discussed in this chapter, achieved rapid economic growth even during the oil crises. Indeed, in the 1970s, GDP growth rates in the two countries were 8.2 percent and 9.2 percent per annum, respectively. The economic progress of Malaysia and Singapore can be assessed as phenomenal, considering that over the same period, the economic growth rate of the two countries' former suzerain state, the United Kingdom, was only 2.7 percent and faced economic stagnation. As is well-known, these economic developments in East Asia attracted the attention of the World Bank, leading to the publication of the controversial report "The East Asian Miracle."[1] In this report, the World Bank stated that East Asian countries, including Malaysia and Singapore, achieved some of the highest growth rates in the world while also making significant social progress, such as reducing economic inequality and poverty and increasing life expectancy and educational opportunities.[2] Why had the countries of East Asia achieved so much economic development? This was the fundamental question running through the entire report.

In this chapter, I return to this question, once posed by the World Bank, to consider the reasons for economic development in East Asia. However, the research question is slightly changed here, with particular emphasis on the impact of oil on economic growth. The question here is as follows. Why did Malaysia and Singapore achieve high economic growth despite facing the oil crises? This chapter will show the role played by oil in the economic development of both countries.

---

[1] The World Bank, *The East Asian Miracle: Economic Growth and Public Policy* (New York: Oxford University Press, 1993).
[2] The World Bank, *The East Asian Miracle*, 1–5.

1.2. The Oil Curse and Economic Growth

Regarding the relationship between oil and economic growth, the "resource curse" or "oil curse" hypothesis is currently attracting attention. The "oil curse" hypothesis states that, as represented by Middle Eastern countries, oil-producing countries are more politically autocratic, more prone to corruption, and civil war and have lower economic growth rates than non-oil-producing countries.[3] From a political perspective, petro-states (states dependent on oil rents) have fewer incentives to implement policies that consider the welfare of their citizens. This is because, unlike the collection of taxes, which encourages accountability to taxpayers through parliament, oil extraction allows the state to avoid establishing a contractual relationship with its citizens.[4] From an economic perspective, the mechanism by which oil causes economic stagnation is known as the "Dutch disease."[5] This is a phenomenon in which a resource boom causes the national currency to soar while at the same time attracting labor and capital from other sectors of the economy to the resource sector, blocking the path to diversification and industrialization of the economic structure. Thus, the "oil curse" hypothesis emphasizes the political and economic "corruption" of the state by oil.

However, Malaysia, like Canada, Norway, and Australia, is an exceptional case of the "oil curse" hypothesis.[6] This is because Malaysia has achieved high political stability and economic growth rates despite being an oil-producing country. The World Bank data shows that the size of Malaysia's oil rent was well above the global average, exceeding 12 percent of GDP at its peak in 1979.[7] Oil is an inseparable part of Malaysia's economic development. Why has Malaysia achieved economic success without the "oil

[3]   Terry Lynn Karl, *The Paradox of Plenty: Oil Booms and Petro-States* (Berkeley: University of California Press, 1997).
[4]   Mick Moore, "Revenues, state formation, and the quality of governance in developing countries," *International Political Science Review* 25(3) (2004): 297–319; Deborah Brautigam, "Introduction: taxation and state-building in developing countries," in Deborah Brautigam, Odd-Helge Fjeldstad, and Mick Moore, *Taxation and State-Building in Developing Countries: Capacity and Consent* (Cambridge: Cambridge University Press, 2008), 1–33.
[5]   Michael L. Ross, *Extractive Sectors and the Poor* (Oxfam America, 2001).
[6]   Richard M. Auty (ed.), *Resource Abundance and Economic Development* (Oxford: Oxford University Press, 2001); Ross, *Extractive Sectors and the Poor*; Paul Stevens, "Resource impact: curse or blessing? A literature survey," *Journal of Energy Literature* 9(1) (2003): 3–42; Benjamin Smith, "Oil wealth and regime survival in the developing world, 1960–1999," *American Journal of Political Science* 48(2) (2004): 232–46; Halvor Mehlum, Karl Moene, and Ragnar Torvik, "Institutions and the resource curse," *The Economic Journal* 116(508) (2006): 1–20; Michael L. Ross, *The Oil Curse: How Petroleum Wealth Shapes the Development of Nations* (Princeton: Princeton University Press, 2012); James A. Robinson, Ragnar Torvik, and Thierry Verdier, "Political foundations of the resource curse," *Journal of Development Economics* 79(2) (2006): 447–68; Andrew Rosser, *The Political Economy of the Resource Curse: A Literature Survey* (Brighton: Institute of Development Studies, 2006); Patricia Sloane-White and Isabelle Beaulieu, "Beyond 50 years of political stability in Malaysia: rent and the weapons of the power elite," *Canadian Journal of Development Studies/Revue canadienne d'études du développement* 30(3–4) (2010): 381–402; Helena Varkkey, "Natural resource extraction and political dependency: Malaysia as a rentier state," in Meredith L. Weiss (ed.), *Routledge Handbook of Contemporary Malaysia* (London: Routledge, 2015), 188–99.
[7]   Data was obtained from the following websites. "Oil rents (% of GDP)." World Development Indicators, The World Bank Group. https://data.worldbank.org/indicator/NY.GDP.PETR.RT.ZS. Accessed September 15, 2022. Oil rents are defined as the difference between the value of crude oil production at regional prices and the total production costs.

curse"? This is a crucial question for this chapter, which discusses the relationship between oil and economic growth.

Recent studies have rejected the claim that oil resources automatically lead to inevitable social consequences.[8] In other words, oil-producing countries are not necessarily led to low economic growth. In explaining the diversity of economic fortunes of oil-producing countries, several studies have focused on equitable development policies and the quality of political institutions capable of implementing such policies as factors linking oil and economic growth.[9] While the studies by Mick Moore and Deborah Brautigam referred to earlier emphasized that oil forms political corruption and weak bureaucracy,[10] a political environment and competent economic bureaucracy conducive to equitable development have developed in Malaysia.[11] When analyzing the relationship between oil and economic growth, it may be helpful to focus on the state capacity[12] to carry out development (Section 2).

However, the mystery remains as to why Malaysia was able to build the strong state capacity needed for economic development and link oil to economic development. In this regard, Benjamin Smith raised the issue of the timing of oil's incorporation into the domestic political and economic environment.[13] His research showed that if the institutions of the developmental state were formed before the economy became dependent on oil, the chances of successfully using oil for economic development increased. Relatedly, some studies pointed out that a solid developmental state[14] framework was already in place in Malaysia before the 1970s, when oil output surged, to overcome threats to the state.[15] The presence of "threats" that prompted the formation

---

[8]   Gwenn Okruhlik, "Rentier wealth, unruly law, and the rise of opposition: the political economy of oil states," *Comparative Politics* 31(3) (1999): 295–315; Auty ed. 2001; Jonathan DiJohn, *Mineral-Resource Abundance and Violent Political Conflict: A Critical Assessment of the Rentier State Model* (Crisis States Research Centre, London School of Economics and Political Science, 2003); Rosser, *The Political Economy of the Resource Curse.*

[9]   Zainal Abidin Mahani, "Competitive industrialization with natural resource abundance," in Richard M. Auty (ed.), *Resource Abundance and Economic Development* (Oxford: Oxford University Press, 2001), 147–64; Ross, *Extractive Sectors and the Poor*; Stevens, "Resource impact: curse or blessing?"; Mehlum et al., "Institutions and the resource curse"; Robinson et al., "Political foundations of the resource curse."

[10] Moore, "Revenues, state formation, and the quality of governance in developing countries"; Brautigam, "Introduction: taxation and state-building in developing countries."

[11] Adrian Leftwich, "Bringing politics back in: towards a model of the developmental state," *The Journal of Development Studies* 31(3) (1995): 400–27.

[12] State capacity comprises a complex of coercive or military, fiscal, administrative, legal and infrastructural elements. This chapter also takes a composite and multidimensional view of state capacity to implement development policy. For a survey of state capacity, see Luciana Cingolani, "The role of state capacity in development studies," *Journal of Development Perspectives* 2(1–2) (2018): 88–114.

[13] Smith, "Oil wealth and regime survival in the developing world, 1960–1999."

[14] In this chapter, following Adrian Leftwich, the developmental state is defined as "states whose politics have concentrated sufficient power, autonomy and capacity at the centre to shape, pursue and encourage the achievement of explicit developmental objectives, whether by establishing and promoting the conditions and direction of economic growth, or by organising it directly, or a varying combination of both." See Leftwich, "Bringing politics back in," 401.

[15] Richard Stubbs, "War and economic development: export-oriented industrialization in East and Southeast Asia," *Comparative Politics* 31(3) (1999): 337–55.
     Richard F. Doner, Bryan K. Ritchie, and Dan Slater, "Systemic vulnerability and the origins of developmental states: Northeast and Southeast Asia in comparative perspective," *International Organization* 59(2) (2005): 327–61; Dan Slater, *Ordering Power: Contentious Politics and*

of the developmental state and the "timing" of when Malaysia began to benefit from oil is of particular interest in this chapter in that they shaped the preconditions for Malaysia's ability to use oil for economic development.

On the other hand, Singapore, unlike Malaysia, is not an oil-producing country. However, as discussed below, Singapore, like Malaysia, benefited significantly from oil exports. The two countries also overlap in that the motivation to form a robust developmental state existed prior to the oil crisis. The cases of Malaysia and Singapore had similarities in that the threats enhanced state capacity, and oil could be used for economic development based on such high capacity.

1.3. State Capacity and the East Asian Oil Triangle

As the World Bank report written on the East Asian Miracle claimed, the economic growth of the East Asian countries was not achieved through the development efforts of one country alone. Andrew Rosser once pointed out that the high economic performance of oil-producing countries was driven by the geopolitical and external economic environment, using Malaysia as an example. He highlighted, in particular, the close trade relations that Malaysia and Singapore had with Japan, whose economy was developing rapidly in the 1970s. As in his study, it is essential to emphasize in this chapter that the countries of East Asia have embarked on a trajectory of economic growth in an interrelated manner.

My task is to analyze economic growth in East Asia, focusing on the role of oil. For this purpose, I would like to extend Kaoru Sugihara's theory of the oil triangle.[16] While his argument was pioneering in discussing the relationship between the creation of "global" trade relations through oil and Japan's industrialization, it is also helpful in understanding the relationship between the formation of the oil cycle at the "regional" level of East Asia and the economic development of Malaysia and Singapore. The oil triangle at the East Asian level, which exchanges oil for industrial goods and crude oil for refined oil, played a critical role in encouraging economic development in both countries. I would like to name this "the East Asian Oil Triangle" (Section 3).

Importantly, Kaoru Sugihara focused only on the physical aspects of the oil cycle and did not touch on the financial aspects. However, it is worth pointing out that establishing economic relations through oil at the East Asian level went beyond the exchange of trade goods. The Asian dollar market, which facilitated economic growth in East Asia, developed due to the inflow of oil dollars from the rest of the world into Asia. The Asian dollar market increased the fiscal capacity of East Asian countries and

---

Authoritarian Leviathans in Southeast Asia (Cambridge: Cambridge University Press, 2010); Erik Martinez Kuhonta, *The Institutional Imperative: The Politics of Equitable Development in Southeast Asia* (Redwood City: Stanford University Press, 2011).

[16] Kaoru Sugihara, "Japan, the Middle East and the world economy: a note on the oil Triangle," *Japan Forum* 4(1) (1992): 21–31.

enabled their economic development. Furthermore, Sugihara did not refer to the above-mentioned political factors linking oil to economic development or state capacity. Economic development would only have occurred with state efforts to link oil to development.

Section 2 of this chapter describes the role of the developmental state in Malaysia and Singapore, which was a precondition for economic development. Section 3 provides an overview of the trends in economic growth through oil, summarizing various statistics. Through Sections 2 and 3, both domestic and international factors in the economic growth of the two countries will be understood. Finally, Section 4 refers to the divergence in the trajectories of economic development in Malaysia and Singapore.

2. The Developmental State and the Oil Crises

2.1. Institutional Framework of the Developmental State Formed Before the Oil Crises

Halvor Mehlum, Karl Moene, and Ragnar Torvik refuted the "resource curse" or "oil curse" hypothesis, which states that countries rich in natural resources cause economic stagnation, arguing that specific resource types are not necessarily linked to specific social outcomes.[17] They argued that the economic performance of resource- or oil-producing countries depends on the factor of "institutional quality," which synthesizes five dimensions: the rule of law, quality of bureaucracy, government corruption, risk of expropriation, and risk of contract breakdown by the government.[18] According to their analysis, institutional quality in Malaysia is high, considered one of the critical factors in overcoming the "oil curse." Several other studies discuss the relationship between institutional quality and the "oil curse."[19] Note that the institutional quality of Singapore, which has achieved high economic growth in a non-oil-producing country, also ranks high globally.[20]

Relatedly, research on the developmental state makes much the same argument as the above studies. These studies have focused on the reasons for the rapid economic growth of countries with different histories and cultures in East Asia, such as Japan, South Korea, Taiwan, Hong Kong, Singapore, and Malaysia, focusing on bureaucracy

---

[17] Mehlum et al., "Institutions and the resource curse."
[18] Their concept of "institutional quality" is a synthesis of the following indices provided by Political Risk Services: (1) the rule of law index, (2) the bureaucratic quality index, (3) the corruption in government index, (4) the risk of expropriation index, and (5) the government repudiation of contracts index. For more information on Political Risk Services data, see also Jeffrey D. Sachs and Andrew M. Warner, "Sources of slow growth in African economies," *Journal of African Economies* 6(3) (1997): 335–376. Note that these data are as of 1980.
[19] Daron Acemoglu, Simon Johnson, and James A. Robinson, "An African success: Botswana," in Dani Rodrik (ed.), *In Search of Prosperity: Analytic Narratives on Economic Growth* (Princeton, New Jersey: Princeton University Press, 2003), 80–119; Robinson et al., "Political foundations of the resource curse."
[20] Mehlum et al., "Institutions and the resource curse."

and other institutional factors that promote development. Chalmers Johnson, for example, discussed in detail the industrial policy led by the Ministry of International Trade and Industry (MITI) behind Japan's economic growth.[21] The Economic Planning Unit in Malaysia and the Economic Development Board in Singapore also fall under such economic bureaucracies.[22]

What factors could have given rise to these strong institutional apparatuses of the developmental state, which formulate and implement economic policies autonomously from social pressures? Several recent studies have highlighted how state-shaking "threats," such as wars and large-scale domestic conflicts, created strong state institutions to control society and helped pursue economic growth.[23] These studies apply Charles Tilly's thesis on European state formation, "Wars make the states," to East Asian countries while at the same time extending the argument by including the outbreak of civil war as well as inter-state war as an essential factor in shaping state organization.[24]

Richard Stubbs pointed out that the countries that have experienced rapid economic growth and a shift to export-oriented industrialization, such as Japan, South Korea, Taiwan, Hong Kong, Singapore, Malaysia, and Thailand, all experienced a series of wars and threats that gripped these regions since the post-war period.[25] The main point of his argument is that one of the critical conditions for a successful export-oriented industrialization strategy in East Asia was a robust institutional state linked to the business community, which adopts and fully implements the necessary policy reforms, and that such a "strong state" was formed in the process of facing inward threats. Indeed, in Malaysia and Singapore, communist forces posed a major political and military threat in the post-war period, and confrontation with them led to the development of a bureaucracy and the mobilization of all resources, including financial and human resources. In this process, workers' and left-wing organizations were repressed, and the authoritarian political system was established in which the government exercised power with relative autonomy from social pressures. In addition, the project of building a "strong economy" in response to the communist threat became widely accepted.

Even after the communist threat had been put to rest, internal threats continued to arise in both countries. The main reason for such domestic unrest was whether the Malay-led United Malays National Organisation (UMNO) or the Chinese-led People's Action Party (PAP) would take political leadership.[26] Underlying these heightened

[21] Chalmers Johnson, *MITI and the Japanese Miracle: The Growth of Industrial Policy, 1925–1975* (Stanford, California: Stanford University Press, 1982); "The developmental state: odyssey of a concept," in Meredith Woo-Cumings (ed.), *The Developmental State* (Ithaca, New York: Cornell University Press, 1999), 32–60.

[22] Leftwich, "Bringing politics back in."

[23] Stubbs, "War and economic development"; Doner et al., "Systemic vulnerability and the origins of developmental states"; Slater, *Ordering Power*; Kuhonta, *The Institutional Imperative*.

[24] Charles Tilly, "War making and state making as organized crime," in Peter B. Evans, Dietrich Rueschemeyer, and Theda Skocpol (eds.), *Bringing the State Back In* (Cambridge: Cambridge University Press, 1985), 169–91.

[25] Stubbs, "War and economic development."

[26] Slater, *Ordering Power*.

political tensions was a marked widening of the economic gap between Malays and non-Malays, even though Malaysia[27] experienced high economic growth rates in the post-war period.[28] Malaysia had a markedly segregated racial occupational structure, with Malays concentrated in the low-income agricultural sector and non-Malays in the commercial and industrial sectors, leading to unacceptable levels of inequality in terms of income, unemployment, and poverty rates. For example, in terms of poverty rates, at the time of independence from Britain in 1957, there was a huge difference between the poverty rate of 70.5 percent for the Malays and 27.4 percent for the Chinese, a situation that remained largely unchanged until 1970.

In 1965, Singapore and the PAP were expelled from Malaysia when Lee Kuan Yew launched his own "Malaysia" initiative. However, in the national elections of May 1969, Alliance[29] formed a majority but lost a significant number of seats, from 89 to 66, as the Chinese party Gerakan and the Democratic Action Party (DAP), which had links with the PAP, increased their strength. The impact of these political consequences on the Malays was so great that the same year, riots and ethnic massacres erupted, with an estimated 178 people, mainly Chinese, killed.[30] The political challenge to Alliance throughout the 1960s and the impact of the 1969 race riots resulted in fears that competitive democratic politics was destabilizing rather than orderly in Malaysia and led people to accept a more robust authoritarian regime.[31] In the 1970s, the previous laissez-faire era came to an end as the institutional framework of a more developmental state was needed to improve the economic welfare of the Malays.[32]

On the other hand, the loss of its "hinterland," Malaysia, increased Singapore's economic vulnerability as a small country and reinforced the need for more extraordinary development efforts.[33] In addition, the earlier-than-expected withdrawal of British troops, which severely damaged Singapore's economy, provided the impetus for the country to develop as a global city by promoting export-oriented industrialization and fostering a global financial market under the one-party rule of the PAP.[34]

Chalmers Johnson pointed out that East Asian developing countries that experienced rapid industrialization had the overriding goal of "economic development" widely shared by their people.[35] This was brought about in the process of overcoming

---

[27] The country's name is unified here under "Malaysia" regardless of the period.
[28] Faridah Jamaludin, "Malaysia's New Economic Policy: Has it been a success?," in William Darity and Ashwini Deshpande (eds.), *Boundaries of Clan and Color: Transnational Comparisons of Inter-Group Disparity* (London: Routledge, 2003), 152–74.
[29] "Alliance" refers to a political alliance centered on UMNO.
[30] Kuhonta, *The Institutional Imperative*.
[31] Slater, *Ordering Power*.
[32] Kuhonta, *The Institutional Imperative*.
[33] Jun Jie Woo, *The Evolution of the Asian Developmental State Hong Kong and Singapore* (London: Routledge, 2018).
[34] Gregg Huff, "The developmental state, government, and Singapore's economic development since 1960," *World Development* 23(8) (1995): 1421–38.
[35] Johnson, "The developmental state: odyssey of a concept," 52–3.

the political and economic vulnerabilities brought to those countries,[36] as discussed in this section. In addition, in both countries, authoritarian political regimes were also accepted, as historically the experience of competitive democratic politics was perceived by the people to be country-breaking. The political stability of UMNO in Malaysia and the PAP in Singapore was strong,[37] and the stability of these parties enabled both countries to pursue long-term visionary economic development. As discussed below, Malaysia and Singapore benefited economically from the oil crises. This was because the institutional framework of the developmental state, which did not presuppose the existence of oil, was already in place before the oil crisis. The issue of the timing of the formation of the developmental state is considered crucial in overcoming the "oil curse."[38]

2.2. The New Economic Policy and Oil

After the 1969 race riots, parliamentary democracy was temporarily suspended, leading to centralized decision-making by the National Operations Council. However, the subsequent formation of a broad multi-racial coalition party called Barisan Nasional (BN), led by UMNO, set in motion a system of development policies that aimed to reduce racial political tensions and remove the economic inferiority of the Malays. It is important to note that while the policy after the race riots primarily focused on establishing the economic dominance of the Malays, BN was never intended to exclude non-Malay parties. Rather than a "zero-sum" policy of increasing political tension by depriving non-Malays of political and economic rights, the Government of Malaysia aimed to "distribute through growth" to the Malays. The New Economic Policy (NEP), which lasted for 20 years from 1971, epitomized such political trends.[39]

Although the NEP only outlined a broad set of goals in the beginning and offered few concrete measures to consolidate the economic position of the Malays,[40] from the

---

[36] Doner et al., in "Systemic vulnerability and the origins of developmental states" highlighted that "systemic vulnerability" was a factor in shaping the developmental state. In this study, they explained that the systemic vulnerabilities faced by Singapore were stronger than those faced by Malaysia, which led to Singapore being characterized as a more fully developed state.

[37] Allen Hicken and Erik Martinez Kuhonta, "Shadows from the past: party system institutionalization in Asia," *Comparative Political Studies* 44(5) (2011): 572–97.

[38] Although there is no reference to the developmental state, see Smith, "Oil wealth and regime survival in the developing world, 1960–1999," for an argument that the "oil curse" was overcome in countries where national integration takes place when oil revenues are scarce.

[39] Kuhonta, *The Institutional Imperative*. The claim that an institutional framework for a developmental state was put in place in Malaysia after the 1969 race riots is an almost standard view in various studies. See, for example, Noorhayati Mansor and Roseni Ariffin, "Public administration in Malaysia: origins, influence and assessment," in Meredith L. Weiss (ed.), *Routledge Handbook of Contemporary Malaysia* (London: Routledge, 2015), 103–15. However, there are some objections to the view that the pre-NEP period was regarded as laissez-faire, as there was a certain scale of income distribution policy for Malays before the NEP. On this issue, see R. Thillainathan and Kee-Cheok Cheong, "Malaysia's new economic policy, growth and distribution: revisiting the debate," *Malaysian Journal of Economic Studies* 53(1) (2016): 51–68.

[40] D.G.S.D. Stafford, "Malaysia's new economic policy and the global economy: the evolution of ethnic accommodation," *The Pacific Review* 10(4) (1997): 556–80.

mid-1970s onward, policies gradually emerged to give substance to the NEP. The NEP was a form of affirmative action targeting Malays, and the rise of Malay nationalism after 1969 culminated in the Petroleum Development Act (PDA) of 1974, the Industrial Co-ordination Act (ICA) of 1975, and the establishment of the Yayasan Pelaburan Bumiputera (YPB) in 1978. The PDA was enacted to enable centralized state control of Malaysia's oil resources, and the other, ICA, required that a certain percentage of the assets of companies with capital above a certain level be distributed to Malay interests and that some of the managers be Malays. Finally, the YPB was an agency to encourage Malay shareholding. Through these institutional frameworks, the NEP intended to restructure employment patterns and ownership of the corporate sector in Malaysia.[41]

Of the above measures adopted by the Government since the mid-1970s, the PDA was particularly important in relation to the theme of this chapter. Malaysia's relationship with oil is long-standing, with hydrocarbon discoveries in the 1870s on the island of Borneo, now Malaysian territory, and commercial production by Shell in the early 1900s. Two world wars then boosted this oil production, and discoveries and exploration activity in offshore oil fields continued and expanded after the war, making Malaysia a hotspot of international oil companies (IOCs). Following the increase in oil prices after the 1973 oil crisis, the Government of Malaysia changed its relationship with foreign oil companies to utilize more of their profits for the NEP. The PDA was to force IOCs such as Shell and Esso to relinquish their concessions and sign Production Sharing Contracts to establish a national oil company, Petronas.[42]

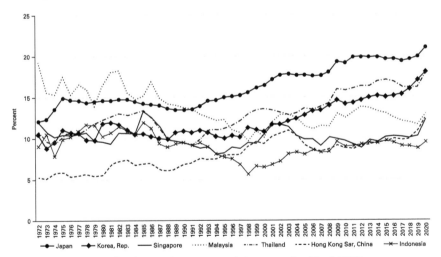

Figure 5.1 Trends in fiscal expenditure in East Asian countries (% of GDP).
Source: The World Bank, "World Development Indicators."

[41] Takashi Torii, "The New Economic Policy and the United Malays National Organization: with special reference to the restructuring of Malaysian society," *Developing Economies* 35(3) (1997): 209–39.
[42] Leslie Lopez, "Petronas: reconciling tensions between company and state," in David G. Victor, David R. Hults, and Mark C. Thurber (eds.), *Oil and Governance: State-Owned Enterprises and the World Energy Supply* (Cambridge University Press, 2011), 809–35.

The establishment of Petronas was highly significant in terms of policy management in that it provided a substantial financial resource for the NEP. Figure 5.1 provides data on the evolution of fiscal expenditure in Asian countries that have experienced rapid economic growth. It shows that Malaysia's fiscal expenditure was extremely high from the 1970s to the mid-1980s. This was due to the preferential treatment of Malays through the NEP, which pushed the size of the exchequer to a higher level.[43] As discussed in the next section, these vast financial outlays were supported by the financial resources generated by Petronas.[44] A surge in oil exports from Malaysia against high oil prices drove this increase in oil revenues. The considerable oil rents enabled income distribution to the Malays without economic sacrifice to other ethnic groups and ensured a rare degree of political stability.[45]

Of course, the growing dependence on oil resources had the potential to put Malaysia under the "oil curse." However, following the 1969 race riots, Malaysia sought to rebuild Malay employment patterns through industrialization, promising a more robust non-resource-based economy. In addition, the political elite involved in Petronas in the 1970s avoided the "oil curse," using neighboring Indonesia's Pertamina as a point of reference. Pertamina's transformation into a private plaything of Suharto and Ibn Sutowo in August 1974, just as Malaysia was preparing for Petronas, led to massive debt, which plunged Indonesia into its worst economic crisis. The Pertamina scandal made Petronas' management realize the need to assemble a strong group of technocrats and subsequently established a strong management base.[46] Furthermore, as is well-known, Malaysia's industrialization developed as export-oriented with the active involvement of foreign capital, which curbed the deviation from market discipline in Malaysian economic policy.[47] Oil was not an impediment to Malaysia's non-resource-based industrialization but a complement to it.

2.3. Global City and Oil

Singapore was in an economic quagmire following its separation from Malaysia and the withdrawal of British troops from the country, just as Malaysia experienced major national upheaval during the 1969 race riots. In particular, the fear of losing Malaysia, a hinterland rich in natural resources, was an important motivating factor in pushing Singapore, a small country, to become a developmental state.[48] However, unlike Malaysia, Singapore did not face a challenge in implementing affirmative action in

---

[43] Greg Felker, "Malaysia's development strategies: governing distribution-through-growth," in Meredith L. Weiss (ed.), *Routledge Handbook of Contemporary Malaysia* (London: Routledge, 2015), 133–47.

[44] Note that although the data was limited to Southeast Asian countries, Malaysia had the highest tax revenues in the 1970s. On this point, see Mukul G. Asher, *Revenue Systems of ASEAN Countries: An Overview* (Singapore: Singapore University Press, 1980).

[45] Sloane-White and Beaulieu, "Beyond 50 years of political stability in Malaysia."

[46] Lopez, "Petronas: reconciling tensions between company and state."

[47] Stafford, "Malaysia's new economic policy and the global economy"; Mahani, "Competitive industrialization with natural resource abundance."

[48] Lee Kuan Yew, *From Third World to First: The Singapore Story, 1965–2000: Singapore and the Asian Economic Boom* (New York: HarperCollins Publishers, 2000).

favor of certain ethnic groups. They aimed for a more open "global city," where export-oriented industrialization using foreign capital and the development of an Asian dollar market were promoted.[49] In order to foster an international financial center, the Government of Singapore was required to build an efficient government, including compliance with the law, an independent judiciary, and sound macroeconomic policies.[50] Singapore's characteristic pursuit of efficient and simplified government can also be confirmed by comparing the size of fiscal expenditure between Malaysia and Singapore in Figure 5.1.

An important issue with this chapter is that oil was involved in the industrialization of Singapore and the development of the Asian dollar market. Singapore was blessed with a natural harbor, and in addition to entrepôt trade and ship repair, oil refining was also active.[51] As of 1973, Shell, Exxon, Mobil, British Petroleum, and Singapore Petroleum were operating oil refineries, making Singapore the largest in Asia.[52] As discussed in the next section, the largest industrial exports in Singapore in the 1970s were refined petroleum products. The Asian dollar market, on the other hand, has grown into a primary industry due to the Singapore government's systematic nurturing of it, whereas its international financial market rival, Hong Kong, was cautious about attracting Eurodollars.[53] By the late 1980s, the financial and business sector had the most significant single GDP share,[54] and by 1993, the Asian dollar market was the fourth largest foreign exchange market in the world after London, New York, and Tokyo.[55]

Although the direct inflow of oil dollars into the Asian region was not significant in size, there is no doubt that oil dollars facilitated the development of the Asian dollar market when indirect inflows via other regions were taken into account. Following the oil crises, OPEC countries received significant oil revenues, of which surpluses were again transferred to other regions in search of investment opportunities. This is known as "oil money recycling," and Singapore has also benefited from this.[56] This means that Singapore benefited from oil not only from a trade perspective but also from a financial perspective.

As discussed above, the achievement of non-resource-based economic growth was recognized by the political elites in Malaysia and Singapore due to the political and economic vulnerabilities experienced prior to the oil crisis. The fact that oil was positioned solely to complement their developmental states was essential in avoiding

---

[49] Huff, "The developmental state, government, and Singapore's economic development since 1960"; Woo, *The Evolution of the Asian Developmental State Hong Kong and Singapore*.

[50] Lee, *From Third World to First*.

[51] IMF Archives. SM/75/203. Singapore—Recent Economic Developments. July 30, 1975.

[52] IMF Archives. SM/74/145. Singapore—Recent Economic Developments. June 21, 1974.

[53] Seung Woo Kim, "The Asian dollar market," in Stefano Battilossi, Youssef Cassis, and Kazuhiko Yago (eds.), *Handbook of the History of Money and Currency* (Singapore: Springer, 2020), 315–33; Catherine R. Schenk, "The origins of the Asia dollar market 1968–1986: regulatory competition and complementarity in Singapore and Hong Kong," *Financial History Review* 27(1) (2020): 17–44.

[54] IMF Archives. SM/88/203.

[55] Huff, "The developmental state, government, and Singapore's economic development since 1960."

[56] Hisao Tanaka (ed.), *Oil-Asian Dollar and International Financial Market* [Oilu-Azian dolaa to Kokusai Kinyuu Shijyou] (in Japanese) (Institute of Developing Economies, Japan External Trade Organization, 1978).

the "oil curse." In the next section, what has been discussed so far is shown objectively through the various statistics. Note that East Asian countries did not achieve economic growth in isolation as the World Bank's "East Asian Miracle" theory suggests. The following section therefore analyzes the economic linkages among East Asian countries, with a particular focus on oil. The analysis includes the existence of inter-Asian oil trade through "the East Asian oil triangle" and the formation of inter-Asian financial links through the Asian dollar market. The formation of these inter-Asian oil-mediated trade and financial links are points that has not been discussed in previous studies and are explored.

3. Formation of Inter-Asian Trade and Financial Links Through Oil

3.1. Inter-Asian Trade Through Oil: The East Asian Oil Triangle

As is well-known, Malaysia and Singapore experienced rapid economic growth through export-oriented industrialization. Export-oriented industrialization efforts in Malaysia are thought to have already started around the time of enacting the Investment Incentives Act of 1968. However, the full-scale initiation of export-oriented industrialization began after the race riots of 1969. Among these, the efforts initiated by the Penang Development Corporation in the early 1970s to attract US electronics companies triggered the rapid development of Malaysia's manufacturing sector. Establishing a free trade zone in 1972 attracted foreign companies, particularly in the textile and electronics industries, and in later years, Malaysia became the world's largest

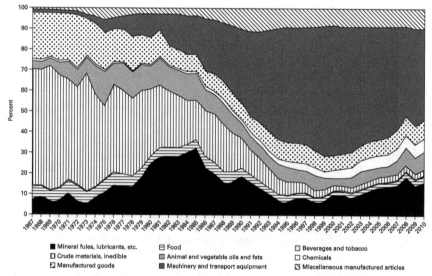

Figure 5.2 Long-term trends in the composition of Malaysia's exports (1967–2010). Source: Department of Statistics, Malaysia, *Malaysia Economic Statistics Times Series*, 2015.

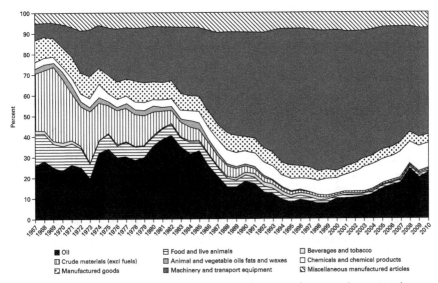

Figure 5.3 Long-term trends in the composition of Singapore's exports (1967–2010). Source: Department of Statistics Singapore, *Merchandise Trade: Detailed Statistical Time Series*.

producer of semiconductors.[57] Malaysian bureaucrats selectively attracted these textile and electronics industries from Japan and the USA because they were labor-intensive and export-oriented.[58] On the other hand, following its separation from Malaysia, Singapore similarly had to move aggressively toward foreign markets, emphasizing attracting the electronics industry as an engine of growth.[59]

Throughout the 1970s, the industrialization of Malaysia and Singapore progressed rapidly, but not all at once (Figures 5.2 and 5.3). In 1967, the share of exports of raw materials such as rubber and tin (under the heading "Crude Materials, Inedible") was well over 50 percent, and the Malaysian economy depended on these exports. However, after the onset of the oil crisis and the nationalization of the oil industry,[60] oil exports

[57] Anita Doraisami, "Has Malaysia really escaped the resource curse? A closer look at the political economy of oil revenue management and expenditures," *Resources Policy* 45 (2015): 98–108. FTZs had the advantage of not only receiving tax incentives but also being exempt from the abovementioned requirements imposed on companies by the ICA. On this point, see Bryan K. Ritchie, "Coalitional politics, economic reform, and technological upgrading in Malaysia," *World Development* 33(5) 2005): 745–61.

[58] James V. Jesudason, *Ethnicity and the Economy: The State, Chinese Business, and Multinationals in Malaysia* (Singapore: Oxford University Press, 1989).

[59] Huff, "The developmental state, government, and Singapore's economic development since 1960." In the mid-1990s, Malaysia accounted for a quarter of outward FDI inflows into ASEAN, second only to Singapore. On this point, see Jayant Menon, "Growth without private investment: what happened in Malaysia and can it be fixed?," *Journal of the Asia Pacific Economy* 19(2) (2014): 247–71.

[60] Crude oil production increased rapidly after 1975 when a production-sharing arrangement was made between the state oil company Petronas and the multinational oil companies Shell and ESSO. On this point, see IMF Archives. SM/80/142. Malaysia—Recent Economic Developments. June 18, 1980.

proliferated and replaced raw material exports as Malaysia's main export. Importantly, as the graphs show, oil exports bought time for industrialization to shape from the 1980s onward. As the price of oil plummeted and the oil component declined, exports of industrial products ("machinery and transport equipment") increased rapidly. In Malaysia, there was a sequential shift from rubber and tin exports to oil exports and, from the mid-1980s onward, to exports of industrial products. In short, oil exports acted as a "mediator" to industrialization. Natural rubber, Malaysia's main export product, faced significant price declines due to increased competition from synthetic rubber.[61] Without oil exports, Malaysia's industrialization must have been a tough road, as rubber and tin prices, its main exports until the 1960s, were very volatile.

As shown in Figure 5.3, Singapore followed a similar path to Malaysia. Until the 1960s, Singapore, like Malaysia, relied on raw material exports for many of its exports. The bulk of this raw material export was crude rubber imported from Malaysia and Indonesia, which Singapore re-exported to other countries.[62] However, after the oil crises, oil exports increased and, at their peak in 1982, accounted for 40 percent of exports. Oil exports declined as oil prices had fallen, but the economy did not return to its previous dependence on raw material exports. From the mid-1980s onward, Singapore's exports of industrial goods grew to replace its oil exports. As in Malaysia, oil exports played an intermediary role in industrialization.

So far, we can see that oil exports played a pivotal role in the industrialization of both countries, but the role of oil was not limited to that. The fact that oil acted as a "catalyst" for forming new trade links within East Asia was significant. Table 5.1 shows the trade statistics of Malaysia by the trading partner in 1979. The first thing noted from this table is that trade relations with Malaysia, Japan, Singapore, and the USA were established in 1979. In 1970, trade relations with the United Kingdom, the former suzerain, still accounted for a certain proportion of the total.[63] However, trade links with the UK declined rapidly as time passed, and new trade links were formed in the East Asia and Pacific regions. These countries alone accounted for more than half of Malaysia's exports and imports trade. It is worth noting that Malaysia exported oil to Japan, Singapore, and the USA while importing industrial goods from Japan and the USA. As the production structure changed from raw materials to industrial goods, demand for intermediate and investment goods used in the manufacturing process increased.[64] Malaysia used the foreign currency earned from oil to buy machinery and equipment and then pursued its development plans.

Odd as it may seem, Malaysia exported oil while importing it from Singapore and the rest of the world. The oil available to the economy for industrialization is refined oil, but Malaysia did not have sufficient technology to refine crude oil. As a result, Malaysia exported crude oil to Singapore, while Malaysia purchased large quantities of refined petroleum from Singapore.[65] This trade was based on the exchange of oil for oil. In

[61] Thillainathan and Kee-Cheok, "Malaysia's new economic policy, growth and distribution."
[62] IMF Archives. SM/74/145.
[63] Department of Statistics, Malaysia, *Malaysia Annual Statistical of External Trade*, 1970.
[64] IMF Archives. SM/80/142.
[65] IMF Archives. SM/87/163. Malaysia—Recent Economic Developments. July 15, 1987.

Table 5.1 Trade structure by trading partner country in 1979

Export

	Food	Beverages and tobacco	Crude materials, inedible	Mineral fuels, lubricants, etc.	Animal and vegetable oils and fats	Chemicals	Manufactured goods	Machinery and transport equipment	Miscellaneous manufactured articles	Miscellaneous transactions and commodities	Composition ratio (%)
Australia	4.7		1.4	0.8	1.6	2.6	1.9	2.2	3.8	13.5	1.7
Canada	0.3		1		1		0.7	0.5	1.1	1.4	0.7
France	0.6		3.1		0.6	0.2	0.3	2.2	6.1	0.9	1.7
Germany	8.8		3.9		3	2.1	2.5	6.1	18.1	2.2	3.7
India	0.2		0.6		13	0.2	1.7			3.2	2.1
Italy	0.7		2.9		1.6		2.4	0.2	1.4	0.3	1.7
Japan	19.2		28.1	43.2	6.5	5.9	19.7	5.2	7.9	9.3	23.4
Netherlands	7.9		5.3		11.3	0.1	12.9	0.2	3.1	3.3	5.6
Singapore	33	80.9	16.8	18.8	23.5	44	7.9	15.4	13	11.9	17.5
Thailand	1.4		0.7	4	0.4	5.4	0.5	1.1	0.4	2.1	1.3
U.S.S.R.			3.3		2.9		5.4			1.6	2.3
United Kingdom	5.2		3.1		8.4	1.1	5.4	4	8.2	13.2	3.9
United States	3.6		6	27.4	8.7	5.9	24.8	47.5	16.5	9	17.3
Rest of the World	14.4	19.1	23.8	5.8	17.5	32.5	13.9	15.4	20.4	28.1	17.1
Total Value (Million)	1081.9	20.9	9024.9	4345.8	3016.4	131	3314.5	2535.4	603.8	147.4	24222

(Continued)

Table 5.1 Continued

Import

	Food	Beverages and tobacco	Crude materials, inedible	Mineral fuels, lubricants, etc.	Animal and vegetable oils and fats	Chemicals	Manufactured goods	Machinery and transport equipment	Miscellaneous manufactured articles	Miscellaneous transactions and commodities	Composition ratio (%)
Australia	24.6	0.6	29.8	0.6	15.3	2.1	5.3	0.9	2.1	2.7	6.1
China	10.1	2.6	5.3	0.2	5.6	2.2	4	0.4	5.2		2.8
France	0.6	30.5	0.1			2.6	1.4	2.7	1	1.3	2
Germany	0.3	0.3	1.3	0.1	4	14.1	3	9.2	8.8	4.5	5.9
Hong Kong	0.5	11	0.4		3.3	1.1	3.1	1.1	7.7	2.4	1.6
India	3	0.2	0.8		2.7	0.5	0.8	0.9	2.5	3.9	1.1
Indonesia	2.5	0.6	6.9	0.3	0.7	1.1	0.8	0.1	0.4	0.2	1
Japan	3.3	0.4	4.8	0.6	9.9	18.1	35.6	34.6	18	5.8	22.3
Netherlands	1.6	0.4	0.1	0.1	5.6	1.4	0.5	0.8	0.7	0.4	0.8
Singapore	4.9	4.8	3.5	34.6	32.1	4.9	6.7	4.8	10.4	26.2	9.2
Thailand	20.6		11.1		0.3	0.3	1.2	0.8	1	0.4	3.6
U.S.S.R.			0.2		0.3	0.9	0.1				0.1
United Kingdom	2	7.2	1.2	0.4	5.6	10	5.7	9	11.7	10.1	6.4
United States	4.7	36.2	7.6	0.4	2.3	22.7	6.6	24.7	18.2	15.6	14.9
Rest of the World	21.3	5.2	26.9	62.7	12.3	18	25.2	10	12.3	26.5	22.2
Total Value (Million)	2015.5	185.2	850.3	2076.7	30.2	1747.4	2919.8	6373.6	791	135.4	17161.1

Source: Department of Statistics, Malaysia, Malaysia Annual Statistical of External Trade, 1980.

addition, Singapore exported refined petroleum to Japan and the USA while importing industrial products from these countries for industrialization.[66] Note that Malaysia and Singapore imported significant amounts of refined petroleum and crude oil from the Middle East. Therefore, if Malaysia and Singapore had not been able to export crude oil and refined petroleum, the balance of payments would have resulted in a significant deficit, and they would have had to rely on substantial external debt.

The transformation of the trade structure in Malaysia and Singapore after the oil crises is here named "the East Asian oil triangle" (Figure 5.4). As mentioned above, Kaoru Sugihara discussed the relationship between creating a global oil cycle and Japan's economic growth. However, as discussed in this section, such a global oil cycle did not promote economic growth in the Asia-Pacific and East Asia regions on its own but had to be complemented by the existence of "the East Asian oil triangle." This was created by the trade relationships within the Asia-Pacific and East Asia that exchanged crude oil, refined petroleum products, and industrial goods, which stimulated economic growth in East Asia.

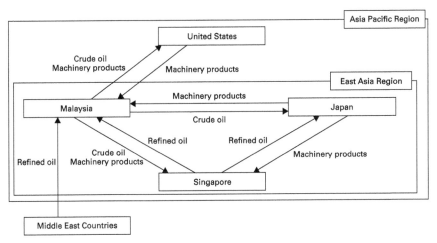

Figure 5.4 Formation of the East Asian oil triangle after the oil crisis.
Source: Created by the author.

3.2. Expanded Fiscal Capacity and Formation of Financial Links Through Oil

The East Asian oil triangle improved not only the import and export capacity of Malaysia and Singapore but also the fiscal capacity of both countries. This was because the East Asian oil triangle led to a diversification of tax revenues for economic development. Also known as oil dollar recycling, oil revenue surpluses of OPEC countries flowed into the Eurodollar market, which Malaysia and Singapore actively used for economic development.

---

[66] Department of Trade, Ministry of Trade & Industry, Republic of Singapore, *Annual Report, 1979/1980*, 1980.

Table 5.2 shows the IMF staff's analysis of Malaysia's fiscal structure, focusing on oil-related tax revenues. The table shows that in the 1980s, Malaysia received an average of more than 30 percent of its tax revenue from oil-related taxes alone. For example, in 1985, corporate, excise, import, and export taxes on oil extraction companies together generated RM 5,726 million in tax revenue. In addition to this, there was a revenue of RM 1,549 million from dividends from Petronas and petroleum royalties. As mentioned above, Petronas is a public oil company owned by the Government of Malaysia, which

Table 5.2 Malaysia's fiscal capacity and oil-related revenues (in millions of ringgit)

		1981	1982	1983	1984	1985
Tax revenue	Taxes on petroleum	3,669	3,964	4,208	5,023	5,726
	Of which: Oil production companies	1,978	2,075	1,998	2,570	3,130
	Of which: Excises on petroleum products	276	305	436	487	537
	Of which: Import duties on petroleum products	174	233	297	337	420
	Of which: Export duties on petroleum	1,241	1,351	1,477	1,629	1,639
	Other taxes	9,417	9,200	11,708	12,185	11,733
	Of which: Taxes on international trade	3,055	2,451	2,709	2,819	2,298
	Of which: Taxes on goods and services	228	2,425	3,291	3,459	3,319
	Of which: Taxes on net income and profits	3,846	3,981	5,270	5,412	5,681
	Of which: Non-oil companies	2,756	2,617	3,451	3,432	3,920
	Of which: Individuals	1,088	1,362	1,815	1,975	1,749
	Other tax revenues	288	343	438	495	475
Non tax revenue	Dividends by Petoronas	950	1,450	500	980	930
	Petroleum royalties	417	425	491	581	619
	Other	1,244	1,516	1,587	1,819	1,920
Foreign grants		6	12	8	59	4
Petroleum revenue (as percent of total revenue, excluding loans)		32.1%	35.3%	28.1%	32.0%	34.7%
Financing	External loans	3,419	4,880	4,570	3,119	956
	Domestic loans	4,665	5,779	2,190	2,228	3,314
	Of which: Banking system	1,168	1,671	-156	1,055	-2,854
	Of which: Nonbanks	3,497	4,128	2,346	1,173	6168
	Of which: Employees' Provident Fund	1,733	2,154	1,947	2,773	3403
	Of which: Petronas	1,772	1,900	-177	-2,043	1402
	Of which: Other	8	74	576	434	1363

Source: IMF Archives. SM/86/173, SM/87/163.

later became a national symbol.[67] Moreover, oil also increased Malaysia's borrowing capacity. Tax revenues alone were insufficient to finance the development programs that Malaysia pursued at the time, which were filled by external and internal borrowing. Looking at domestic borrowing, it is noteworthy that the government also borrowed heavily from Petronas in addition to the Employees' Provident Fund. Oil profits were used to control debt through Petronas. The Government of Malaysia distributed the revenues obtained in this way throughout the country to carry out its development plans.

On the other hand, it was also true that Malaysia had to resort to external borrowing to pursue its massive development programs. Figure 6 shows Malaysia's external borrowing from 1965 to 1985 by major currency, which shows that borrowing from the market had increased since the oil crises. A particularly noteworthy fact was borrowing in US dollars, which accounted for less than 20 percent of external borrowing in 1965 but rose sharply after that, reaching more than 70 percent in 1975. In absolute terms, borrowing in US dollars increased about 8.5 times from RM 1,409 million in 1979 to RM 12,008 million in 1984. This increased borrowing of dollar funds was due to the inflow of Eurodollars into Malaysia, which increased rapidly after the oil shock.

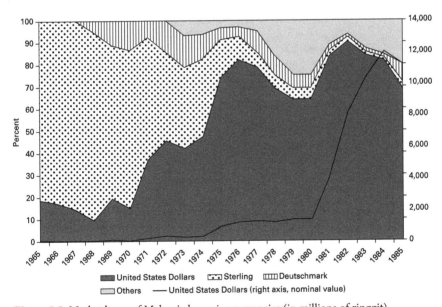

Figure 5.5 Market loans of Malaysia by major currencies (in millions of ringgit). Source: The Treasury, Government of Malaysia, *Economic Report*, 1975; 1981; 1985; 1986.

---

[67] For more information on Petronas, see Fred R. von der Mehden and Al Troner, *Petronas: A National Oil Company with an International Vision* (The James A. Baker III Institute for Public Policy of Rice University, 2007).

Table 5.3 shows that most of the international banks involved in Malaysia's Eurodollar borrowing were large Western banks such as Chemical Bank, Chase Manhattan Bank, and Lloyds Bank. However, Malaysian banks were also involved and jointly borrowed Eurodollar with these Western international banks to finance Malaysia's economic development (e.g., Amanah-Chase Merchant Bank Berhad). It can be seen from here that local Malaysian banks acted as catalysts to bring the Eurodollar into the Malaysian economy. Secondary refluxes of the oil dollars to the Asian region between 1974 and 1977 were estimated to have been around USD 2.4 billion.[68] Although the exact size is not clear, given the increase in Eurodollar borrowing after the oil crises, there is no doubt that the oil dollar underpinned Malaysia's development finance. It should also be noted that Middle Eastern countries jointly established banks

Table 5.3 Eurodollar finance of Malaysia after the oil crisis

Year 1975	May	July	Dec.
Borrower	Government of Malaysia	Government of Malaysia	Government of Malaysia
Leading Financial Institutions	Chemical Bank	Chase Manhattan Bank N. A.	Chase Manhattan Ltd.
	First National Bank of Chicago	Orion Pacific Ltd.	Morgan Guaranty Trust Co.
	Manufacturers Hanover Ltd.	Amanah-Chase Merchant Bank Berhad	Toronto Dominion Bank
	Morgan Guaranty Trust Co.	Westdeutsche Landesbank Girozentrale	Westdeutsche Landesbank Girozentrale
	Toronto Dominion Bank		Amanah-Chase Merchant Bank Berhad
	Wells Fargo Bank N. A.		Kuhn, Loeb & Co. Asia
	United Malaysian banking Corp. Bhd.		N. M. Rothschild & Sons Ltd.
	Asia International Merchant Bankers Bhd.		Grindlays Bank Ltd.
			Manufacturers Hanover Ltd.
			Lloyds Bank International Ltd.
			United California Bank
			Wells Fargo Bank, N. A.
Amount in Millions	150	75	200
Term (Years)	5	5	5.5
Interest (Percent)	1.625	1.625	1.5
Remarks	To finance internal economic development	To finance internal economic development	— (no description)

Source: The World Bank, *Borrowing in International Capital Markets: Foreign and International Bond Issues: Publicized Eurocurrency Credits*, First Quarter 1975; Second Quarter 1975; Third Quarter 1975.

[68] Tanaka ed. 1978.

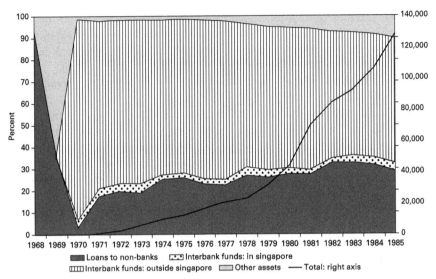

Figure 5.6 Trends in the size of the Asian dollar market (in millions of US dollars).
Source: Monetary Authority of Singapore, *Annual report*, various year editions.

with Malaysia, such as the Arab-Malaysian Development Bank Berhad, and used oil dollars for Malaysia's development.[69]

As mentioned above, since the oil crises, Singapore's economic activities have been underpinned by the export of refined petroleum. In addition, the Government of Singapore decided to diversify its economic structure through the oil dollar. What differed from the Malaysian case was that the Government of Singapore actively used the oil dollar to foster an international financial market and tried to make it the cornerstone of its economy. The Government's desire to develop Singapore as a financial center led to several incentives, most notably the exemption of non-residents from the 40 percent withholding tax on interest earned on Asian dollar deposits, which was an important factor in the market development.[70] Figure 5.6 shows the size of the Asian dollar market that Singapore fostered to attract and operate Eurodollars. From just USD 2 million in 1968, the Asian dollar market expanded rapidly to USD 128.4 billion in 1985.

One of the key factors behind the significant expansion of the Asian dollar market was the surplus of funds from OPEC countries. The largest source of funds came from the euro currency market in London, but after the oil crises, Middle Eastern countries became increasingly crucial as net suppliers of funds. In terms of demand for funds, it was estimated that more than 75 percent of new loans were to the Asian region in 1979. These funds were used to cover the balance of payments deficits associated with the

---

[69] The World Bank, *Borrowing in International Capital Markets: Foreign and International Bond Issues: Publicized Eurocurrency Credits*, first half 1980.
[70] Monetary Authority of Singapore, *Annual Report*, 1973.

East Asian countries' oil imports[71] and finance development expenditures, including oil refining projects. In the early years, the Asian dollar market was dominated by short-term loans and interbank lending, but gradually long-term, non-bank lending increased.[72] Changes in lending to non-banks can also be seen in Figure 5.6. It is important to note that oil played a significant role in the source and use of funds in the Asian dollar market.

As a background to the economic development of East Asia as one coherent region, the establishment of financial linkages in East Asia through the Asian dollar market may be mentioned. Figure 5.7, prepared by the Bank of Japan, confirms this point. First, funds in the Asian dollar market were not only used for interbank transactions but were also lent to governments, central banks, and companies to finance the development of Asian countries. Secondly, interestingly, the Asian dollar market was closely linked to the international financial market in Hong Kong, contributing significantly to the

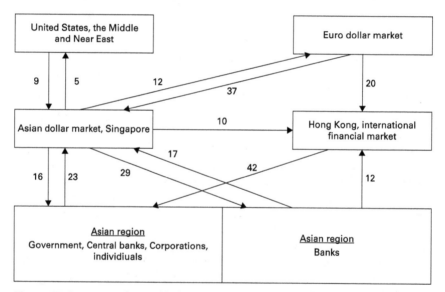

Figure 5.7 Inter-Asian financial link and Asian dollar market (in billion dollars, end of 1974).

Source: Bank of Japan, Research and Statistics Department, "Asian dollar market in Transition and Hong Kong's International Financial Transactions" [Tenkanki no Azian dalaa Shijyou to Honkon no Kokusai Kinyuu Torihiki] (in Japanese), *Nippon Ginko Chousa Geppou* 27(2) (1976): 8.

[71] The current account balance in the Asian region, except for oil-exporting countries Malaysia and Indonesia, faced substantial deficits, increasing the need for foreign capital procurement. On this point, see Bank of Japan, Research and Statistics Department, "The development of Hong Kong and Singapore as international financial markets: with a focus on their role in the circulation of oil money since the last oil crisis," [Kokusai Kinyuu Shijyou toshite no Honkon, Shingapouru no Hatten ni tsuite: Zenkai Sekiyu Kiki ikou no Oilu Manei Kanryuu ni Hatashita Yakuwari wo Chuushin ni] (In Japanese), *Nippon Ginko Chosa Geppou* 31(5) (1980): 1–20; Kenneth Bernauer, "Asian dollar market," *Economic Review (Federal Reserve Bank of San Francisco)* (1) (1983): 47–63.

[72] Monetary Authority of Singapore, *Annual Report*, 1980.

development of Asia. Funds flowing into the Asian dollar market from the Eurodollar market were lent to the international financial market in Hong Kong, from where they further flowed out to other Asian countries, creating a highly complex situation. Singapore's Asian dollar market attracted funds from outside Asia, while Hong Kong managed the funds so collected, thus dividing its role as an international financial market.[73]

4. Conclusion: Diverging Trajectories of Economic Development in Malaysia and Singapore

As described above, in Malaysia and Singapore, the formation of a trade structure based on the exchange of oil for oil and oil for industrial products, and the transformation of the economic structure in financial terms using oil money, were underway. These expanded the export and financial capacities of both countries while simultaneously helping to achieve economic growth in the region as a whole by creating trade and financial links across East Asia through oil. The remarkable economic growth of both countries in the 1970s, when the developed world was in economic stagnation, was largely due to the fact that both countries were able to benefit from the oil crises.[74] And despite the substantial economic gains through oil, they did not stop their efforts to diversify further their economic structures because both countries had experienced political and economic threats that shook the state before the oil crisis and institutionalized the developmental state. The East Asian Miracle thus arose.

However, while Malaysia and Singapore experienced rapid growth after the oil crises, it is also true that the economic trajectories of the two countries differed in direction. There is no evidence that oil has reduced economic growth in Malaysia,[75] but not all projects through oil have been successful. The competitive industries in Malaysia were the electronics and textile industries based on low-cost Malay labor, but the comparative advantage in labor costs gradually shifted to other countries.[76] In addition, foreign capital developed these industries in free trade zones, which failed to create linkages between industries. In response to this situation, in the 1980s, Mahathir bin Mohamad established HICOM to develop heavy industries such as steel, cement, automobiles, and chemicals. The motivation for establishing HICOM was to engage Malays in higher value-added industries and to form linkages between local industries

---

[73] Bank of Japan, Research and Statistics Department, "The development of Hong Kong and Singapore as international financial markets."
[74] For an assessment of the good economic performance of Malaysia and Singapore after the oil crisis, see the following literature: IMF Archives. SM/75/183; SM/80/142.
[75] There is no statistical evidence that oil has reduced economic growth. See, for example, Ramez Abubakr Badeeb, Kenneth R. Szulczyk, and Hooi Hooi Lean, "Asymmetries in the effect of oil rent shocks on economic growth: a sectoral analysis from the perspective of the oil curse," *Resources Policy* 74 (2021): 1–11.
[76] Already in 1980, it was recognized that Malaysia's electronics industry was losing its comparative advantage. See IMF Archives. SM/80/142.

to overcome the so-called "enclaves," which ultimately failed to create self-sustaining industries and resulted in huge losses. Importantly, significant oil revenues supported heavy industrial projects through HICOM, and from the 1980s onward, politicians often used Petronas for these reckless policies.[77]

It is also said that various Malay preferential policies through the NEP have created distortions in the Malaysian economy. For example, ethnic quotas have been applied to a certain percentage of admissions to higher education institutions. This has forced non-Malays who were denied admission to study abroad, hindering the development of talented industrialists.[78] This situation contrasts with Singapore, where an emphasis on education and training and active upskilling has shifted the economic structure from labor-intensive industries to higher value-added sectors and wages.[79] Although there has been no quantitative development program in Singapore since the First Development Plan of 1961–4, the Finance Minister's Budget Speech in 1972 stated that Singapore would be transformed into a regional center of "the brain industry" within ten years.[80] Upgrading education and skills were vital in directing Singapore's economic development. On the other hand, Malaysia is in the so-called "middle-income trap," where it does not have the competitive comparative advantage of low wages and has failed to upgrade to the production of skill-based, high-value-added goods.[81]

As noted above, the Government of Malaysia was able to generate significant oil revenues, which allowed it to progress a major development program. In the past, the development policy without taxation had been able to gain public support and build a stable political system.[82] However, from a long-term perspective, it can be noted that this has destabilized Malaysia's fiscal structure and political system. Successive Malaysian governments have repeatedly proposed introducing a value-added tax called Goods & Services Tax (GST) to create a more stable fiscal structure, given the shortcomings of oil revenues being dependent on trade trends and the endemic budget deficit. These proposals were repeatedly rejected, but in 2015 the GST was introduced, the latest in Southeast Asia.[83] Nevertheless, the first change of government occurred when the opposition coalition led by former Prime Minister Mahathir Mohamad announced the abolition of GST. The public has not accepted the GST, and establishing a stable fiscal base has yet to be achieved, as the funding from oil has served to avoid

---

[77] Ritchie, "Coalitional politics, economic reform, and technological upgrading in Malaysia"; Lopez, "Petronas: reconciling tensions between company and state."

[78] Ritchie, "Coalitional politics, economic reform, and technological upgrading in Malaysia"; Menon, "Growth without private investment."

[79] IMF Archives. SM/88/203. Singapore—Recent Economic Developments. September 1, 1988.

[80] IMF Archives. SM/75/203.

[81] Anita Doraisami, "Economic crisis and policy response in Malaysia: the role of the new economic policy," *Asian-Pacific Economic Literature* 26(2) (2012): 41–53.

[82] Varkkey, "Natural resource extraction and political dependency"; Sloane-White and Beaulieu, "Beyond 50 years of political stability in Malaysia."

[83] Suresh Narayanan, "The challenges of raising revenues and restructuring subsidies in Malaysia," *Kajian Malaysia* 25(2) (2007): 1–28; Mohammad Fajar Ikhsan, Norsyuhada Azwin Aziz, and Emil Mahyudin, "Case study on the implementation of Goods and Services Tax (GST) in Malaysia and Singapore," *Journal of International Studies* 18 (2022): 159–89.

the tax burden on most Malaysians.[84] It should also be remembered that dependence on oil revenues has led the Malaysian government to avoid accountability to the public and fostered a secretive political culture.[85] This is in contrast to Singapore, which introduced the GST in 1994 and built a more accountable polity.

Malaysia and Singapore benefited from each other's economic development through oil, which was complimentary. However, it is also true that, from a long-term perspective, their political and economic performance diverges. Oil is seen as a factor that could explain the background to economic growth in East Asia as a whole, as well as the political and economic differences.

---

[84] Doraisami, "Has Malaysia really escaped the resource curse?"
[85] DiJohn, *Mineral-Resource Abundance and Violent Political Conflict*; Ross, *The Oil Curse*.

6

The 1970s Macrocycle: Eurodollars, Petrodollars, Credit Booms, and Debt Busts, 1973–82

Mark Metzler

Whether one focuses on the nexus between oil and the US dollar, or on geopolitical shifts, or on geo-cultural currents, the "sixties" as a world-historical moment ended in the year 1973 and gave way to the "seventies." The interval from 1973 to 1979 was in the Western countries an in-between time, when the reigning policy paradigms of the long postwar boom seemed to become dysfunctional while also maintaining a basic inertial force. For many commodity-exporting countries, it seemed a moment of possibility, as relative prices shifted in favor of raw-material producers while historically high volumes of credit-capital flowed in from US and European banks. This "interregnal" moment began to close with the combined monetary, energy, and political shocks of 1979–80. The great credit wave and the great commodity-price wave then came crashing down in 1982, opening a new phase of international debt crisis and depression. In the global-conjunctural view presented here, the 1970s was an era of two dollar-oil crises; two waves of inflationary price revolution; and one international lending wave, which ended in the fourth major international debt crisis of the modern capitalist era.

It is good to begin this essay on the 1970s by considering the unfolding global economic conjuncture of the 2020s. When I drafted early ideas for this paper in August 2020, many commentators were already anticipating the return of a 1970s-type combination of inflationary credit conditions, supply shocks, and "stagflation."[1] *Easy money*, including the lowest interest rates and biggest debt bailouts in the entire historical record, has been the story of the twenty-first century to date. Until recently though, this was a kind of central-bank Keynesianism for the financial sector that was coupled with popular austerity. In 2020 and 2021, for the pandemic season at least, popular austerity was lifted. *Supply shocks* simultaneously reverberated across the global economy. Even more reminiscent of the 1970s, these now include energy shocks, beginning with natural gas, whose prices in Asia and Europe increased by four or five times in the six months from spring to autumn 2021. Coal prices also increased by four or five times in 2021, as did prices for chemical fertilizers. The February 24, 2022

---

[1] This paper grew out of a series of workshops organized by Shigeru Akita in 2020–22. I would like to express my appreciation also to the late Kiren Aziz Chaudhry for comments on a much earlier statement of the ideas presented here.

Russian invasion of Ukraine brought on a still greater surge of energy, food, and fertilizer prices.[2] World inflation reached levels not seen since the 1970s, and a 1970s-style international strike wave seems to be in the making. *Stagnation* has not arrived as of this writing though it is widely predicted. Comparisons to the 1970s fly around the popular financial media.

This chapter offers a schematic picture of the 1970s that is *conjunctural* in the classic sense of the term, taking economic fluctuations as a key to historical periodization and to structural analysis. The history of prices and of credit/debt cycles is especially fundamental. Pricewise, the 1970s was dominated by two global inflationary waves coinciding with the two oil shocks of 1973–4 and 1979–80. Superficially, the oil shocks seemed exogenous to the international economic system, originating in the specific politics of the Middle East. Deeper examination reveals a picture of economically endogenous, globally systemic dynamics—from the beginning of this period to its end, shifts in the money system were tightly coupled with shifts in the oil system. We can also compare these years to earlier sequences of *international commodity booms* → *international lending booms* → *international debt crises* as seen in the international boom-bust cycle of the 1920s–1930s and that of the 1860s–1870s. These cross-time comparisons clarify essential dynamics of the 1970s. They may also produce insights into the unfolding dynamics of the 2020s.

This chapter views "the 1970s" as the decade (or novennium) from February–March 1973 to August 1982. It thus corresponds to the "rise and fall of the Third World project," as described by Dane Kennedy, also in this volume. The focus here is on three turning points. In *1973*, the long boom of the 1950s and 1960s ended and "the sixties" as a cultural and political moment gave way to "the seventies." In *1982*, the international inflationary wave and the conjoined Eurodollar lending wave ended. Mexico's default on its dollar debts in August of the year signaled the start of the "third world" debt crisis and of the deepest international depression since the 1930s. Midway between these two points came a major change of phase after *1977–8*, when a new round of US dollar depreciation culminated in a second dollar-oil crisis in 1978–9. This temporal framing—*1973, 1977–8, 1982*—is a global economic periodization but these turning points were political and cultural ones as well.

1. Periodizing History: A Bretton Woods Era in Oil, Money, and Grain

What changed in the 1970s? One explanation is that the coordinated system of institutions and technologies that sustained the long international boom of 1950–73 reached a series of limits that brought that system into crisis and inaugurated an

[2] Prices for natural gas (LNG Japan/Korea Marker) rose from around $6 or $7 per million BTUs in early 2021, to over $30 in late 2021, to over $50 in August-September 2022. European natural gas prices went much higher. Fertilizer prices moved in parallel with natural gas prices. Benchmark coal prices (Australian Newcastle coal futures) were mostly between $60 and $100 per ton in the 2010s, reached $200 in late 2021, and surpassed $400 in the spring of 2022.

epochal shift. Most analysts who take this view identify the long postwar boom with "Fordist" modes of industrial regulation and Keynesian modes of macroeconomic regulation.[3] In international monetary relations, this was the "Bretton Woods era," when major currencies were fixed to the gold-linked US dollar. In a resource and energy view, it was the age of cheap oil, sustained by production from the Persian Gulf oil fields, and of cheap food production based on a new package of petroleum- and petrochemical-based technologies. We can therefore describe the dominant techno-economic paradigm as a *petro-Fordist-Keynesian* one.

The postwar monetary regime and the postwar energy regime took form together in the late 1940s, and they broke down together in 1971–3. The international monetary conference at Bretton Woods in July 1944 aimed to re-establish fixed exchange rates among the world's major currencies in place of the international fragmentation that had followed the breakdown of the gold standard in 1931–3. This goal was achieved in a de facto way between 1947 and late 1949, when the US dollar took the place that had formerly been held by gold and the gold-linked British pound.[4] Other currencies were pegged to the US dollar, which itself was legally fixed to gold. The Japanese yen, to take a pivotal example, was fixed to the dollar in April 1949 at ¥360 to $1. This rate remained unchanged until August 1971.[5] The German mark was only slightly less fixed.

Simultaneously an oligopolistic, US-sponsored "fixed-rate" regime was established in the international oil trade, which had suffered from excessive competition and damaging price collapses in the 1930s depression.[6] As a result, oil prices between 1947 and 1970 were not only relatively low but also extremely stable. In 1947, the price of benchmark Arabian Light crude was $1.90 per barrel (bbl). In 1970, amazingly, it was $1.80/bbl.

One can also identify a *postwar food regime* from the late 1940s to 1972–3.[7] The International Wheat Agreement of 1949 inaugurated a period of exceptionally stable and low wheat prices that continued until the first half of 1972 (initially around $2/bushel and then declining still further). This price regime was anchored by the government-subsidized stockpiling of large US grain surpluses combined with large

---

3 E.g., "Regulation school" theorists such as Michel Aglietta; "social structures of accumulation" theorists such as David M. Gordon; and neo-Schumpeterian analysts such as Christopher Freeman and Carlota Perez. As noted below, the earliest statements of these ideas date from the 1970s.
4 Armand van Dormael, *Bretton Woods: Birth of a Monetary System* (New York: Holmes & Meier, 1978); Eric Helleiner, *States and the Reemergence of Global Finance: From Bretton Woods to the 1990s* (Cornell University Press, 1994), 25–77. "Dollar" in this chapter means US dollars.
5 Mark Metzler, *Capital as Will and Imagination: Schumpeter's Guide to the Postwar Japanese Miracle* (Cornell University Press, 2013), 132–6.
6 David S. Painter, "Oil and the Marshall Plan," *Business History Review* 58(3) (1984): 359–83; David S. Painter, *Oil and the American Century: The Political Economy of U.S. Foreign Oil Policy, 1941–1954* (Baltimore: Johns Hopkins University Press, 1986); David S. Painter, "The Marshall Plan and oil," *Cold War History* 9(2) (2009): 159–75; Daniel Yergin, *The Prize: The Epic Quest for Oil, Money, and Power* (New York: Simon & Schuster, 1991), chapter 21; Laura E. Hein, *Fueling Growth: The Energy Revolution and Economic Policy in Postwar Japan* (Harvard University Press East Asia Center, 1990).
7 Emma Rothschild, "Food politics," *Foreign Affairs* 54(2) (1976): 285–307; Harriet Friedmann, "The political economy of food: the rise and fall of the postwar international food order," *American Journal of Sociology* 88 (Supplement, 1982): S248–86; Philip McMichael, "A food regime genealogy," *Journal of Peasant Studies* 36(1) (2009): 139–69; Fridolin Krausmann and Ernst Langthaler, "Food regimes and their trade links: a socio-ecological perspective," *Ecological Economics* 160 (2019): 87–95.

US grain exports—one-half of all world wheat exports in the early 1960s; one-third in the late 1960s. US Public Law (PL) 480 subsidized the export of food grains to poorer countries.[8] This "export fix" for US agriculture also reduced grain self-sufficiency in many importing countries.

The international dollar crises of August 1971 and February-March 1973 announced the breakdown of the Bretton Woods monetary order. Beginning in mid-1972 and extending through 1973 came an international food crisis and the breakdown of the postwar food regime. Then in late 1973 and 1974 came the first oil crisis and breakdown of the postwar oil regime.

2. Endogenous Shocks: The Dollar Shock Came First

The first big trade imbalances of the decade were caused by European and Japanese trade surpluses, combined with the first US trade deficits since the 1890s. This too was connected to oil, as US domestic oil production peaked in 1970 and US oil imports began to increase in the second half of 1971. In May 1971, heavy selling of US dollars in the European foreign-exchange markets, fed by speculative "Eurodollar" credit-creation, forced an upward valuation of the German mark and brought a windfall to the banks who had sold dollars to buy marks. In July and early August 1971, amidst another wave of dollar selling, there was a kind of "run" on the US dollar as British and French monetary authorities asked the United States to convert hundreds of millions in dollar claims into gold (whose official price remained at $35 per ounce).[9] It was probably inevitable by then that the US government would suspend the dollar's convertibility into gold, but the actual announcement of this was nonetheless a shock. For domestic US audiences, the most salient part of President Richard Nixon's nationally televised speech on the evening of Sunday, August 15, 1971 was his ordering of a ninety-day freeze on wages, prices, and rents. These were the first US wage and price controls since the Korean War. They were in fact a classic wartime emergency measure (though not described as such) responding to a wartime inflation at a moment when well over 100,000 US troops remained in Vietnam. Nixon's simultaneous suspension of the dollar's convertibility into gold was also a classic wartime measure, reminiscent of President Woodrow Wilson's suspension of gold convertibility fifty-four years earlier during World War I.[10] Now, however, the suspension was permanent, and

---

[8]   Shigeru Akita, "The Green Revolution in India, the World Bank, and the oil crises in the 1970s—focusing on chemical fertilizer problems," this volume.

[9]   James L. Butkiewicz and Scott Ohlmacher, "Ending Bretton Woods: evidence from the Nixon tapes," *Economic History Review* 74(4) (2021): 922–45; Paul A. Volcker and Toyoo Gyohten, *Changing Fortunes: The World's Money and the Threat to American Leadership* (New York: Times Books, 1992), 75–81; Francis J. Gavin, *Gold, Dollars, and Power: The Politics of International Monetary Relations, 1958-1971* (Chapel Hill: University of North Carolina Press, 2003), 194–6; Ronan Manly, "British requests for $3 billion in US Treasury gold—the trigger that closed the gold window," *BullionStar* (bullionstar.com/blogs), August 16, 2021 [accessed August 17, 2021]; George P. Shultz and Kenneth W. Dam, *Economic Policy Beyond the Headlines* (W.W. Norton, 1977), 110–15.

[10]   Simon Bytheway and Mark Metzler, *Central Banks and Gold: How Tokyo, London, and New York Shaped the Modern World* (Ithaca: Cornell University Press, 2016), 45–7, 71–3.

it ended the final vestige of the historic gold standard. Economist Robert Triffin called it "the collapse of the Bretton Woods system," though efforts to maintain the Bretton Woods principle of fixing currency exchange rates would continue for another eighteen months.[11]

The US suspension of gold convertibility set off a series of seismic readjustments of world currency values. Japan was especially affected by this "Nixon shock," which also included an emergency 10 percent surcharge on imports into the US. One could read a direct message to Japan into it, as August 15 happened to be the twenty-sixth anniversary of the Japanese surrender in World War II. Adding to the picture of systemic shifts, this is also when the international pound-sterling system finally ended, with the winding up of the Sterling Area between August 1971 and June 1972. For London banks, international lending in British pounds was largely replaced by Eurodollar lending, about which more below.[12]

Countries responded to the 1971 monetary crisis by launching a wave of national stimulus policies, which fed an internationally synchronized inflationary boom.[13] This turned out to be the finale of the long postwar boom. British industry faced a deepening structural crisis and the UK was early in experiencing "stagflation," but on the financial side there developed after 1971 "a mood of euphoria approaching mania," under the combined effects of government stimulus and easing by the Bank of England, magnified by Eurodollar credit creation.[14] The London stock market reached a speculative peak in May 1972 and the property market grew into a bubble. The United States simultaneously experienced a speculative boom in real estate investment trusts (REITs). In Japan, the "high-speed growth" boom of 1955–73 culminated in a phase of super-stimulus under Prime Minister Tanaka Kakuei's 1972 "Plan to Remodel the Japanese Archipelago," which brought a doubling of land prices.[15] Asset prices in all of these countries then deflated sharply in 1974–5. The inflationary monetary and fiscal policies of 1972 also coincided with the first of a series of supply shocks.

[11] Robert Triffin, "Gold and the dollar crisis: yesterday and tomorrow," *Essays in International Finance*, No. 132 (Department of Economics, Princeton University, 1978), p. 3.
[12] Herman van der Wee, *Prosperity and Upheaval: The World Economy 1945–1980* (University of California Press, 1986 [1984]), 491; Catherine R. Schenk, "The sterling area and economic disintegration," *Geschichte und Gesellschaft* 39(2) (2013): 177–96; P. J. Cain and A.G. Hopkins, *British Imperialism: Crisis and Deconstruction, 1914–1990* (London: Longman, 1993), 293; Carlo Edoardo Altamura, "A new dawn for European banking: the Euromarket, the oil crisis and the rise of international banking," *Zeitschrift für Unternehmensgeschichte / Journal of Business History* 60(1) (2015): 33.
[13] Philip Armstrong, Andrew Glyn, and John Harrison, *Capitalism since 1945* (Oxford: Basil Blackwell, 1991 [1984]), 215–20.
[14] E.g., *The Economist*, "Rampant stagflation," October 17, 1970, pp. 63–4. Quotation from Anthony Sampson, *The Money Lenders: Bankers and a World in Turmoil* (New York: Viking, 1982), 129–30.
[15] Japan Institute of International Affairs, *White Papers of Japan 1973–74* (Tokyo: Japan Institute of International Affairs, 1975), 190–2.

3. Dollars and Climate: The Food Price Shock Came Second

In the 1960s, a run of good harvests together with agricultural subsidies, heavy use of chemical fertilizers, and surplus production in North America and Europe brought low international crop prices and apparently general agricultural overproduction. International price-fixing arrangements were loosened in 1968, and between 1968 and 1970 wheat acreage in the US, Canada, Australia, and Argentina was reduced from 50 million to 30 million hectares, reducing wheat production from 80 million to 60 million tons. Policy turned from maintaining the largest grain stocks in previous history to a new phase of maintaining much smaller stocks.[16] Then, in the northern summer of 1972, an exceptionally strong El Niño–Southern Oscillation (ENSO) event caused droughts and bad harvests in Russia, China, India, Southeast Asia, Australia, and the Sahelian countries in Africa. Total world grain production declined by 36 million tons in 1972. The pioneering climate historian H. H. Lamb described it as the first actual drop in total world food production since World War II.[17] The El Niño also caused the collapse of the Peruvian anchovy fishery, which had become in the 1960s the world's main source of fishmeal protein for animal feed.[18]

The Soviet Union faced a large grain deficit, made worse by a domestic policy of increasing meat consumption that had led to a 40 percent increase in the use of feed grains between 1968 and 1971. In July 1972, Soviet buyers took advantage of the diplomatic détente with the United States to quietly make large, hitherto unprecedented grain purchases in US markets. In total the Soviet Union imported more than 21 million tons of grain in 1972–3 and another 9 million tons in 1973–4, a scale of purchasing that in Harriet Friedmann's judgment "tipped the balance of the international food order."[19] It also set off a US agricultural boom. From mid-1972, Japanese general trading companies were also buying up commodities overseas and stockpiling them, encouraged by the Japanese government which sought to reduce Japan's net trade surplus and hold down the value of the yen against the dollar.

In Southeast Asia, the severe ENSO drought of 1972 abruptly reversed recent optimism over the "Green Revolution" in rice farming, and in April 1973 Thailand, Asia's largest rice exporter, restricted its rice exports in order to assure food security at home. "For a very scary nine months, there was no world rice market," in Peter Timmer's words.[20] When Thai rice exports fully resumed in January 1974 they were priced four times higher than before the embargo. In Cambodia, harvest failures interacted with

---

[16]   Friedmann, "Political economy of food," p. S275.
[17]   H. H. Lamb, *Climate, History and the Modern World* (Methuen, 1982), 307; John A. Schnittker, "The 1972–73 food price spiral," *Brookings Papers on Economic Activity* 2 (1973): 498–500.
[18]   César N. Caviedes, "El Niño 1972: its climatic, ecological, human, and economic implications," *Geographical Review* 65(4) (1975): 493–509; Gregory Ferguson-Cradler, "Fisheries' collapse and the making of a global event, 1950s–1970s," *Journal of Global History* 13 (2018): 399–424; Kristin A. Wintersteen, *The Fishmeal Revolution: The Industrialization of the Humboldt Current Ecosystem* (Berkeley: University of California Press, 2021), chapter 5.
[19]   Lyle P. Schertz, "World food: prices and the poor," *Foreign Affairs* 52(3) (1974): 513–14; Friedmann "Political economy of food," S249, S272–3.
[20]   C. Peter Timmer, "Reflections on food crises past," *Food Policy* 35 (2010): 2.

war in an extremely vicious cycle. In newly independent Bangladesh, famine took the lives of tens of thousands of people who depended on market sources of food. Many tens of thousands of people who depended on local food supplies in Ethiopia and the West African Sahel starved to death.[21]

Coming in an already inflationary monetary context, these supply shortfalls and massive buying operations caused international grain prices to increase by nearly four times between late 1972 and early 1974.[22] Notably, this was the same magnitude by which oil prices would subsequently increase between late 1973 and early 1974.

Negative price shocks for some were positive price shocks for others. World prices of primary commodities of all kinds more or less doubled in the year that preceded the October 1973 oil shock. This was the biggest terms-of-trade shift in favor of primary commodity producers since the Korean War—and, "for the first time since the Korean War rising food prices were a major factor in fueling the world's rate of inflation."[23] For US farmers, this was the beginning of a "golden age" comparable to the farm boom of the 1910s.[24] The same was true for US coal miners and for agriculture and mining in other countries. India as a commodity importing country was squeezed by high prices, but most Latin American, African, and Southeast Asian countries looked to be in a newly advantageous position. As Angus Hone judged it, on the eve of the oil shock, "the trade prospects for the developing world are thus considerably better in 1973 than they were in 1951 or even in 1960. The balance of advantage has shifted toward the primary producers."[25] Or so it seemed at the time.

4. By Now, Overdetermined: The Oil Shock Came Third

The year 1973 opened with a series of international political and economic shifts. The Paris peace agreement between the United States and North Vietnam was signed on January 27, 1973. Two weeks before that, President Nixon had lifted most US wage and price controls. For Americans the war was ending, and there was a great mood shift. There was also a new round of heavy dollar selling on the foreign exchanges, which forced West German authorities to impose emergency foreign-exchange controls on February 3. Authorities in Tokyo put an emergency stop to foreign-exchange trading on February 9, and then on February 12 came the general closure of European foreign-

---

[21] Amartya Sen, *Poverty and Famines: An Essay on Entitlement and Deprivation* (Delhi: Oxford University Press, 1981 [reprint, 1999]). Christian Gerlach suggests a much higher number of deaths ("Famine Responses in the World Food Crisis 1972–5 and the World Food Conference of 1974," *European Review of History—Revue européenne d'histoire* 22(6) (2015): 930).

[22] Simon Harris, "Cereals," in Cheryl Payer, ed., *Commodity Trade of the Third World* (New York: Wiley and Son, 1975), 86–8.

[23] Angus Hone, "The primary commodities boom," *New Left Review* (81) (September–October 1973): 85; Angus Hone, "World raw materials trade: trends and forecast for 1974–1980," *Economic and Political Weekly* 9(11) (March 16, 1974): 439; Richard N. Cooper and Robert Z. Lawrence, "The 1972–75 commodity boom," *Brookings Papers on Economic Activity* (3) (1975): 671–723. Quotation from Harris, "Cereals," 79.

[24] Wendong Zhang and Kristine Tidgren, "The current farm downturn vs the 1920s and 1980s farm crises: an economic and regulatory comparison," *Agricultural Finance Review* 78(4) (2018): 396–411.

[25] Hone, "Primary commodities" (quotation from 92); Hone, "World raw materials."

exchange markets. On February 13, the US dollar was devalued by a further 10 percent relative to gold and major currencies.[26] US stock markets turned down sharply on February 15, and financial speculation turned all the more to currencies and to primary commodities. Free-market gold prices soared. In the UK, a great strike wave was simultaneously underway in reaction to the government's anti-inflationary austerity program.

Dollar selling intensified in the last week of February, forcing Japanese, European, and London foreign-exchange markets to close again on March 2. This was the end of efforts to maintain the fixed exchange-rate system of the Bretton Woods era. On March 12, West Germany, France, Belgium, Luxemburg, and the Netherlands agreed to peg their currencies to each other and jointly float them against the dollar and other currencies. This was supported by the Bank of Japan. When the European foreign exchanges reopened March 19 this "floating" system went into operation—seemingly a temporary expedient, it was in fact the inauguration of a new international monetary order. It was also a major step toward the establishment of a common European currency twenty-six years later. On March 27, the G20 finance ministers and central bank governors effectively approved these new arrangements. The German mark, which anchored this floating "currency snake," rose in early 1973 to more than 70 percent above its pre-1969 par value while the Japanese yen rose more than 25 percent above its old pre-1971 par.[27]

These post-Vietnam War monetary shifts—though they are rarely analyzed as "postwar" events—coincided with geopolitical shifts. On March 29, North Vietnam released remaining US prisoners of war and the last US combat troops left South Vietnam. The easing of "East–West" relations included the normalization of Japan's diplomatic relations with the People's Republic of China, also in March, and the normalization of West Germany's relations with communist-ruled East Germany and Czechoslovakia in May.

There were simultaneous rumblings in the international oil trade, happening against the background of nationalization or quasi-nationalization of foreign petroleum operations by Algeria and Libya in 1971–3, by Iraq in 1972–3, and by Iran in early 1973. On May 15, 1973, Libya, Iraq, Kuwait, and Algeria jointly made a temporary demonstrative halt to their oil shipments to Western countries, to protest their support for Israel. The devaluation of the US dollar also created its own pressures by devaluing the large dollar holdings of oil-exporting states, above all Saudi Arabia.

In the summer of 1973 came a more substantive export embargo—by the United States. As a knock-on effect of the 1972 fishmeal shock, the prices of soybeans and other oilseeds used for livestock feed tripled in early 1973, causing meat prices to soar. At the end of March 1973, President Nixon ordered new price controls on beef, pork, and lamb. Then on June 27, Nixon ordered a surprise embargo on the export of soybean

---

[26] *Current History*, 1973, various issues; Harold James, *International Monetary Cooperation Since Bretton Woods* (Washington, DC: International Monetary Fund/New York: Oxford University Press, 1996), 241–2.

[27] Van der Wee, *Prosperity and Upheaval*, 491–3; James, *International Monetary Cooperation*, 242–3; *Current History*, various issues.

and cottonseed products. The United States then supplied more than 90 percent of the world's soybean exports, and Japan was the biggest importer. In July the US government widened its export restrictions to include oil seeds in general, animal fats, edible oils, livestock feed, and scrap metal. This new "Nixon shock" also induced a coordinated push by Japan's government and general trading companies to develop an export-oriented soybean farming sector in Brazil, driving forward Brazil's modern soybean boom.[28]

Then came the oil shock. On October 6, 1973, Egypt and Syria launched the fourth Arab-Israeli war with Saudi foreknowledge and cooperation. Arab oil embargoes during the wars of 1956 and 1967 had been ineffective because the United States could serve as the world's petroleum supplier of last resort. The rapid increase of US oil imports after 1971 changed the balance. On October 17, 1973 members of the Organization of Arab Petroleum Exporting Countries (OAPEC) declared an embargo of oil exports to the United States and other countries that supported Israel.[29] The fighting ended on October 25 with another Israeli victory. This brief regional war, coming when and where it did, had global economic effects. The oil embargo continued, with modifications, into early 1974. Simultaneously OPEC, acting as a whole, raised oil prices from just under $3/bbl before the war to nearly $12/bbl in early 1974.[30] Within a span of weeks, oil prices thus went from lagging the inflationary price revolution to leading it.

The generalized supply-side effects were profound. Petroleum fueled transportation by land, sea, and air. Oil-fired power plants generated one-fourth of world electric power. Petroleum, with natural gas, was a basic feedstock to the petrochemical industry, so the oil shock was also a petrochemical shock and a fertilizer shock particularly. World fertilizer prices increased by four or five times between 1972 and 1974. For India, notwithstanding a good monsoon and good harvest in 1973, the food-price pressure of 1972–3 thus continued, as discussed in Shigeru Akita's contribution to this volume. Coal and natural gas prices also surged. World grain prices soared to new peaks in 1974. Sugar prices quintupled. There was panic buying of toilet paper in Japan and elsewhere as shortage psychology spread in pandemic fashion.[31]

For the already-industrialized countries, the oil shock triggered the first of a series of major industrial recessions. In fifty years' retrospect, we can see also that it marked a limit in the trajectory of heavy industrialization in those countries. For Japan, which

[28] Saburo Okita, "Natural resource dependency and Japanese foreign policy," *Foreign Affairs* 52(4) (1974): 714–24; Michael Hudson, *Super Imperialism: The Origin and Fundamentals of U.S. World Dominance* (second edition, Pluto Press, 2003 [first edition, 1972]), 370; Raj Patel, *Stuffed and Starved: The Hidden Battle for the World Food System* (Portobello Books/Melville House Publishing, 2007), 180–4.

[29] Joe Stork, "Oil and the international crisis," *MERIP Reports* (32) (November 1974): 3–20, 34; Rüdiger Graf, "Making use of the 'oil weapon': western industrialized countries and Arab petropolitics in 1973–74," *Diplomatic History* 36(1) (2012): 185–208.

[30] Very roughly, one could translate these numbers into 2022 dollars by adding another zero. Oil prices in the late 2010s were around $50/bbl and in 2022 were closer to $100/bbl.

[31] Akita, "Green Revolution" (this volume); Eiko Maruko Siniawer, "'Toilet paper panic': uncertainty and insecurity in early 1970s Japan," *American Historical Review* (June 2021): 530–54.

after 1955 had boomed more than any other country, the year 1973 was the all-time peak in the sheer mass of material resources used per capita and the beginning of a gradual lightening of per capita material use that has continued to the present.[32] The year 1973 thus stands out in an ecological-economic view also.

5. 1973 as Historical Watershed

Big thoughts on the epochal character of the shifts of the 1970s began early in the decade. Appearing soon after domestic oil production peaked in the United States, the Club of Rome's 1972 *Limits to Growth* report gained international attention for its computer-modeled argument that world industrialization was overshooting its resource base and faced collapse in the twenty-first century. This was part of a public intellectual moment. The Sierra Club-sponsored bestseller *The Population Bomb* (Paul and Anne Ehrlich, 1968) predicted mass starvation in the 1970s. A "whole earth" message of restraint and downsizing was spread by other bestsellers like *Diet for a Small Planet* (Frances Moore Lappé, 1971), which criticized the livestock-industrial complex, and *Small is Beautiful* (E. F. Schumacher, 1973), which advocated a Buddhist-inspired economics. These ideas were powerful narrative-makers and might be considered secular versions of the story told by the even bigger US bestseller *The Late Great Planet Earth* (Hal Lindsey, 1970 and later editions), which read current events in the Middle East and Europe as signs that the biblical Book of Revelations was now playing out in real time. The great Japanese bestseller of 1974 was the disaster story *Japan Sinks* (*Nippon chinbotsu*, by Komatsu Sakyō, 1973). Closer to the subject of the current chapter was the idea that the world capitalist system had now entered its late phase, as presented by Ernest Mandel (*Der Spätkapitalismus*, 1972; published in English as *Late Capitalism* in 1975).

Mandel's account was notable for rehabilitating in Marxist terms the idea of economic long waves formulated by N. D. Kondratiev in the 1920s and extended by Joseph Schumpeter and by Mandel's countryman Léon Dupriez among others.[33] Dupriez in 1978 returned to this theme and interpreted "1972–74 as the focal point in a decisive turn of the long wave," an upper turning point comparable to 1920, or 1872, or 1818. (These are dates to be noted again below.) He thought that the dynamics of

[32] Fridolin Krausmann, Simone Gingrich, and Reza Nourbakhch-Sabet, "The metabolic transition in Japan: a material flow account for the period 1878 to 2005," *Journal of Industrial Ecology* 15 (2011): 877–92; Dominik Wiedenhofer, Elena Rovenskaya, Willi Haas, Fridolin Krausmann, Irene Pallua, Marina Fischer-Kowalski, "Is there a 1970s syndrome? Analyzing structural breaks in the metabolism of industrial economies," *Energy Procedia* 40 (2013): 182–91; Mark Metzler, "Japan: the arc of industrialization," in Laura Hein, ed., *The New Cambridge History of Japan, Volume III* (Cambridge University Press, 2023), 293–337.

[33] Ernest Mandel, *Late Capitalism*, transl. Joris De Bres (London: NLB, 1975 [revised edition of *Der Spätkapitalismus*, 1972]); N. D. Kondratjew [Kondratiev], "Die langen Wellen der Konjunktur," *Archiv für Sozialwissenschaft und Sozialpolitik* 56(3) (1926): 573–609, partially translated by W. F. Stolper as "The long waves in economic life," *Review of Economics and Statistics* 17(6) (November 1935): 105–15. Schumpeter's statement came in his 1,000-page book *Business Cycles* in 1939; that of Dupriez in *Des mouvements économiques généraux* in 1947.

credit creation were fundamental to these movements.[34] Writing in 1977, the radical economist David M. Gordon extended Schumpeter's idea that these long waves reflected a succession of technical-industrial revolutions, arguing that the long international boom of the 1950s and 1960s had been sustained by a specific "social structure of accumulation" based on an oligopolistic capital–labor settlement and supported by cheap oil; this system reached a point of crisis in 1973 and was now dissolving.[35] This view is substantially similar to that of the French "Regulation" school, "all of [whose] members have reached the same conclusion, ... [that] *the break with previous economic trends after 1973* derived from the *crisis of Fordism* as an economic, social, and technical principle of organization," in Robert Boyer's words.[36]

Political and cultural tendencies that we think of as part of "the sixties" also reached an initial limit in 1972–3, and later analyses have continued to see that moment as a temporal watershed. Historian Judith Stein, for instance, called the US presidential election of November 1972 "the last election of the 1960s,"[37] while the "seventies" presidencies of Gerald Ford (August 1974–January 1977) and Jimmy Carter (January 1977–January 1981) had a strongly in-between or interregnal character. In Japan, to take another instance, the leftwing movement in general and the new "women's lib" movement particularly peaked in the first years of the 1970s and faded quickly after 1972, to be replaced by a conservative counter-movement after 1977.[38] Considering cultural and intellectual styles, the literary historian Fredric Jameson also identified 1973 as a point of systemic transition associated with the fading of 1960s liberation movements and the end of the long postwar boom. The urban theorist David Harvey later discerned a "sea-change" in cultural and political-economic practices "since around 1972," a "cusp in intellectual and cultural history when something called 'postmodernism' emerged." Jameson linked that idea to Mandel's theory by describing postmodernism as "the cultural logic of late capitalism."[39] Postmodernism is well to the side of the present story, but the idea of a comprehensive turning point in systemic functioning is at the heart of it. The shifting of the international monetary regime deserves special attention.

[34] Léon Dupriez, "1974 a downturn of the long wave?" *Banca Nazionale del Lavoro Quarterly Review* 31 (September 1978): 199–210. For two of those earlier turning points, see Mark Metzler, "The correlation of crises, 1918–20," in Urs Matthias Zachmann, ed., *Asia after Versailles: Asian Perspectives on the Paris Peace Conference and the Interwar Order, 1919–33* (Edinburgh University Press, 2017), 23–54, and Mark Metzler, "Japan and the world conjuncture of 1866," in Robert Hellyer and Harald Fuess, eds., *The Meiji Restoration: Japan as a Global Nation* (Cambridge University Press, 2020), 15–39.

[35] David M. Gordon, "Up and down the long roller coaster," in Crisis Reader Editorial Collective, ed., *U.S. Capitalism in Crisis* (New York: Union for Radical Political Economics, 1978), esp. 32–4.

[36] Robert Boyer, *The Regulation School: A Critical Introduction*, transl. Craig Charney (New York: Columbia University Press, 1990), 25, my emphasis.

[37] Judith Stein, *Pivotal Decade: How the United States Traded Factories for Finance in the 70s* (New Haven: Yale University Press, 2011), chapter 3.

[38] Ochiai Emiko, *The Japanese Family System in Transition: A Sociological Analysis of Family Change in Postwar Japan* (Tokyo: LTCB International Library Foundation, 1996 [1994]), 85–99; Jean-Marie Bouissou, *Japan: The Burden of Success* (Boulder: Lynne Rienner, 2002), chapter 5.

[39] Fredric Jameson, "Periodizing the 60s," *Social Text*, No. 9/10, The 60's without Apology (Spring-Summer, 1984): 178–209; David Harvey, *The Condition of Postmodernity: An Enquiry into the Origins of Cultural Change* (Cambridge, MA: Blackwell, 1990), vii, 1, 4.

6. Credit Fix: The Eurodollar Lending Boom

With the quadrupling of oil prices, "petrodollar" purchasing power in the hands of developing-country oil exporters jumped from about $30 billion (BN) in 1973 to more than $100BN in 1974, and the need to "recycle" these funds seemed acute to economic policymakers in the industrialized countries. The term *recycling* can also be misleading, for more than a recirculation of already-existing dollars, this was a matter of newly created dollar claims. "The explosion of oil prices," Robert Triffin explained in 1978, was "financed by a corresponding explosion of international financing, mostly by commercial banks"—that explosion began before the oil shock and involved dollar-credit-creation by "offshore" banks. Stated simply, "*petrodollars are Eurodollars*," as Murau, Rini, and Haas put it.[40]

Eurodollar lending, meaning the unregulated creation of new US-dollar means of payment by private banks outside of the United States, is fundamental here. The viewpoint of the present chapter agrees with that of Murau, Rini, and Haas (2020), that in a historical view of successive international monetary regimes, the Bretton Woods system was replaced after 1973 by a new "Offshore US-Dollar System."[41] The term *offshore dollars* is a synonym for the 1970s term *Eurodollars*, and "Eurocurrency" or "Euromoney" means offshore money (not to be confused with Europe's Euro currency created in 1999).[42] It took time for this privatized offshore-dollar system to be recognized as a system, and its operations and dimensions have remained mysterious. Its centrality and its hiddenness were revealed most dramatically in the global financial crisis that followed the "Lehman shock" of 2008, as noted in the conclusion to this chapter. When we look back to the early 1970s, we are therefore looking back to the origin the present international monetary regime with its manifest tendencies toward crises on a world scale.

From its origins early in the Cold War, Eurodollar banking was a device for evading the oversight of the US government. Offshore US dollar credits were created above all in London, especially by large US banks operating out of their London branches, and the "Euromarket" was dominated by a few very large banks.[43] By 1970, total

[40] Triffin, "Gold and the dollar crisis," 10–11; Steffen Murau, Joe Rini, and Armin Haas, "The evolution of the offshore US-dollar system: past, present and four possible futures," *Journal of Institutional Economics* 16 (2020): 773, my italics.

[41] Murau, Rini, and Haas, "Evolution"; Steffen Murau, "Offshore Dollar Creation and the Emergence of the post-2008 International Monetary System," IASS Discussion Paper, Institute for Advanced Sustainability Studies, Potsdam, 2018. See also Ikuto Yamaguchi, "Privatisation of international development finance: oil-money, emerging Euro-dollar market and developing countries in the 1970s," this volume; Carlo Edoardo Altamura, *European Banks and the Rise of International Finance: The Post-Bretton Woods Era* (Abingdon: Routledge, 2017); Jeffry Frieden, *Banking on the World: The Politics of American International Finance* (New York: Harper & Row, 1987), chapter 4. Paul Einzig in *The Euro-dollar System* (1964 and several later editions) gave a series of approbatory treatments, and *Euromoney* magazine (since 1969) publishes from the standpoint of market participants.

[42] To say *offshore dollars* as opposed to *Eurodollars* is also less confusing to audiences of people other than monetary historians. The present chapter uses the two terms interchangeably.

[43] Catherine R. Schenk, "The origins of the Eurodollar market in London: 1955–1963," *Explorations in Economic History* 35 (1998): 221–38; Marcello de Cecco, "Inflation and structural change in the Euro-dollar market," EUI Working Paper No. 23 (Florence: European University Institute Department of Economics, August 1982), 31; Miguel S. Wionczek et al., *LDC External Debt and the World Economy* (Colegio de México, Center for Economic and Social Studies of the Third World, 1978), 76–7.

Eurocurrency (mainly Eurodollar) lending by European based banks already came to an estimated $105BN. By 1972, it had grown to $183BN.[44] Warnings were made at the time. Euromarket lending was "*a new dollar creating mechanism of great power*"— these were the words of Federal Reserve chair Arthur Burns in May 1971, in closed-door conversation with his fellow G10 central bankers where he spoke more frankly about private money creation than central bankers speak in public.[45] In 1972, the economist Fritz Machlup described "the manufacturing of US dollars in Europe"— that is, "*dollar creation by lending activities of commercial banks in Europe*"—as a case of unregulated "stateless money." Machlup, a friend and countryman of Joseph Schumpeter, shared Schumpeter's clear-eyed view of the way that banks create money by the act of lending it, a process that Machlup once described as "monetary witchcraft."[46] When banks created new Eurocurrency balances, they were also free of the reserve requirements that limited their domestic credit creation. Machlup guessed that the extent of leverage in Eurodollar operations was 80 percent, versus a guess by Milton Friedman that it was more like 97 percent.[47] No one really knew. This was the magic bag that would fund the wave of international credit creation in 1973–82.

European central banks facilitated this process and actually had a leading role in the expansion of the Euromarkets in 1971–3, in effect priming the pump for the next phase in which "petrodollars" had a leading part. There were also official efforts, particularly by the German authorities, to regulate the Eurodollar system and institute the kinds of reserve requirements that banks were subject to in their domestic lending. British representatives resisted this, reflecting the standpoint of London-based banks.[48] Machlup in 1972 noted also that even central bankers who utilized the Eurodollar markets saw only parts of the whole and were repeatedly surprised by the unanticipated consequences of their own actions. One example is seen in the way the Euromarkets funded speculation in the foreign-exchange markets. Machlup further foresaw that the central banks would have to bail out their client private banks in the event of a crisis. This is what happened in the summer of 1974, on a scale of hundreds of millions of dollars. It happened repeatedly after 1982 on a scale of billions, and then on a scale of trillions in the global financial crisis of 2008.

The oil price hikes suddenly worsened the balance of payments of European oil-importing countries, putting them into a potentially deflationary and depressionary

[44] Carlo Edoardo Altamura, "The paradox of the 1970s: the renaissance of international banking and the rise of public debt," *Journal of Modern European History* 15(4) (2017): 536, citing BIS estimates.
[45] Quoted in Altamura, *European Banks*, 90, my italics.
[46] Fritz Machlup, "The Eurodollar system and its control," in American Enterprise Institute for Public Policy Research, *International Monetary Problems* (Washington, DC: American Enterprise Institute for Public Policy Research, 1972), 3–63, my italics; Fritz Machlup, "Forced or induced saving: an exploration into its synonyms and homonyms," *Review of Economics and Statistics* 25(1) (1943): 26–39; Metzler, *Capital as Will and Imagination*, 36–61 for the larger question of credit-money creation.
[47] Milton Friedman, "The Euro-dollar market: some first principles" (Federal Reserve Bank of St. Louis, July 1971), 16–24; also De Cecco, "Inflation."
[48] Altamura, *European Banks*, 35–8, 89–98; William Glenn Gray, "Learning to 'recycle': petrodollars and the West, 1973–5," in Elisabetta Bini, Giuliano Garavini, and Federico Romero, eds., *Oil Shock: The 1973 Crisis and its Economic Legacy* (I. B. Tauris, 2016), 172–97.

situation. Conscious policy decisions were taken not to deflate. Thus, IMF Managing Director H. J. Witteveen in early May 1974 stated that the normal response to a deficit in a nation's balance of payments would be "internal deflation, or import restraint" but said this was not appropriate in the case of petroleum imports.[49] The main policy response was instead to rely on the Euromarkets—a choice, in effect, for adjustment via private, bank-generated credit inflation. Debate over imposing reserve requirements was tacitly shelved. In the first phase of this process in 1974, the biggest new Eurocurrency credits actually went to Japan and to European countries including the UK and France.[50] Like the acceptance of floating rates a year earlier, this de facto handing off of the business to the international private banks was now a kind of default policy response. It was also in harmony with early bubblings of neoliberal economic thinking, which in many ways was applied first in the field of international finance.[51]

The first serious banking crisis of the new offshore-dollar era began in London in December 1973, when the Bank of England quietly brought the big London banks together in a "lifeboat" operation to bail out and restructure the smaller "secondary" banks.[52] Bank crises began also in the United States. In June–July 1974, there was an open Euromarket crisis with the failures of Bankhaus Herstatt and the Italian banks associated with Michele Sindona including Franklin National Bank in New York state, which had become a center of trans-Atlantic dark-money operations. The European central banks quietly stepped in to offer informal lender-of-last-resort assurances in September 1974. The US Federal Reserve, in Hyman Minsky's words, "by 'paying off' all of Franklin National Bank's Eurodollar liabilities before closing the bank,... implicitly underwrote the bank liabilities of all American banks in the Eurodollar market." In November 1974, the Bank of England was directly bailing out London banks.[53]

These banking crises caused new Eurodollar credit creation temporarily to decline in late 1974. Recession in Europe and the United States also induced European and US banks to seek other, more profitable places to invest. Supported by high commodity prices, economic growth for the developing middle-income countries as a whole continued to be strong.[54] High commodity prices also promoted talk of producers' cartels on the model of OPEC and of a "New International Economic Order" based on

---

Altamura, "New dawn," 35–6; Altamura, *European Banks*, 101–3. Yamaguchi, "Privatisation" (this volume) refers to discussions within the OECD on this same point.

Gerald A. Pollack, "Are the oil-payments deficits manageable?," *Essays in International Finance*, (International Finance Section, Department of Economics, Princeton University, 1975), 3–5; Altamura, *European Banks*, 100–2; Simone Selva, *Before the Neoliberal Turn: The Rise of Energy Finance and the Limits to US Foreign Policy* (London: Palgrave Macmillan, 2017), 241; Simone Selva, "Recycling OPEC oil revenues and resurrecting the dollar, and the US international payments position in American foreign policy, 1970–1975," *Federal History* (2020): 29–52.

Helleiner, *States*, 115–22.

Margaret Reid, "The secondary banking crisis—five years on," *The Banker* 128 (December 1978): 21–30.

Sampson, *Money Lenders*, 130–9; R.T. Naylor, *Hot Money and the Politics of Debt* (third edition, McGill-Queen's University Press, 2004), 51–4; Altamura, *European Banks*, 109–10; Hyman P. Minsky, "Financial markets and economic instability, 1965–1980," *Nebraska Journal of Economics & Business* 20(4) (1981): 9.

Miles Kahler, "Politics and international debt: explaining the crisis," *International Organization* 39(3) (1985): 20; Carlos Ominami, "North-south relations in the 1980s: the return of imperialism?" *International Journal of Political Economy* 18(4) (1988/9): 80–112.

third-world commodity sovereignty, as called for in the UN General Assembly's resolution of May 1, 1974.[55] This new economic order did not materialize, but for a few years the new offshore-dollar system did funnel new spending power to a substantial subset of developing countries. In the longer run, this extension of credit came to appear more as a kind of neocolonial Trojan horse.

In 1975, Eurodollar lending to developing countries surged, now featuring "jumbo" loans of over $100 million. In 1976, it exceeded lending to the industrialized countries. Especially big loans went to Mexico and Brazil, which in the 1970s came to be considered, with Taiwan and South Korea, as part of a cohort of "newly industrializing countries." This lending exploded in 1977 and 1978, with some individual "jumbo loans" now as large as $1BN.[56] By this point, the "offshore" banking operations of many US banks were also a legal fiction, supposedly conducted through offshore offices in places like the Bahamas but actually done out of banks' own back offices in the United States.[57]

For borrowing countries, private Eurocurrency loans were free of the spending restrictions and other political and economic conditions that were attached to official loans. High inflation also meant that real interest rates (interest rates minus inflation rates) were low in the mid-1970s. The international banks reduced their own risk of losses on these loans by joining with other banks to syndicate loans, by setting up new specialized consortium banks, and, crucially, by structuring large long-term loans as roll-over credits with floating interest rates that were reset every few months.[58]

All of this seemed innovatory at the time, but lending to the world's "peripheral" commodity-exporting countries had a much longer, highly episodic history. The previous great international lending wave had been in the 1920s; it ended with the defaults of most countries of Eastern Europe and Latin America in the 1930s.[59] US banks did not return to lending to Latin America for thirty or more years after that, when the disasters of the 1930s were beyond the memory of all but the oldest generation of financiers. In fact, a conspicuous feature of the new cohort of international bankers was their youth and inexperience: "The more loans the banks made, the faster middle management passed into the hands of the baby-boom generation."[60]

[55] Dane Kennedy, "The oil crises as fulcrum for the rise and fall of the Third World project," this volume; Joan Edelman Spero, *The Politics of International Economic Relations* (fourth edition, New York: St. Martin's Press, 1990), 286–98; Andre Gunder Frank, *Crisis: In the World Economy* (New York: Holmes & Meier Publishers, 1980), 263–304.

[56] Wionczek et al., *LDC External Debt*, 72–5; Altamura, *European Banks*, 113–20; and for an engaging firsthand account, S. C. Gwynne, *Selling Money* (New York: Penguin, 1986).

[57] Gwynne, *Selling Money*, 75–8, 82–5; Donald D. Hester, *The Evolution of Monetary Policy and Banking in the US* (Springer, 2008), 74.

[58] Stephany Griffith-Jones, *International Finance and Latin America* (Routledge [reissue], 2014 [orig. 1984]), 44–5; Altamura, *European Banks*, 104–6; Sebastian Alvarez, *Mexican Banks and Foreign Finance: From Internationalization to Financial Crisis, 1973-1982* (Palgrave Macmillan, 2019), 12–23.

[59] Ilse Schueller Mintz, *Deterioration in the Quality of Foreign Bonds Issued in the United States, 1920–1930* (New York: National Bureau of Economic Research, 1951).

[60] Gwynne, *Selling Money*, 16.

Total annual capital flows of all kinds to developing countries increased from $9.5BN in 1970, when most of it was official aid and foreign direct investment, to a peak of $69BN in 1982, with the increase due almost entirely to private Eurodollar lending. US banks alone used the new Eurodollar facilities to lend a total $480BN to developing countries between 1973 and 1982. Of this, $300BN went to Latin America. Total foreign debt of all kinds owed by developing countries increased to $600BN.[61] By 1978 the excessive production of dollar means of payment was also bringing on a new round of US dollar depreciation. This in turn provoked a strong restorationist response.

7. The Second Dollar Crisis and the Second Commodities-and-oil Shock

The US presidential administration of Jimmy Carter, inaugurated in January 1977, was the most "globalist" yet, and it promoted a kind of international Keynesianism. President Carter himself, and almost all of his leading officials, were members of the Trilateral Commission organized by David Rockefeller in July 1973. Part of the novelty of this "trilateral" initiative was its inclusion of Japan in a hitherto "Atlanticist" club.[62] The Carter administration also returned to a policy of letting the dollar slide. In 1978, the slide turned into a dive, yielding a new dollar crisis that finally forced the United States to begin doing some of the adjusting.

In the 1975–8 lull between the two oil shocks, oil prices remained stable at around $13 or $14 per barrel. This was a historically high level, but relative to the ongoing inflation in the prices of other goods, oil prices were actually falling back. For oil exporters, the inflation and dollar depreciation of 1977 thus seemed to repeat the situation of 1971–3. Now, however, the economic slowdown in Europe restrained the demand for oil, while new non-OPEC oil production increased in the North Sea after 1975 and in Alaska's North Slope and Mexico's new offshore fields after 1977. Even China and Malaysia briefly emerged as oil suppliers.[63] By 1978, current-account balances of the biggest Persian Gulf oil exporting countries had shrunk nearly to pre-oil shock levels. For all the OPEC countries together, current-account surpluses fluctuated as follows:[64]

1973	1974	1975	1976	1977	1978	1979	1980
$7 BN	$68 BN	$35 BN	$40 BN	$30 BN	$2 BN	$69 BN	$114 BN

---

[61] Barbara Stallings, "The role of foreign capital in economic development," in Gary Gereffi and Donald L. Wyman, eds., *Manufacturing Miracles: Paths of Industrialization in Latin America and East Asia* (Princeton University Press, 1990), 66; Griffith-Jones, *International Finance*, chapter 5; World Bank, *World Debt Tables, 1992–93, External Finance for Developing Countries* (two volumes, Washington, DC: World Bank, 1992), 3.

[62] Stein, *Pivotal Decade*, 158–75; Kazuhiko Yago, "Before the 'locomotive' runs: the impact of the 1973–1974 oil shock on Japan and the international financial system," *Financial History Review* 27(3) (2020): 418–35.

[63] Kazushi Minami, "The global energy crises and China's oil diplomacy, 1973–1983," this volume; Shigeru Sato, "Industrialization in Southeast Asia and the oil triangle: the cases of Malaysia and Singapore," this volume.

[64] Altamura, "Paradox of the 1970s," citing IMF data.

Here too the year 1978 stands out, as a collective OPEC surplus of $30BN in 1977 fell to only $2BN.

Simultaneously another imbalance in international payments was building up, as Japanese industrial growth recovered after 1975, now led by exports of fuel-efficient automobiles, lightweight consumer electronic goods, and the world's most energy-efficient production of steel. Japan's trade surpluses with the US, Canada, and Western Europe grew from $2BN annually in 1973–5 to more than $10BN in 1977. From Japan's side, these higher export earnings continued to be balanced by heavy payments for imported oil, creating an *"oil triangle"* between Japan, the Middle East, and the Western industrialized countries, which now became the world's largest multilateral settlement mechanism.[65]

As the dollar slid against other currencies in late 1977, OPEC members considered whether to shift their oil pricing from dollars to Special Drawing Rights (SDRs) or a basket of currencies. This talk grew in early 1978. In the Eurobond market, investors now wanted bonds denominated in German marks. Central banks and governments including those of Venezuela and Saudi Arabia quietly moved more of their currency reserves out of dollars.[66] Dollar selling intensified, boosting daily foreign-exchange trading to the historic high volumes last seen in early 1973. In October 1978 the dollar fell to its lowest level of the decade against the Japanese yen (¥190 to the dollar, down from ¥300 at the end of 1975). In the seven years since August 1971, the dollar had thus lost nearly half its value against the Japanese yen. The US dollar/German mark and US dollar/Swiss franc exchange rates moved similarly but with even greater amplitude.

This great depreciation of the US dollar is not usually described as a *partial default* on US external debts, but from the standpoint of holders of US dollars, that effectively is what it was.

Again commodity prices surged. World wheat and rice prices traced a saddle-shaped peak in the 1970s, first surging to historic highs in 1972–4, then falling back in 1976–7 to some 50 percent below their 1974 highs, and then surging again. This second sharp increase started in early 1978. By 1980, wheat and rice prices were back nearly to their 1974 highs.[67] The autumn of 1978 was also an interim low point for the real price of oil.

At this critical point, the US government reversed course and asked Japan and Germany to help support the dollar. The resulting international dollar "rescue package"

[65] Kaoru Sugihara, "Japan, the Middle East and the world economy: a note on the oil triangle," *Japan Forum* 4(1) (1992): 27; Kaoru Sugihara, "East Asia, Middle East and the world economy: further notes on the oil triangle," Working Paper Series No. 9, Kyoto: Afrasian Centre for Peace and Development Studies, 2006, p. 1 (I have converted yen figures into dollars at then-current exchange rates).

[66] "A European scheme to defend the dollar," *Business Week*, March 13, 1978, p. 36; "The dollar fades as a reserve currency," *Business Week*, March 20, 1978, p. 150.

[67] Jonas Joerin and Robert Joerin, "Reviewing the similarities of the 2007–08 and 1972–74 food crisis," Working paper, Swiss Federal Institute of Technology ETH Zurich, 2013, pp. 14–16; Sue Horton, "The 1974 and 2008 food price crises: déjà-vu?," Economic Research Paper: 2009-06, Laurier Centre for Economic Research & Policy Analysis, Wilfrid Laurier University, 2009; Geoffrey Bastin and John Ellis, *International Trade in Grain and the World Food Economy*, EIU Special Report No. 83 (London: Economist Intelligence Unit Ltd., 1980), Charts.

of November 1, 1978 was a watershed. The Federal Reserve raised its discount rate to the historically high level of 9.5 percent and opened big new currency swap arrangements with the German Bundesbank, the Bank of Japan, and the Swiss National Bank (SNB). The US government simultaneously promoted voluntary price and wage controls. Remarkably, it also issued "Carter bonds" denominated in Japanese yen and German marks. This was the decade's low point for the US dollar against the Japanese yen, though the low point against the German mark would not come until 1980.[68]

Simultaneously the revolution in Iran was entering its climactic phase. The rise of oil prices after 1973 helped create the conditions for revolution, as the boom engendered disruptive social changes, fueled the shah's megalomania, and pushed up the cost of living.[69] In late 1978, mass demonstrations in Iranian cities were accompanied by strikes in the oilfields that throttled back oil production. The victory of the revolutionaries in January and early February 1979 then set off an international scramble to buy oil and build inventories. Iranian oil production dropped by almost 5 million barrels per day (7 percent of world production) between October 1978 and January 1979, though most production was restored in early 1979.[70] Simultaneously, however, OPEC again raised prices, which over the course of 1979 went from around $15 to nearly $30/bbl. In absolute dollar terms, the second oil shock was thus a bigger shock than the first. The crisis was prolonged by Iraq's September 22, 1980 invasion of Iran and attempt to seize the Khuzestan oil fields, and oil prices remained around $35/bbl through 1982.

As a trend, however, OPEC was losing its control over oil prices. The years from 1970 to 1977 were in fact the moment of "peak OPEC," when OPEC's share of world oil production exceeded 50 percent. The year 1973 was actually the highest point for OPEC's share. By 1978 and 1979, OPEC's share had fallen to just less than half of world production, and it fell to less than a third in the early 1980s. International oil sales after the second oil shock tended to shift from contracted sales to the spot market, also increasing price volatility.[71]

The 1979 dollar-oil crisis thus repeated in part the pattern of the 1973 crisis: first came dollar depreciation and commodity price increases, then an apparently exogenous political crisis in the Middle East and a sudden oil price spike. Now, however, the underlying balance of forces was different. The inflationary "fix" adopted after the first oil shock no longer seemed viable in either Europe or the United States—"the difference in the international mood following the first oil shock in 1974 and the second in 1979

[68] R. Taggart Murphy, *The Weight of the Yen* (W. W. Norton, 1997), 128–9; James, *International Monetary Cooperation*, 303–6; Robert Guttmann, *How Credit Money Shapes the Economy: The United States in a Global System* (Armonk: M.E. Sharpe, 1994), 146; Van der Wee, *Prosperity and Upheaval*, 492.
[69] Robert E. Looney, "The inflationary process in prerevolutionary Iran," *Journal of Developing Areas* 19(3) (1985): 329–50; Peyman Jafari, "Reasons to revolt: Iranian oil workers in the 1970s," *International Labor and Working-Class History* (84) (Fall 2013): 195–217.
[70] Yergin, *The Prize*, chapters 33–4; James D. Hamilton, "Historical oil shocks," in Randall E. Parker and Robert M. Whaples, eds., *Routledge Handbook of Major Events in Economic History* (Routledge, 2013), 252–4.
[71] Catherine R. Schenk, *International Economic Relations Since 1945* (Routledge, 2011), 56–7; Yergin, *The Prize*, 718–24.

was in this respect striking," as London insider Andrew Shonfield wrote in 1979. In effect, authorities now chose to adjust by means of deflation and recession.[72]

As a strategic defeat for the United States, the Iranian revolution was compared to the defeat in Viet Nam. It was also described, for a time, as another 1960s-style national-liberation revolt against US imperialism, like the Nicaraguan revolution of July 1979. The dollar again fell against other currencies in January 1979 and the international dollar "rescue" initiative faltered. Gold prices spiked from $200/oz. at the beginning of 1979 to an all-time high of $875/oz. a year later. Other systemic shifts coincided. The new European Monetary System (EMS) in March 1979 linked the currencies of European Community countries to a common European Currency Unit (ECU), a step toward a single European currency that the UK opted not to join. On May 4, 1979 the Conservative party won the UK elections, making Margaret Thatcher prime minister with an avowed neoliberal and anti-inflationary agenda.

Momentous shifts were also happening in the cost of capital. The US Federal Reserve continued to increase its discount rate to historical highs, but so far these increases seemed to be tracking inflation rather than stopping it. The dollar's international primacy still seemed endangered. The really big movement began in October 1979, when the new Federal Reserve chair Paul Volcker dramatically shifted policy from targeting interest rates to targeting the money supply by controlling the level of bank reserves. This effectively raised interest rates to the highest levels in US history. A key feature of Volcker's monetary squeeze announced October 6, 1979 was the imposition of an 8 percent reserve requirement for US banks' additional borrowings including Eurodollar borrowings. Its first effect, however, was to induce an anticipatory rush of Eurodollar borrowing by US banks in London in August and September "producing one of the sharpest such expansions of credit yet seen," as net balances in the London Eurocurrency market expanded by $15BN.[73] The new policy also made interest-rate movements extremely volatile. Ultimately, interest rates on long-term US government bonds rose above 14 percent in September-October 1981 while prime US corporate bonds reached 15 percent. Interest rates on Eurodollar deposits rose from 9 percent in late 1979 to 21 percent in late 1981.[74] The floating interest rates that developing countries paid on Eurodollar loans rose to double their mid-1970s levels, to an average of 18 percent per annum in 1981.[75]

These contractionary measures finally brought US consumer price inflation down from a peak of 14 percent per annum in early 1980 to under 4 percent by the end of 1982 and partially restored the value of the US dollar. In July 1982, the Fed eased

---

[72] Andrew Shonfield, "The world economy 1979," *Foreign Affairs* 58(3) (1979): 596, 607 (quotation), 620.

[73] Hester, *Evolution of Monetary Policy*, 57–60; William Ellington, "Billions in Eurodollars were borrowed by U.S. banks before Fed credit squeeze," *Wall Street Journal*, October 19, 1979, p. 36. These reserve requirements were raised still further in April 1980, after the Carter administration put in new credit controls in March. They were ended on July 24, 1980 (Hester, *Evolution*, 61).

[74] Sidney Homer and Richard Sylla, *A History of Interest Rates* (third edition, New Brunswick, NJ: Rutgers University Press, 1991), chapter 18; Jeffry Frieden, "Classes, sectors, and foreign debt in Latin America," *Comparative Politics* 21(1) (October 1988): 1.

[75] Griffith-Jones, *International Finance*, 54–5.

substantially, ending thirty-three months of the tightest money policy in Federal Reserve history.[76] In August 1982, the international debt bubble burst.

Amid the monetary refluxes and wild speculative movements of 1979–81, there had been a last great surge of private international lending. By this point, borrowing countries were covering their existing debts by taking out short-term high-interest loans that had continually to be rolled over. Japanese and European banks now tended to supplant US banks in lending to the big developing-country borrowers. Japanese bank loans outstanding to Mexico jumped from $5BN in 1980 to $27BN in 1982, with 70 percent of that going to the private sector.[77]

The defaults began in a piecemeal way. Peru and Bolivia ran into debt-repayment crises early, in 1980. In the socialist countries of Eastern Europe, the economic squeeze was also connected to the increase in oil prices. In April 1981, Poland was unable to make its foreign debt payments, and in September Western banks halted further credits to Romania.[78] Costa Rica, Jamaica, and Senegal also defaulted in 1981.

In many places where the lending and borrowing did continue, it now looked more like financial looting, as newly created credits fed a historic wave of capital flight from borrowing countries back to lending countries. In Mexico, the biggest developing-country borrower of the decade, an estimated $30BN of new debt was taken on in 1981 and the first part of 1982. Simultaneously perhaps $20BN took flight, mostly re-routed to US banks or into US real estate. An estimated $14BN fled Venezuela during 1982 and 1983. Latin America's total external debt thus doubled in the four years between 1978 and 1982, to $331BN, while more than $100BN somehow made a round trip back to the United States.[79]

8. The Fall of Commodity Prices, the Debt Crisis, and the Great Depression of 1982

While anti-inflationary policies in the United States and Europe depressed demand, new sources of commodity supply also came online. In the spring and summer of 1980, oil prices reached their highest levels of the twentieth century at more than $38/bbl for

[76] William Greider, *Secrets of the Temple: How the Federal Reserve Runs the Country* (New York: Simon & Schuster, 1987), 505–7.

[77] Frances McCall Rosenbluth, "Japanese banks in Mexico: the role of government in private decisions," *International Journal* 46(4) (1991): 674–5.

[78] Fritz Bartel, "Fugitive leverage: commercial banks, sovereign debt, and Cold War crisis in Poland, 1980–1982," *Enterprise & Society* 18(1) (2017): 72–107; David Shirreff, "Romania tries bankers' nerves," *Euromoney* (November 1981): 15–24; also Michael De Groot, "The Soviet Union, CMEA, and the energy crisis of the 1970s," *Journal of Cold War Studies* 22(4) (2020): 4–30, and David S. Painter, "The oil crises of the 1970s and the Cold War," this volume.

[79] Frieden, "Classes, sectors," 11, 13; Jeremy Adelman, "International finance and political legitimacy: a Latin American view of the global shock," in Niall Ferguson, Charles S. Maier, Erez Manela, and Daniel J. Sargent, eds., *The Shock of the Global: The 1970s in Perspective* (Harvard University Press, 2011), 124; Albert Fishlow, "Some reflections on comparative Latin American economic performance and policy," in Tariq Banuri, ed., *Economic Liberalization: No Panacea. The Experiences of Latin America and Asia* (Oxford: Clarendon Press, 1991), 153.

West Texas Intermediate. They then began gradually to decline. At the end of 1980, prices for wheat, sugar, and other agricultural commodities reached their second great peak of the decade and then fell sharply in 1981.

For world commodity prices in general, this was the beginning of a twenty-year decline. Indebted commodity-exporting countries were now caught in a scissors effect between soaring interest rates and falling prices for their products. This was the story for commodity producers in general. US agricultural exports also reached a peak in 1981, and the farm debt crisis of the 1980s followed. In a long view, 1973–81 thus stands out as a boom era for US agriculture, comparable to the historic farm booms of 1910–19 and 2003–13.[80] For the group of Latin American countries that would have to reschedule their international debts in the 1980s, prices received for export goods declined relatively modestly in 1981 and 1982, down 7.6 percent, while the total monetary value received for exports declined 8.5 percent. Declines were much steeper for cotton (down 22 percent), Brazilian coffee (down 26 percent), and especially sugar (down 71 percent).[81]

In Mexico, companies whose revenues were mainly in Mexican pesos had been taking on debt in US dollars. Mexican banks had been borrowing in interbank markets at floating interest rates. Then in mid-1981 they were hit by a major retrenchment of US interbank lending. The situation became untenable after the 30 percent devaluation of the peso in February 1982.[82] The Mexican government's announcement on August 13, 1982 that it could not make upcoming payments on its $85BN foreign debt was the signal for a wider crisis.

By October 1983, twenty-seven countries in Latin America, Africa, and Eastern Europe could not pay their external debts and were attempting to reschedule them.[83] This was the fourth great international debt crisis of the modern era. Simultaneously recession verged into structural depression in industrial "rust belts" across wide regions of Europe and North America. It was in fact the worst general economic depression since the 1930s.

In Latin America, Venezuela and Mexico as high-borrowing oil exporters experienced the most extreme boom-and-bust cycles (Figure 6.1). Across Latin America and the Caribbean, GNP per capita fell by 17 percent between 1981 and 1985. Brazil's downturn was judged by Peter Evans to be "the worst industrial recession in [Brazil's] recorded history." Eichengreen and Lindert called the years after 1982 the "worst recession of the twentieth century" in Latin America.[84]

[80] Barry J. Barnett, "The U.S. farm financial crisis of the 1980s," *Agricultural History* 74(2) (2000): 366–80; Zhang and Tidgren, "Current farm downturn."
[81] Eliana Cardoso and Ann Helwege, *Latin America's Economy: Diversity, Trends, and Conflicts* (MIT Press, 1992), 117; Gary P. Green, *Finance Capital and Uneven Development* (Routledge, 1987), 108, citing Inter-American Development Bank data.
[82] Sebastian Alvarez, "The Mexican debt crisis redux: international markets in financial crisis, 1977–1982," *Financial History Review* 22(1) (2015): 79–105.
[83] Altamura, *European Banks*, 230–1.
[84] World Bank, *World Tables, 1994* (Baltimore: Johns Hopkins University Press, 1994), Table 1; Kahler, "Politics and international debt," 35; Barry Eichengreen and Peter H. Lindert, "Overview," in Eichengreen and Lindert, eds., *The International Debt Crisis in Historical Perspective* (Cambridge, MA: MIT Press, 1989), 1.

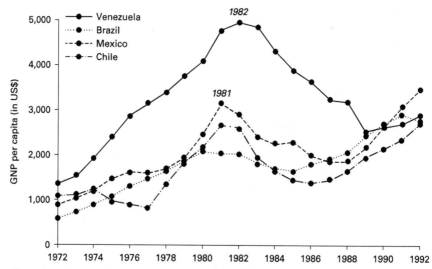

Figure 6.1 GNP per capita in Venezuela, Brazil, Mexico, and Chile, 1972–92, showing the effects of the 1980s depression. (Data from World Bank, *World Tables, 1994*, Table 1.)

In Africa, private Eurodollar lending was not a significant factor for most countries, but a parallel and in many ways more severe debt crisis played out. For sub-Saharan Africa as a whole, GNP per capita dropped by 38 percent between 1982 and 1987 (Figure 6.2). Nigeria as a highly indebted oil-exporting country experienced one of the most extreme boom-bust cycles. National experiences diverged, as described in Gareth Austin's contribution to this volume, but at least twenty-seven sub-Saharan countries had per capita declines in a dramatic "reversal of development."[85]

Economic recoveries were less synchronized. Brazil and Uruguay began to recover as early as 1985, but by 1992, when the next major international business-cyclic downturn was getting underway, ten Latin American countries[86] still had not regained the income levels of the early 1980s. Others barely exceeded them. The downturn that began in 1981–2 thus came to appear as a new structural condition rather than a passing conjunctural downturn.

The debt crisis affected most of Eastern Europe, all of Latin America, and almost all of Africa. In its next phase in the early 1990s, the debt crisis affected much of the Middle East and the former Soviet bloc as well. Asia, except for the Philippines, was much less affected. The exceptional position of Asia is a fundamental point in

[85] Gareth Austin, "Ghana and Kenya facing the 1970s commodity price shocks: the national and the global," this volume; Dharam Ghai and Cynthia Hewitt de Alcántara, "The crisis of the 1980s in Africa, Latin America, and the Caribbean: an overview," in Dharam Ghai, ed., *The IMF and the South, The Social Impact of Crisis and Adjustment* (London: Zed Books/United Nations Research Institute for Social Development, 1991), 14; Alejandro Portes and A. Douglas Kincaid, "Sociology and development in the 1990s: critical challenges and empirical trends," *Sociological Forum* 4(4) (1989): 479–503.

[86] Uruguay, Paraguay, Peru, Ecuador, Colombia, Venezuela, Nicaragua, Honduras, Guatemala, and the Dominican Republic.

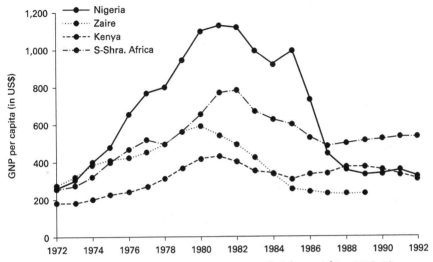

Figure 6.2 Growth and decline of GNP per capita in sub-Saharan Africa, 1972–92. (Data from World Bank, *World Tables, 1994*, Table 1.)

considering the new departures of the 1980s, when Japan replaced the United States as the world's largest net creditor nation while export-oriented industrialization accelerated across the region. At the same time, the offshore US-dollar system remained more than ever at the center of the international monetary system.

9. Conclusions: Time-structures in the History of Capitalism

To recapitulate the argument of this chapter, the "Bretton Woods era" in international monetary history, from the late 1940s to 1971–3, was also a distinct era in the international oil trade, and in the international grain trade. The postwar monetary regime, the postwar food regime, and the postwar energy regime all ended in the early 1970s, while the long international boom that began in the 1950s ended in the international recession of 1973–5. Simultaneously a great wave of international offshore-dollar lending got underway. That lending wave, with its unevenly distributed inflationary boom effects, peaked in a series of crises at the beginning of the 1980s, giving way to the recessions and depressions of the early 1980s.

The first oil shock of 1973–4 was in fact a comprehensive dollar-oil crisis. So too was the second oil shock of 1979–80. In both cases, the dollar-depreciation shock came first, followed by a surge in the prices of grain and other commodities, and then by a surge of oil prices. The "reverse" oil shock—that is, the oil price collapse—of 1985–6 was another type of dollar-oil crisis, associated with the great depreciation of the US dollar that followed the Plaza Accord of September 1985.[87] It too was accompanied by a collapse of grain prices.

---

[87] Duccio Basosi, Giuliano Garavini, and Massimiliano Trentin, eds., *Counter-Shock: The Oil Counter-Revolution of the 1980s* (London: I.B. Tauris, 2018).

For commodity producers, the commodity price booms of the 1970s were thus followed in the 1980s by commodity price crashes and negative terms-of-trade shocks, initiating a generation-long period of depressed commodity prices. The next big, general increase in international commodity prices did not come until 2003, stimulated by China's hyper-industrialization boom and by the US invasion of Iraq. For many commodity-exporting regions, 2003 marked the end of the long downswing that had begun in 1982.

9.1. When was the 1970s?

This chapter has argued that "the sixties" as an economic, political, and cultural era gave way to "the seventies" in 1973. Early 1973 was a watershed, with the ending of the US–Vietnam war in January followed in February by the devaluation of the US dollar and fall in US stock markets, followed in March by the international shift to floating exchange rates. The October 1973 oil shock then compounded these events into a comprehensive energy and industrial crisis.

When did the 1970s end? For purposes of the present analysis, the biennium 1979–80 was the beginning of the end. In January 1979 came the Iranian revolution and second oil shock. In May, Margaret Thatcher was elected prime minister of the UK. After October 1979, the Federal Reserve System enforced its contractionary policy turn much more stringently. Oil prices reached their twentieth-century high point in May and June 1980, while prices for wheat and other agricultural commodities peaked in the autumn of that year. Ronald Reagan was elected US president in November. International inflation and the Eurodollar lending wave nonetheless continued in 1981 and then collapsed in 1982. This concatenation of political and economic turning points was accompanied by a generational and cultural shift.

Thinking of the history of international finance, C. Edoardo Altamura offers the same periodization I have offered here for the "seventies," 1973–82. He also describes that decade using a term I have long associated with the seventies in my own thinking— as an *interregnum*, when the old order was faltering but a new one had not yet emerged.[88] Or, if we disaggregate the different aspects of this succession of orders: a new *international financial order* indeed emerged in the years after 1973, centered on the offshore US-dollar system. Industrially, the Fordist order was slipping its gears, but the emergence of a new technical-economic paradigm centered around microelectronics was more a story of the 1980s. The 1980s is also when the whole panoply of neoliberal governance fully emerged.

9.2. From the Fourth International Lending Wave to the Fourth International Debt Crisis

A wider time vista opens when we turn to the history of credit/debt cycles. The debt crisis of the 1980s could have been predicted—this is the thrust of Christian Suter's

---

[88] Altamura, *European Banks*, 247.

seminal study of the subject, which detailed three earlier waves of international credit creation, each ending in a cascade of defaults. These multi-decadal credit/debt cycles shared some remarkable structural similarities and exhibited a classic long-wave chronology (Figure 6.3).[89] Each new lending wave was associated with a burst of banking innovation and deregulation. Each debt crisis struck "peripheral" commodity-producing regions—the same places repeatedly. Each debt crisis unfolded in a conjunctural context of monetary constraint and falling world commodity prices.

The first international lending wave of the industrial capitalist era culminated in the speculative peak and crash of 1825. It involved lending out of London, particularly to the newly independent republics of South America. In the debt crisis that followed, a total of fifteen countries defaulted. In a follow-on wave of defaults after 1837, almost all of the southern states of the United States also defaulted.

The second, greater international lending wave reached a peak in the first years of the 1870s and it centered on British, French, and other European lending to the Americas, the Ottoman Empire, and Egypt. It ended in the depression of 1873–9. A total of seventeen countries defaulted in 1875–82. There was a follow-on wave of defaults in the 1890s.

The third great international lending wave in the 1920s focused on central and Eastern Europe and yet again on South America. US banks now took the lead. In the great debt-deflation crisis of the 1930s, twenty-four countries defaulted.

The credit boom and debt bust of the 1970s and 1980s thus followed a classic pattern, although the defaults were managed defaults of a new sort. Thirty-three countries defaulted in 1982–6, including much of the "second world" of socialist Eastern Europe and most of the "third world" as then understood, except for the Asian countries. There was a follow-on wave of defaults in the 1990s, which is when world prices for oil and other commodities declined to their lowest levels of the late twentieth century.

In these successive debt crises, Suter noticed a remarkable regularity in the number of countries defaulting—in each case about one-third of the independent states then existing. The peaks of each lending wave—in the early 1820s, the first years of the 1870s, in the mid-1920s, and in the mid to late 1970s—came at the peaks or initial downturn stages of posited economic long waves. Suter explained these lending booms in terms of both "pull" and "push" factors. "Pull" factors included favorable conditions in borrowing countries, above all high prices for various primary products. An important "push" factor was the deterioration of investment opportunities in the lending countries: "Capital flows into the periphery occur in later stages of the long wave when markets of the core are saturated and profit rates begin to decline."[90] Both types of factors operated in the 1970s.

---

[89] Christian Suter, "Long waves in the international financial system: debt-default cycles of sovereign borrowers," *Review* (Fernand Braudel Center) 12(1) (1989): 26–7, 37; Christian Suter, *Debt Cycles in the World-Economy, Foreign Loans, Financial Crises, and Debt Settlements, 1820–1990* (Boulder, CO: Westview Press, 1992); also Carlos Marichal, *A Century of Debt Crises in Latin America: From Independence to the Great Depression, 1820–1930* (Princeton University Press, 1989).

[90] Suter, "Long waves," 6. Suter's full data tables are given in the German edition, *Schuldenzyklen in der Dritten Welt: Kreditaufnahme, Zahlungskrisen und Schuldenregelungen peripherer Länder im Weltsystem von 1820 bis 1986* (Frankfurt am Main: Anton Hain, 1990).

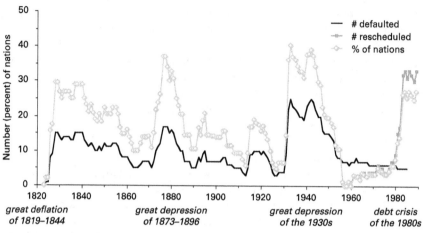

Figure 6.3 Debt-default cycles in the world economy, 1823–1989. [Up to 1956, the number of countries in default; from then, the number involved in multilateral rescheduling arrangements. Also, that number as a percentage of all sovereign states.] (Data from Suter, *Debt Cycles*, 195–9.)

This point connects to the question of international financial "recycling." Kaoru Sugihara's description of the oil triangle of the 1970s and 1980s recalls the debt triangle of the 1920s, which involved a circuit of US international lending, German war indemnity payments, and British and French war debt payments.[91] In naming this a "recycling" operation, Charles Kindleberger noted that the term originated to describe the recirculation of OPEC surpluses after 1973. He also cited three earlier recycling operations:[92]

[1] In *1817–18*, the loan by Barings to the French government "recycled French [war] indemnity payments, and it broadened the horizon of English investors to include foreign lending." As noted, this foreign lending wave culminated in the crash of 1825.

[2] "The same process [was] used in the Franco-Prussian [war] indemnity payment of *1871*," which set off an international investment boom that culminated in the crash of 1873.

[3] It happened again "in the [US-led] Dawes loan of *1924* and with the same side effect of stimulating new investor interest in foreign bonds." The international lending wave of 1924–28 culminated in the world debt crisis of 1929–31.

---

[91] Sugihara, "Japan, the Middle East and the world economy"; Sugihara, "East Asia, Middle East and the world economy"; Charles P. Kindleberger, *The World in Depression, 1929–1939* (second edition, University of California Press, 1986 [orig. 1973]), chapter 2; also Ramaa Vasudevan, "The borrower of last resort: international adjustment and liquidity in historical perspective," *Journal of Economic Issues* 42(4) (2008): 1055–81.

[92] Quoted text from Charles P. Kindleberger, *A Financial History of Western Europe* (Oxford University Press, 1993), 215, my italics.

Each of these initial "recycling" loans, with their strongly political aspects, were the biggest financial operations of their times. We might call them *detonating events* that set off historic international lending booms. The knock-on credit-creation effects were immense, and they set the stage for future debt collapses. No single big loan detonated the lending boom of the 1970s, but there was a kind of herd movement by banks, especially in 1977, which was the year that lending to Latin America really exploded.[93]

One great novelty of the 1980s compared to earlier international debt crises is seen in the managed handling of the defaults, which reflected the existence of powerful global creditor institutions.[94] By contrast, the crisis of the 1930s deeply discredited banks and financiers. Then, the desire to limit the destructive capacities of international financial capitalism shaped the design of the Bretton Woods system, which was notably associated with public rather than private lending to the developing countries. Altogether, the era from the 1930s into the 1970s was one of *national* economic assertion. Contrastingly, the bank-dominated international financial order that took form in the 1970s actually gained new power after the debt crisis of 1982, and has done so in every international financial crisis since then. It was now a case of international financial centers asserting control over national economic policies and over resources in debtor countries.

9.3. International Monetary Regimes: the Offshore US-dollar System

The emergence of the offshore US-dollar system in the 1970s, with its neoliberal principles but ultimate state backing, has structural parallels to earlier systemic shifts. One point not fully considered by writers on this subject is that in each of these earlier instances, the peak of an international lending boom coincided with the establishment of a new international monetary regime:

- In 1817/1821, the "classical" British gold standard came into effect. Articulated with the system of "bills on London," this was the foundation of the world's first truly global credit-money system.
- In 1871–3, the *international* gold standard came into existence, when Germany, France, the United States, and other countries shifted from a bimetallic gold-silver currency basis to a gold-only basis.
- After World War I, the US dollar emerged as the most powerful international currency, and international lending in the 1920s was enmeshed with a campaign to create an international *gold-exchange standard* in which US dollars would serve as a kind of substitute gold.[95] This would-be regime failed after 1931.

[93] See also Carlo Edoardo Altamura and Juan Flores Zendejas, "Politics, international banking, and the debt crisis of 1982," *Business History Review* 94 (2020): 753–78.
[94] Jerome E. Roos, *Why Not Default? The Political Economy of Sovereign Debt* (Princeton University Press, 2019).
[95] Bytheway and Metzler, *Central Banks*, chapters 4–6; Mark Metzler, *Lever of Empire: The International Gold Standard and the Crisis of Liberalism in Prewar Japan* (Berkeley: University of California Press, 2006), chapter 8; Barry Eichengreen, *Golden Fetters: The Gold Standard and the Great Depression, 1919–1939* (New York: Oxford University Press, 1992), chapters 6–7.

In 1973, one remarkable fact is the quiet and seemingly natural way in which the new offshore-dollar system emerged. Concerns over the inflationary effects of Eurodollar credit creation were strongly though often privately voiced at the beginning of the 1970s, including by central bankers. One irony of the era is that as Eurodollar credit creation surged, and as inflation surged, this debate faded. Another fear, that unregulated Euro-credit creation would produce debt crises obliging central banks to be lenders of last resort, also seemed to fade after European central bankers' tacit support for the Euromarkets in 1974–5. These fundamental questions were subject to little or no public debate.

One can draw a line from that moment to the trans-Atlantic financial crisis of 2007–8, when the offshore-dollar system was manifestly at the center of things. "For once," in the words of historian Adam Tooze, "this was a crisis that could not be blamed on the periphery."[96] Tellingly, the day after the collapse of Lehman Brothers was announced, September 16, 2008, as world financial markets began to panic, the matter that topped the agenda of the US Federal Reserve's Open Market Committee meeting in Washington, DC was actually the dollar-funding crisis needs of the European banks. Fed officials feared that if European banks defaulted on their vast US dollar obligations, a leveraged tower of debts built on top of debts, trillions of which continually turned over on a timescale of days, would come crashing down. Acting as lender of last resort for the offshore-dollar system, the US Federal Reserve accordingly gave $2 trillion in direct credits to thirteen large European banks and opened credit lines to the European Central Bank, the Bank of England, and the Swiss National Bank, which passed billions more to the big private banks who were under their care. It was the biggest and most sudden transfer of financial claims in history, and it was "shrouded in as much obscurity as possible."[97] In early 2020, in the financial crisis that broke during the first wave of the coronavirus panic, the Federal Reserve repeated this operation in a bigger, faster, and more practiced manner. One could interpret these bailouts as successful stabilizations. Or one could diagnose a lender-of-last-resort utility that has gone out of control and is bidding up ever bigger bubbles. The scale of these bubble dynamics makes the present moment difficult to compare to earlier historical conjunctures.

9.4. A Turning Point on a Secular Timescale?

A final idea takes in the entire timespan of modern industrialization. Ecological-economic analyses of material and energy flows have given us detailed physically based national accounts that trace the increases in material and energy use that accompanied industrialization. These statistics reveal a conspicuous trend break in the 1970s in most of the already-industrialized countries. Japan presents the most striking case of all, as total material used per capita increased by ten times during the long postwar boom to reach an all-time peak in the year 1973. Per capita material use in Japan has declined

---

[96] J. Adam Tooze, *Crashed: How a Decade of Financial Crises Changed the World* (Viking, 2019), 2.
[97] Tooze, *Crashed*, 154, 202–7, 215–16; Minutes of the Federal Open Market Committee, September 16, 2008, at https://www.federalreserve.gov/monetarypolicy/fomcminutes20080916.htm.

ever since.[98] Japan offers the outstanding example of a turn that happened across the industrialized countries. The Vienna-based team that conducted these analyses named this trend break the "*1970s syndrome*" and asked: "What happened in the 1970s, across so many countries around the world? An endogenous saturation of consumerism and lifestyles? The end of a long-term economic wave? A structural change in the workings of the economic growth engine?"[99] This view of the 1970s as a turning point on a secular timescale is taken from the standpoint of the already industrialized countries. It will appear differently for later industrializing countries. In the 2020s, as we enter a new historical phase with structural resemblances to the 1970s, these questions also affect how we read the dynamics of the present.

---

[98] Krausmann et al., "Metabolic transition"; Metzler, "Arc of industrialization."
[99] Wiedenhofer et al., "1970s syndrome," 189; Marina Fischer-Kowalski and Daniel Hausknost, eds., *Large Scale Societal Transitions in the Past. The Role of Social Revolutions and the 1970s Syndrome*, Social Ecology Working Paper 152, Alpen Adria Universität, 2014.

Part Three

The Cold War, Development, and Aid—Asia and Africa

7

The Global Energy Crises and China's Oil Diplomacy, 1973–83[1]

Kazushi Minami

Oil was a blessing for China.[2] With the help of Soviet technicians, the Chinese developed Karamay and Dushanzi oilfields in Xiangjiang in the 1950s, shattering the Western myth that there was no oil in China.[3] Its oil industry took off with the 1959 discovery of Daqing ("Great Celebration") in Heilongjiang, the country's largest oilfield until it was overtaken by the offshore Bohai oilfield in 2021. Daqing was quickly followed by the other two major oilfields in the Northeast—Shengli ("Victory") in Shandong and Dagang ("Big Port") near Tianjin. These oilfields turned up at a perfect time. The deterioration in Sino-Soviet relations in the late 1950s precipitated a near complete break of economic cooperation in the summer of 1960, when Moscow suddenly withdrew all Soviet technicians from China. Left to itself, the Chinese Communist Party (CCP), under Chairman Mao Zedong, doubled down on "self-reliance" as the cannon of China's economic development. While Soviet oil exports to China tailed off in the 1960s, Beijing imported oil equipment from the Eastern bloc (Hungary, Romania, East Germany, Albania, etc.) and the Western bloc (France, Italy, Japan, etc.) to develop the newly found oilfields, attaining self-sufficiency in oil in the early 1960s.[4] Between the mid-1960s and the late 1970s, Chinese oil production increased more than tenfold, from 0.2 million bpd (barrels per day) to more than 2.1 million bpd. China seemed to be on its way to being an oil giant.

---

[1] Parts of this article have appeared in the following two pieces. Kazushi Minami, "Oil for the lamps of America? Sino-American oil diplomacy, 1973–1979," *Diplomatic History* 41(5): 959–84; and Kazushi Minami, "The bottleneck of the reform: China's oil policy in the 1980s," in Priscilla Roberts, ed., *Chinese Economic Statecraft from 1978 to 1989: The First Decade of Deng Xiaoping's Reforms* (Basingstoke, UK: Palgrave Macmillan, 2022), 297–328.

[2] In this chapter, I refer to the People's Republic of China as "China" and the Republic of China as "Taiwan."

[3] Chu-yuan Cheng, *Economic Relations between Peking and Moscow: 1949–63* (New York, 1964), 33, 36; Sidney Klein, *The Road Divides: Economic Aspects of the Sino-Soviet Dispute* (Hong Kong, 1966), 56; Tatsu Kambara and Christopher Howe, *China and the Global Energy Crisis: Development and Prospects for China's Oil and Natural Gas* (Northampton, MA, 2007), 11.

[4] Arthur Klinghoffer, "Sino-Soviet relations and the politics of oil," *Asian Survey* 16, no. 6 (1976): 542–3; Chad Mitcham, *China's Economic Relations with the West and Japan, 1949–79: Grain, Trade and Diplomacy* (New York, 2005), 118–19, 122, 142–3, 156–7, 180–1; Kim Woodard, *The International Energy Relations of China* (Stanford, CA, 1980), 528–33, 546, 550.

Table 7.1 China's oil production and consumption (thousand bpd)[5]

Year	Production	Consumption	Year	Production	Consumption
1965	227	215	1981	2033	1625
1966	292	277	1982	2051	1614
1967	279	273	1983	2130	1654
1968	320	298	1984	2295	1713
1969	437	401	1985	2508	1807
1970	616	554	1986	2625	1925
1971	791	753	1987	2694	2048
1972	915	865	1988	2745	2203
1973	1077	1058	1989	2764	2315
1974	1302	1217	1990	2778	2297
1975	1548	1342	1991	2831	2491
1976	1746	1534	1992	2845	2705
1977	1880	1625	1993	2892	3013
1978	2090	1819	1994	2934	3069
1979	2132	1827	1995	2993	3342
1980	2122	1707			

The oil shock of 1973 turned Chinese oil into a diplomatic asset. Unaffected by the global energy crisis, Beijing profited handsomely from the oil price hike as it expanded oil exports from 26,000 bpd in 1972 to 284,000 bpd in 1979. The foreign currency revenues allowed the Chinese to purchase equipment for the "four modernizations" in agriculture, industry, science and technology, and national defense, the brainchild of Premier Zhou Enlai. Oil riveted the capitalist bloc to China. Desperate to find an alternative source of oil outside the Middle East, oil companies in the United States, Western Europe, and Japan were transfixed by the potential of China, a vast country with enormous natural resources. Fueling this optimism was the 1968 oceanographic survey conducted by the UN Economic Commission for Asia and the Far East, which concluded that the continental shelf in the East China Sea, untested by the drill, might contain "one of the most prolific oil and gas reservoirs in the world, possibly comparing favorably with the Persian Gulf area."[6] As Beijing improved diplomatic relations with capitalist countries in the early 1970s, Chinese policymakers dangled the country's offshore resources to awe their counterparts. Little did they know that China was about to face its own energy crisis.

This chapter analyzes how the oil crises of the 1970s and 1980s reshaped China's economic statecraft. It argues that the opportunity and the threat posed by the crises facilitated China's economic and political opening to the capitalist bloc through technological cooperation, which evolved from equipment trade to joint ventures. This cooperation, carried out in the spirit of "self-reliance," helped China avert a major

---

[5] BP Statistical Review of World Energy 2022 (data can be downloaded at https://www.bp.com/en/global/corporate/energy-economics/statistical-review-of-world-energy.html).

[6] Kenneth Emery et al., "Geological structure and some water characteristics of the East China Sea and the Yellow Sea," in Coordinating Committee for Geoscience Programs in East and Southeast Asia (CCOP) *Technical Bulletin*, 2 (1969): 41.

Table 7.2 China's oil exports (thousand bpd)[7]

Year	Exports	Year	Exports
1970	7.63	1980	351.64
1971	12.65	1981	372.32
1972	30.73	1982	393.41
1973	60.05	1983	396.22
1974	131.54	1984	556.48
1975	240.58	1985	727.78
1976	209.86	1986	681.99
1977	222.31	1987	646.04
1978	270.71	1988	619.33
1979	330.55	1989	584.99

economic crisis in the 1980s and undergirded "Reform and Opening-Up" (*gaige kaifang*). This chapter first discusses the worldwide euphoria about Chinese oil in the wake of the first oil shock, which soon dissipated. Next, it examines Beijing's imports of oil equipment, initiated by Mao Zedong and accelerated by his successors, which formed the economic basis for the new US–China relationship in the late 1970s. The chapter then turns to the energy crisis that threatened China in the advent of the reform era. The remedy that Beijing prescribed itself after extensive internal debate was joint offshore ventures, which helped its economy hobble along despite the deteriorating energy balance. It closes with a brief discussion on how China escaped the same economic fate as the Soviet bloc in the 1980s.

1. "Another Middle East"

Beijing deployed oil for strategic goals. In late 1973, Japan, severely affected by the Oil Shock, became the first non-communist country to import Chinese oil—a meager 7.3 million barrels for that year, approximately one-fifth of Japan's weekly consumption. Beijing was apparently trying to seduce Tokyo out of the energy development project in Siberia, for which Moscow was seeking foreign technology and capital. China also exported oil to its fractious "friends," North Korea and Vietnam, and US regional allies, Thailand and the Philippines, both of them maintaining diplomatic relations with Taiwan.[8] The Chinese hinted that more was on the way. When a US business delegation visited China in late 1973, an oil company executive expressed interest in "assisting China with onshore and offshore oil and gas exploration, as well as petroleum

---

[7] These figures are converted from Larry Chuen-ho Chow, "The changing role of oil in Chinese exports, 1974–89," *The China Quarterly*, no. 131 (September 1992), 751.

[8] Jeronim Perović and Dunja Krempin, "'The key is in our hands:' Soviet energy strategy in détente and the global oil crises of the 1970s," *Historical Social Research* 39, no. 4 (2014): 117–19, 123–8, 131; Arthur Klinghoffer, *The Soviet Union and International Oil Politics* (New York, 1977), 261–2, 276–7; Woodard, *International Energy Relations*, 504–5.

production and refining facilities."[9] Vice Premier Li Xiannian responded by equivocating that the Chinese were still calculating the country's oil potential. "In fact," he quipped, "Chinese technicians had been directed to drill very deep into the earth in the search for oil reserves, but to refrain from drilling too deep so as not to drill through to the United States."[10] These words tantalized oilmen around the world.

The Americans debated whether China would be the next oil giant. There was no doubt about it if the continental shelf in the East China Sea, disputed by China, Japan, and Taiwan, offered a bonanza as promised. "No oil company will withdraw from that part of the world until oil has been found and we've forced a resolve," stated an executive of Gulf Oil, one of the US firms that had begun investing in that region. "Not until the claims have been resolved and we've been told by the governments concerned. Finding oil would act as a catalyst."[11] Raymond Cox, Vice President of Geospace, the first company to sell advanced seismic exploration equipment to China, summarized the sentiment of oil companies across the United States: "I think China is another Middle East, but it's going to take a while. They are moving fast, however."[12] Yet the Middle East analogy was challenged by many. Mao's ideology of self-reliance seemed to warrant only a slow pace of offshore development. Granting that China's oil production increased over time, China's domestic demand would preclude rapid expansion of oil exports. Richard Nixon pledged to diversify the sources of oil imports in late 1973, but US firms reached no oil purchase agreement with Beijing before 1978. By the mid-1970s, the Middle East analogy had passed its prime.

China was never meant to be an oil giant. As predicted, the increase in China's oil production was closely trailed by the increase in domestic demand, with exports hovering below 200,000 bpd between 1975 and 1977, infinitesimal compared with Saudi Arabia's exports of 8 million bpd. The Central Intelligence Agency (CIA) was right to observe in late 1975 that if the Chinese were to export a significant amount of oil, they would have to sacrifice economic growth at home and accept joint oil ventures with foreign companies, both apparently unacceptable for Beijing.[13] For a brief period in mid-1975, however, joint venture was not out of the question. In his twenty-point industrialization plan, Vice Premier Deng Xiaoping, China's chief economic planner in 1975, espoused a joint venture scheme in the East and South China Seas, wherein Beijing would sell the oil produced by foreign oil companies to pay for technology imports from capitalist countries.[14] This bold plan was soon scrapped by the Gang of

---

[9] Remarks of Andrew Gibson, November 6, 1973, "Special Reports #6 The Peking Report March 1974," box 158, United States-China Business Council (hereafter USCBC), Gerald R. Ford Library (hereafter GFL); General Discussion, November 7, 1973, "Special Reports #6 The Peking Report March 1974," box 158, USCBC, GFL.

[10] Summary of Meeting with Li Hsien-nien, November 8, 1973, "Special Reports #6 The Peking Report March 1974," box 158, USCBC, GFL.

[11] Selig S. Harrison, "Time bomb in East Asia," *Foreign Policy*, no. 20 (Fall 1975), 14, 20–1.

[12] James Sterba, "Peking purchasing U.S. oil equipment to step up output," *New York Times*, November 28, 1975, p. 63.

[13] CIA, *China: Energy Balance Projections*, November 1975, "Special Reports #15, Energy Balance Projections for the PRC, 1975–1985," box 158, USCBC, GFL.

[14] Deng Xiaoping, "Guanyu jiakuai fazhan gongye de ruogan wenti (taolun gao)" ["Some questions on accelerating the development of industry (discussion draft)"], September 2, 1975.

Four, a group of Deng's political rivals, who insisted on a dogmatic reading of "self-reliance," but the vice premier's comeback would give it a second life in the late 1970s.

Even without the domestic political turmoil, Mao Zedong's foreign policy would have hobbled China's oil exports. In 1974, Beijing began to trumpet the chairman's Three Worlds Theory, which divided the world into the United States and the Soviet Union (First World), their allies in Europe and Asia (Second World), and the vast swaths of developing countries (Third World), including China.[15] According to this theory, China must join the Arab nations in their energy war against the United States. Siding with "the oppressed peoples and oppressed nations" around the world, Deng Xiaoping, at the UN General Assembly in 1974, denounced the US and Soviet superpowers, which were "vainly seeking world hegemony," as "the source of a new world war."[16] Exporting a large amount of oil to the United States and its allies would have contradicted the Three World Theory. Symbolically, when a Chinese drillship successfully operated in the East China Sea in 1974, the crew were extolled not for taking the first step in search of offshore resources, but for performing "the great political responsibility of opposing U.S. and Soviet maritime hegemonies."[17] In the mid-1970s, politics took precedence over economics in China's oil policy.

2. Redefining Self-Reliance

For China, "self-reliance" was a contested notion that meant different things at different times. The definition of the term became more rigid than before during the peak years of the Cultural Revolution (1966–8), when Beijing made a bid for autarky. Yet the slowdown of economic growth forced China's trade policy to bounce back. As Wang Yaoting, president of the China Council for the Promotion of International Trade (CCPIT), told American businessmen in 1973, self-reliance no longer meant that China would "keep its door closed."[18] Particularly so in oil industry, in which Chinese technology lagged behind the world's modern standard by half a century.[19] In 1972, Beijing resumed importing oil equipment from the capitalist bloc, from seismic exploration systems to large computers to jack-up rigs, totaling millions of US dollars. As one energy expert observed at a 1976 conference on China's oil industry in Houston, "sole reliance on indigenous creativity" now made little sense. China, he claimed,

[15] CCP Central Archives and Manuscript Division, ed., *Mao Zedong waijiao wenxuan* [*Collection of Mao Zedong's Diplomatic Manuscripts*] (Beijing, 1994), 600–1; Kuisong Yang and Yafeng Xia, "Vacillating between revolution and détente: Mao's changing psyche and policy toward the United States, 1966–1976," *Diplomatic History* 34, no. 2 (April 2010): 415–22.

[16] "Excerpts from Chinese address to U.N. Session on Raw Materials," *New York Times*, April 12, 1974, p. 12.

[17] The Industry and Transportation Team of the Shanghai Municipal Revolutionary Committee, ed., *Gongjiao qingkuang* [Transportation Report], no. 296, August 30, 1974, B246-2-1030-188, Shanghai Municipal Archive (hereafter SMA).

[18] Summary of National Council Meeting with CCPIT, November 7, 1973, "Special Reports #6—The Peking Report," box 158, USCBC, GFL.

[19] Smil, "Energy in China: achievements and prospects," *The China Quarterly* 65 (March 1976), 59.

should seek "some Western know-how" to facilitate the shift in its oil industry from "a Russian technology way" to "a Western technology way."[20]

The death of Mao Zedong in 1976 accelerated this shift. At the 1977 national industrial conference at Daqing, his hand-picked successor, Hua Guofeng, rolled out an overly ambitious vision for rapid industrialization based on modern technology imports. The new chairman stated: "If we have more . . . great successes like Daqing, we should be able to catch up and surpass the world's modern economic and technological standards." He then pledged to build "some ten Daqing oilfields" by 1980 and achieve 5 million bpd in oil production before the end of the Sixth Five-Year Plan in 1985.[21] These numbers would soon turn out to be little more than a fantasy, but Hua enshrined technology imports as the kingpin of China's new oil policy. When the CCPIT's delegation toured around the United States later that year, it hardly hid its interest in oil technology, an American forte. "By self-reliance we don't mean self-seclusion so we have the interest to take in the advanced technology from foreign countries," said Wang Yaoting. "It is beneficial to speed up the industrialization in China."[22]

The redefinition of self-reliance was more of a necessity than a choice. A US petroleum equipment delegation in late 1977 was shocked by the obsoleteness of drilling rigs in Northeast China, as outdated as the 1945 US standard. "The Chinese could use everything the West has to offer in drilling," they analyzed.[23] Another delegation in late 1978 that toured 1,500 oil wells in Daqing also concluded: "They have practically nothing." One report on China's most advanced oilfield, which was interlarded with adjectives like "crude," "antique," and "old-fashioned," found it "rather apparent they are going to have to go outside and buy equipment."[24] The Chinese knew that the Americans had the best petroleum technology in the world. Although the US share in China's energy technology imports remained only 10 percent, partly due to the lack of diplomatic relations before 1979, Beijing became an avid customer of US oil technology in the late 1970s, purchasing Armco's offshore drilling rigs ($15–20 million), Digital Resources' seismic exploration system ($3.7 million), and Hughes Tool's drilling bits and cutters ($17 million), among others.[25] So hectic was this technological shopping spree that China accepted long-term loans from Japanese and Western European banks to finance a whopping trade deficit of more than $1 billion against the United States.[26] Self-reliance had now acquired a new meaning: borrow money, import equipment, and internalize technology.

---

[20] Jan-Olaf Willums, "The development of China's petroleum industry," June 23, 1976, "Conference on China's Oil Industry and the Prospect for United States Trade, Houston, 6/20/76, speeches," box 118, USCBC, GFL.

[21] "Zhongguo gongchandang zhongyang weiyuanhui zhuxi guowuyuan zongli Hua Guofeng tongzhi zai quanguo gongye xue Daqing huiyi shang de jianghua (May 9, 1977)" ["Chinese Communist Party Central Committee Chairman and State Council Premier Comrade Hua Guofeng's speech at the national conference on 'learn from Daqing in industry'"] *People's Daily*, May 13, 1977, pp. 2, 3.

[22] CCPIT Business Meeting, September 8, 1977, "September 1977—CCPIT from China, Business Meeting (2)," box 125, USCBC, GFL.

[23] Stephen Harner's Trip Report, undated, "Delegations Department, Petroleum Industry Delegation, 11/77, Trip Report (1)," box 107, USCBC, GFL.

[24] B. R. Dixon to China File, December 1, 1978, "Delegations Department, Petroleum Industry Delegation, 9/78, Trip Report," box 111, USCBC, GFL.

[25] Woodard, *International Energy Relations*, 82, 548–9.

[26] Min Song, "A dissonance in Mao's revolution: Chinese agricultural imports from the United States, 1972–1978," *Diplomatic History* 38(2) (2014): 428–9; and De Pauw, *U.S.-Chinese Trade Negotiations*, 5.

Table 7.3 China's exports and imports (million USD)[27]

Year	Export	Import
1965	2,200	2,000
1966	2,400	2,300
1967	2,100	2,000
1968	2,100	1,900
1969	2,200	1,800
1970	2,300	2,300
1971	2,600	2,200
1972	3,400	2,900
1973	5,800	5,200
1974	7,000	7,600
1975	7,300	7,500
1976	6,900	6,600
1977	7,600	7,200
1978	9,700	10,900
1979	13,700	15,700
1980	18,300	19,600

3. Leaning to the United States

Oil became a strategic fulcrum for US–China relations in the late 1970s. In the United States, National Security Advisor Zbigniew Brzezinski, an anti-Soviet hawk, replaced Cyrus Vance, a détente advocate, as Jimmy Carter's primary advisor. In China, Deng Xiaoping, who was restored to previous positions in July 1977, superseded Hua Guofeng as the de facto national leader, a process that culminated in the Third Plenum of the CCP Central Committee in December 1978. Brzezinski and Deng shared an abhorrence against the expansion of Soviet influence in the developing world, particularly in the Middle East and Vietnam. They agreed that the Soviet Union, out of its thirst for oil, might invade countries in the Persian Gulf region, which would cause another energy crisis in the capitalist bloc.[28] It was time to send "an immediate and strong message to the Soviet Union." In July 1978, Frank Press, the president's science and technology advisor and Brzezinski's ally, led a large delegation of government officials to China and submitted an official proposal for scientific cooperation, something that Washington had never done before.[29] Deng's only complaint was that the proposal was not "concrete" enough. In November, the Presidential Directive 43 set energy, education, space, agriculture, medicine, geoscience, and commerce as areas of US cooperation with China.[30]

---

[27] National Bureau of Statistics, *Zhongguo tongji nianjian* [*Statistical Yearbook of China*] 1988, 721.
[28] For a more detailed discussion about this perception of Soviet threat, see chapter 1 in this volume by David S. Painter.
[29] Memo, Press to Brzezinski, March 13, 1978, "China (PRC), 2-5/78," box 8, Country Files, Brzezinski Material, National Security Adviser, JCL.
[30] Presidential Directive 43, November 3, 1978, *FRUS*, 1977–80, vol. XIII, doc. 150.

Beijing also found two influential American allies—Chairman of the Senate Energy Committee Henry "Scoop" Jackson and Secretary of Energy James Schlesinger—who cemented the US–China partnership against the Soviet Union, anchored in oil. The two had vocally opposed détente and insisted on forming a tacit alliance with China through oil technology cooperation. In February 1978, Jackson travelled to China and met Deng Xiaoping for the second time. "Seriously, it is in our interest to help you develop your oil," he stated. "We have the finest technology in oil and coal development and can help."[31] The vice premier nodded in agreement, vowing to "import modern technology and experience from around the world." "If Sino-American relations normalize early, the pace of development in Sino-American trade can become much faster," he added.[32] That October, Schlesinger visited China as part of government-to-government science and technology cooperation that Frank Press had initiated. He negotiated with Vice Premier Yu Qiuli, godfather of China's oil industry, an informal agreement on energy cooperation, which would become part of the science and technology cooperation signed by Jimmy Carter and Deng Xiaoping in January 1979.[33] Schlesinger and Yu concurred that the projected downturn in Soviet oil production might prompt Moscow to invade the Persian Gulf region, a fear that gave energy cooperation a political significance.[34] With oil, Jackson and Schlesinger fired up US–China relations.

Chinese oil, which American oilmen had coveted since 1973, finally came along on November 21, 1978, when Coastal States Gas Corporation announced the first US crude oil purchase from China. The paltry volume—3.6 million barrels—amounted to less than one-sixth of the total US oil supply per day. In fact, China was selling most of its oil to Asian neighbors, including Japan, with which it agreed to export 345 million barrels of oil in five years.[35] China's oil shipment to the United States was a token of the strategic partnership against the Soviet Union. The two countries normalized diplomatic relations in January 1979, and around the same time, the Chinese made sizable purchases of American oil technology, including twelve large computers from CDC ($69 million), seven drilling rigs from LTV ($40 million), and seismic recording systems from Geosource, Surcel, and Texas Instruments ($39 million). Three decades after China leaned toward the Soviet Union, it leaned back to the United States, and oil lubricated this process.

---

[31] Mao Lin, "Sino-American relations and the diplomacy of modernization: 1966–1979" (PhD diss., University of Georgia, 2010), 447.

[32] *Deng Xiaoping sixiang nianbian*, 105–6.

[33] Memo, Schlesinger to Carter, November 27, 1978, FRUS, 1977–1980, vol. XIII, doc 157; and Government Printing Office, ed., *Public Papers of the Presidents of the United States: Jimmy Carter, 1979* (Washington, D.C., 1979), 200–2.

[34] CIA, *The International Energy Situation: Outlook to 1985*, ER 77-10240 U, April 1977; CIA, *Prospects for Soviet Oil Production*, ER 77-10270, April 1977; CIA, *Prospects for Soviet Oil Production: A Supplemental Analysis*, ER 77-10425, July 1977; and the Ministry of Petroleum Industry, Waishi qingkuang fanying [External Affairs Report] no. 36, October 27, 1978, B76-4-1105-69, SMA.

[35] Kevin Fountain, "The development of China's offshore oil," *China Business Review* 7, no. 1 (January–February 1980), 36; and Andrew Malcom, "Japan and China sign 8-year pact for $20 billion industrial deals," *New York Times*, February 17, 1978, A10.

4. Going Offshore

In the late 1970s, Beijing decided to tap China's offshore resources to boost oil production. Offshore oil was no easy feat. It required modern technology far more sophisticated than the outdated Soviet equipment that Chinese engineers were using to extract onshore oil in the Northeast. Even more exacting was the complex process for offshore oil industry—from seismic survey to exploratory drilling, well construction to service provision, transportation to worker training—which cost billions of US dollars in total. Managing this process also required administrative skills that would take shape only after years, or even decades, of experience. Beijing bought Japanese, Singaporean, Norwegian, and US jack-up rigs—a mobile platform for offshore drilling—in the early and mid-1970s, which could drill much deeper than its domestic rigs, but they hardly eased the challenges facing China's offshore business.[36] Possessing neither equipment nor capital nor know-how, the Chinese could not do it by themselves—and they knew it. The only alternative was to invite foreign oil companies— "yesterday's paragons of capitalist evil" in the words of energy expert Vaclav Smil—to joint offshore ventures.[37]

The year 1978 ushered in a new era for China's oil industry. In January, a group of Chinese officials led by Vice Minister of Petroleum Industry Sun Jingwen and Vice Director of the State Planning Commission Li Renjun toured Japan and the United States, surveying modern oil technology. Kang Shi'en understood the significance of this delegation. When its trip report landed on his desk, Kang organized a study group consisting of leading energy officials, which revised the report before submitting it to the CCP leadership. The final report proposed the production-sharing scheme as the only way for Beijing to accelerate offshore exploration and development, while asserting that foreign companies should buy Chinese equipment and employ Chinese engineers whenever possible. These innovative suggestions arrested Chinese leaders. On March 26, Chairman Hua Guofeng chaired a high-profile meeting to discuss the report, in which he espoused offshore cooperation to achieve his ambitious plan to increase China's annual oil production to 3.45 million bpd by 1985. "This issue does not affect sovereignty," said Hua. "On principle ... we can make a firm decision to do it." Ye Jianyin, Li Xiannian, and other senior officials seconded Hua's view.[38] The March 26 meeting set foreign cooperation as the mainstay of Beijing's offshore strategy.

Beijing made a move that spring. Reversing its long-held aversion to foreign offshore cooperation, the Ministry of Petroleum openly invited American, Japanese, and French oil companies to Beijing in order to discuss joint exploration and development of China's offshore resources, a decision that the *Oil and Gas Journal* called "something of a revolution."[39] This unprecedented move dazzled American oilmen.[40] J. Hugh Liedtke

---

[36] Woodard, *International Energy Relations*, 204.
[37] Vaclav Smil, *Energy in China's Modernization: Advances and Limitations* (Armonk, NY, 1988), 98.
[38] Qin Wencai, *Xin ji lan jiang* (Beijing: Xinhua chubanshe), 37–8.
[39] Larry Auldridge, "Watching the World," *The Oil and Gas Journal*, September 4, 1978, 56.
[40] Kenneth Lieberthal and Michel Oksenberg, *Policy Making in China: Leaders, Structures, and Processes* (Princeton, NJ, 1988), 219.

of Pennzoil speculated: "My guess is that this has an extremely high priority [in the Chinese government], and the pressure is on to get something done."[41] The Chinese, in essence, were holding an international race for production-sharing contracts. Zhang Wenbin, president of China Petroleum Corporation, told an American businessman that Beijing was encouraging foreign companies "to compete with each other in a given area, to have a race to see who discovers oil first."[42] The Ministry of Petroleum soon began to negotiate with more companies, while dispatching delegations to the United States, Britain, France, Norway, Japan, and Brazil to study their offshore technology. The international competition for the continental shelf was on.

Foreign oilmen were quick to jump in. The Japan National Oil Corporation (JNOC) became the first company in late 1978 to obtain the right to conduct a geophysical survey in the southern Bohai Gulf. JNOC was closely followed by dozens of competitors. A few months after normalization of US–China relations, ARCO, AMOCO, Citco, and Union reached similar agreements with the Chinese.[43] In 1979 and 1980, 33 firms from 17 countries followed suit. They would spend $200 million in total in seismic surveys, and the Chinese would acquire their data for free. If the data showed subterranean structures that might contain oil and gas, the company that conducted the survey was given preferential rights for development. In December 1979, Beijing awarded the first offshore development contracts to Japanese and French firms—JNOC and the Société Nationale Elf Aquitaine in the Bohai Gulf, and Compagnie Française des Pétroles (Total) in the northeastern part of the Gulf of Tonkin. These contracts did not look like a model contract, however. First, the Chinese had already drilled and developed these oilfields, and the contracts stipulated that the Japanese and the French would simply share the cost of production. Second, these proven oilfields were located much shallower, and thus easier to develop, than potential oilfields in such unexplored areas as the South China Sea. Third, these companies were completely or partially state-owned, and could bear higher risks than private firms. At the end of the 1970s, foreign oilmen were still trying to gauge what China's joint offshore ventures would look like.

5. China's Energy Crisis

Beijing embarked on joint offshore ventures at a propitious moment. Just as China embarked on "Reform and Opening-Up" in late 1978, it found its oil industry in deep trouble. After decades of exploitation using water pressure, combined with the lack of technological updates and failure to find new wells, China's onshore oil production plateaued between 2 million and 2.1 million bpd between 1978 and 1983. Oil production at Daqing increased only ten percent in the early 1980s, from 1 million bpd

---

[41] Hobart Rowen, "China's Oil: Peking Turns to West for Its Technology," *Washington Post*, August 11, 1978, pp. A1, A8.

[42] Meeting with China Petroleum Corporation, September 23, 1978, "Subject File, CHP Visit to Peking, 9/78," box 338, USCBC, GFL.

[43] "Exporter's Notes," in *China Business Review* 6, no. 1 (January-February, 1979), 66–8; no. 2 (March-April, 1979), 36; no. 3 (May-June, 1979), 41.

in 1981 to 1.1 million bpd in 1985. Hua Guofeng's fallacy of "some ten Daqings" was laid bare. This sudden slump, largely unforeseen by the Chinese before it became imminent, resulted in China's failure to honor its oil sale agreement with Japan in the early 1980s. Beijing feared that it was a beginning of a nightmare. Kang Shi'en, China's energy tsar and director of the State Economic Commission, who led the country's oil policy in the 1970s and 1980s, stated in 1981 that energy officials were debating whether they could keep the current production level and maintain the country's status as an oil exporter in the future. "If [China] becomes an oil importer, it would be a problem," Kang intoned.[44] Once projected to become "another Middle East," China now seemed to be on the cusp of backsliding into an energy-poor country.

The energy crisis threatened Reform and Opening-Up. Although China relied on coal for about three-fourths of its total energy consumption, Beijing viewed oil as a key natural resource for the domestic energy needs in the 1980s, a decade in which China's industrial output more than tripled; the population mushroomed from 980 million to more than 1.1 billion; and the energy consumption increased more than 60 percent. Equally important, an oil shortage would disrupt Beijing's plans for technology imports. Despite the stagnation in Chinese oil exports, the Second Oil Shock of 1979, which more than doubled the world oil prices, increased the revenues from $1.2 billion in 1978 to $4.7 billion in 1981—more than one-fifth of the total export earnings.[45] Still, however, Beijing faced an acute shortage of foreign currency due to hasty plant and equipment purchases, which formed a massive trade deficit, reaching $15 billion in 1985. The Chinese estimated that to finance technology imports and achieve the four modernizations, they had to keep exporting oil amid the rising demand at home.

A failure to do so would be costly. Chinese leaders resolved that Reform and Opening-Up should never be reversed, but oil shortage would not only derail their economic planning, but also shatter the myth of self-reliance, a refrain of China's political discourse since the discovery of Daqing. The result might be another power struggle and then another Cultural Revolution, a scenario that no one desired. Beijing had three options to deal with the crisis. First, it could suppress the domestic

Table 7.4 China's energy composition, 1970 and 1980 (percent)[46]

| | 1970 | | 1980 | |
	Production	Consumption	Production	Consumption
Coal	81.6	80.9	69.4	72.2
Oil	14.1	14.7	23.8	20.7
Other	4.3	4.4	6.8	7.1

[44] Kang Shi'en, *Kang Shi'en lun Zhongguo shiyou gongye* (Beijing: Shiyou gongye chubanshe, 1995), 365–6.
[45] Larry Chuen-ho Chow, "The changing role of oil in Chinese exports, 1974–89," *The China Quarterly* 131 (September 1992), 757.
[46] National Bureau of Statistics, *Zhongguo tongji nianjian 1990*, 453.

consumption of oil. In 1979, Beijing launched a nationwide campaign to reduce the household consumption of oil, partly by encouraging the use of coal. "Where conditions permit, all oil-burning boilers should be converted to coal-burning units this year," Kang Shi'en insisted.[47] Second, Beijing could slow down the pace of economic development. To the frustration of foreign investors, Chinese leaders often cancelled technology imports in the early 1980s, whenever they deemed the purchases too hasty. These two measures, effective as they were, fell short of resolving the fundamental tension in oil supply and demand. The third, and ideal, solution to the energy problem was to find new sources of oil—along China's 2,800-mile coastline.

6. Debating Offshore Cooperation

Not surprisingly, China's offshore policy aroused a controversy within the CCP. While rationalizing foreign offshore cooperation based on China's lack of technology, capital, and experience, Kang Shi'en believed that the production-sharing scheme was not tantamount to giving up the country's maritime and energy sovereignty. He emphatically proclaimed that "sovereignty is still in our hands."[48] His argument carried the day, but not without pushback. In February 1978—when the Chinese were still debating the wisdom of enlisting foreign oilmen's help in their offshore enterprise— Vice Premier Li Xiannian wrote to the "energy clique," including Kang Shi'en, Yu Quili, and Vice Premier Gu Mu, expressing his fear that foreign "capitalists" and "imperialists" might take advantage of China's "insufficient international [business] knowledge"— "not a little insufficient but very insufficient." "[T]o haggle with wolves, you should learn to howl like a wolf," he maintained. "We do need to learn to howl." Moreover, continued Li, offshore cooperation might render China dependent on foreign companies, particularly for technology. "We should import the world's modern technology based on the premise of self-reliance," he insisted.[49] Li's misgivings were not merely a reflection of his personal angst; they were widely shared among Chinese officials, particularly the conservatives.

Two incidents in 1979 and 1980 further complicated China's foreign offshore cooperation. On November 25, 1979, a heavy storm, combined with misguided responses to it, destroyed Bohai II, a jack-up rig in Bohai Bay, killing 72 out of 74 workers on board. The tragedy caused a political storm. Minister of Petroleum Song Zhenming was dismissed, and four other officials were imprisoned. Yu Qiuli was transferred from the State Planning Commission to the newly created State Energy Commission, and Kang Shi'en resigned as director of the State Economic Commission and succeeded Song as the new minister of petroleum, a shakeup widely considered

[47] Kevin Fountain, "The development of China's offshore oil in the next decade," *China Business Review* 7(1): 23–36.

[48] The State Council, *Haishang shiyou kantan gongzuo xietiaohui jianbao* [Report on the coordination meeting on offshore oil exploration], November 8, 1979, B1-9-67-122, SMA; Zhou Yongkang, ed., *Kang Shi'en lun Zhongguo shiyou gongye* [Kang Shi'en Discusses China's Oil Industry] (Beijing, China), 348.

[49] *Jianguo yilai Li Xiannian wengao*, vol. 4 (Beijing: Zhongyang wenxian chubanshe, 2011), 84.

demotions. On January 25, 1980—less than two months after the Bohai II incident—
China Daily News, a Chinese American newspaper in New York, criticized the Sino-
Japanese contract in Bohai Bay, falsely claiming that the term allowed JNOC to retrieve
the cost of investment in a few months and enjoy a free supply of oil until 2000, worth
hundreds of billions of US dollars. As the article gained popularity in some quarters in
China, the State Energy Commission and the State Import and Export Administration
Commission, under Deng Xiaoping's instruction, reaffirmed the economic merit of the
JNOC deal.[50] The Bohai II accident and the *China Daily News* incident both highlighted
the political risks involved in the offshore business.

Perhaps the most difficult adjustments that the Chinese had to make were
ideological. In 1980, Chen Yun, a conservative critic of Deng Xiaoping's economic
reform, argued that China should build not only "a material civilization" based on
modernization, but also "a spiritual civilization" based on socialism. China, in other
words, should only import capitalist technology, not the ideas embedded in it. Chen
Yun's words reverberated in the oil industry. Vice Minister of Petroleum Qin Wencai,
for instance, stated that Chinese engineers who worked with foreign counterparts
should "be on guard against the influence and corrosion of capitalist thoughts," while
cautioning that they should not consider all foreign engineers "proxies of capitalists"
and foreign cooperation "capitulation."[51] Li Xiannian's distrust of foreign capitalists
stemmed from the same concern as Chen's. Li wrote to Yu Qiuli in 1981 that the
"importance and complexity" of offshore cooperation "far surpasses" anything that
Beijing had tried with foreign companies, including Baoshan Iron and Steel
Corporation, a company founded with the assistance of Nippon Steel of Japan. Li
warned that Beijing must keep in mind that "foreign capitalists are also capitalists"—or
it might "get the short end of the stick on [the issues of] sovereignty, resources, and
economics."[52] The Chinese thus kept on debating joint offshore ventures, leaving
foreign oilmen with no clue about their next move.

7. The Bidding

The Chinese had to make a decision. In mid-1980, foreign companies completed all the
geophysical surveys agreed upon since 1979, exploring 430,000 square meters in the
Pearl River Mouth (northern part of the South China Sea) and Yinggehai Basins
(southern part of the Yellow Sea). With the data, Chinese energy officials brooded over
the oil potentials in these areas. In January 1981, they held a series of meetings on
foreign offshore cooperation, which reached a conclusion after 17 days: Beijing should
prepare for international bidding on offshore acreage. Whoever wins the bidding
would obtain the right to explore, develop, and produce in that area. Although the
financial, legal, and technical complexities of offshore ventures postponed the bidding

---

[50] Qin, *Xin ji lan jiang*, 206.
[51] Qin, *Xin ji lan jiang*, 12–13.
[52] *Jianguo yilai Li Xiannian wengao*, vol. 4, 225.

for almost a year, Chinese officials remained cautiously optimistic. Kang Shi'en estimated that China would shift its main sources of oil from onshore to offshore after 1985. According to his plan, some oilfields in Bohai Bay and the Gulf of Tonkin would begin production in 1986 and reach their full potential shortly, while oilfields in the South China Sea would require several more years.[53] The Chinese were pinning their hopes offshore.

After many months of waiting, foreign oilmen were losing patience. The Iranian Revolution and the Soviet invasion of Afghanistan in 1979 urged them to ramp up their efforts to find new sources of oil, while a worldwide recession in oil industry in the early 1980s created an urgent need for cash. No one knew the exact amount of China's offshore oil reserves—the numbers varied from the conservative US estimate of around 39 billion barrels, comparable to China's proven onshore reserves, to Beijing's unsubstantiated claim of 100 billion barrels, rivaling Saudi Arabia. The US estimate still exceeded the reserves in the North Sea (10–30 billion barrels) or in the United States (30 billion barrels), but extracting resources in the continental shelf along the Chinese coast would be far more daunting. Foreign oilmen had a hunch that China's offshore ventures would not fly as high as the thriving North Sea. Still, they remained arrested by China's offshore oil, as long as Beijing was determined to tap it with foreign technology.[54]

A breakthrough came in early 1982. In January, Beijing enacted the "Regulations of the People's Republic of China on Sino-Foreign Cooperation in the Exploration of Offshore Petroleum Resources" and rolled out the "model contract," a basic framework for offshore cooperation. The next month, Beijing established the China National Offshore Oil Corporation (CNOOC), a legal entity responsible for offshore ventures, with Qin Wencai as president. A day after CNOOC's founding, Beijing announced the first round of bidding for acreage in the northern part of the southern Yellow Sea and part of the Pearl River Estuary. That March, it opened more areas for bidding, including the southern part of the southern Yellow Sea, the southern part of the Gulf of Tonkin, and the western part of the Yinggehai Basin. Due to territorial disputes with Japan, Beijing left the entire East China Sea closed for bidding, but the designated areas in the southern Yellow Sea and the South China Sea covered 58,000 square miles. Invited for the bidding were 46 companies from a dozen countries that had participated in the 1979–80 surveys. With cautious excitement, most of these companies sent representatives to Beijing that May to pick up the bidding package.

Foreign oilmen opened the package and winced at the contract terms. They were obliged to conduct offshore exploration within five to seven years, bearing all the expenses, from seismic survey to exploratory drilling. If they found oil, they would negotiate production-sharing with CNOOC. Foreign companies and CNOOC would use 50 percent of produced oil as "cost oil" to recover the cost of exploration, development, and production. When all costs were recovered, they would split "profit oil," with CNOOC taking 51 percent and the foreign counterpart 49 percent. With the

[53] Kang, *Kang Shi'en*, 373–5.
[54] Thomas J. Lueck, "Plumbing China Oil Reserves," *New York Times*, August 18, 1983, pp. D1, 2.

12.5 percent royalty tax and the 5 percent sales tax, China's offshore oil seemed to be a risky business without guaranteed profit. Beijing also demanded all technologies, from design to software to data, transferred to the Chinese side after the termination of the contract. There was more. Foreign companies had to use Chinese equipment and personnel whenever possible, an arrangement that allowed Chinese engineers to learn technical and managerial skills.[55] Put simply, Beijing would win it all—it would put the financial burden on foreign firms, internalize offshore technology, and, if lucky, get oil. Foreign oilmen balked at making a long-term commitment to a precarious offshore enterprise in a country with rising domestic energy demand and a record of political instability—especially when the crude oil prices were declining. At the end of the day, however, they had little choice but to stay in the game. In August 1982, dozens of companies, including fifteen from the United States, applied for the bidding.

After months of silence, Beijing awarded the first offshore contract in May 1983—an area in the Pearl River Estuary—to an international group of oil companies led by British Petroleum (BP). Although BP estimated that large-scale production in this area, if possible at all, would require at least a decade, the deal elated the oilmen. Wilbert Hopper, Chairman of Petro-Canada, a member of the BP group, called the venture "very profitable."[56] "Our thinking is that offshore Chinese reserves represent at least another North Sea, and perhaps more," BP spokesperson Russ Hill enthused. "What we're looking at in China has very, very attractive potential."[57] BP's agreement was soon followed by several others involving US, Japanese, and French firms. Contrary to their public statements, these oil companies were far from euphoric. The triple whammy of rigorous contracts, declining oil prices, and slim prospects of finding oil had rendered China's offshore business more risky and less profitable than ever before. "The key point is to find oil," one US executive commented. "Both sides want to discover oil as quickly as possible."[58]

8. Walking the Energy Tightrope

Unfortunately, there was little oil. In the first half of the 1980s, foreign companies spent more than $1.7 billion in offshore exploration in the continental shelf near China. They drilled 150 exploratory wells, about one-third of them hitting oil or gas. Most of these fields, however, proved commercially infeasible due to the scanty amounts of production. No giant field with more than 1 billion barrels of oil reserves was discovered, and only three oilfields were profitable enough to develop—Total's Weizhou 10-3 in the Gulf of Tonkin and the Japan-China Oil Development Corporation (JCODC)'s Chengbei oilfield and BZ28-1 in Bohai Bay. Small wonder that Beijing's announcement of the second round of bidding in November 1984 attracted significantly less attention from foreign oilmen than did the first one. Worse, China's proven oil

---

[55] Stephanie R. Green, "Offshore business," *China Business Review* 9(3): 17–19.
[56] Christopher S. Wren, "China sets offshore oil accord," *New York Times*, May 11, 1983, pp. D1, 6.
[57] Lueck, "Plumbing China oil reserves."
[58] Kim Woodard, "The drilling begins," *China Business Review* 10(3): 25.

Table 7.5 Oil production at Daqing oilfield (thousand bpd)[59]

Year	Production
1970	365
1971	460
1972	526
1973	580
1974	708
1975	797
1976	867
1977	867
1978	868
1979	875
1980	887

Table 7.6 World crude prices (current USD per barrel)[60]

Year	Price	Year	Price
1970	1.80	1983	29.55
1971	2.24	1984	28.78
1972	2.48	1985	27.56
1973	3.29	1986	14.43
1974	11.58	1987	18.44
1975	11.53	1988	14.92
1976	12.80	1989	18.23
1977	13.92	1990	23.73
1978	14.02	1991	20.00
1979	31.61	1992	19.32
1980	36.83	1993	16.97
1981	35.93	1994	15.82
1982	32.97	1995	17.02

reserves plateaued between 1985 and 1988, hovering just over 17 billion barrels, before declining in 1989. The most fatal blow was the world crude prices, which fell precipitously from $27.6 per barrel in 1985 to $14.4 per barrel in 1986, obviating offshore ventures in many parts of the world. China's oil dream all but evaporated.

The energy balance in China was once again on the line, and Beijing rushed to cultivate other sources of oil. The best hope lay in what had motivated offshore ventures in the first place—the existing onshore oilfields in the Northeast. At the beginning of the 1980s, the Chinese could not detect or extract oil at greater depths and in more complex and remote structures in these fields due to severe lack of investment. To reinvigorate onshore oil production, CCP General Secretary Hu Yaobang and other high-ranking officials called for major technological updates.[61] Between 1981 and

---

[59] Chen Guangyu, *Daqing youtian zhi* [Daqing oilfield gazette] (Harbin: Heilongjiang renmin chubanshe, 2009), 264.

[60] BP Statistical Review of World Energy 2022.

[61] David Denny, "China's oil industry charts a new course," *China Business Review* 12(1): 14–18.

1984, Beijing spent more than $26 million, partially using loans from the World Bank, to buy more than 400 submersible water pumps from the United States, which enabled it to boost Daqing's production and dig new wells in the area.[62] Moreover, Minister of Petroleum Tang Ke and Daqing President Li Yugang toured the United States in 1984 to study onshore oil technology. Upon their return, Beijing dramatically increased equipment and service purchases from the United States, which peaked at $372.6 million in 1985. With the new investments, Daqing could maintain a steady production of 947,000–965,000 bpd until the turn of the twenty-first century.

That—combined with the development of new oilfields and coalmines—bought some time for China's offshore soft landing. In 1987, China's offshore oil production reached 142,000 bpd, approximately five percent of the total oil production, with Chengbei producing 72,000 bpd and Weizhou 10-3 7,000 bpd. That same year, a consortium of Agip (Italy), Chevron, and Texaco signed a contract to develop Huizhou 21-1 in the Pearl River Basin, which would produce 20,000 bpd in the early 1990s. In 1988, JCODC's BZ28-1 in Bohai Bay came into operation, with a production capacity of 22,000 bpd. These modest successes kept foreign oilmen's hopes afloat. When Beijing declared parts of the East China Sea under China's undisputed sovereignty open to preliminary survey in 1989, Exxon, BP, and Phillips quickly expressed interest. All the while, Beijing was internalizing offshore technology as fast as possible. In 1987, CNOOC found and developed an oilfield in the northern Bohai Gulf, named Suizhong 36-1. The Ministry of Geology also drilled sixteen wells of its own in the East China Sea between 1980 and 1990, of which thirteen hit oil or gas. The offshore business was no longer a black box for the Chinese.

Beijing successfully walked the energy tightrope. In the 1980s, oil production increased from 2 million bpd to 2.8 million bpd, and coal production rose from 700 million tons to 1.2 billion tons. This rapid expansion fell short of reversing the worsening of China's energy balance, let alone generating a large amount of foreign currency through exports. It, however, more than offset the offshore sector's less-than-ideal performance. Between 1980 and 1990, foreign companies invested $2.7 billion in China's offshore industry ($2.25 billion for exploration and $450 million for

Table 7.7 Oil production by oilfields in 1985 (bpd)[63]

Oilfield	Production
Huabei	175.78
Daqing	923.04
Shengli	396.52
Liaohe	130.97
Xinjiang	77.55
Dagang	54.63
Changqing	24.47

---

[62] Christopher S. Wren, "China's race to keep pumping oil," *New York Times*, April 22, 1984, p. F9.
[63] National Bureau of Statistics, *Zhongguo tongji nianjian* 1986, 342.

development), surveying 400 kilometers of seismic lines and drilling 220 wells. They found 6.34 billion barrels of oil and 120 billion cubic meters of gas.[64] At the end of the decade, however, only three wells were producing oil; two wells were under construction; and six gas wells were under development. These results were disappointing, but not disastrous. In those ten years, CNOOC earned $1.8 billion from oil sales and service contracts, accumulating capital and technology to expand its own offshore operation.[65] The Chinese offshore dream collapsed under its own weight, but Beijing's—and foreign oilmen's—efforts to reach that dream did pay off, at least partially.

9. Conclusion

The oil shocks of the 1970s and 1980s—the steep rise and fall of the world crude prices—transformed China's economic statecraft. Before 1973, China was an outcast, interacting with the world economy within the strict boundary of "self-reliance." The global energy crises of the 1970s caused a facelift. The fantasy about Chinese oil, shared by foreign oilmen and the Chinese, who promoted technology trade to turn the fantasy into reality, gradually incorporated China into the capitalist bloc, economically and politically. Even before the official launch of Reform and Opening-Up, China's energy sector ushered in a new era of joint ventures, a point of no return for a country that had permitted minimum foreign economic presence in its territory for almost two decades. Although self-reliance survived as a discursive device, its concept became more and more plastic and expansive. By the end of the 1980s, China had placed itself firmly on track to being integrated further into the global economy, and the Tiananmen Square Massacre of 1989 only slowed down the process.

By no means was China's economic success preordained. When China faced its own energy crisis in the late 1970s, there was a chance that it would slip into a predicament similar to the one that triggered the demise of the Soviet bloc. The Soviet Union profited handsomely from the global energy crisis of the 1970s, but its satellite states in Eastern Europe, which relied on Soviet oil exports, suffered from it. The plunge in the oil prices in the mid-1980s and the subsequent troubles in Soviet finances left the entire Soviet bloc deeply indebted to the West, which occasioned economic reforms that would eventually tear down socialism.[66] China, too, was more indebted than ever before at the close of the 1970s due to the technological shopping spree, and its largest source of income was the revenues from oil exports, inflated by the upheavals in the Middle East. When the oil bubble burst in the mid-1980s, the Chinese were beset by the double trouble of energy shortage and foreign currency shortage, much like the Russians and the Eastern Europeans. The Chinese persevered nonetheless. Throughout the 1980s, onshore reinvestments and offshore ventures allowed them to maintain a modest yet steady increase in oil production and an inexpensive flow of technology

---

[64] Kang, *Kang Shi'en*, 543.
[65] Qin, *Xin ji lan jiang*, 27.
[66] On this point, see, for example, Michael De Groot, "The Soviet Union, CMEA, and the energy crisis of the 1970s," *Journal of Cold War Studies* 22(4): 4–30.

transfer. By the time China became an oil importer in 1993, it was making headway to becoming the factory of the world, racking up trade surpluses with the rest of the world.

All this begs the question: how did China avoid the fate of the Soviet Union? China's oil strategy was not planned—until the mid-1980s, it was largely predicated on a pipe dream that the continental shelf in the East and South China Seas would one day turn China into an oil giant. In pursuing that pipe dream, however, the Chinese had to take a delicate balance between the need to absorb foreign technology and the visceral aversion to forming dependency, an aporia that caused heated debates within the CCP leadership. Beijing never tilted to one side. If it forsook self-reliance altogether and obtained more loans and credits from overseas, Reform and Opening-Up could have ended abruptly due to a financial crisis, similar to the ones that engulfed Latin America in the early 1980s. If, on the other hand, Beijing hit the brakes hard on technology imports and joint ventures, it could have suffered enormously from the energy crisis and regressed into isolation from the world economy. The ad hoc, incremental nature of China's oil policy in the 1970s and 1980s, crafted by policymakers with diverse lines of economic thinking, enabled China to navigate through the energy crisis without falling into the pitfalls along the way. In this sense, China's economic rise was indeed a "miracle."

8

India's Green Revolution, the World Bank, and the Oil Crises in the 1970s—Focusing on Chemical Fertilizers

Shigeru Akita

This chapter reconsiders progress in India's Green Revolution, specifically agricultural development in the 1970s within the context of the two oil crises. How did India achieve de facto self-sufficiency in food production in the 1970s despite the critical impact of the oil crises? What factors contributed to India's agricultural development in the 1970s?

In the middle of the 1960s, India managed to overcome a serious food crisis through international aid, especially through the United States' (US) PL480 for foreign food aid.[1] During the food crisis, the Indian government changed its policy priorities regarding economic development from heavy industrialization for the production of capital goods to agricultural development. This could be called the start of India's Green Revolution from the late 1960s.[2]

However, in 1973–4, India faced another critical economic situation caused by the first oil crisis, which led to a shortage of the most basic inputs for agricultural development—chemical fertilizer. Chemical fertilizer is a major by-product of the petrochemical industry.[3] How did the Indian government solve this shortage in a global economic crisis? This chapter first focuses on external economic aid to India, especially from the World Bank (WB) group—specifically, the International Bank for Reconstruction and Development (IBRD) and the International Development Association (IDA)—led by its President Robert McNamara (1968–81),[4] and then

8

[1] See, Shigeru Akita, Teikoku kara Kaihatsu-Enjyo e: Sengo Ajia Kokusai-Chitsujyo to Kougyouka [From Empires to Development Aid: International Economic Order of Asia and Industrialization in the 1950s–60s] (Nagoya: Nagoya University Press, 2017); David C. Engerman, The Price of Aid: The Economic Cold War in India (Cambridge, Massachusetts: Harvard University Press, 2018).
[2] C. Subramaniam, Hand of Destiny: Memoirs, Vol. II: The Green Revolution (Bombay: Bharatiya Vidya Bhavan, 1995); Nick Cullather, The Hungry World—America's Cold War Battle against Poverty in Asia (Cambridge, Massachusetts: Harvard University Press, 2010).
[3] Michael Tanzer, The Political Economy of International Oil and the Underdeveloped Countries, (London: Temple Smith, 1965), chap. 19.
[4] Patrick Allan Sharma, Robert McNamara's Other War: The World Bank and International Development (Philadelphia: University of Pennsylvania Press, 2017).

considers its implications in the context of the Green Revolution and the transformation of international economic order in Asia in the 1970s. After the first oil crisis (1973–4), India overcame its critical economic situation through strong efforts to expand exports and invisible incomes. India recorded exceptionally favorable trade balances between 1974–5 and 1976–7 when exports grew at an average annual rate of 27 percent and a dramatic increase remittance from the Gulf countries. This steady growth was overturned in 1979 during the second oil crisis. How did India manage to recover from this second economic turmoil in the early 1980s? In the last section, we explore the Indian government's distinctive approaches to the two oil crises in the 1970s.

1. India's Economic Development in the 1970s: from Industrialization to Agricultural Development

In the late 1960s and early 1970s, India shifted its policy priorities for economic development from industry to agriculture after the food crisis and the threat of famine in 1965–7. At the latter stage of the Third Five-Year Plan (1961–5), India, faced with the slow pace of heavy industrialization, focused on the production of capital goods. Concurrently, India suffered two successive years of food shortages and drought due to poor monsoon seasons. Under these critical economic conditions, the Indian government was forced to declare a "Plan Holiday" to reconsider the content and economic strategies of the upcoming Fourth Five-Year Plan. Three Annual Plans were drawn during this intervening period (1966–9).

The long-awaited revised Fourth Five-Year Plan was finally tabled in the Indian Parliament on April 21, 1969. This was the product of a new team appointed in September 1967 at the Planning Commission (deputy chairman D. R. Gadgil). They had taken good advantage of the three-year hiatus in five-year planning to make a fundamental reassessment of the Indian economy's capabilities and requirements after fifteen years of planned development effort. The most striking features of the Fourth Five-Year Plan were: (1) the relatively modest size of public sector expenditure and expectations for gross foreign aid, which shifted the financing of public sector development expenditure from a heavy reliance on foreign aid and deficit financing to a greater reliance on domestic resources; and (2) the significantly greater role assigned to private sector investment, particularly in agriculture, small-scale industries, and transportation.

As for the financing of the Fourth Plan, the reduction of net aid as a proportion of total financing to 17.5 percent (28 percent in the Third Plan, 29 percent in the original Fourth Plan, and about 40 percent during the three years of Annual Plans)[5] was

---

[5]   In September 1968, American ambassador C. Bowles pointed out the same statistics of 41 percent for 1966/67 and 45 percent for 1967/68, but he still emphasized the importance of foreign aid, which provide well over one-third of the financing for the Indian government development program in the 1968/69 Annual Plan. See Airgram A-1454 from AmEmbassy NEW DELHI to Department of State, September 13, 1968, "GOI Annual Plan for 1968–69," by Chester Bowles, p. 4, E 2-2 GER-E 1/1/67 BOX 624 [The US National Archives and Research Administration, College Park-Maryland: NARA II].

presented as a reflection of India's determination to achieve self-reliance. Except for concessional food aid—expected to be phased out after 1971 because of increased domestic availability—the decline in net aid also reflected a more realistic assessment of the availability of foreign aid as well as the mounting burden of debt repayment.[6] The year before the start of the revised Fourth Five-Year Plan, domestic food production in India recovered and achieved the level of 95 million tons, and then exceeded 100 million tons in 1971–2. Through this drastic increase in domestic food production, the volume of grain imports, especially imports through PL480 channels, tended to decrease. Although food imports were not completely terminated, as shown in Table 8.1, India started to move toward greater self-reliance in the production of grains from the late 1960s, This marked the beginning of the Green Revolution.[7]

In the latter half of the 1960s, PL480 aid from the US government played a crucial role in India's economic development during the food crisis. The Johnson administration used PL480 as political leverage to influence India's economic policies, especially its agricultural policy. The Johnson administration's "short tether" policy was very effective in moving India's agricultural policies into a more liberal direction.[9]

However, even if we recognize the effective external factors, domestic and internal factors were prerequisite for the transformation of the Indian economy, especially the modernization and self-reliance of Indian agriculture. India's food crisis ended with the improvement in weather patterns (monsoon) in 1967–8. The strenuous efforts to reform agricultural policies started toward the end of the Third Five-Year Plan under the Shastri administration and the liberal leadership of the Minister of Food and Agriculture (C. Subramaniam), the Planning Minister (Ashok Meta), a prominent financial official, later Governor of the Reserve Bank of India (J. K. Jha), and the Finance

Table 8.1 Indian food production and food imports in the 1960s

Year	Domestic production	Whole imports	PL 480
1964–5	8,070	625 (7.7)	543 (6.7)
1965–6	8,940	744 (8.3)	635 (7.1)
1966–7	7,320	1,031 (14.1)	806 (11.0)
1967–8	7,420	866 (11.7)	596 (8.0)
1968–9	9,501	567 (6.0)	421 (4.4)
1969–70	9,400	382 (4.1)	257 (2.7)
1970–1	9.950	355 (3.6)	245 (2.5)
1971–2	10,842	201 (1.9)	121 (1.1)

Note: Unit: 10,000 ton (percent).[8]

---

[6] Airgram A-299 From AmEmbassy NEW DELHI to Department of State, May 1, 1969, "India's Revised Fourth Five-Year Plan" by Whathesby, pp. 2–14, E 5 INDIA 1/1/67 BOX 624.

[7] Bruno Dorin and Frédéric Landy, *Agriculture and Food in India: A Half-century Review from Independence to Globalization* (New Delhi: Manohar, 2002), chapter 3; Nick Cullather, *The Hungry World—America's Cold War Battle against Poverty in Asia*, chapter 9.

[8] Government of India, *Economic Survey 1964-65~1971-72* (New Delhi: Government Printing Office, 1965-72).

[9] Shigeru Akita, "The Aid-India Consortium, the World Bank, and the International Order of Asia, 1958–1968," *Asian Review of World Histories* 2-2 (2014): 217–48.

Minister and (later) Deputy Prime Minister under the Indira Gandhi administration (Morarji Desai). India's ambassador to the US, B. K. Nehru, who had initiated the Aid India Consortium, also tried to mediate between the Indian government and the Johnson administration, in collaboration with prominent US officials, such as W. W. Rostow, the National Security Special Adviser to the President, and Chester Bowles, US ambassador to India.[10] Their skillful economic diplomacy enabled the acquisition of financial resources for the construction of Indian infrastructure.

For a smooth start and continuation of the Green Revolution, three prerequisites were crucial: (1) the introduction of high-yielding seed varieties (HYVs), (2) intensive use of chemical fertilizers,[11] and (3) an improvement in irrigation practices, especially the development of tube wells and electric power for pumps. In this chapter, among these three requirements of the Green Revolution, we focus on chemical fertilizer because of its linkage to India's industrialization (petrochemical industries) and its close relationship with oil imports during the oil crises of the 1970s.

In the multilateral framework for aid to India, the Aid India Consortium led by the WB was crucial for the acceleration of economic development, especially to overcome the Food Crisis. The WB organized the Food Consortium in April 1967 in Paris and urged Consortium members as well as non-member countries to cooperate to provide India with food aid. In 1968, Robert McNamara succeeded George Woods as the president of the WB. McNamara's long presidency (1968–81) drastically transformed the mission and activities of the WB in the 1970s.[12] Under his leadership, the WB group, especially the IDA, dramatically expanded their lending to developing countries, including India, more than ten times more than before.[13] The mission of the WB changed from profit-motivated industrial lending and support to capital-intensive industrialization, to support agricultural and social development, and poverty-

---

[10] Chester Bowles, *Promises to Keep—My Years in Public Life 1941–1969* (New York and London: Harper & Row, Publishers, 1971), Part IV: Ambassador to India; Chester Bowles, *A View from New Delhi—Selected Speeches and Writings by Chester Bowles* (New Haven and London: Yale University Press, 1969), Section 2.

[11] Nitrogen fertilizers (N) are made from ammonia (NH_3), which is sometimes injected into the ground directly. The ammonia is produced by the Haber-Bosch process. In this energy-intensive process, natural gas (CH_4) usually supplies the hydrogen, and the nitrogen (N_2) is derived from the air. This ammonia is used as a feedstock for all other nitrogen fertilizers, such as anhydrous ammonium nitrate (NH_4NO_3) and urea ($CO(NH_2)$). All phosphate fertilizers (P) are obtained by extraction from minerals containing the anion PO_4^{3-}. In rare cases, fields are treated with the crushed mineral, but most often more soluble salts are produced by chemical treatment of phosphate minerals. The most popular phosphate-containing minerals are referred to collectively as phosphate rock. Potash (K) is a mixture of potassium minerals used to make potassium (chemical symbol: K) fertilizers. Potash is soluble in water, so the main effort in producing this nutrient from the ore involves some purification steps; e.g., to remove sodium chloride (NaCl) (common salt). Sometimes potash is referred to as K_2O, as a matter of convenience to those describing the potassium content. In fact potash fertilizers are usually potassium chloride, potassium sulfate, potassium carbonate, or potassium nitrate.

[12] Patrick Allan Sharma, *Robert McNamara's Other War: The World Bank and International Development*.

[13] S. Guhan, "The World Bank's lending in South Asia," in Devesh Kapur, John P. Lewis, and Richard Webb (eds.), *The World Bank: Its First Half Century*, vol. 2, *Perspectives* (Washington DC: Brookings Institution Press, 1997), chapter 8, 317–84.

reduction efforts such as public health, elementary education, and family planning. In particular, agricultural development in developing countries was emphasized as an important target of the lending program. In this context, we examine the close relationship between the Green Revolution and the supply and production of artificial fertilizers in India in the 1970s.

2. The World Fertilizer Crisis and the Active Role of the World Bank

Before the first oil crisis, developing countries experienced a so-called fertilizer crisis. The WB Report, *Fertiliser Requirements of Developing Countries in 1975*,[14] reported that the critical shortage in fertilizers was a global problem from the early 1970s. Since 1971-2, the higher demand for fertilizer, coupled with an increase in the price of raw materials and energy, resulted in fertilizer shortages and unprecedented high prices. The *Report* highlighted four reasons for the sharp rise in fertilizer prices after 1971: (1) the slowdown in investment in fertilizer production facilities, (2) severe droughts and crop failures in various parts of the world, (3) a substantial increase in energy and raw material prices, and (4) a build-up and augmentation of fertilizer stocks in several developing countries as a hedge against inflation. The *Report* noted that the greatest impact of the shortage was felt in importing developing countries. Two-thirds of developing countries' fertilizer requirements were imported at the time, and it was in this market that the major shortages and hence highest prices occurred. The sharp upward movement of fertilizer prices after 1972 is shown in the *Report's* price chart of Figure 8.1.[15]

> Whatever the reasons for the high prices and fertilizer shortages, it became clear early in 1974 that many developing countries would not manage to produce adequate quantities of fertilizers and that therefore urgent international action was required. The most seriously affected countries were in the weakest position due to their inability to pay for the needed imports from their own resources or to mobilize them through bilateral or multilateral aid.[16]

In terms of fertilizer investment and providing technical help on fertilizer production and use, the WB group was the most active of all the bilateral and international lending institutions in investing in new capacity in developing countries:

> Up to the end of 1973 the Bank Group had made total investments of nearly US$300 million in 19 fertilizer projects in 17 countries, of which US$147 million were approved between 1970–1973 for six projects. During 1974 alone, the Bank

---

[14] Report No. 830: *Fertilizer Requirements of Developing Countries—Revised Outlook in 1975*, July 1975, Industry Projects Department, the International Bank for Reconstruction and Development/ International Development Association.
[15] "Export price indications for some major fertilizer materials," in ibid., 15.
[16] Ibid., 3–4.

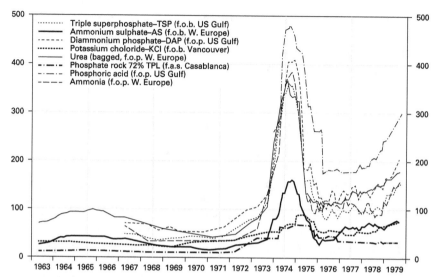

Figure 8.1 Export price trends for selected fertilizer materials (US$ per ton of product) current prices.

Group made commitments in the amount of US$ 329 million for seven projects in six countries, and in the first half of 1975 a further US$ 329 million for seven fertilizer projects were approved. All these projects together (excluding potash) represent an annual capacity of 4.4 million tons of nutrients, or about 13% of the nitrogenous and phosphatic fertilizer capacity currently installed or firmly committed in the developing countries.

4.02

Although the Bank has financed projects for the production of all three fertilizer nutrients (nitrogen, phosphates and potash), the greatest help has been directed toward the production of nitrogenous fertilizers and, in particular, ammonia and urea. This emphasis has been justified by the fact that it has been in the nitrogen area that the principal shortages have occurred and are likely to continue in the next few years. Also, although all three nutrients are required over a period of time to achieve a balanced enrichment of the soil and thus optimum crop response, the regular application of nitrogen is needed most of all in the early years of major fertilizer use to give maximum crop yields.

4.03

This *Report* recommended that:

the Bank Group plans for the next five years should contain about US$ 1 billion for new fertilizer production facilities and the related marketing and distribution network to meet additional fertilizer demands in developing countries after 1980. This compares with about US$ 775 million approved over the last five years (FY

1971–75) and about US$ 720 million in the last three years (FY 1973–75). The Bank/IDA operations program for FY 1976–79 included US$ 0.5 billion for fertilizers (nitrogen fertilizers US$ 165 million; phosphate fertilizer US$ 155 million; phosphate rock US$ 60 million; potash US$ 30 million; and unspecified US$ 120 million).

5.14

This also suggested that the WB group adopted an increasingly comprehensive approach to fertilizer development aimed at responding flexibility to changing requirements in all aspects of fertilizer production and use in developing countries. For the WB group, financing fertilizer projects in developing countries became an important lending target during the first oil crisis.

3. The First Oil Crisis and India's Economy

India's economy went through a difficult period in 1972/73. In addition to stagnation in the industrial sector, agricultural production was severely impacted by a drought in 1972/73. Despite a favorable monsoon in 1973 and a good autumn harvest, India's food situation remained challenging. The crop shortfall was the result of acute shortages in fertilizers and electric power and diesel to run irrigation systems, as well as poor winter rainfall. Shortfalls in agricultural production were the primary contributors to inflation—the inflation rate was around 25 percent in 1974, compared only 4–5 percent a few years ago.

After the balance of payments crisis of the late 1950s, a shortage of foreign exchange constituted a critical constraint on the development of India's economy. The increase in global commodity prices added to these problems. Petroleum was a very prominent item in the import bill. In 1972/73, imports of crude oil and petroleum products amounted to US$ 265 million, equivalent to 10 percent of merchandise imports; estimates for 1973/74 were US$ 625 million (18 percent), and for 1974/75 US$ 1,300 million (26 percent). The Indian government undertook several measures to cope with the situation. The short-term focus was to reduce consumption by increasing the price of petroleum products and converting oil-burning equipment to coal wherever possible.

Since the bulk of petroleum consumption was concentrated in vital sectors as agriculture (as inputs for fertilizer production and as fuel for irrigation systems and mechanized farming), transport, and industry, lower oil supplies were bound to depress overall economic production. However, the higher oil price was only one element in India's widening trade deficit. The need for large food and fertilizer imports at exceptionally high prices in 1973, and the price increases in oil, steel, non-ferrous metals, and other vital imports increased India's import bill by 37 percent in 1973/74. This increase was partly offset by a 14 percent increase in exports, but the estimated trade gap was about US$ 650 million compared with US$ 50 million in 1972/73. Total imports were expected to increase by a further 40 percent if prices remained at their present level. Exports continued to do well, which reduced the impact of the enlarged import bill. However, there was a critical need for external assistance, mainly from the IDA, at a much higher level than the US$ 1.3 billion of the previous year, which was itself 45 percent (US$ 400 million) higher than the year before.

As a result of substantial borrowing in the past, India's external public debt stood at US$ 9.9 billion on March 31, 1973. Debt services in 1973/74 were estimated at US$ 700 million, equivalent to around 24 percent of export receipts. The Consortium extended debt relief to India from 1968/69 onward to mitigate the negative effects of such a high burden of external debt on growth. In 1973/74, the amount of debt relief was about US$ 185 million. On the assumption that India would obtain its new financing requirements on appropriately soft terms, debt service was expected to grow more slowly in the 1970s to around 20 percent of export receipts by 1980.[17]

4. India's Fertilizer Industry after the First Oil Crisis

The WB usually made an appraisal on all credit financing to India. The US was the largest fertilizer exporter to India. The US embassy's agricultural attaché, Ivan E. Johnson, regularly sent *Fertilizer Survey of India*, from New Delhi to the US Department of Agriculture in Washington DC. The *World Bank Appraisal Report* and *American Fertilizer Survey of India* provide details on fertilizer production, their use in Indian agriculture, and the implications and impact of the first oil crisis.

The agricultural sector and fertilizer production were the focal points of the IDA's lending. Based on the WB's *Appraisal Report*,[18] the IDA became involved in India's fertilizer industry in 1970. Since it was impossible to identify a private sector project, the IDA concentrated on projects in the public sector that were focused on the modernization and/or expansion of existing plants with external engineering. During the Fourth Plan (1969–74), seven public sector projects were started, including four assisted by the IDA.

As shown in Figure 8.2, fertilizer production in India increased rapidly after 1954, and continued to increase for the following two decades. Under the Third Five-Year Plan, the procurement of fertilizer tended to shift from imports to domestic production through the construction of many fertilizer plants. In this section, we observe the development of India's fertilizer industry during and after the first oil crisis.

4.1. Fertilizer Production: the Largest Heavy Industry in India in the Mid-1970s

After the first oil crisis (1973–4), India's government requested an IDA credit of US$ 105 million to improve existing plants' capacity utilization. The total cost of this

---

[17] Report No. P-1460-IN, "Report and Recommendations of the President to the Executive Directors on a Proposed Credit to the Government of India for the Trombay IV Fertilizer Expansion and Plant Operations Improvement Project," June 3, 1974, 1240623: Fertilizer Expansion and Plant Operation Project-Trombay Fertilizer-Credit 0481-P009685-Correspondence, World Bank Archives.

[18] Report No. 928-IN, "Appraisal of a Project to Improve Fertilizer Production Fertilizer Industry Credit; India," November 24, 1975, Industrial Projects Department, the World Bank.

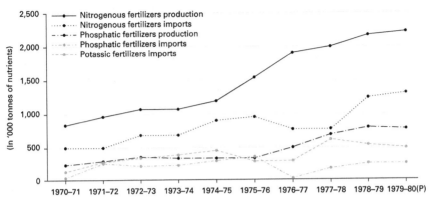

Figure 8.2 Import and domestic production of three major artificial fertilizers in India.
Source: The Government of India, *The Economic Survey of India, 1970–1979* (New Delhi).

program was estimated at US$ 239 million, including US$ 92 million in foreign currency. This credit represented the WB group's ninth project since 1967 in fertilizer production facilities, including two by the IFC (International Finance Cooperation) and seven by the IDA.

In India, there were sixteen major fertilizer companies with twenty operating plants. In 1975, they have a total capacity of about 2.8 million tons of nitrogen (N) and 0.8 million tons of phosphate (P), with sixteen additional plants under construction and five in a planning phase. The industry was expected to have a total capacity of about 6.4 million TPY (tons per year) by 1979—55 percent in the public sector, 27 percent joint public–private ventures, and 18 percent in the private sector. The total capacity would include 5.1 million TPY of nitrogen content in fertilizers and 1.3 million TPY of phosphate content in fertilizers.[19]

However, India was only able to achieve 60 percent overall capacity utilization in the fertilizer industry. Imports were still required to meet about half of the country's demand, thus further aggravating India's severe balance of payments situation.

The US *Fertilizer Survey of India for 1976* noted that India's fertilizer industry, with a total investment of Rs. 10,680 million at the end of November 1975, was one of the largest and most vital industries in India. India's government continued to emphasize public sector expansion entailing excessive use of unproved domestic engineering capacity and overburdened management. Despite these problems and an economy that was unable to provide all the needed inputs and infrastructure (principally shortages in electric power, raw materials, transportation systems, and equipment replacement), India's fertilizer industry was still in a relatively good position compared to other developing countries. The *Fertilizer Survey of India for 1976* reported:

---

[19] Report No. 928-IN, "Appraisal of a Project to Improve Fertilizer Production Fertilizer Industry Credit; India," 3.12, 9–10.

Some domestic engineering capacity has been established; Indian capacity in equipment, construction, and civil works has expanded greatly in the last few years; foreign exchanges costs are about half those of projects in countries such as Indonesia, Philippines, and Arabian Gulf countries; and total foreign exchange requirements are only about 30–40 percent of a project's cost compared with about 60–80 percent elsewhere. However, deliveries from the equipment manufacturing industry frequently take longer than desirable.[20]

4.2. India's Fertilizer Investment Program in the mid-1970s

The WB's *Report* of 1975 described India's domestic fertilizer production as follows: "The forecast assumes that gradually India will become virtually self-sufficient in nitrogen fertilizer (N) production, but keep importing some amount of phosphate (P) and all of its potash (K) requirements. To meet its increasing demands for fertilizer, the Government is making efforts to increase the output from existing plants and is undertaking an ambitious program to add new capacity (2.08)."[21]

India's fertilizer industry continued to expand: from 3.6 million TPY in 1975 to about 6.4 million TPY nutrient capacity by 1979. As shown Table 8.2, the Indian government's contribution would account for more than two-thirds of the total costs. The Indian government's funds during 1976–9 accounted for an annual average of about US$ 0.5 billion or about 15–20 percent of India's annual development capital budget (4.04, 13).

The investment program faced some risk. The management and technical capabilities of the industry were significantly stretched with additional projects. The capital goods industry, still experiencing difficulties in supplying fertilizer equipment on time, was hard pressed to keep up with orders. Most importantly, government funding constraints further delayed the completion of several projects.

Table 8.2 Financing sources for the fertilizer investment program (US$ million)[22]

| Fiscal year (March 31) | Through 1975 | Disbursement period | | | |
		1976–9	1980	Total	%
IBRD/IDA	45	395	–	440	11
Other external credits	180	320	–	500	12
Local financial institutions	–	200	–	200	5
Internal enterprise funds	40	130	–	170	4
Government of India	485	2,010	290	2,785	68
Total	750	3,055	290	4,095	100

[20] RG166 BOX59: Fertilizer Survey of India for 1976, In-6045, May 21, 1976, by Ivan E. Johnson, Agricultural Attachê, NARA II.

[21] Report No. 928-IN, "Appraisal of a Project to Improve Fertilizer Production, Fertilizer Industry Credit; India," November 24, 1975, Industrial Projects Department, the World Bank, 4.

[22] Report No. 928-IN, "Appraisal of a Project to Improve Fertilizer Production, Fertilizer Industry Credit; India," 13.

Notwithstanding the anticipated easing of the supply and a consequential decrease in international fertilizer prices, there were several factors that justified capital investment to increase domestic fertilizer production in India, either by modernizing or expanding existing plants or by building new factories:

> Firstly, even with expected lowering of international fertilizer prices, the economic return on capacity additions in India is still expected to be satisfactory. Secondly any shortage in the international market, even temporary, has a major adverse effect on the balance of payments of countries who rely on imports to fill a large portion of their requirements. During 1972 to 1975, India depended on imports for 45 to 50% of fertilizer nutrient consumption. When prices almost tripled between 1974 and 1976, the fertilizer import bill jumped from US$355 million in 1974 to an estimated US$1,090 million in 1976. Such large and unexpected drains on the scarce foreign exchange resources of a country creates strains on the economy and disrupts economic development programs. Considering the cyclical nature of the fertilizer industry, such disruption may happen again unless steps are taken now to reduce major dependence on imports.
>
> 8.03[23]

In the face of other demands on the available foreign exchange, for example, the demand for petroleum, oil, and lubricants (POL), foodgrain imports, and debt servicing, the US government projected India's need for more long-term financial credit in 1976 as follows: "India is quite likely not only to take advantage of any available long-term credit for the purchase of fertilizer and fertilizer-feedstock import requirements, but also to regularize these needs at more stable price levels through the conclusion of bilateral trade agreements covering these and other import requirements in exchange for guaranteed markers for Indian agricultural, semi-manufactured, and manufactured products."[24]

4.3. Oil as Feedstock for the Fertilizer Industry

To increase domestic production of fertilizers, India utilized a wide range of raw materials in ammonia production, including natural gas, naphtha, fuel oil, coal, lignite, coke-oven gas, and electrolytic hydrogen. As long as domestic gas was available, it was used, although India had small reserves of natural gas, it was sufficient to provide feedstock for only two fertilizer plants, the FCI (Fertilizer Corporation of India) Namrup plant in Assam and the IFFCO (Indian Farmers Fertilizer Corporative) Kalol plant in Gujarat. All the other fertilizer plants relied on petroleum products, namely naphtha and fuel oil, provided by the oil industry. Traditionally, naphtha was used as feedstock. The naphtha conversion process to produce ammonia was a well-known process and was the only one commercially available for the manufacturer of nitrogen fertilizer from petroleum feedstock.

---

[23] Report No. 928-IN, "Appraisal of a Project to Improve Fertilizer Production, Fertilizer Industry Credit; India," 26.
[24] RG166 BOX59: Fertilizer Survey of India for 1976, In-6045, May 21, 1976, by Ivan E. Johnson, Agricultural Attaché, NARA II.

The Indian government, through the Ministry of Petroleum and Chemicals, had decided in 1971 to adopt fuel oil as the feedstock for all ammonia plants built in India. Although they were aware of the additional capital cost required, the higher price of naphtha, when compared to fuel oil, and the availability of surplus fuel oil in the local market, appeared to be sufficient reason to justify the decision from both an economic as well as a supply point of view. The US *Fertilizer Survey of India for 1976* made the same observation:

> As for the feedstock of fertilizer production, most Indian fertilizer plants are fuel-based. Prior to the sharp rise in the price of crude oil in late 1973, the industry's plans were based on an increase in petroleum refining capacity commensurate with the natural growth in demand and the anticipated surpluses of light distillates. As a consequence of the price increase, considerations have increasingly been given to the use of heavy fuel oil and coal. The present quandary is one facing the refining industry as much as the fertilizer industry. Despite the additional capital cost involved, the higher price of naphtha when compared to fuel oil and the expectation of ample surpluses of fuel oil in the local market were viewed by the Government of India in 1971 as sufficient bases upon which to decide to adopt fuel oil as the feedstock for all ammonia plants to be built in India.[25]

In the *Appraisal Credit Report* of 1975, the WB pointed out the substitution of fuel oil with coal: "Recently, the Indian government has attempted to reduce the use of crude oil by substituting fuel oil with coal, and the resultant prospective surplus of heavy fuel oil would warrant, in their view, the establishment of a new generation of fertilizer plants based on fuel oil rather than naphtha." In India, the choices for new capacity were therefore limited to naphtha, fuel oil, or coal. This situation changed again in favor of naphtha after the discovery of oil and gas reserves off Bombay in 1977.

The priorities for feedstock in India's fertilizer industry fluctuated between naphtha, fuel oil, coal, and natural gas based on the price of crude oil before and after the first oil crisis. By 1979, of the estimated 5.1 million TPY of total nitrogen (N content of fertilizer) installed capacity, 37 percent was based on naphtha, 31 percent on fuel oil, 13 percent on coal, 12 percent on gas, and 7 percent on other sources (3.18).[26] More than 60 percent of the feedstock of India's fertilizer industry depended on petroleum. This heavy dependence on imported oil from the Middle East (Iran, Iraq, and Saudi Arabia) was greatly influenced by the spike in oil prices during the first oil crisis.

In terms of fertilizer production, India was projected to approach nitrogen self-sufficiency by 1980, while maintaining phosphate imports at about 200,000–400,000 TPY and increasing potash imports to about 800,000 TPY (all in nutrients). Import costs, including raw materials, were expected to average about US$ 900 million annually between 1977 and 1981, on the assumption that ongoing projects were

---

[25] RG166 BOX59: Fertilizer Survey of India for 1976, In-6045, May 21, 1976, by Ivan E. Johnson, Agricultural Attaché, NARA II.

[26] Report No. 928-IN, "Appraisal of a Project to Improve Fertilizer Production, Fertilizer Industry Credit; India," November 24, 1975, Industrial Projects Department, the World Bank, 12.

completed on schedule. Despite the rapid progress in import substitution and the expansion of domestic fertilizer production, external connections in trade and development finance or economic aid were still needed for India's agricultural development in the late 1970s.

5. The Second Oil Crisis and India's Agreement with the IMF in 1981

India made a quick recovery from the economic recession that followed the first oil crisis; however, in 1979–80, India once again experienced a sharp deterioration in its economy due to a combination of several adverse factors. First, the economy faced a severe drought. Second, it ran into constraints imposed by the poor performance of its infrastructure sectors such as power, coal, and transport where shortages could not be overcome by imports. Third, political instability for a major part of the year produced a lack of effective direction from the government. Last, and most crucially, the substantial rise in petroleum prices and disruption in supply caused both direct and indirect damage to the economy. India faced the second oil crisis in this complex entanglement of political economy.

5.1. The Recovery in the Balance of Payments, Remittances from the Middle East, and a Complex Entanglement of Political Economy

India's government clearly recognized a difference in the international economic order between the first oil crisis (1973) and the second oil crisis (1979–80):

At present, India is placed in a different situation from that in 1973 when the first major increase in oil prices took place. In the years that followed the fourfold increase in petroleum prices in 1973, the balance of payments difficulties were tackled through a highly successful export performance. Exports increased at an average annual rate of 27% between 1974–75 and 1976–77. We organized domestic production and fashioned export policy to take advantage of the relatively favorable trading conditions which prevailed after the first oil crisis, including especially the sharp increase in the import demand of oil exporting countries. We also benefited from the large demand from these countries for our skilled and unskilled services. The situation today is distinctly unfavorable in comparison because the world trading environment is much more unpropitious and because domestic supply constraints are a much greater inhibition to increasing exports. Also the demand for our workers abroad seems to be slackening.[27]

---

[27] Government of India, *Economic Survey of India, 1979–80*, New Delhi, 1980, Outlook for 1980–81, 64.

From the above description, we identify two important factors that contributed positively to India at the time of the second oil crisis: the size of India's food stock (14 million tons) and the high level of foreign exchange reserves (Rs. 4890 crores on May 30, 1980). Substantial foreign exchange reserves offered some cushioning for taking medium-term adjustment measures.

From 1975 to 1977, improvements in exports, imports, and invisibles brought about a significant improvement in India's foreign exchange reserves, as shown in Figure 8.3 —notably a spurt in net invisible receipts from remittances emerged due to a large increase in the number of Indians working abroad in the Gulf's oil-producing countries.[28] Private transfers were the largest single item and these receipts had increased to Rs. 696 crores from Rs. 233 crores in 1976.[29] To encourage the flow of funds from abroad, the government introduced a scheme on November 1, 1975 to encourage the flow of funds from Indians and aliens of Indian origin residing abroad.

> This scheme permits persons of the category to maintain deposit accounts in certain foreign currencies and to claim interest and repayment in the same currencies. The Scheme, thus, ensures convertibility and provides protection against exchange rate risk. Deposits under the scheme are accepted for periods ranging from 91 days to 61 months and carry tax-free interest at rates varying from 5.5 to 10.0 per cent. Government have also, in another measure, liberalized the provisions for repatriation of investments by non-resident Indians abroad, subject to certain safeguards.[30]

These fiscal policies led to the successful and rapid recovery of India's balance of payments before the second oil crisis.

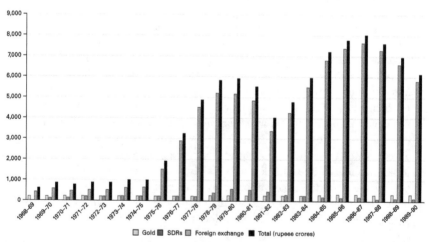

Figure 8.3 India's foreign exchange reserves, 1968–89 (Rs. crores).

[28] Government of India, *Economic Survey of India, 1977–78*, New Delhi, 1978, chapter 7, 39.
[29] Government of India, *Economic Survey of India, 1978–79*, New Delhi, 1979, chapter 7, 45.
[30] Government of India, *Economic Survey of India, 1975–76*, New Delhi, 1976, chapter 7, 41.

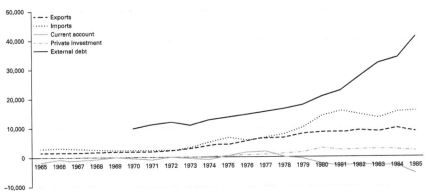

Figure 8.4 India's balance of payments, 1965–85 (Rs. crores).
Source: The Government of India, *The Economic Survey of India, 1965–1989* (New Delhi).

However, due to the second oil crisis in 1979, the situation changed for the worse, as shown in Figure 8.4. The growth in foreign remittances had already started to level off in 1978–9 and "in view of the considerable uncertainties regarding ability of the Gulf countries to absorb more labor, a continued growth under this head cannot be expected."[31] After two years of good rainfall, a severe drought occurred in the *kharif* season in 1979–80 in the Punjab, Haryana, Rajasthan, Uttar Pradesh, Bihar, West Bengal, Madhya Pradesh, and Andhra Pradesh. This led to a decline of about 14 million tons in the grain production, equivalent to a 10 percent decline in agricultural production. However, despite these challenges, "the agrarian economy in India has gained in basic strength over the years. This fact testifies to the basic soundness of the strategy for agricultural development adopted since the late sixties, encompassing expansion of irrigation with improved water management, better seeds, a greater use of fertilizer, and the adoption of improved cultural practices."[32] After ten years of experimenting with the Green Revolution in India, agriculture had developed a degree of resilience against recurring droughts. However, this appreciable increase in fertilizer consumption increased the financial burden of subsidies on the government budget and a higher import bill.

5.2. Borrowing Rs. 815 Crores (SDR 791 Million) from the IMF

In 1980–1, India's economy continued to be constrained by the delayed effect of a severe drought, continuing infrastructural problems, and adverse external factors. However, from the middle of the fiscal year 1980–1, the economy was able to recover most of the ground lost during 1979–80. Agricultural production increased 19 percent and GDP grew by 6.5 percent. Inflationary pressures continued to be strong in the first quarter of 1980–1 but decelerated significantly after July 1980. India's balance of payments remained under severe strain during 1980–1. Trade deficits exceeded Rs

[31] Government of India, *Economic Survey of India, 1980–81*, New Delhi, 1981, chapter 8, 54.
[32] Government of India, *Economic Survey of India, 1979–80*, New Delhi, 1980, 2 and 5.

4000 crores due to the rising prices of oil and other imports, and export growth remained sluggish.

As for agriculture, although the sharp decline in agricultural production during 1979–80 still pointed to the substantial impact of adverse weather conditions on agriculture production, the recovery during 1980–1 confirmed the growing strength and resilience of India's agricultural sector. The price of crude oil and petroleum products increased in June 1980 and again in January 1981 to adjust for higher international prices. Consequently, the price of fertilizer also increased in line with the higher price of imports, increase in input costs, and the need to reduce the budgetary subsidy.

Inflationary pressures in India's economy moderated somewhat but persisted and lower inflation remained an important objective of economic policy. The single most important factor accounting for the deterioration in the payments position was the doubling of oil prices between December 1978 and January 1980. This price increase, and the associated increases in price of other critical imports, such as fertilizer, meant a sharp increase in the value of imports even though import volumes increased only modestly. Out of the increase of Rs 4500 crores in the total import bill over the next two years, the increase in POL imports alone accounted for Rs 3,923 crores or about 87 percent.

In India's seventh general election in January 1980, Indira Gandhi of the Indian National Congress Party won a majority and returned to power after three years in opposition. Her new government applied for loans from the International Monetary Fund (IMF),[33] and obtained SDR[34] 525.5 million (Rs. 541 crores) from the Trust Fund of the IMF in August 1980, which provided balance of payments relief on concessional terms. The IMF has also agreed to a purchase of foreign exchange by the government of India under the Fund's compensatory financing facility because of an export shortfall experienced during the twelve-month period ending March 1980. The purchase was equivalent to SDR 266 million (Rs. 274 crores) or 23.2 percent of India's quota in the Fund.[35]

To approve the *Purchase Transaction-Compensatory Financing Facility* and *Trust Fund Loan*, the IMF authorities clearly recognized the crucial role of India's agricultural sector: "Policies to promote agricultural development have been stepped up in recent years. It is necessary to recapture the momentum of agricultural development following the setback in 1979/80, if India is to achieve its growth, employment, and income distribution objectives."[36] The steady progress of India's Green Revolution offered a

---

[33] International Monetary Fund (IMF), "India—Request for Trust Fund Loan," prepared by the Asian Department, July 25, 1980; "India—Request for Trust Fund Loan," TR/80/25, July 28, 1980.

[34] Special drawing right of the IMF (SDR): the SDR is an international reserve asset created by the IMF to supplement the official reserves of its member countries. The SDR is not a currency. It is a potential claim on the freely usable currencies of IMF members. As such, SDRs can provide a country with liquidity. A basket of currencies defined the SDR such as the US dollar, the British pound, West the German mark, and Japanese yen in those days.

[35] Government of India, *Economic Survey of India, 1980–81*, New Delhi, 1981, 54; IMF, Minutes of Executive Board Meeting, EBM/80/122, August 7, 1980, 1–31.

[36] IMF, The Acting Chairman's Summing Up at the Conclusion of the 1980 Article IV Consultation with India, EBM/80/122, August 7, 1980, and August 11, 1980-80/185.

solid foundation for getting financial support from international institutions. This was the first step in complicated negotiations with the IMF.

5.3. Extended Arrangements of SDR 5 Billion with the IMF for Structural Adjustments

The approval of the three-year agreement for SDR 5 billion (US$ 5.75 billion) in November 1981 extended arrangements with the IMF. This was the largest single EFF (extended fund facility) in the history of the IMF, although India's balance of payments improved quickly, so the whole sum was not drawn.[37] As a result of rapid worldwide inflation, the real value of existing IMF quotas fell, which led to quota enlargement. The quota basis of the Fund had increased 2.3 times over five years: SDR 39 billion (US$ 47.4 billion) in October 1978, SDR 60 billion (US$ 78.1 billion) in November 1980, and SDR 90 billion (US$ 95 billion) in March 1983.[38] Compared with the increasing pace of IMF quota enlargements, India's arrangement was too large to ignore their politico-economic significance to both the Indian government as well as to the IMF. The Bank of England also explicitly acknowledged India's exceptional request: "The EFF which India is seeking—worth a maximum SDR 5 billion over three years—would be the largest IMF facility to date and would represent an exceptional drawdown on Fund monies."[39]

The IMF debated the suitability and legitimacy of this huge arrangement with India at the Fund's executive board meetings on November 9, 1981. R. D. Erb, who represented the US government, heavily criticized the arrangements on behalf of the US Government (Reagan administration) and finally abstained from voting on India's request.

The debates focused on the scale of the arrangements and their financial implications for the IMF. India's Minister of Finance, Narasimham, first emphasized the seriousness of India's balance of payments deficit, saying, "Fund assistance in this case would provide the critical mass of finance for implementing the structural adjustment program."[40] At two successive board meetings on November 9, 1981, the essence of India's request was debated. Was it a balance of payments rescue plan or financial aid for development? The Alternate Executive Director, C. Taylor, pointed out the following: "the adjustment program was being accompanied by an ambitious development and investment program. It was in that respect, as in others, that the request was unusual and indeed rather exceptional. Much of the program's impact on productivity and the

---

[37] The IMF launched the EFF in 1975 to create a longer-term framework (drawings over three years and repurchases over four to eight years), as a measure for a serious structural transformation. See, Harold James, *International Monetary Cooperation Since Bretton Woods* (New York: Oxford University Press, 1996), 328 and 333. The Indian government stopped the drawing of IMF funds in May 1984. The total drawings were SDR 3.9 billion.

[38] Harold James, *International Monetary Cooperation*, 338–40.

[39] "India, the IMF and the World Bank," from the Bank of England, P. N. Mayes to A. J. Coles, South Asia Department, FCO, October 13, 1981, FCO37/2506, the National Archives (TNA).

[40] IMF, "Statement by Mr. Narasimham on India," EBM/81/138, November 9, 1981, EBM/81/138 (11/9/87), 2.

trade balance would not be felt until after the end of the extended arrangement."[41] R. D. Erb was opposed to the proposal:

> Interpreting the policy too loosely could threaten the Fund's liquidity position and impinge on the availability of resources for future borrowers. Of more importance, such an evolution could significantly alter the character of the Fund. In effect, the Fund could become more a medium-term financial intermediary than a revolving monetary fund standing ready to provide temporary balance of payments financing on a contingent basis.[42]

The chairman and the managing director of the IMF, J. de Larosiere, confirmed the IMF's position as follows: "the Fund should be in a position to provide assistance to its members in a nondiscriminatory way and in accordance with its established lending policies; it is in that spirit that we have been backing the operation that you have been considering today." India's case was not considered a precedent. He emphasized five key elements that deserved very particular attention during the reviews: (1) India's sharp increase in public savings, (2) interest rate and, more generally, monetary policies, (3) external performance, (4) the opening up of the economy, and (5) the investment program.[43] The US's Reagan administration took a critical stance against the Indian government in 1981. The US executive director abstained from voting. C. Taylor had reservations about the admissibility of India's request, but gave India the benefit of the doubt. The United Kingdom's (UK) executive director supported India's application, suggesting a need for the program to be monitored carefully.[44] Despite some directors' criticism, the SDR 5 billion arrangement with India was approved.

In 1981–2, India's economy showed significant improvement, with encouraging performances from both the agricultural and industrial sectors. India's inflation rate improved significantly although pressures persisted in certain essential commodities. The major factor underlying the difficult balance of payments situation was the deterioration in the trade account. The sharp increase in import values, particularly those for POL and fertilizers, had increased from Rs. 2098 crores in 1978–9 to Rs. 6240 crores in 1980–1. To address the severe balance of payments problem in the short term, it would be necessary to redouble efforts to increase exports and achieve faster import substitution in critical areas such as crude oil, fertilizer, steel, cement, edible oil, newsprint, and aluminum. In this regard, the increase in domestic crude oil production from 10.5 million tons in 1980–1 to 15.9 million tons in 1981–2 was crucial and noteworthy.

---

[41] Remarks by Mr. Taylor, IMF, Minutes of Executive Board Meeting, EBM/81/138, 10:00 a.m., November 9, 1981, 40–5.

[42] IMF, Minutes of Executive Board Meeting, EBM/81/139, 3:00 p.m., November 9, 1981, 12–13.

[43] IMF, Minutes of Executive Board Meeting, EBM/81/139, 3:00 p.m., November 9, 1981, 38–42; "The Chairman's Concluding Remarks with Regard to India's Request for an Extended Arrangement," EBM/81/139, November 9, 1981, and November 16, 1981-81/193.

[44] "IMF-INDIA," from Chancellor of Exchequer to Lord Carrington, Secretary of State for FC Affairs, 6 November 1981, FCO37/2507 Aid to India-Policy, the National Archives (TNA).

The current account deficit in 1980–1 was more than Rs. 2700 crores. This was financed by net aid flows of about Rs. 1058 crores, Rs. 815 crores in drawings under the IMF's Trust Fund and Compensatory Financing Facility, and a drawdown of Rs. 342 crores in foreign currency assets. The Government of India pointed out the crucial role of IMF SDR drawings as follows:

> In view of the medium-term nature of the balance of payments problem, and the need to finance a large current account deficit for some years, it was essential to resort to additional financing beyond the normal flows of external assistance. Accordingly, the Government entered into an extended arrangement under the IMF's Extended Fund Facility/Enlarged Access Policy remaining period which enabled India to purchase up to the equivalent of SDR 5 billion over a three-year period which spans the fiscal years 1981–82 to 1984–85. Purchases under this arrangement (which is equivalent to 291% of India's quota of SDR 1717.5 million) will be financed in part from the Fund's ordinary resources (SDR 2404.5 million) and in part from resources borrowed by the Fund under the policy of enlarged access (SDR 2595.5 million). Of the total amount of the arrangement, the schedule envisages that the equivalent of SDR 900 million can be made available until June 30, 1982; not more than SDR 1800 million up to June 30, 1983; leaving SDR 2300 million for the remaining period of the programme. An amount of SDR 600 million has been drawn under the first year's allocation by the end of January 1982.[45]

India was in a better position for further initiatives to achieve the necessary structural adjustments in the medium term. A sustained growth in agricultural production was an essential requirement not only for price stabilization, but also the longer-term growth potential of the economy. Food production in 1981–2 was expected to reach 134 million tons, whereas the average annual level in the 1970s was about 114 million tons against 83 million tons in the 1960s. Much of this increase was due to higher yields, which reflected the success of the basic agricultural strategy of extending irrigation, improved seeds, fertilizers, credit, and other inputs. This was a great achievement of the Green Revolution.

5.4. Resilience Against the Economic Downturn and Concessional Borrowings

In 1982–3, prices remained stable with the annual inflation rate fluctuating around 2.0 percent from the beginning of September 1982. Exports increased significantly by 16.2 percent in 1981–2. In short, the economy showed an appreciable degree of resilience in agriculture, despite growing constraints on resources and continued strains on balance of payments.

The use of chemical fertilizers accelerated in the early 1970s and became an important factor in raising agricultural productivity. The appearance of high-yielding,

---

[45] Government of India, *Economic Survey of India, 1981–82* (New Delhi, 1982), 60–2.

fertilizer-responsive seed varieties and greater use of irrigation systems assisted this growth. Total consumption of fertilizers (nitrogenous, phosphatic, and potassic fertilizers) increased from 294,000 tons in 1960–1 to 2.26 million tons in 1970–1 and 5.5 million tons in 1980–1. As a result of this rapid increase in fertilizer consumption, India was ranked fourth globally (after China, the US and the Soviet Union) in the consumption of nitrogenous fertilizers, and sixth among phosphatic fertilizers users. With India's the substantial increase in locally produced fertilizer, imports of fertilizers decreased significantly. India, however, continued to be a major importer of fertilizers and exerted a significant influence on international fertilizer prices.

External assistance in the form of loans and cash and commodity grants from normal sources became an important source of finance in India's balance of payments. In 1982–3, the Aid India Consortium members pledged assistance to the amount of SDR 3.4 billion (US$ 3.73 billion), of which the WB group (the IDA and the IBRD) pledged US$ 2.2 billion (60 percent). While India's current account deficit increased, there was a prospect of a reduction of concessional assistance from normal sources in the future. It therefore became necessary to resort to additional external borrowing to meet the residual financing requirements of the balance of payments. As a result, India's government entered into an extended arrangement with the IMF to the extent of SDR 5 billion over three years (1981–2 to 1984–5), and also resorted to commercial borrowings on a selective basis to supplement resources available from multilateral and bilateral sources of Rs. 1204 crores.

In February 1982, the British government assessed the Indian market as follows:

> The IMF loan (or 'line of credit' as the Indian authorities prefer to call it) should be regarded as a trust factor. India will doubtless have balance of payments problems over the medium term and the EFF will not only act as a financial pin but as a mark of confidence which should encourage other lenders. The Indians have made the point that they might very well not drawn down the whole facility although the first tranche was taken immediately.[46]

The underpinning effect of the IMF loan, the resilience of India's agricultural sector, and the bright prospects of oil suggested that India's medium-term prospects were much improved; moreover, India had not defaulted on any debt in the 1970s and early 1980s.

The *Economic Survey of India for 1982–3* summarized India's position within the world economy and in the context of the Asian international economic order as follows:

> While for a continental economy like India, an export-led growth strategy is neither relevant nor feasible, there is no gainsaying the importance of expanding the export base in order to meet payments for essential imports. --- India's policies of selectivity and caution in regard to external borrowings have been more than

---

[46] "India: Market Assessment," Export Credit Guarantee Department, February 1982, T442/43—INDIA—Aid/Trade Provision, the National Archives (TNA).

vindicated by recent experience of several countries, which are now facing increasing difficulties in servicing past debt. --- The oil importing countries have been the most severely affected by these [unemployment/zero growth/high inflation] and other developments. Their current account deficits, which had reached alarming levels, after the escalation in prices of oil in 1979, have further deteriorated because of a decline in the prices of their exports. Development plans in many countries have had to be drastically curtailed. Sustained price stability has proved elusive, and growth rates have declined. India is one of the few oil importing countries which, in the last three years have been able to maintain the tempo of planned development and also achieve a significant reduction in the rates of inflation. Growth rates in the first three years of the Plan are likely to be about 5% per annum despite the set-back in agricultural production this year. The years ahead are difficult and challenging. The economy now has the necessary strength and the resilience to cope with these.[47]

The Indian government's observations are quite interesting and insightful. As a continental economy with large domestic market, India never considered an export-led growth strategy or export-oriented industrialization (EOI) in the 1970s and early 1980s. However, to cover the rapidly increasing trade deficit due to higher imports and to address India's deteriorating balance of payments, the Indian government had to rely on not only concessional loans from the WB group, but also favorable borrowings from the IMF, beyond the normal flows of external assistance. Commercial borrowings from privatized financial markets were strictly managed as alternative supplementary external financing sources and kept within the limits of debt servicing.

6. Conclusion

In this chapter, we examined the chemical fertilizer problems of India in a global context of a changing international economic order in the 1970s and early 1980s during the oil crises in 1973–4 and 1979–80. India was one of the most severely affected countries. We would like to highlight the following three observations.

First, from these analyses, we can clearly see the strong and active role played by the WB group in the expansion of India's fertilizer industries through financial aid for projects under the presidency of Robert McNamara. After the decline and contraction of US economic aid to India in the early 1970s, including PL480 under the Nixon Administration, the WB became the leading donor to India. Most of the Bank's lending was allocated to fertilizer projects. Of course, the largest contribution for investment in fertilizer programs came from the Government of India (68 percent), but the contribution of the IBRD/IDA (11 percent) and other external financial institutions (12 percent) cannot be ignored during the oil crises of the 1970s. The financial aid (cheap credit) offered by the WB group through the IDA and technical assistance for

---

[47] Government of India, *Economic Survey of India, 1982–83* (New Delhi, 1983), 68–72.

improving existing fertilizer factories in India buffered India against the financial and economic impact of the oil crises.

Second, the second oil crisis inflicted more damage on India, and India lapsed into a serious balance of payments crisis in 1979–80. The critical situation deteriorated even further due to a severe drought in the *kharif* season and political instability, which caused a complex entanglement of political economy. Remittances from Indian workers in the Middle East—an important source of earnings on the invisible accounts—and external assistance through normal channels (e.g., the Aid India Consortium) could not curb the increasing current account deficit. To weather this difficulty, the Indira Gandhi administration negotiated an IMF rescue program of SDR 5 billion arrangements for three years. This political decision to utilize IMF facilities managed to solve India's financial crisis, followed by the general rules of IMF's "structural adjustments." However, India's program was not imposed in any manner from outside, but was self-imposed. The policy mix chosen by India's government was perceived by the government and the country as providing support for its implementation.[48] India's government continued its developmental policies and exerted autonomous policy initiatives, although through consultations with the IMF. In this sense, India's experience was quite different from structural adjustment policies for Latin American countries after a series of defaults. India's case provides new historical insight into the meaning of structural adjustment in the 1980s.

Third, a heavy dependence on petroleum by-products for fertilizer production affected India's use of fertilizers for agricultural development, and the high prices of fertilizers temporarily discouraged Indian farmers from the intensive use of fertilizers. However, the Indian government initiated the Green Revolution as a strategy for agricultural development and tried to pursue self-sufficiency in grains. Agricultural development was not interrupted even during the balance of payments crisis, which crucially absorbed some of the impacts of the oil crises. Compared to East Asian and Southeast Asian countries, India's developmental achievements in the 1970s are sometimes evaluated in a negative light because of the stagnation in heavy industry-based (capital goods) industrialization and relatively slow economic growth during the Indira Gandhi administrations. However, we should consider the substantial progress of the Green Revolution in India in the context of the rapid transformation of international economic order of Asia.

---

[48] M. Narasimham, *World Economic Environment and Prospects for India* (New Delhi: Sterling Publishers, 1988), 76–7.

9

Ghana and Kenya Facing the 1970s Commodity Price Shocks: The National and the Global[1]

Gareth Austin

The 1970s, especially 1973–5, saw a transition in the economic growth of post-independence Sub-Saharan Africa: from slow growth in the 1960s to stagnation and actual decline in the 1980s and early 1990s (Figure 9.1).[2] There is a strong case for seeing this transition as accelerated, and in part caused, by the oil-price shock of 1973–4, consolidated by that of 1979. The focus in this chapter, however, is not the oil shocks themselves. Taking them as "global" phenomena, albeit (as usual with global events and processes) originating among a specific group of countries, the aim here is to explore national variations in economic and political reactions and outcomes. This chapter presents a comparative analysis of two countries in the region which, though possessing similar characteristics in several important respects, nevertheless experienced contrasting economic outcomes. If differences between the terms of trade shifts cannot account for the contrast, is it attributable to divergent policies; and if so, why were policies different?

On the principle that good comparators have enough in common to make the differences significant, Ghana and Kenya make a good pair. In the 1970s neither were oil producers, though Kenya had a refinery from which petroleum products were exported to neighboring countries, so the OPEC oil-price rises were indeed major adverse shocks to their economies, starting with major impacts on import bills and

---

[1] Earlier drafts of this essay were presented at three workshops organized by Professor Akita on this project (online, August 31–September 1, 2020; Heidelberg, Germany, November 5, 2021; Washington DC, March 22–3, 2022) and finally at our session at the World Economic History Congress in Paris (July 29, 2022). I am grateful for the comments received on all these occasions, and especially for a suggestion from Mark Metzler as the discussant at the first workshop.

[2] The reality of African average growth before the mid-1970s is spotlighted in Morten Jerven, *Economic Growth and Measurement Reconsidered in Botswana, Kenya, Tanzania, and Zambia, 1965–1995* (Oxford: Oxford University Press, 2014), 9–13. The data in Figure 9.1 come from World Bank, *Africa Development Indicators 2012–2013* (Washington DC, 2013). Jerven also rightly highlights the weaknesses of national income accounts in Africa. My chapter makes much use of these sources. In general, however, I would say that the Ghana-Kenya contrasts shown in the sources are so large as to be unlikely to be purely statistical phenomena; especially as the numbers tend to be roughly in line with other sources.

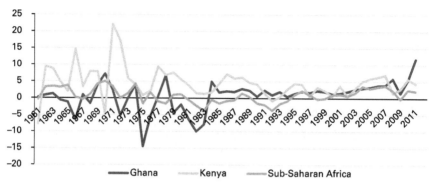

Figure 9.1 GDP annual growth rate (percent) 1961–2010: Ghana, Kenya, Sub-Saharan Africa (World Bank, *Africa Development Indicators 2012–2013*).

inflation. For their exports, both countries relied on beverage crops. Ghana began the decade as the world's largest producer of cocoa beans, while Kenya was a major producer of coffee and tea. This reflected their comparative advantage in the production of these commodities: at official exchange rates, domestic resource costs per unit of foreign exchange from export crops were 0.30 for Ghana (1972) and 0.44 and 0.67 respectively for Kenyan coffee and tea (1975).[3] Thus, while 1973 brought a huge shock in terms of the soaring price of a large and vital import, both economies stood to gain from a boom in the prices of beverage crops, from 1976 to 1978.[4] The countries were on a similar demographic scale: by 1980, Ghana had nearly 11 million people, Kenya over 16 million.[5] While Kenya, with its much larger area, was the more extreme in the internal diversity of its physical environment—from mountain to desert (with a quarter of its territory classified as "wilderness")[6]—the vast majority of its population lived in the same three kinds of zones as the population of Ghana: savanna, forest and coast. Both countries were former British colonies, independent in 1957 (Ghana) and 1963 (Kenya) respectively. In a ranking of African countries by GNP per capita, they were literally next to each other at the end of the 1970s, at the bottom of the World Bank's class of "medium-income" countries: at then-current prices, Ghana on 400 US dollars, Kenya on 380.[7] Finally, the comparison is uncomplicated by trade links between them, as these were virtually non-existent.

[3] World Bank, *Accelerated Development in Sub-Saharan Africa: an Agenda for Action* (Washington DC, 1981), 65. This publication is best known as "the Berg Report," after its main author, Elliot J. Berg.
[4] Jeffrey M. Davis, "The economic effects of windfall gains in export earnings, 1975–1978," *World Development* 11:2 (1983), 119–39.
[5] World Bank, *Africa Development Indicators 2017* (updated August 2, 2017), (Washington DC).
[6] As against zero in Ghana. The figures are for 1985 and are for areas larger than 4,000 square km (World Bank, *Sub-Saharan Africa: From Crisis to Sustainable Growth—A Long-Term Perspective Study* (Washington DC: World Bank, 1987, 280–1).
[7] World Bank, *Accelerated Development*, 143. The figures are weighted averages of income, converted into current US dollars, for 1977–9, divided by the estimated population at mid-1979 (ibid., 188–9).

1. Different Colonial Pasts and Decolonizations

Already in the 1960s and 1970s, both countries attracted considerable scholarly literature on their colonial pasts and their post-independence political economies.[8] This attention was partly inspired by, and focused upon, their respective statuses as epitomes of particular kinds of colonial history. This is where contrast replaces similarity. Ghana was the most economically successful exemplar of colonial development based on agricultural exporting by African producers,[9] whereas Kenya had a substantial presence of European settler-farmers, who enjoyed strong discriminatory support from the colonial government, despite a proclamation from London that African interests should be paramount.[10]

With no significant European ownership of land, Ghana's passage to independence was relatively peaceful and early. "Relatively" is the word: in 1948 an incident in which police fired on a protest march of army veterans about pension rights sparked riots in the major towns, targeting European-owned stores. The imperial government in London responded with a commission of inquiry, whose report led to a definitive acceleration of the timetable for independence, preceded by joint rule between colonial officials and elected African ministers (1951) and then internal self-government (1954). Following the elections for the latter, the Convention People's Party (CPP) government announced that the price paid to farmers for their cocoa beans would be fixed for four years. At a time when cocoa prices had been rising on the world market, this decision provoked the formation of an opposition party, the National Liberation Movement. The NLM demanded a federal constitution, to enable the export-producing regions to retain the lion's share of the revenues. Based in Ashanti, the largest cocoa-producing region, the NLM failed to win majority support in the second-largest cocoa region, Eastern Region: essentially because the Movement was strongly backed by the Asantehene's palace, and was perceived as a vehicle for the restoration of the dominance that the former kingdom of Asante (Ashanti) had exercised before the colonization of what became Ghana.[11]

In my view, the outcome of the CPP-NLM struggle defined the political economy of independent Ghana until the 1980s. During the first half of the century, a powerful tradition of independent cocoa-farmers' associations had emerged in Ghana: in 1937–8 they had fought a European cocoa-buying cartel to a standstill by withholding the crop from the market.[12] But in the mid-1950s, the movement became fatally divided,

---

[8] Indicatively, Bob Fitch and Mary Oppenheimer, *Ghana: End of an Illusion* (New York: Monthly Review Press, 1966) and Colin Leys, *Underdevelopment in Kenya: the Political Economy of Neo-colonialism* (London: Heinemann, 1975).

[9] Polly Hill, *The Migrant Cocoa-Farmers of Southern Ghana* (Cambridge, 1963: 2nd edn with preface by Gareth Austin, Hamburg: LIT, 1997). More recently, Gareth Austin, *Labour, Land and Capital in Ghana: From Slavery to Free Labour, 1807–1956* (University of Rochester Press, 2005); Austin, "Vent for surplus or productivity breakthrough? The Ghanaian cocoa take-off, c.1890–1936," *Economic History Review*, 67:4 (2014), 1035–64.

[10] Paul Mosley, *The Settler Economies: Studies in the Economic History of Kenya and Southern Rhodesia 1900–1963* (Cambridge: Cambridge University Press, 1983); Bruce Berman and John Lonsdale, *Unhappy Valley: Conflict in Kenya and Africa* (London: James Currey, 1992).

[11] The major study of the NLM is Jean Marie Allman, *The Quills of the Porcupine: Asante Nationalism in an Emergent Ghana* (Madison: University of Wisconsin Press, 1993).

[12] The best introduction remains John Miles, "Rural protest in the Gold Coast: the cocoa hold-ups, 1908–1938," in Clive Dewey and A. G. Hopkins, eds., *The Imperial Impact: Studies in the Economic History of India and Africa* (London: Athlone Press, 1978), 152–70, 353–7.

with the Ashanti association siding with the NLM and the southern association backing the CPP. That split, coupled with the fact that Nkrumah decisively won the pre-independence elections of 1956, "marked the effective end of the tradition of independent cocoa farmers' associations."[13] It gave the centralizing government of the newly independent state political freedom to extract as large a share as it wished of the cocoa revenue. How far and with what effects it would exercise that option remained to be seen over the following quarter-century.

The party conflict during decolonization in Ghana was rough but not deadly. In contrast, in Kenya a major guerrilla war was fought by the Land and Freedom Army (the "Mau Mau") from 1952 to 1956, in which some 25,000 people died.[14] The guerrillas came overwhelmingly from the largest single ethnic group living in central Kenya, the Kikuyu. The rest came from two smaller groups culturally and politically related to the Kikuyu, the Embu, and the Meru.[15] The conflict was both a national liberation struggle and a Kikuyu civil—specifically, a class—war. Despite lacking modern weapons, the guerrillas proved that independence under a white minority government was unsustainable in local terms as well as in the context of British and Cold War politics in the 1950s–60s. The leading role of Kikuyu "loyalists" in the defeat of Mau Mau, however, created the political possibility of an independent, non-socialist, African (and Kikuyu-led) government under Jomo Kenyatta with whom the British and other Western governments, and Western companies, would be reasonably happy to do business.[16]

At independence, while both countries were poor, in bilateral terms it was the Kenyan economy that had catching up to do. Whereas the potential of African peasant and small-capitalist farming had been unleashed during the colonial period in Ghana, when it was largely the result of African economic initiatives that Ghana became the world's largest cocoa producer, in Kenya only a small licensed minority of Africans were legally permitted to grow either of the two major cash crops, coffee and tea, and Europeans occupied the lion's share of land suitable for their cultivation. The one respect in which settler colonies in Africa tended to outgrow colonies in which Africans kept control of most of the land was in manufacturing.[17] But Ghana's performance in export agriculture was so superior that, at Independence, as Table 9.1 shows, while its

---

[13] Gareth Austin, "National Poverty and the 'Vampire State' in Ghana," *Journal of International Development*, 8:4 (1996), 553–73, at 563.

[14] The contrast between the two transitions to independence is very well conveyed, with excellent interviews with protagonists, in the Ghana and Kenya episodes of the Granada Television documentary film series *End of Empire* (Manchester, 1985). For an introduction to Mau Mau, see Wunyabari O. Maloba, *Mau Mau and Kenya: an Analysis of a Peasant Revolt* (Bloomington: Indiana University Press, 1993).

[15] An excellent analysis of the economic basis of the conflicts between the guerrillas and the settlers, and the guerrillas and the "loyalists," is Robert H. Bates, "The demand for revolution: the agrarian origins of Mau Mau," in Bates, *Beyond the Miracle of the Market: the Political Economy of Agrarian Development in Kenya* (Cambridge: Cambridge University Press, 1989), 11–44, 157–63.

[16] The major study of the "loyalists" is Daniel Branch, *Defeating Mau Mau, Creating Kenya: Counterinsurgency, Civil War, and Decolonization* (New York: Cambridge University Press, 2009).

[17] Peter Kilby, "Manufacturing in colonial Africa," in Peter Duignan and L. H. Gann, eds., *Colonialism in Africa 1870–1960*, vol. IV, *The Economics of Colonialism* (Cambridge: Cambridge University Press, 1975), 4; Gareth Austin, Ewout Frankema, and Morten Jerven, "Patterns of manufacturing growth in Sub-Saharan Africa: from colonization to the present," in Kevin O'Rourke and Jeffrey G. Williamson, eds., *The Spread of Modern Industry to the Poor Periphery since 1870* (Oxford: Oxford University Press, 2017), 345–73.

Table 9.1 Ghana and Kenya as of 1960: population, income, manufacturing

	Population (million)	Gross domestic product ($ million)	Income per capita ($)	Manufacturing output ($ million)	Share of manufacturing in GDP (%)
Ghana	6.8	1,503	222	94.7	6.3
Kenya	8.1	641	79	60.9	9.5

Source: Peter Kilby, "Manufacturing in colonial Africa," in Peter Duignan and L. H. Gann, eds., *Colonialism in Africa 1870–1960*, vol. IV, *The Economics of Colonialism* (Cambridge: Cambridge University Press, 1975), 472.

manufacturing sector was smaller than Kenya's as a share of their respective GDPs, it was much the larger in absolute terms.

The Kenyan catch-up can be said to have begun with land titling, and continued with land resettlement. In response to Mau Mau, in 1955, the colonial administration began distributing land titles to African smallholders, abolished the restrictions on African entry to coffee and tea production, and began redistributing land to [loyalist] Kikuyu farmers. As part of the Independence settlement, Britain lent the Kenyan government money to buy out the European landowners—who were concentrated in the "White Highlands" of the Rift Valley—at the generous market prices of 1959. The creation of the "White Highlands" had been at the expense of Luo, Maasai and Kalenjin as well as Kikuyu land claims. Now, as in Ghana in 1954, a new party was created to fight for a federal constitution, so that regional governments would control the crucial fruit of Independence: in Kenya, not so much revenue from agricultural exports (important as that was to become), but access to the land vacated by European settlers. However, as in Ghana, the incumbent nationalist leader defeated the new opposition: in this case, not just before Independence but a year or so afterwards, resulting, as in Ghana, in a strongly centralized state.[18] Kenyatta proceeded to enable Kikuyus to acquire most of the land transferred in the Rift Valley, while his Kalenjin ally, Daniel Arap Moi, was compensated with some land elsewhere for his own clients.[19] Most of the largest estates, deemed to be characterized by significant scale economies, were acquired intact by members of the new Kikuyu power elite, who thereby became a "gentry."[20] The smaller ("medium-sized") European farms, engaged in mixed farming (maize, beverage crop and dairy cattle), were acquired by smaller-scale Kikuyu farmer-entrepreneurs, often combining in syndicates or cooperatives.

William House and Tony Killick estimated the distribution of ownership of the former settler farms as of about 1978 as follows. Non-citizens still owned 73 percent of the 1,640,000 hectares under plantations and ranches. The rest had been acquired by Africans. It was different with the 1,760,000 hectares of mixed farms. Less than 6 percent of this hectarage remained in non-citizen hands. Just over 24 percent was now owned by Africans who continued to run them as single large farms; 45 percent had been officially transferred to smallholdings; while over 24 percent (often bought by cooperatives or groups of farmers) had been informally divided into smallholdings or

[18] The struggle over land, and the significance of the constitutional question within it, is sharply analyzed by Bates, *Beyond the Miracle of the Market*, 52–63.
[19] Branch, *Kenya: Between Hope and Despair*, 86–98.
[20] Bates, *Beyond the Miracle of the Market*, 148.

else cultivated collectively.[21] It is important to note that the land transferred constituted about a quarter of the "best-potential" land, i.e., "about 3 per cent of the nation's total stock of agricultural land."[22] Thousands of Kikuyu, especially former guerrillas, remained landless.[23]

Meanwhile, the great success story of the Kenyan economy in the later 1950s and 1960s was the growth of smallholder agriculture,[24] especially in Central Province and Rift Valley Province, i.e., partly on shambas in the former "Kikuyu Reserve," now that African smallholders were free to grow beverage crops, and partly on shambas established on resettled land. Smallholder production of coffee reached 30,400 tons in 1970, 52 percent of the total crop, and continued to expand, more slowly, in the new decade. Smallholders started later in tea, because the state had believed that it was technically unsuitable for them. Smallholder production of tea had reached 53,300 tons in 1972, and jumped to 86,300 in 1977, 32 percent of the national crop: helped by more farmers adopting tea, and higher output per hectare.[25]

On the other side of the continent, Ghanaian cocoa farmers—often described as small-scale, but actually of varied scales and making much use of hired labor[26]—expanded the planted area in the 1950s, resulting in a new output boom, and a world record cocoa crop in the farming year 1964/5. By then world cocoa prices were falling, however, while Nkrumah's pursuit of import-substituting industrialization had entailed the costs but not the desired returns.

2. Economic Growth and Inflation in the 1970s

Despite the strong similarities in the nature and magnitude of the external trade shocks that impacted them, the reactions to and effects of the external shocks, negative and positive, were very different in Kenya and Ghana. Figure 9.2 puts the 1970s growth record in the context of the preceding and following periods.

---

[21] William J. House and Tony Killick, "Inequality and poverty in the rural economy, and the influence of some aspects of policy," in Killick, ed., *Papers on the Kenyan Economy* (Nairobi: Heinemann, 1981), 157–79, at 167–8.

[22] Ibid., 168.

[23] Branch, *Kenya: Between Hope and Despair*, 90–5.

[24] According to government statistics in 1977, the mean size of smallholdings was 2.33 hectares (Peter Wyeth, "Economic development in Kenyan agriculture," in Tony Killick, ed., *Papers on the Kenyan Economy* [Nairobi: Heinemann, 1981], 299–310, at 301. The focus of my chapter is export agriculture, but smallholders' output expanded much more broadly, notably regarding maize. The World Bank reported a 1974 survey which found that "over a wide range of mixed farming on land of medium to high potential, smallholders have proven to be superior in Kenya": not only in higher output per hectare (predictable because of higher labor inputs per hectare) but also in total factor productivity (World Bank, *Accelerated Development*, 51).

[25] Hazlewood, *Economy of Kenya*, 44–5.

[26] In the largest cocoa-growing region the ratio of cocoa-farm owners to the hired laborers they employed was 1.89:1 according to a major survey during the 1956/7 cocoa season (Austin, *Labour, Land and Capital*, 319–20). Beckman, using the now lost purchasing records of the state monopsonist, calculated that in 1963/4 the largest 5 percent of producers were responsible for 31 percent of output; the smallest 18 percent produced just 2 percent. See his table, originally presented in Beckman, "The distribution of cocoa income, 1961–1965," Staff Seminar Paper no. 13, Department of Economics, University of Ghana, Legon (1970), conveniently reproduced in Piet Konings, *The State and Rural Class Formation in Ghana* (London: KPI, 1986), 76.

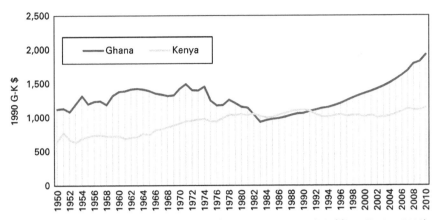

Figure 9.2 Real GDP per head in Ghana and Kenya, 1950–2010 (Maddison Project 2013).

The early years of Kenyan independence had seen marked economic growth: GDP per head was 23.39 percent higher in 1969 than in 1963, an average annual growth rate of 3.34 percent.[27] In the same seven years, Ghana's GDP per head fell almost seven percentage points. If we widen the period slightly, to compare 1962, the year before Kenyan independence, with 1970, both countries look better: Kenya grew at 3.39 percent per year, while Ghanaian growth edged into positive territory, averaging 0.125 percent per year. Ghana in 1970 recovered its previous highest level of real income per head, that of 1963. There was also a contrast in economic stability. Whether in the seven or the nine-year period Kenya only once experienced a fall compared to the year before, whereas Ghana suffered five annual falls in succession.

Coming to the OPEC intervention in 1973, it should be noted that the higher oil prices began to be felt strongly in 1974, which partly explains why in both countries GDP per capita was higher in that year than in 1973. Thus 1973 *as such* was not a turning-point in the evolution of output per head. However, taking 1970–80 as a whole, Ghana's gross domestic product (GDP) per head for 1980 was 18.75 percent below its 1970 level; Kenya's was 14.86 percent above. Ghana ended the oil shock years of 1973–80 with an economy 20.74 percent smaller; Kenya's economy was 8.35 percent larger (Figure 9.3). In short, in the 1970s Ghana suffered an economic disaster, while Kenya managed modest growth.

The inflation story was different, in that both countries entered the 1970s with consumer prices rising only slowly. As Figure 9.4 shows, however, they began to diverge sharply after 1974. The lag after the oil-price shock, and especially the fact that Kenya's inflation rate stayed fairly low, suggest that Ghana's burst of hyperinflation cannot be attributed to OPEC. In 1977, Ghana's consumer price inflation was 116 percent, 7.75 times the Kenyan level—and over 100 percentage points more.

---

[27] The underlying data in this paragraph and the next. as well as in Figure 9.2, come from the Maddison Project Database 2013 (Groningen Growth and Development Centre). See Jutta Bolt and Jan Luiten van Zanden, "The Maddison Project: collaborative research on historical national accounts," *Economic History Review*, 67:3 (2014), 627–51.

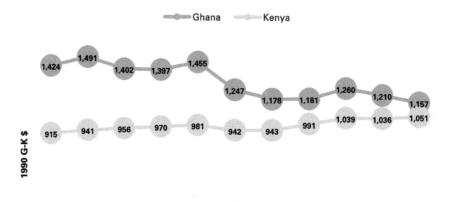

Figure 9.3 Real GDP per head in Ghana and Kenya, 1970–80 (Maddison Project 2013).

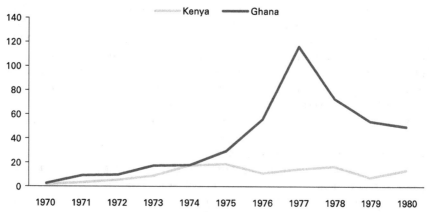

Figure 9.4 Consumer prices in Ghana and Kenya, 1970–80: annual rate of increase (percent).

Source: World Bank, World Development Indicators 2017.

3. Political Conflict, Continuity, and Instability in the 1970s

The political story of the 1970s roughly corresponded to the economic one (we will consider the direction of causation later). The decade saw four changes of regime in Ghana: one conventional military coup, led by senior officers; one palace coup to replace a very embarrassing soldier with a more respectable one; one junior ranks' coup (or "revolution"); and one democratic election. In Kenya, by contrast (see Table 9.2), even when the sitting president died in office, with his patronage network in

Table 9.2 Successive governments in Kenya and Ghana in the 1970s

Year of accession	Means of accession	Leader	Type of regime
KENYA			
1963	Independence election	J. Kenyatta	Civilian (became one-party)
1978	Constitutional succession	D. A. Moi	Civilian one-party
GHANA			
1969, October	Election	K. A. Busia	Civilian
1972, January	Coup	I. K. Acheampong	Military
1975	Internal rearrangement	Ditto	Ditto
1978	Palace coup	F. Akuffo	Ditto
1979, June 4	Junior ranks' coup ("revolution")	J. J. Rawlings	"Revolutionary," military
1979, September 24	Elections	H. Limann	Civilian
1981, December 31	Junior ranks' coup ("revolution")	J. J. Rawlings	"Revolutionary," partly civilian

place, and his political lieutenants—all from Kenyatta's home district of Kiambu—strategically placed to safeguard the interests that Kenyatta had represented, those lieutenants decided to allow the constitutional process to take its due course: the vice-president, Moi, a Kalenjin, was allowed to succeed.

The appearance of striking continuity and orderly political succession in post-independence Kenya was profoundly deceptive in that it hid major conflicts and crises which challenged the durability of the Kenyatta government. That there was opposition to Kenyatta was underlined by the very fact that he imposed a *de facto* one-party state, suppressing a powerful socialist party, the Kenya People's Union, which had been formed by Kenyatta's former vice president, Oginga Odinga, when he left the government in 1966. Odinga was temporarily detained. Worse was the fate of the two leading challengers to the regime from within the ruling party. Tom Mboya, who in ability and charisma was the natural successor to Kenyatta had he not been from a different ethnic group, the Luo, was assassinated in 1969. J. M. Kariuki, himself both Kikuyu and successful in business, was a former member of the Land and Freedom Army who became the most prominent critic of the inequity of the government's land policy, particularly the fact that many settler estates had been bought intact by relatives and clients of Kenyatta, rather than divided between the landless, especially former Mau Mau fighters. "JM," as Kariuki was popularly known, won exceptionally big personal majorities in his constituency in the 1969 and 1974 parliamentary elections. Following the latter, he was sacked as a junior minister.

In March 1975, "JM" was himself assassinated. When the news was confirmed, amid popular fury, parliament defied the government by insisting on appointing its own select committee to investigate the murder. This defiance had the effect, intended or otherwise, of buying time for the government during which the immediate popular anger was diffused and displaced. This was ironic because the eventual report was damming, implying that senior members of the government had probably been involved in the assassination of Kariuki, and explicit that they had obstructed the inquiry into it. This was a regime-threatening crisis, during which Kenyatta temporarily lost his authority over his cabinet as well as over parliament, and his popular legitimacy probably never recovered.[28] Kenyatta's non-Kikuyu opponents perhaps missed their chance by underestimating quite how popular "JM" had been, and how unpopular the government had become, in Kikuyu districts other than Kiambu.[29]

If Kenyatta could have fallen in 1975, the fact that after his death he was succeeded by the vice-president, Moi, was ultimately not a constitutional given but a political decision, and one which some of those who made it had cause to regret. For if the grandees of the Kenyatta regime, his "Kiambu clique" as the historian William Ochieng' put it,[30] led by the Attorney-General Charles Njonjo, thought they could contain Moi, they were confounded. Over his first six years as president, 1978–84, Moi engineered their downfall, and systematically deconstructed their and Kenyatta's patronage network, while expanding his own, thereby consolidating his power base in western Kenya.[31] So Kenya was not as politically stable as it appeared, but despite the political crises of 1975 and 1978, the same Kenyan state remained afloat throughout the decade when Ghana's Second Republic, and the military government that overthrew it, both sank.

Ghana entered the 1970s having already had two changes of government since independence: the military coup that deposed President Kwame Nkrumah in 1966, overthrowing the first republic, and the 1969 election by which K. A. Busia, one of Nkrumah's old opponents, became prime minister in the Second Republic. While the 1966 coup was popular, it should be noted that Busia's campaigning challenge was eased by the fact that the outgoing military government forbade Nkrumah's former party from competing. In 1972 there was a second coup, led by Colonel I. K. Acheampong, which displaced Busia and the Second Republic. The regime had an internal restructuring in 1975, followed by a palace coup in 1978, in which the embarrassingly corrupt Acheampong was replaced by another senior officer, "Fred" Akuffo. The government had faced, and continued to face, strong protests from civil society, notably university students and the Professional Bodies Association, demanding a return to civilian government. By 1979 Akuffo was steering the military government toward a handover of power to an elected civilian government. Before the scheduled elections took place, however, there was a dramatic junior ranks' coup, proclaimed as the June 4 Revolution. This brought to power the Armed Forces Revolutionary Council, led by Flight-Lieutenant J. J. Rawlings. The AFRC launched a whirlwind and violent campaign against corruption, black marketeering and inflation. The three surviving

---

[28] Daniel Branch, *Kenya: Between Hope and Despair, 1963–2011* (New Haven: Yale University Press, 2011), 89–120.

[29] Here I may well be relying too much on my own youthful impressions at the time, teaching in a secondary school near Othaya in Nyeri District of Central Province. I witnessed the junior Kenyan teachers, all locals, respond to the news of JM's murder by making speeches at assembly exhorting the students to be ready to "go to the hills"—following the precedent of the Mau Mau—in resisting the government. However, traveling on buses around other provinces during the next school break, the people I met seemed unaware that Kenyatta's Kikuyu base was so weakened.

heads of military governments were among eight senior officers summarily executed. Meanwhile the general and presidential elections went ahead as scheduled, and the AFRC handed over, in September 1979, to President Hilla Limann and his broadly Nkrumahist People's National Party.

Both countries had armed uprisings early in the 1980s, but—in line with their post-independence records to that date—the attempted (very) junior ranks' air force coup of August 1, 1982 in Kenya was easily suppressed, whereas Rawlings' "Second Coming," the December 31 Revolution of 1981, succeeded. Even when political instability became visible in Kenya, the constitution held; in Ghana, it fell again.

4. Interactions of Economics and Politics

So how did economic discontent and political instability (or their partial opposites) interact in these contrasting national experiences? In the case of the combination of economic decline and political instability in Ghana, one can say that economic crises, felt by the mass of the population, specifically including those in the capital city, set the agenda, even the schedule, for regime change. Economic crisis drove Busia, eventually, to a "desperately large"[32] devaluation of the currency; Colonel Acheampong used both the crisis and the government's response to justify his coup. Akuffo's palace coup of 1978, removing Acheampong, took place in the context of extreme shortages of everyday commodities, which had helped motivate the demands for a return to civilian rule. The same applied a year later, by when the new head of state had failed to deliver material improvements, leading to the June 4 Revolution, and then confirmation of the military decision to hold elections and restore civilian government.

Fundamental as the unfolding economic disaster was to the political instability of 1970s Ghana, the link was not unmediated. Opposition to devaluation seems to have stemmed primarily from fears about the cost of living, perhaps especially in the towns, but there was also a tendency to see the value of the national currency as a matter of national dignity. By 1978 and 1979, popular anger took a "moral economy" form, expressed in a new word of uncertain origin, *kalabule*, which described corruption and economic cheating with visceral contempt.[33] The word was directed at a range of targets, from traders who sold goods at multiples of the price set by the state, to the rulers themselves, who were seen not only as presiding over the mess but also as themselves the biggest recipients of ill-gotten gains. The anger against traders, specifically market women, was manifested dramatically in the implementation of the

---

[30] William R. Ochieng', "Structural and political changes," in B. A. Ogot and W. R. Ochieng', *Decolonization and Independence in Kenya 1940–93* (London: James Currey, 1995), 102.

[31] Branch, *Kenya: Between Hope and Despair*, 120–59, 331–4; B. A. Ogot, "The politics of populism," in B. A. Ogot and W. R. Ochieng', *Decolonization and Independence in Kenya 1940–93* (London: James Currey, 1995), 187–201, at 213.

[32] Tony Killick, *Development Economics in Action: A Study of Economic Policies in Ghana* (London: Heinemann, 1978), 107.

[33] Jonathon H. Frimpong-Ansah, *The Vampire State in Africa: the Political Economy of Decline in Ghana* London: James Currey, 1991), 111, 116, suggests it derived from the Hausa *kara bude*, "keep it quiet."

June 4 Revolution, when Makola No. 1 Market, the largest marketplace in the country, was demolished by soldiers.[34] There and elsewhere market women were subjected to corporal punishment if suspected of selling goods at above control prices. If such acts were targeted in a specifically gendered way, conversely, the former military rulers who were executed on Accra beach in the same month, in what was seen as the most vivid blow against *kalabule* from above, were all male.

In Kenya, by contrast, despite the slowing of economic growth compared to the 1960s, there was no macroeconomic crises of the extreme kind suffered by Ghanaians, repeatedly and with increasing severity. The most politically sensitive economic issue was not the price and availability of goods or foreign currency, but rather the regionally and socially unequal distribution of the "fruits of uhuru"—the material benefits of independence. The political salience of this was not limited to the fact that the Kikuyu areas had received preferential treatment in the allocation of government spending and jobs. There was also the issue that, within the Kikuyu homeland of Central Province, Kiambu district enjoyed the lion's share of the patronage; and the continuing landlessness of thousands of people in the areas in which the Mau Mau rising had happened. As in Ghana, objective poverty and inequality did not serve as political forces in themselves:[35] in Kenya, they were animated as issues by very strong feelings of unfairness and injustice[36]—a fact which defies Paul Collier's reductionist attempt to distinguish "greed" and "grievance."[37]

On the direction of causality, the primary link was overwhelmingly from economic hardship to political discontent, such that standard-of-living challenges created opportunities for ambitious opportunists with guns to hand, as with Acheampong. Crucially, when the hardship became much worse, and the sense of injustice deeper, there was a greater likelihood that some members of the armed forces would feel obliged to risk their lives in trying to seize power for a "cleansing" moment: as with Rawlings and others in the junior ranks of the Ghanaian armed forces in 1979. In Kenya, despite the inequalities of class, ethnicity and region, the delivery of sustained economic growth in the 1960s and even through the 1970s reduced the opportunity for a coup. The second oil shock of 1979 combined with drought to spread economic discontent at the start of the 1980s. While these circumstances clearly contributed to the motivation for the coup attempt of 1982, the difficult economic conjuncture presumably counted for less in the minds of the security forces who put down the airmen than the positive long-run economic trend.

---

[34] For a first-hand account, see Nii K. Bentsi-Enchill, "Destruction of Accra's Makola market," *West Africa*, August 27, 1979.

[35] The general point was given classical expression half a century ago but needs reiteration today. See E.P. Thompson, "The moral economy of the English crowd in the eighteenth century," *Past & Present* 50:1 (171), 76–136.

[36] Among many possible examples, see Ngũgĩ wa Thiong'o's *Petals of Blood* (London and Nairobi: Heinemann, 1977), a novel which read at the time like a bitter opposition documentary.

[37] Paul Collier, "Doing well out of war," in Mats Berdal and David M. Malone, eds., *Greed and Grievance: Economic Agendas in Civil Wars* (Boulder: Lynne Rienner, 2001), 91–111; Paul Collier and Anke Hoefler, "Greed and grievance in civil wars," *Oxford Economic Papers* 54:4 (2004), 563–95. For a critique, see David Keen, "'Greed': economic agendas," in Keen, *Complex Emergencies* (Cambridge: Polity Press, 2008), 25–49.

It should be added that there was a secondary causal link from political (in)stability to economic performance. John Dunn commented at the time that "Nothing … destabilizes like instability."[38] I have argued elsewhere that the rapid succession of regimes in Ghana in the 1970s sharply raised the discount rate for new rulers: if corrupt, they needed to seize their share of the shrinking cake while they could, at the expense of policy reforms that might enlarge the cake but only beyond their time horizon.[39] This is consistent with the military regime's slide into seemingly ever-deeper kleptocracy the longer it stayed in office, in whichever form (1972, 1975, 1978). In contrast, the marked continuity of office-holding in Kenya surely benefitted the economy, by making it easier for investors, from small farmers to large foreign companies, to assess the prospects: they faced risk more than uncertainty. But the content of policy was surely much more important than continuity by itself. Before examining policy differences between the two countries, however, let us return to external trade.

5. Can Terms-of-trade Shifts Explain the Contrast in Economic Performance?

Both countries were fully dependent on oil for their net energy imports, which in each case contributed between 21 and 22 percent of energy consumption.[40] But Ghana had the important advantage of the Volta dam, which limited the country's need for oil. In 1973 the proportion of electricity derived from oil was merely 1 percent in Ghana, compared to 42.7 percent in Kenya. Conversely, hydro contributed 99 percent in Ghana and 45 percent in Kenya.[41] Thus, in this respect, Ghana was significantly less exposed to the OPEC price shock than Kenya. Even so, it may still be suspected that the contrast between Ghana's economic disaster and Kenya's economic stability was the result of some sort of variation between their commodity terms of trade, that is, in the ratio between the prices of exports and imports (how many units of imports could be purchased with the proceeds of one unit of exports).

To wit, Frankema and van Waijenburg assert of Ghana that "the collapse of international cocoa prices after the first oil crisis led to a sharp economic decline in the years 1973–85, as it eroded the expanding production volumes of cocoa of the 1950s and 1960s."[42] Actually the volume of Ghana's cocoa exports had peaked already in 1964/5, and reached its trough in 1982/3. More important in the present context, to attribute Ghana's economic collapse to an adverse shift in the net barter terms of trade is to overlook the boom in beverage crop prices in 1976–8. Over the 1970s as a whole,

[38] Dunn, "Conclusion," in John Dunn, ed., *West African States: Failure and Promise* (Cambridge: Cambridge University Press, 1978), 212.
[39] Austin, "National poverty," 565, 568.
[40] World Bank, *World Development Indicators 2017*, updated August 2, 2017.
[41] Ibid.
[42] Ewout Frankema and Marlous van Waijenburg, "Africa rising? A historical perspective," *African Affairs* 117:469 (2018), 557.

Table 9.3 Terms of trade shifts 1970–9: annual average growth, Ghana and Kenya (percent)

	Net barter terms of trade	Income terms of trade
Ghana	6.9	−0.8
Kenya	2.2	0.9

Source: World Bank, *Accelerated Development in Sub-Saharan Africa: An Agenda* for Action (Washington DC, 1981), 155.

as Table 9.3 shows, the net barter terms of trade of both countries actually improved; moreover, Ghana's improved much more than Kenya's. This is not surprising, because the average annual percentage growth rates of the key commodity prices over 1970–80 were as follows: 18.2 for oil; -2.8 for tea, 3.9 for coffee, and 7.5 for cocoa.[43]

To explain how Ghana had a fall in its income terms of trade despite a boost to its net barter terms of trade,[44] it might be supposed that Kenya was sacrificing food security in order to boost exports, while Ghana made the opposite trade-off, accepting a decline in export agriculture in the cause of food production. This would be consistent with Acheampong's flagship program "Operation Feed Yourself."[45] But, actually, food output per head fell in both countries, in that the three-year average index for 1977–9 was lower than that for 1969–71. And the fall in Ghana was over twice that in Kenya: 18 percent compared to 8 percent.[46] During the five years 1975–9, with Ghana's GDP contracting, both countries received small quantities of food aid: Ghana received ten times more per head (averaging just over 5.4 kg per year, compared to Kenya's almost token 0.54 kg).[47] So Ghana had a particularly dismal decade in foodstuff production, and needed to make small but significant use of food aid. According to FAO data, the total volume of agricultural output grew over the decade by more than 4 percent per year in Kenya but fell in Ghana.[48]

6. The Contrast in Economic Policy

Douglas Rimmer's excellent analysis of Ghana's economic descent before Structural Adjustment attributed it primarily to two institutional innovations. One, a colonial legacy dating back to 1939, was the statutory state monopoly on the export of cocoa

[43] World Bank, *Accelerated Development*, 157.
[44] The income terms of trade are the total value of imports a country can buy with its exports. A fall in income terms of trade despite a rise in the commodity (net barter) terms of trade implies a greater fall in the volume of exports.
[45] Douglas Rimmer, *Staying Poor: Ghana's Political Economy 1950–1990* (Pergamon Press for the World Bank: Oxford, 1992), 135, 163–4.
[46] World Bank, *Accelerated Development*, 143.
[47] Ibid., 166. The figures are for cereals only (ibid., 192).
[48] Ibid., 50.

beans, exercised through a marketing board. The other, from the Nkrumah era, was the creation of an autonomous monetary system. The first steps were the establishment of a central bank and national currency in 1957.[49] Both Rimmer's arguments are highly plausible in single-country terms. It will be argued in this section, however, that comparison with Kenya shows that it is necessary to be more specific: the problem was not having a marketing board and monetary independence as such; rather, it was the particular policies which those institutions were used to implement in Ghana—but not in Kenya—which is the proximate explanation for Kenya's decidedly better economic performance during the 1970s.

Kenya, too, had agricultural-export marketing boards enjoying statutory monopolies, such as the coffee board which was established in 1946, plus a central bank and a national currency, both introduced in 1966. The origins of the Kenyan marketing boards reflected not only the interests of government but perhaps especially those of European growers.[50] In British West Africa, the introduction of a statutory monopoly had been intended to create a mechanism for preventing a collapse of producer prices during the world war. Unlike in Kenya, the farmers, who were African, were not directly represented in the discussions which led to this move. Their influence was considerable, however, in that the main concern of the Gold Coast government was to avoid unrest which might lead to farmers withholding their crop from the market, as had happened as recently as 1937-8.[51] By 1970, however, in both countries the export marketing boards had been transformed into actual or potential tools of taxation, extracting a surplus from the differential between the world price on one hand, and the producer price plus marketing costs on the other. In partial recompense, the state offered the farmers various inputs at a subsidized price, such as insecticide. Marketing boards have been pilloried by economic liberals for their fiscal role, because of the disincentive it creates for producers: famously by P. T. Bauer, and later by Rimmer as well in the Berg Report, the World Bank's manifesto for Structural Adjustment.[52]

Table 9.4 presents International Monetary Fund data for the price paid to producers as a share of the world price (to be precise: the border—FOB—price). The figures show that in Kenya the marketing boards were used only minimally as a fiscal instrument. In contrast, Ghana used the marketing board to tax cocoa farmers heavily. To make the comparison more informative, I have included in the table the figures for Ghana's neighbor, Côte d'Ivoire. It will be seen that Ghana's taxation of cocoa exports via the marketing board[53] was not much heavier than Côte d'Ivoire's during the early 1970s,

---

[49] Rimmer, *Staying Poor*, esp. 199–212.

[50] E.g., Alan Rufus Waters, "Change and evolution in the structure of the Kenya coffee industry," *African Affairs* 71:283 (1972), 163–75.

[51] Rod Alence, "Colonial government, social conflict and state involvement in Africa's open economies: the origins of the Ghana Cocoa Marketing Board, 1939–46," *Journal of African History* 42:3 (2001), 397–416.

[52] P.T. Bauer, *West African Trade: A Study of Competition, Oligopoly and Monopoly in a Changing Economy* (Cambridge: Cambridge University Press, 1954); Rimmer, *Staying Poor*; World Bank, *Accelerated Development*.

[53] Including an explicit element of cocoa export duty, within the general marketing board surplus.

Table 9.4 Producers' share of border price* at official exchange rates, 1971–80

	1971–5 (%)	1977–80 (%)
Kenya coffee	96.80	94.50
Kenya tea	90.60	100.25
Ghana cocoa	44.40	47.50
Côte d'Ivoire cocoa	52.40	40.00

Note: *Export price at national border.

Source: "African Historical Producer Price" dataset constructed by Tom Westland from the International Monetary Fund archives, "Recent Economic Developments" series. I am very grateful to Dr Westland for making this source available. Kenyan data are not available for 1976, hence my comparison excludes that year.

and was actually lighter than theirs in the late 1970s. Despite the Ghanaian marketing board paying producers a higher share of the world price than its Ivorian counterpart, at the official exchange rate, it was during the late 1970s that Côte d'Ivoire overtook Ghana as the world's largest producer of cocoa. Thus, the Ghana Cocoa Marketing Board was not the main reason for the decline of the industry over which it presided. The key was the exchange rate.

To investigate effective taxation of export agriculture, we need to consider how far exchange rate systems affected the difference between the nominal and real shares of the world price received by Kenyan and Ghanaian farmers. There was a vital contrast here, made possible by the different ways in which the two countries used their central banks and national currencies.

In 1961 Ghana introduced comprehensive exchange controls. This effectively ended the free convertibility of the national currency with sterling.[54] Thereby, four years after Independence, the country shifted from a "liberal" to a "closed" foreign exchange regime.[55] By definition, in a liberal regime, prices are used to control exports and imports; starting with the exchange rate. Convertibility has to be maintained. This constrains the fiscal deficit, because large deficits will lead to domestic inflation and weaken the currency. If the situation is allowed to become severe, the government is likely to have to choose between devaluation and abandoning convertibility. Conversely, in a closed foreign exchange regime, budget deficits can be funded by central bank credit (effectively, printing money). The resultant balance of payments deficit can be tackled by devaluation or by import quotas: conserving foreign exchange by quantity restrictions rather than price adjustments. Allowing the currency to become non-convertible becomes an option.

[54] Rimmer, *Staying Poor*, 205.
[55] Francis Teal, "The foreign exchange regime and growth: a comparison of Ghana and the Ivory Coast," *African Affairs* 85:339 (1986), 267–82, at 272. See, further, J. Clark Leith, *Foreign Trade Regimes and Economic Development: Ghana* (New York: National Bureau of Economic Research, 1974).

Francis Teal contrasted Ghana's move to a closed foreign exchange regime, and its persistence with it until Structural Adjustment,[56] with Côte d'Ivoire's continued membership of the CFA franc zone, which precluded devaluations and inflationary finance. Ghana came out very badly from this comparison with respect to economic growth.[57] However, Kenya presents an intermediate case. Like Ghana, Kenya was not only monetarily independent, in principle, but also occasionally exercised the options of devaluation and even exchange controls. Yet there was a big difference: Kenya avoided spectacular budget deficits and its money-supply expansions were comparatively modest. Essentially as a result, while inflation was about the same in the earlier 1970s, Kenya avoided the major escalation of inflationary finance that the Ghanaian government staged in the later 1970s, leading to the hyperinflation reflected in Figure 9.4 (above).[58] The most extravagant Kenyan monetary expansion was very tame by comparison. It occurred at much the same time, when the balance of payments surplus created by the coffee and tea "windfall" of 1976–9 was allowed to expand the money supply (for the result, again see Figure 9.4). This context of relative monetary restraint arguably explains why the Kenyan devaluation of 14.5 percent in October 1975[59] worked, in the sense of checking the growth of the differential between the official and parallel exchange rates of the Kenyan shilling.[60] In contrast, as Rimmer observed, Ghana's "occasional devaluations had only transitory effects … While the nominal exchange value of the cedi was lowered in 1967, 1972 and 1978, its real official value appreciated on trend from 1962 to 1983."[61]

In industrial economies the economic significance of the exchange rate is usually understood in terms of the competitiveness of a country's products against foreign competition (devaluation giving them an edge), and in inflation (devaluation making imports more expensive in the domestic currency). For countries whose principal exports are staple commodities, the prices they receive are determined as well as denominated in dollars or other external currencies: devaluation does not affect their competitiveness compared to rival suppliers. Overvaluation makes imports cheaper and could thus assist import-substituting industrializers with cheaper capital goods and raw materials; but by making exports more expensive, it would hinder export-oriented industrialization. For predominantly agricultural economies, however, the main significance of the exchange rate is domestic: overvaluation works as an implicit tax on exporters.

[56] Leith notes that, after the overthrow of Nkrumah, Ghana made a rather half-hearted attempt to liberalize imports, an experiment abandoned with Acheampong's coup in 1972. See Leith, *Foreign Trade Regimes*, 109–62. For an incisive analysis by an insider, see Frimpong-Ansah, *Vampire State*, 100–8. Frimpong-Ansah was the governor of the Bank of Ghana under Busia.

[57] Teal, "Foreign exchange regime."

[58] Ghana's money supply rose nearly nineteen times between 1971, the year before Acheampong's coup, and 1980 (Rimmer, *Staying Poor*, 149).

[59] Tony Killick and Maurice Thorne, "Problems of an open economy: the balance of payments in the Nineteen-Seventies," in Killick, ed., *Papers on the Kenyan Economy* (Nairobi: Heinemann, 1981), 59–70, at 68.

[60] Arthur Hazlewood suggested that the Kenyan shilling became somewhat overvalued during the beverage-crop price boom that followed. On the parallel market (admittedly much narrower than its Ghanaian counterpart), it was worth several times more than the Tanzanian or Ugandan shillings, with which it was officially at par. Hazlewood, *The Economy of Kenya: the Kenyatta Era* (Oxford: Oxford University Press, 1979), 130–1.

[61] Rimmer, *Staying Poor*, 208, commenting on his table of nominal and real exchange rates (209).

Having achieved monetary independence, Ghana and Kenya faced the likelihood that their independent currencies would soon face downward pressure, given that they were on their own—unlike the countries, such as Côte d'Ivoire, which had adopted the African franc, linked to the French franc (and later the euro) and supported by the Bank of France. Both the Ghanaian cedi and the Kenyan shilling faced such pressure, as was reflected in the emergence of parallel exchange rates: in other words, illegal markets in which the national currency was traded at below its official exchange rate. In both cases, the parallel market premium—the differential—between the official and unofficial exchange rates was initially small.

In Kenya, the premium remained modest during the 1970s despite the oil price shocks. This is attributable to a combination of greater fiscal and monetary discipline, both of which were easier when exports were strong, specifically including avoiding the currency becoming heavily overvalued. Kenya, too, having like Ghana forsaken the kind of fully liberal foreign exchange system represented by Côte d'Ivoire, was willing to impose quantity controls on imports, in 1972,[62] which, as in Ghana, was through a licensing system. The difference was that, not only were the restrictions less severe, the control system never had to do the main work in balancing imports with exports: that was done by encouraging exports and avoiding extreme expansions of the money supply. The continued availability of long-term capital inflows was also important, as we will see below.

In Ghana, the downward trend in the volume of cocoa exports after 1965 meant that, sooner rather than later, the existing exchange rate would be hard to sustain. In December 1971, Busia's government finally decided, very reluctantly, to devalue. By then they felt the devaluation needed to be dramatic: 78 percent, from 1.02 to 1.82 cedis to the US dollar.[63] Having used the devaluation as his excuse for a coup, Acheampong reversed it, though only partially: revaluing the cedi by 29 percent, to 1.28 to the dollar. A year later, in February 1973, a US devaluation left the official rate at 1.15 cedis to the cedi.[64] In the rest of the decade, despite rapidly falling cocoa exports and the massive hikes in the price of oil, the official exchange rate was reduced only once more: in 1978, to 2.75 cedis to the dollar.[65]

As a result of these divergent performances and policies, the parallel market premium for Kenya and Ghana in the 1970s averaged 16.8 and 66.3 percent respectively.[66] The one time the premium soared in Kenya during the decade was at the start, when the government was putting pressure on the Asian community to emigrate,

---

[62] A. T. Brough and T. R. C. Curtin, "Growth and stability: an account of fiscal and monetary policy," in Tony Killick, ed., *Papers on the Kenyan Economy* (Nairobi: Heinemann, 1981), 37–51, at 40, 41, 42; Hazlewood, *Economy of Kenya*, 152.

[63] Yaw Ansu, "Macroeconomic aspects of multiple exchange rate regimes: the case of Ghana," in Miguel A. Kiguel, J. Saul Lizondo and Stephen A. O'Connell, eds., *Parallel Exchange Rates in Developing Countries* (Houndmills UK: Macmillan, 1997), 188–220, at 189.

[64] Ibid., 190.

[65] Ibid., 190.

[66] Miguel Kiguel and Stephen A. O'Connell, "Parallel exchange rates in developing countries," *World Bank Research Observer* 10:1 (1995), 21–52, at 23. The average concerned is the median end-of-year value, from data provided by International Currency Analysis Inc.

"without allowing them to take their capital with them,"[67] so obliging them to buy foreign exchange even at disadvantageous rates. Conversely, at the end of 1977—the height of the coffee boom—the premium was, briefly, negative.[68] The fact that the premium was usually quite low meant that parallel market's coverage was also low, with the brokers rarely extending beyond the generally criminal community. Though Kenya was monetarily independent, the government was willing to devalue when the official exchange rate became completely incompatible with the maintenance of convertibility. While convertibility was not always unlimited, in the middle of the decade it was possible to walk into a Kenyan bank and exchange Kenyan shillings for foreign currency, without requiring a license; something inconceivable at the time in Ghana.[69] Again, the central bank was used for inflationary finance on a much bigger scale in Ghana than in Kenya.[70]

In Ghana the parallel market currency premium took off during the later 1970s, and attained wide coverage, with parallel market transactions occurring way beyond what were generally considered the criminal part of the society. The ratio of the parallel market exchange rate to the official exchange rate averaged 1.66 in 1970 and 1.73 in 1975. But it jumped to 8 in 1977 and, after an official devaluation, stood at 5.77 in 1980.[71] Toward the end of the decade many of the prices that most people paid were parallel market prices, often reflecting, directly or indirectly, the unofficial exchange rate, even if the majority of the population had no occasion themselves to change money.[72] Ernesto May attempted to calculate the size of the parallel economy by first estimating the amount of money derived from cocoa smuggling. He suggested that, as a share of Ghana's official GDP, the parallel economy rose from 0.32 percent in 1970 to a still insignificant 1.11 percent in 1976, before ballooning to 11.51 percent in 1979 and 24.45 percent in 1980.[73]

7. Contrasting Outcomes: Trends in Export Agriculture and Beyond

The implications for the taxation of exports in Ghana and Kenya were dramatically different. In Kenya, the fact that the parallel market premium was relatively low in value and very modest in coverage meant that what might be called the implicit

---

[67] Jean-Paul Azam, *Trade, Exchange Rate and Growth in Sub-Saharan Africa* (Cambridge: Cambridge University Press, 2007), 79.

[68] Judging from the graph in ibid., 78.

[69] I had exactly that experience in Kenya in 1975. Conversely, in order to obtain an entry permit to Ghana in 1977, it was necessary to buy "cedi vouchers," buying Ghanaian currency at the official exchange rate. Having done this, a single tomato in Accra turned out to cost as much as £2.

[70] For Ghana, see Ansu, "Macroeconomic aspects," 196–7; for Kenya, note the moderation of the critique of monetary policy in Brough and Curtin, "Growth and stability."

[71] Calculated from Rimmer, *Staying Poor*, 209.

[72] The most detailed examinations of the overvaluation of the cedi in this period are May, *Exchange Controls*, and Ansu, "Macroeconomic aspects."

[73] Ernesto May, *Exchange Controls and Parallel Market Economies in Sub-Saharan Africa: Focus on Ghana*, IMF Staff Paper no. 711 (Washington DC, 1985), 129. May sets out his calculations at 81–91.

"overvaluation tax" on exports was almost negligible. Thus the low tax rates implied by the marketing boards' pricing policies were close to the real tax rates, explicit plus implicit, experienced by Kenyan producers of coffee and tea. In Ghana, in contrast, the widening gap between the official and unofficial exchange rates, and the increasing prevalence of the latter when it came to most people buying imported goods, multiplied the effective tax rate on exports. In 1976–80, as we have seen, Ghanaian cocoa farmers officially received an average of 47.5 percent of the sum the Cocoa Marketing Board received for their produce (minus transport costs, etc.). Applying the ratios between the official and unofficial exchange rates noted above, this meant that farmers received only a few percent of what the marketing board received for their crop. The results, shown in Figures 9.5 and 9.6, were predictable.

The difference the exchange rate made to farmers' behavior is strikingly seen in smuggling of cocoa beans from Ghana to its coastal neighbors, Côte d'Ivoire and Togo. During the period 1976–80, the nominal producer price of Ghanaian cocoa, as a share of the world price, was actually higher than in Côte d'Ivoire. Whether it was higher or

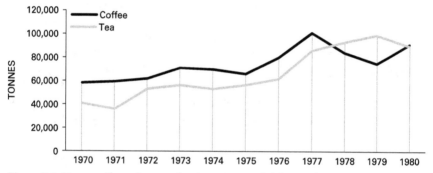

Figure 9.5 Kenya coffee and tea production, 1970–80 (FAO, March 1, 2020).

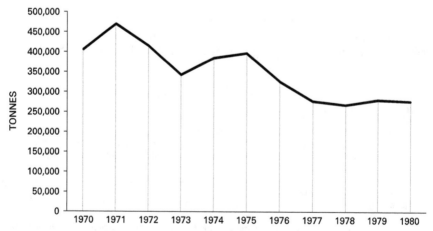

Figure 9.6 Ghana cocoa production, 1970–80 (FAO, March 1, 2020).

lower than in Togo is disputed between the IMF and World Bank figures.[74] None of this was decisive when the overvaluation of the cedi is taken into account. When the smuggler received the Ivorian or Togolese producer price, paid in CFA francs, and exchanged them for Ghanaian cedis on the parallel market, the product was a sum in cedis far greater than that proffered by the Ghana Cocoa Marketing Board for the same quantity of beans. The ratio between the cedi price of cocoa beans sold on the Ivorian side of the border and that paid by the Ghana Cocoa Marketing Board was 2.06 in 1975, 4.36 in 1977 and after a dip to a "mere" 3.3 in 1979 – reached 5.54 in 1980. For cocoa smuggled to Togo, the ratios for the same years were 1.35, 2.86, 2.52 and 4.37 respectively.[75] Franco made the most careful estimates of the annual volumes of cocoa smuggled from Ghana (to both Togo and Côte d'Ivoire) to the crop year 1978/79. His figures give an annual average of 38,500 tonnes over the nine years 1970/71 to 1978/9, with a climb from 31,000 in the first year, and a low of 30,000 in 1974/75, to a record 50,000 in the last year.[76]

The overvaluation tax made the difference between a tax rate that was high but maintained incentives to farmers to reinvest, and one that was punitive, destroying the incentive to replant and even to harvest and prepare for market an existing crop. Franco concluded that even after the 1978 devaluation, it would be impossible to revive Ghanaian cocoa production at the prevailing exchange rate (2.75 cedis: US$1), because the nominal producer price required would have to be higher than the world price.[77] It is difficult to be sure in which year Côte d'Ivoire overtook Ghana as the world's largest producer of cocoa beans, because Côte d'Ivoire would have become the biggest exporter, helped by re-exporting beans from Ghana, before its own rising output passed Ghana's declining production. It should be added that Kenya's coffee exports included a certain amount smuggled from Uganda, attracted by the same producer prices as motivated Kenyan coffee growers themselves.[78]

Though this chapter focuses on export agriculture, it should be noted that the contrasting Ghanaian and Kenyan exchange-rate policies had correspondingly divergent effects on the rest of their economies, directly and via the effects on agricultural exports. In Ghana, the punitive overvaluation tax discouraged all exports, not just cocoa. Though the overvalued official exchange rate made imports cheap in principle, acting on it required obtaining the necessary license. In this context, the licensing system created rents for those who administered it. The shortage of imports, stemming from declining

---

[74] Presumably because Tom Westland's IMF figures in Table 9.4 are FOB (though adjusted for processing costs, where figures are available), whereas the World Bank figures deduct transport, marketing and processing costs. For the three countries in Table 9.4, the differences between the IMF and World Bank figures are small; I preferred the former because they have fewer missing years. But for Togo, the producer price, as an average of the world price 1976–80, was 25 percent according to the Bank, but 74 percent according to the IMF data. Sources: IMF/Westland, as Table 9.4; World Bank, *Accelerated Development*, 56.

[75] May, *Exchange Controls*, 129.

[76] G. Robert Franco, "The optimum producer price of cocoa in Ghana," *Journal of Development Economics* 8:1 (1980), 77–92, at 85–6. Franco's calculations combine the best data available with a plausible cocoa supply function.

[77] Franco, "Optimum producer price of cocoa in Ghana."

[78] Killick and Thorne, "Problems of an open economy," 64.

export volumes and the control systems, badly disrupted the industries that depended on imported capital goods and spare parts, such as motor transport and mining. Thus Ghana was unable to take advantage of the fact that, even more than cocoa, the price of gold was buoyant during the years following the United States' departure from the gold standard in 1971. The price realized per unit of gold from Ghana rose more than seven times from 1973 to 1980, but the volume of output nearly halved.[79] Timber exports collapsed much faster: in 1980 sawn timber exports were 37.6 percent of their 1971 level, while logs were at 21.86 percent. In 1980, the volume of diamonds, manganese, and bauxite production in Ghana was down to 37.90, 39.56, and 56.03 percent percent, respectively, of their 1971 levels.[80] Output in manufacturing also declined,[81] with under-utilization of capacity rising: from about 50 to about 80 percent by the end of the decade, according to James Ahiakpor, though Rimmer quotes 26 percent as the figure for "large-scale" manufacturing (perhaps three-quarters of the sector) in 1980.[82] This was to a large extent as a result of shortages of imported inputs such as spare parts.[83] A rare positive story was the emergence of Suame, a district of the second city, Kumasi, as a center of micro workshops making spare auto parts and simple machines for artisans, items which were otherwise unobtainable.[84] Overall, manufacturing declined in Ghana from 13.23 percent of GDP in 1970 to 8.10 percent of a smaller GDP in 1980.[85] In Kenya, manufacturing output rose.[86] The informal workshop sector advanced, often focused on metal working.[87] As a share of GDP, manufacturing in Kenya edged upwards from 11.98 percent in 1970 to 12.84 percent in 1980.[88]

Critically, contrasting policies and agricultural-export performance had corresponding effects on the fiscal foundations of the state. In Kenya, the government's share of gross national income rose over the decade, helped partly by the recycling of coffee and tea earnings into consumption, thereby raising sales tax receipts. In Ghana, the tax take shrank as the parallel market expanded. According to Rimmer, government revenue as a share of GDP fell from 19.3 percent in 1970 to 8.0 percent in 1980.[89] The overvalued currency meant that the export tax rate was remarkably high, but this was

[79] Rimmer, *Staying Poor*, 144–5.
[80] Ibid., 145.
[81] For an excellent comparison of the performance of manufacturing in both countries in this period see Miatta Fahnbulleh, *The Elusive Quest for Industrialisation in Africa: A Comparative Study of Ghana and Kenya, c1950–2000* (PhD dissertation, London School of Economics, 2005), 195–204.
[82] James C. W. Ahiakpor, "The success and failure of Dependency theory: the experience of Ghana," *International Organization* 39:3 (1985), 535–52, at 539; Rimmer, *Staying Poor*, 153 (cf. 118).
[83] Fahnbulleh, "Elusive Quest," 199. Also Ahiakpor, "Success and failure," 549; Rimmer, *Staying Poor*, 153. Further, Fahnbulleh shows that Kenyan manufacturing, overall, made greater use of domestic resources, and was therefore less import-dependent, 197.
[84] This local industry predated the import famine of 1972 onwards, but greatly expanded during it. Jonathan Dawson, "The development of small-scale industry in Ghana: a case study of Kumasi," in Hank Thomas, Francisco Uribe-Echevarría and Henry Romijn, eds., *Small-Scale Industry: Strategies for Industrial Restructuring* (London: Intermediate Technology Publications, 1991), 173–207.
[85] World Bank, *World Development Indicators 2017*, updated August 2, 2017.
[86] Jerven, *Economic Growth and Measurement* Reconsidered, 111–15; more generally, see Hazlewood, *Economy of Kenya*, ch. 5.
[87] Kenneth King, *Jua Kali Kenya: Change and Development in an Informal Economy 1970–95* (London: James Currey, 1996).
[88] World Bank, *World Development Indicators 2017*, updated August 2, 2017.
[89] Rimmer, *Staying Poor*, 207.

grossly outweighed by the declining volume of output, especially of cocoa, and by the increasing propensity for output to be smuggled, thereby becoming subject to tax only in the neighboring countries. Printing money itself functions to increase a government's share of national income, but in this case a high proportion of cedis were spent and re-spent in the parallel economy, often on goods unavailable at official prices. With the means to pay salaries shrinking, it is hardly surprising that there was a massive exodus of teachers and other mostly state-employed professionals, including university lecturers, to Nigeria and (especially in the case of doctors) far beyond.

Kenya had larger inflows of aid and investment from overseas during the decade. This was important for the country's balance of payments. Except for the peak year of the coffee boom, 1977, Kenya ran a deficit on its current account; which in most years, was covered by a net inflow of capital.[90] The comparison with Ghana highlights the endogeneity of these external sources of income, in that their scale was to a considerable extent a function of government policy in the receiving economy; decisively so for private sector lenders and investors, less so for government and multilateral donors. On coming to power, so more than a year before the 1973 oil price shock, Acheampong took unilateral action on Ghana's backlog of suppliers' credits from the Nkrumah era. He repudiated the accumulated interest and one third of the principal (together, $170 million out of $366 million) and suspended payments on the rest for ten years.[91] Given this precedent, along with exchange controls, a non-convertible currency and the stagnant and then falling GDP, it is hardly surprising that Ghana did not receive loans from foreign commercial banks during this decade.[92] Even so, in the Cold War era, military dictatorship and even economic implosion did not deny a country official development assistance, bilateral and multilateral: such aid represented 3.00 percent of Ghana's GDP during 1973–80. Kenya received rather more aid, though: the equivalent figure was 4.56 percent.[93] By the end of the decade, Ghana governments could have used huge loans, but they were unable to get them: debt-service payments averaged 7.57 percent of exports during 1975–80.[94] Kenya, on the other hand, was able to borrow even from long-term private lenders.[95] Debt service payments averaged 17.26 percent of exports over 1975–80, and reached 21 percent in 1980,[96] during the end-of-decade economic squeeze prompted by higher oil prices plus drought. The latter figure presumably includes a loan of $55 million from the World Bank: a modest beginning to what became known as Structural Adjustment.[97] Thus Kenya had the beginnings of

[90] Killick and Thorne, "Problems of an open economy," 60–1.
[91] Lt-Colonel Acheampong, "Statement on Ghana's external debts," February 5, 1972, in Eboe Hutchful, ed., *The IMF and Ghana: the Confidential Record* (London: Zed and Institute for African Alternatives, 1987), 281–6.
[92] Cf. Bartholemew Armah, "Trade structures and employment growth in Ghana: a historical comparative analysis, 1960–1989," *African Economic History* 21 (1993), 21–36, at 27.
[93] World Bank, *World Development Indicators 2017*, updated August 2, 2017.
[94] Ibid.
[95] Killick and Thorne, "Problems of an open economy," 67.
[96] World Bank, *World Development Indicators 2017*, updated August 2, 2017.
[97] Structural adjustment "did not become an important part of economic management" in Kenya until 1986 (Joseph Kipkemboi Rono, "The impact of the structural adjustment programmes on Kenyan society," *Journal of Social Development in Africa* 17:1 [2002], 81–98, at 82). In contrast, Ghana began a much more fundamental adjustment, agreed with the World Bank and International Monetary Fund, in April 1983.

a debt service problem, albeit on a manageable scale. There is no suggestion in this chapter that Kenyan economic policies in the 1970s were perfect for economic growth; but the comparison with policy-making in Accra puts any failings in Nairobi into perspective.

The episode in Kenya's macroeconomic management that has come in for most criticism is the surge in earnings from coffee and tea when their prices were high in 1976–8. Three claims have been made, as we will see: that the government deserved no credit for the boom; that the farmers did nothing to earn it either, and therefore did not deserve the extra money; and that the government should have taken more of the income in order to limit the farmers' share, in the interests of restraining inflation. These charges particularly interest me because the inspiration for this chapter came from my memory of revisiting a coffee-growing valley in Nyeri district, Kenya, in 1978, three years after I had taught in a school nearby. Walking on the road over the crest of one of the surrounding hills and seeing the view, for a moment I was disoriented, and wondered if it was the same place. As before, the valley exhibited the dispersed but dense settlement characteristic of the region: plenty of shambas, with the people living on the farms not in villages. But whereas in 1975 most of the roofs were thatched, now most home-owners had upgraded to metal. The sight was doubly striking because of the contrast with a cocoa-growing area of Ghana, in which I had done research in 1977: where metal roofs where fairly frequent, but by then badly dilapidated. My desire to explain this contrast, knowing that world cocoa prices had boomed like world coffee prices, was the motive for this chapter.

Daniel Branch, in his enthralling overview of Kenya's post-colonial history, asserts that the "causes" of the country's coffee-fueled "return to prodigious economic growth … lay not in government policy, but instead" in the frost in Brazil that destroyed the crop there in 1975.[98] The distinguished development economists Tony Killick and Maurice Thorne wrote shortly after the event that "These were purely fortuitous profits, in no sense a return on past efforts and investments."[99] Their colleague Arthur Hazlewood did not go that far but suggested that the government might have been wise to impose an export tax, perhaps in the form of currency-overvaluation, preferably within a dual exchange rate system, in which the currency would be overvalued for coffee farmers but kept relatively low to help manufacturers in international competition.[100] Overvaluation, or partial overvaluation, might have curbed the surge of private spending that would follow farmers' receipt of the windfall. Branch's remark exemplifies the need for comparison: the preceding sections of this chapter show that government policies cannot be taken as given; unlike their counterparts in Ghana, policy-makers in Kenya provided an environment in which producers would respond to the opportunity presented on the world market. Killick and Thorne's claim, uncharacteristically for the authors, is both patronizing and unrealistic: if you invest capital and labor in rainfed export agriculture, you do so in full knowledge that producer prices (like crops) can and, over time, surely will vary dramatically. The

[98] Branch, *Kenya: Between Hope and Despair*, 126–7.
[99] Killick and Thorne, "Problems of an open economy," 68.
[100] Hazlewood, *Economy of Kenya*, 131.

farmer takes the calculated risk that the bad years will be outweighed by the good years; and that she or he can endure the former in order to be there to enjoy the latter. Moreover, part of the "windfall" was evidently the result of farmers responding to the initial rise in prices to invest additional labor and capital in coffee and tea production.[101] Hazlewood's suggestion (above) raises a more subtle issue. It can reasonably be argued that the government would have been wise either to take the opportunity to raise additional revenue, and/or to hold back part of the farmers' income in order to be able to pay it to them in a time of low world prices. The latter is, after all, exactly what marketing boards across Africa were supposed to do but had very rarely done. Such a policy would have limited monetary expansion and inflation, and the boom in imports. While accepting that income-smoothing could have helped both the farmers and the economy, two points should be added about how the farmers and other beneficiaries used the windfall. David Bevan, Paul Collier and Jan Willem Gunning showed that they saved much of it (and their propensity to save was much higher than the government's). Overall, Bevan and co-authors estimate that "around half of windfall income appears to have been saved whereas prior to the boom the savings rate had averaged around 20 per cent." Morten Jerven notes that "the increase in earnings stimulated manufacturing growth in terms of both demand and the supply of capital goods for new projects."[102] Bevan and colleagues also showed that much of the money was invested in construction.[103] For small farmers, that meant better roofs; for larger operators, as Colin Leys noted, it meant the acquisition of much of the remaining office space in Nairobi that had previously been owned by expatriates. In that sense, the private sector used the coffee boom to further the "Africanization" of the wider economy.[104]

Finally in this section, it should be noted that Kenya responded to OPEC with further investment in hydro, whose contribution to electricity output rose from 45 percent in 1973 to nearly 77 percent in 1979.[105] Ghana had almost nowhere to go in increasing the share of hydroelectricity. However, reflecting the trend of the country's import purchasing-power, rather than a change in energy strategy, from 1973 to 1979 net energy (oil) imports as a share of energy consumption fell 4 percentage points in Ghana, compared to 0.9 of a point in Kenya.

8. The Political Economy of Growth Compared to Decline

An explanation focused on economic policy begs the question why policies were so different in otherwise similar countries facing similar problems. In my view two approaches that stimulated much debate in the 1980s remain particularly useful in

---

[101] David Bevan, Paul Collier and Jan Willem Gunning, "Anatomy of a temporary trade shock: the Kenyan coffee boom of 1976–9," *Journal of African Economies* 1:2 (1992), 271–305, at 273.

[102] Jerven, *Economic Growth and Measurement Reconsidered*, 111.

[103] Bevan, Collier and Gunning, "Anatomy of a temporary trade shock," 84.

[104] Colin Leys, "Capital accumulation, class formation and dependency: the significance of the Kenyan case," *Socialist Register 1978*, 241–66, at 250.

[105] World Bank, *World Development Indicators 2017*, updated August 2, 2017.

thinking about the 1970s comparison undertaken in this chapter. They stand out because both combined an attempt to understand national experiences in a broad theoretical and African-comparative framework with a deep historical and contemporary interest in one or both of Kenya and Ghana. I refer to works by Robert Bates and Colin Leys, which I will treat in reverse-chronological order.

It was Bates who introduced "new institutionalist" political economy to African studies, an approach he has himself refined and extended since; and there have been many additional contributions by other scholars in various disciplines.[106] *Markets and States in Tropical Africa* (1981), along with an essay titled "The nature and origins of agricultural policies in Africa" (1983), remain the most pertinent to the Ghana-Kenya comparison.[107] As a rational-choice political scientist, he accepted the then-new consensus among mainstream economists that the majority of tropical African countries had underperformed in economic growth since Independence, and that this was the result of excessive and economically inefficient government intervention.[108] For Bates, the questions were why they persisted with apparently unsuccessful policies (to make a mistake is not necessarily irrational, but to persist in the mistake is), and why, conversely, the very few African governments to adopt relatively market-friendly policies had done so. Along with Côte d'Ivoire, Kenya was in the latter group, whereas Ghana was among the economically unsuccessful majority, together with the likes of Tanzania and Zambia. Bates assumed that governments are led by entirely self-interested economic maximizers. All the governments that showed continuity in policy were therefore winners in their own estimation. Those who had presided over mainly slow or negative economic growth had rewarded their own political constituencies, albeit not the society as a whole. Those who had presided over rapid economic growth had done the same thing. The difference was that the economic interests of the latter's constituencies coincided closely with the comparative advantage of the economy as a whole.

Concretely, Bates started from the observation that the great majority of the population of these states was agricultural. His thesis is that large numbers of individually small-scale producers are structurally unable to assert their shared economic interests on governments, because of the free-rider problem. Hence, the

---

[106] E.g., Robert H. Bates, *When Things Fell Apart: State Failure in Late-Century Africa* (New York: Cambridge University Press, 2008); Daron Acemoglu and James A. Robinson, "Why is Africa poor?," *Economic History of Developing Regions* 25:1 (2010), 21–50; Catherine Boone, *Property and Political Order in Africa: Land Rights and the Structure of Politics* (New York: Cambridge University Press, 2014).

[107] Robert H. Bates, *Markets and States in Tropical Africa: The Political Basis of Agricultural Policies* (Berkeley: University of California Press, 1981); Bates, "The nature and origins of agricultural policies in Africa," in Bates, *Essays on the Political Economy of Rural Africa* (New York: Cambridge University Press, 1983), 107–33, 164–8.

[108] Until the 1970s, most development economists argued that the state needed to take a leading role in economic development in poor countries. Rimmer was an exception: e.g., Douglas Rimmer, "The abstraction from politics: a critique of economic theory and design with reference to West Africa," *Journal of Development Studies* 5:3 (1969), 190–204. Killick's *Development Economics in Action* is precisely a case study of the role of the earlier development economics in informing government policy, for the case of Ghana up to the Acheampong coup in January 1972.

states which had underperformed economically were those like Ghana in which agricultural (especially export-agricultural) interests were not represented in government, while policy-makers responded instead to the demands of urban interest groups. The exceptions that proved the rule were two countries in which farmers were in power, with the presidents themselves owning large estates: Côte d'Ivoire under Felix Houphouët-Boigny, and Kenya under Jomo Kenyatta. In these countries the movement that took power at Independence "remained strongly centered on a political base made up of commercial farmers." Their governments adopted pricing policies which, compared to Ghana and, say, Zambia, were "highly favorable to farmers."[109]

Bates's analysis is consistent with the respective experiences of Ghana and Kenya in the 1970s. Kenyatta and his trusted collaborators, the "Kiambu clique," had all become landed "gentry," of a fully commercial kind. What was good for their estates was favorable producer prices for export crops, paid at an exchange rate close to the Kenyan shilling's equilibrium rate. This was also good for small-scale export-crop growers. Given Kenya's comparative advantage in coffee and tea production, it was also good for the growth of exports and GDP. Nothing much changed in Moi's first two and a bit years in office, i.e., to the end of 1980, in terms of support for export agriculture, given the circumstances of falling world prices and drought at home.[110] Conversely, farming interests were represented either weakly or not at all in the senior leadership of Ghana under Acheampong, Akuffo, Rawlings, and Limann. Busia's government, however, was elected on a pro-rural program in October 1969, and soon came into serious conflict with the trade unions. Any thought that Bates has misclassified Ghana within his framework is contradicted by the observation that Busia's liberalization of the foreign exchange system, as of the economy in general, was distinctly limited.[111] More so, when the government took strong action in favor of cocoa farmers by a major devaluation (accompanied by a 25 percent increase in the producer price),[112] the army took the opportunity for a coup, with seemingly strong urban support.

As a historian, I find Bates's schema useful not only because it is consistent with the main story, but also because it resonates with important details, such as Kenyatta preferring to base his "court" "primarily at his country home of Gatundu" rather than in Nairobi,[113] and the highly urban character of the consumer anger which propelled soldiers (who were based in central Accra, and felt at the mercy of the market traders)

---

[109] Bates, "Nature and origins," 113.

[110] From his accession to the presidency in August 1978, Moi changed little in policy generally until after securing his position in the 1979 general elections. In later work, Bates argued that Moi consolidated his own agrarian support, in western Kenya, based on maize farmers producing for domestic markets as distinct from Kenyatta's agricultural-export producers in Central Province (*Beyond the Miracle of the Market*, 135–8, 148–9, 183–4). Even so, there is a case to be made for continuity in both policy and outcome (Jerven, *Economic Growth and Measurement Reconsidered*, 109–23). This was indeed what Moi proclaimed with his slogan of *Nyayo* ("footsteps," i.e., following in the footsteps of Kenyatta). Robert Maxon and Peter Ndege argue that continuity from Kenyatta to Moi "was nowhere more apparent than with regard to economic policy": Maxon and Ndege, "The economics of Structural Adjustment," in B. A. Ogot and W. R. Ochieng', eds., *Decolonization and Independence in Kenya 1940–93* (London: James Currey, 1995), 151–86 at 152.

[111] Killick, *Staying Poor*, ch. 6.

[112] Killick, *Development Economics in Action*, 57.

[113] Ochieng', "Structural and political changes," 102.

to destroy Makola market in 1979. Again, earlier, while the Acheampong government supported projects to promote "modern" rice farming in northern Ghana, in the form of mechanization (tractors) or irrigation, these were essentially exercises in subsidizing army officers, civil servants and other men with powerful connections in government to establish large agricultural enterprises on land previously occupied by peasants—without achieving "the expected increase in overall output."[114] In effect, the cocoa farmers—as the main source of government revenue, directly and indirectly—paid for this probable reduction in overall agricultural productivity. Crucially, both the new Ghanaian regimes of 1979—Rawlings and the June 4 Revolution, Limann and the Third Republic—sought to enforce the multiple price and quantity controls in the economy, rather than to allow exporters to receive a high proportion of the value of their produce on the world market.

I have reservations about Bates's classic analysis, but they are about the before and after, rather than the 1970s themselves. I think he underestimates the capacity of small farmers to organize themselves to promote their interests, at least in alliance with larger farmers and chiefs: the Ghanaian cocoa farmers' movement of the colonial period was the biggest example.[115] Again, in positing a high-rent-seeking equilibrium, Bates's framework does not provide a sufficient answer to why so many African countries adopted Structural Adjustment in the 1980s. By doing so, they replaced administrative with market means of allocating resources, thereby reducing the scope for high rent-seeking, i.e., (apparently) sawing off the branch on which they were sitting. This seemingly self-denying move, by the majority of governments in the region, is a surprise in the perspective of *Markets and States*.[116] So, a longer-term view shows that there were other variables involved; but Bates's argument that the type of economic interests represented in the political leadership determined their policy choices, whatever the implications for economic growth, remains a powerful insight, especially for the 1970s.

In the 1960s and early 1970s—before the news to the contrary from South Korea and Taiwan became undeniable—there was a strong case for the proposition that the worldwide spread of industrialization had halted. This observation was theorized by the Dependency school with the argument that subordination to unequal exchange within the world capitalist economy was self-perpetuating, because in dependent economies the circuit of accumulation operated to export surpluses rather than to reinvest them domestically. Flag-independence masked neo-colonialism, the continuation of external exploitation via a local "comprador" bourgeoisie which could do no other than act as the local agent for international capital. The only way to achieve

---

[114] Konings, *The State and Rural Class Formation*, quote at 340.

[115] Gareth Austin, "Capitalists and chiefs in the cocoa holdups in South Asante, 1927–1938," *International Journal of African Historical Studies* 21:1 (1988), 63–95, esp. 92–3.

[116] Bates seems to me to come close to admitting this, albeit only implicitly, in an essay published a decade after *Markets and States*, which reviewed the challenge which new evidence—more recent history—posed for the earlier theories of the politics of agriculture. He was too modest to cite his own 1981 book, the most prominent contribution to that earlier literature. See Robert H. Bates, "Agricultural policy and the study of politics in post-independence Africa," in Douglas Rimmer, ed., *Africa 30 Years On* (London: James Currey, 1991), 115–29.

genuine de-colonization and development was to "de-link" from the world economy.[117] In 1975 Colin Leys published perhaps the best dependency analysis of the historical formation of a newly decolonized African country, *Underdevelopment in Kenya: the Political Economy of Neo-Colonialism*.[118] Three years later, he produced a paper explaining that he had changed his mind. In "Capital accumulation, class formation and dependency: the significance of the Kenyan case," Leys argued that a genuine national capitalism was emerging under Kenyatta.[119] Rapid economic growth had been accompanied by "a steady decline in the non-monetary share of output" and a rising share of wage labor in total employment.[120] In sum, "the relatively high and sustained level of capital accumulation was accompanied by an extension of capitalist relations of production." There was a net inflow of foreign capital, but, he implied, Kenya was no neo-colony. "Africanization" of ownership of the economy, though most complete in agriculture, was proceeding in all sectors. The state played an important role in all this, but Leys implied that it was not autonomous: it "reflected" existing accumulation by the "Kikuyu bourgeoise."[121] African capital was moving into manufacturing from the services and (he seems to imply) agricultural sectors. Whereas decolonization had been a neo-colonial project of international capital, since Independence the story had been "the class project of the indigenous bourgeoisie."[122] The primary engine of growth, he implied, had been the spectacular growth of smallholder production from 1955 onwards, sustained by the resettlement process. By 1977, only 5 percent of the mixed-farming area of the former "White Highlands" remained under expatriate ownership. The smallholdings were themselves not equal, with much of the initial impetus coming from those able to invest and pay wages.[123] Meanwhile, the Kikuyu bourgeoisie was itself buying land and investing in commercial agriculture: by the end of 1977, 57 percent of the area of European-owned coffee plantations was in African hands. These capitalists were also investing in trade, and beginning to invest in manufacturing. Leys argued that the element of corruption and force in the process of accumulation, such as the pressure put on Asian entrepreneurs to sell to Kenyans, should be viewed as a case of Marx's "primitive accumulation": in the context of a poor economy, both market and extra-market means of acquiring wealth were part of the process of capitalist development. Perhaps the most striking example of the ambition and energy of Kenyan capitalism identified by Leys was GEMA Holdings. Founded in 1973, it became a

---

[117] For a sympathetic but critical review of Dependency theory, see Anthony Brewer, *Marxist Theories of Imperialism: a Critical Survey* (London: Routledge and Kegan Paul, 1980). Later editions tracked subsequent developments, but the first edition devotes the most space to the variations of the theory. The major African dependency theorist was the late Samir Amin, e.g., his *Unequal Development: an Essay on the Social Formations of Peripheral Capitalism* (New York: Monthly Review Press, 1976).

[118] London: Heinemann.

[119] Leys, "Capital accumulation."

[120] Ibid., 246.

[121] Ibid. 250–1.

[122] Ibid., 259.

[123] Ibid., 249–50. As he acknowledged, Leys' argument here drew extensively on the research of Michael Cowen, which at the time was mainly available in mimeographs. A more easily accessible presentation of Michael Cowen's research is his "Commodity production in Kenya's Central Province," in Judith Hever, Pepe Roberts, and Gavin Williams, eds., *Rural Development in tropical Africa* (London: Macmillan, 1981), 121–42.

public company in 1977. In addition to investments in [trade, banking and large-scale] farming, it had a tile factory and a newly opened truck assembly plant, co-owned with Fiat.[124]

Leys' shift from a Dependency to a Marxist interpretation of post-independence Kenya attracted a vigorous debate within the general controversy between these two schools over the developmental significance of local capitalisms in the "Third World." The discussion focused on Kenya[125] but broadened into comparative analysis of certain other tropical African economies, such as Cameroon and Nigeria.[126] Ghana did not feature, evidently because its economy was hardly fast-growing, and because it would be difficult to construe its 1970s history as "the class project of the indigenous bourgeoisie."

In my view, Leys' argument fits the evidence for Kenya in the 1970s, and raises important points for comparison with Ghana. First, the Africanization of the economy, and the support for this from the state, are hard to reconcile with the concept of "neo-colonialism." Despite the ghastly economic record and the decline of state capacity in 1970s Ghana, it is even harder to consider the latter as a neo-colony. On the contrary, as Rimmer observed, by 1980 Ghana had gone a long way to fulfil the Dependency theory prescription for a break with the capitalist world system: "de-linking" was well advanced in terms of Ghana's shrinking participation in the world markets for goods and for capital.[127] The two countries had almost identical shares of trade in GDP in 1960. In Kenya, the share remained remarkably stable over the next two decades, increasing slightly during the 1970s. In Ghana the share had plummeted during

Table 9.5 Trade as a percentage of GDP, 1960–80

	1960	1966	1970	1980
Ghana	63.64	34.26	44.04	17.62
Kenya	64.77	63.28	60.49	65.42

Source: World Bank, *World Development Indicators 2017* (updated August 2, 2017).

[124] Leys, "Capital accumulation," 256.
[125] For the view that Leys was right the first time and wrong the second time, see Raphael Kaplinsky, "Capitalist accumulation in the periphery: the Kenyan case re-examined," *Review of African Political Economy* 17 (1980), 83–105. Two incisive contributions to the debate also provided overviews: Björn Beckman, "Imperialism and capitalist transformation: critique of a Kenyan debate," *Review of African Political Economy*, 19 (1980), 48–62; Gavin Kitching, "Politics, method, and evidence in the 'Kenya Debate'," in Henry Bernstein and Bonnie K. Campbell, eds., *Contradictions of Accumulation in Africa: Studies in Economy and State* (Beverly Hills, CA: Sage, 1985), 115–52. Leys offered his own conclusions in "Learning from the Kenya debate," in David E. Apter and Carl G. Rosberg, eds., *Political Development and the New Realism in Sub-Saharan Africa* (Charlottesville, VA: University of Virginia Press, 1994), 220–43, or in Leys, *The Rise and Fall of Development Theory* (1994),
[126] Bruce J. Berman and Colin Leys, eds., *African Capitalists in African Development* (Boulder: Lynne Reiner, 1994).
[127] Rimmer, *Staying Poor*, 147.

Nkrumah's import-substituting industrialization, was partly revived under the more economically liberal governments that followed—and then collapsed during the 1970s.

Second, Leys implied that Kenya's capacity to maintain economic growth despite the 1973 OPEC shock, albeit at a reduced rate, was to a large extent because it had a dynamic indigenous capitalist class, actively supported by the state, resulting in a circuit of accumulation and reinvestment within the country. The irony is that Ghana, more so than Kenya (except at the coast), had a strong indigenous capitalist class, with deep historical roots in trade and production.[128] However, following the fatal division of the cocoa farmers' movement by 1956, Kwame Nkrumah's government was able to complete the political demobilization of the broad base of Ghanaian indigenous capitalism.[129] In Nkrumah's own vision of the Ghanaian economy, as set out in a speech of 1962, large enterprises were considered co-extensive with state and foreign undertakings; there was room for small-scale Ghanaian private enterprises, but implicitly no place for larger indigenous firms.[130] Successor governments in the later 1960s took only modest steps to change this, such as the privatization of the local buying of cocoa beans (from the farmers, for sale to the marketing board). Even that step was reversed under Acheampong. In the 1970s, market conditions worsened and political support for Ghanaian capitalists as a class was absent, in contrast to Kenya during the same decade.[131]

But what happened next raises the question whether Leys had been too optimistic about the stability and potential of the kind of capitalism that had emerged under Kenyatta. Its political vulnerability can be spelled out with "GEMA": Gikuyu-Embu-Meru Association, the organization which gave birth to GEMA Holdings Ltd.[132] GEMA was very much an ethnic political network, and constituted the major force behind the unsuccessful attempt to prevent Moi, as vice-president, from succeeding Kenyatta. The holdings company rapidly acquired new subscribers from within Kenyatta's ruling elite, the value of its asserts rising from 50 million to 50–90 million

[128] Polly Hill, *The Migrant Cocoa-Farmers of Southern Ghana: A Study in Rural Capitalism* (Cambridge, 1963: 2nd ed. LIT and James Currey with International African Institute: Hamburg and Oxford, 1997); Kwame Arhin, "Some Asante views of colonial rule: as seen in the controversy relating to death duties," *Transactions of the Historical Society of Ghana* 15 (1974), 63–84; Arhin, "The economic and social significance of rubber production and exchange on the Gold and Ivory Coasts, 1880–1900," *Cahiers d'études africaines* 20: 77–8 (1980), 49–62; Raymond E. Dumett, "African merchants of the Gold Coast, 1860–1905: dynamics of indigenous entrepreneurship," *Comparative Studies in Society and History* 25 (1983), 661–93; Gareth Austin: "'No elders were present': commoners and private ownership in Asante, 1807–96," *Journal of African History* 37 (1996), 1–30; Austin, *Labour, Land and Capital in Ghana: From Slavery to Free Labour in Asante, 1807–1956* (Rochester NY: University of Rochester Press, 2005).
[129] Björn Beckman, *Organising the Farmers: Cocoa Politics and National Development in Ghana* (Uppsala: Scandinavian Institute of African Studies, 1976).
[130] President Kwame Nkrumah, "Overseas Capital and Investment in Ghana," speech given at the foundation stone laying ceremony of the Kumasi City Hotel, March 24, 1962.
[131] Björn Beckman, "Ghana, 1951–78: the agrarian basis of the post-colonial state," in Judith Heyer, Pepe Roberts, and Gavin Williams, eds., *Rural Development in Tropical Africa* (London: Macmillan, 1981), 143–92.
[132] Gikuyu was an old spelling of Kikuyu.
[133] Ogot, "The politics of populism," 196. Leys, "Capital accumulation," 256, gives a slightly different set of figures for different dates, but the story is the same.

Kenyan shillings between its launch in October 1973 and July 1980.[133] Already in 1979, Moi's new government took legal action against executives of the company over alleged financial irregularities. In 1980, the parent organization was banned, in the name of abolishing "divisive" ethnic associations. The holding company renamed itself Agricultural & Industrial Holdings Ltd,[134] but for the rest of Moi's presidency its priority was survival. It was a casualty of Moi's deconstruction and diminution of Kenyatta's Kiambu-Kikuyu-based patronage network, and of the extension of Moi's own Kalenjin-based network. Kenya did provide more favorable conditions for nationally based capitalists than Ghana, in that the state was not indifferent or hostile to such capitalists in general and, after all, Agricultural & Industrial Holdings was allowed to persist. But even in Kenya, the chance to own capital on more than a small scale was largely a function of access to political patronage, and therefore of the durability of the government of the moment. In that sense the transgenerational accumulation of capital, a feature of family firms in long-established capitalist economies, remained politically vulnerable in principle in both countries in this period, though to different degrees.

9. Conclusion

This chapter has compared the economic and political impact of the oil shocks in two broadly similar countries on opposite sides of tropical Africa. The Ghanaian and Kenyan economies could hardly have performed more differently under the circumstances. In terms of economic growth, and across a range of other criteria, Ghanaians tended to suffer while Kenyans tended to prosper. Both societies were very unequal, but in Kenya prosperity was very unequally distributed, whereas in Ghana the same applied to decline and poverty. The most telling difference was demographic. In 1973–80—the years of and between the oil shocks as such—Ghana's average annual population growth was 1.8 percent, compared to 3.8 percent for Kenya.[135] While Kenya's birth rate was famously high in this period, the main reason for the contrast was clearly net emigration: an exodus of Ghanaians to seek employment in Nigeria, the West, and elsewhere. The economic drama was accompanied by a no less dramatic political one. Kenya was by no means as politically stable as its constitutional continuity suggests. But Ghana's formal instability was a reflection of political reality, based on widespread rejection of the state as inefficient or corrupt.

The contrast cannot be explained by differences in the extent of the trade shocks. Overall, Ghana's commodity terms of trade were more favorable than Kenya's over the decade. As non-producers of oil, both countries were severely hit by the oil price rises; though Ghana had the advantage that 99 percent of its electricity production came from hydro. But, as beverage crop producers, they had the compensation of a major boom in the prices of their own major exports in between the OPEC shocks.

[134] Branch, *Kenya: Between Hope and Despair*, 139, 141; Ogot, "The politics of populism," 195, 197.
[135] World Bank, *Sub-Saharan Africa: From Crisis to Sustainable Growth*, 269.

Economists have described the coffee price-boom as a "wasted opportunity" for Kenya, a case of "mis-management."[136] Comparison with Ghanaian governments' handling of the cocoa price-boom makes this claim largely risible.

It has been argued here that the proximate explanation for the contrast in economic performance is the contrast in economic policies. Specifically, it was not the traditionally maligned marketing board system, nor the choice of monetary independence, but rather the uses to which these institutions were put. A punitive if implicit "overvaluation tax" on exports was the cause of the collapse of Ghanaian cocoa production.

But why did the two countries adopt very different policies, and why did Ghanaian governments stick to theirs after several years of falling exports and GDP? We have seen that Bates's broad "structural" explanation, the presence/absence of farmers in the top political leadership, fits the evidence for the decade in question. It is compatible with another major thesis that is also generally consistent with the evidence from the 1970s, Leys' argument that Kenya was developing along increasingly capitalist lines, with capital being accumulated by the ruling class through both market and non-market methods, and then invested or reinvested productively. If we were to follow the story into the 1980s, questions would arise about the durability of Kenyan exceptionalism. Did Moi's move against GEMA Holdings suggest that the dynamism of Kenyan capitalism was compromised by the patrimonial structure of the political system inherited from Kenyatta, and by the rivalry between ethnic-based networks? Again, under Moi, the Kenyan presidency continued to represent farming interests, but, as Bates highlighted in his later work, the nature of the farming interests had shifted: the influence now lay much more with maize-growers supplying the domestic market than with beverage-crop producers serving the export market. Did that compromise the growth of markets, and thereby weaken the growth of the import-purchasing capacity on which Kenyan industrial prospects partly depended? Conversely, in 1983, defying Bates's (1981) analysis, another strongly urban-based Ghanaian government broke the mold: it made a U-turn toward policies that favored markets in general and export agriculture in particular. But that is a story for another paper.

What remains to be observed here is where the 1960s and especially the 1970s fit into the long-term comparison of the growth rates of these two broadly similar economies. In this period Kenya was steadily closing the gap in GDP per head compared to Ghana that was a legacy of the colonial period. Kenyatta was often accused of taking over the institutions of settler colonialism, but from the mid-1950s until the early 1980s, Kenya did much to overcome the penalty in average African living standards that was a feature of that kind of colonialism, compared to the non-settler, peasant-cum-rural-capitalist variety epitomized by colonial Ghana.[137] As Figure 9.1 shows, both countries grew faster than the average for Sub-Saharan Africa from 1983,

---

[136] Killick and Thorne, "Problems of an open economy," 67; Francis M. Mwega and Njuguna S. Ndung'u, "Explaining Africa growth performance: the case of Kenya," in Benno J. Ndulu, Stephen A. O'Connell, Jean-Paul Azam, Jan Willem Gunning, and Dominique Nijnkeu, eds., *The Political Economy of Growth in Africa 1960–2000* (Cambridge: Cambridge University Press, 2008), 325–68, at 329.

[137] Gareth Austin, "The economics of colonialism," in Célestin Monga and Justin Lin (eds.), *Oxford Handbook of Africa and Economics* (Oxford University Press, 2015), 522–35.

the year Ghana adopted Structural Adjustment, until the 2008–9 Great Recession and beyond. But, to recall Figure 9.2, it was not until 1982 that Kenya's GDP per head overtook Ghana's (which was still falling). In 1992, Ghana regained the "lead." It proceeded to reopen a considerable gap over the next two decades (it makes sense to limit the comparison to the period before Ghana became an oil exporter in 2011), though on a scale smaller than under colonialism. Is the gap to be explained by contingency, or did Ghana possess resource advantages such as a less inelastic supply of fertile land, that made a difference when the contrast in economic policies was largely eliminated under Structural Adjustment?

These are bilateral questions focused on national economies. They reflect the general conclusion of this chapter: national responses were more important than the oil-price shocks themselves in determining the economic histories of African beverage-crop producers in the 1970s.

Notes on Contributors

Shigeru Akita is Distinguished Professor of Global History, Graduate School of Humanities, Osaka University, Japan. He is also the Head of Division of Global History Studies, Institute for Open and Transdisciplinary Research Initiatives, Osaka University. His major publications include (ed.) *American Empire in Global History* (Routledge, 2022); *Teikoku kara Kaihatsu-Enjyo e* [*From Empires to Development Aid*] (Nagoya University Press, 2017); *The Transformation of the International Order of Asia: Decolonization, the Cold War, and the Colombo Plan* (ed. with G. Krozewski) (Routledge, 2015); and *Igirisu-Teikoku no Rekishi—Ajia kara Kangaeru* [*The History of the British Empire from Asian Perspectives*] (Chuokoron-Shinsha, 2012). He received the 20th Ohira Memorial Prize in June 2004, and the 14th Yomiuri-Yoshino Sakuzo Prize in July 2013.

Gareth Austin is Emeritus Professor of Economic History and Director of Research at the University of Cambridge. His previous employers included Kiamuya Secondary School, Kenya, the University of Ghana, the London School of Economics, and the Graduate Institute of Geneva. He has published extensively in African and comparative economic history, including *Labour, Land and Capital in Ghana: From Slavery to Free Labour in Asante, 1807–1956* (Rochester NY, 2005); "Resources, techniques and strategies south of the Sahara: revising the factor endowments perspective on African economic development, 1500–2000" (*Economic History Review*, 61:3 (2008), 587–624); and *Economic Development and Environmental History in the Anthropocene: Perspectives on Asia and Africa* (ed. and au.) (Bloomsbury, 2017).

Hideki Kan is Emeritus Professor of U.S. Diplomatic History at Kyushu University and Invited Visiting Professor at Osaka University, Japan. His major publications include *Reisen Ki Amerika no Ajia Seisaku: "Jiyushugiteki Kokusai Chitsujo" no Henyoo to "Nichi-bei Kyoryoku"* [*American Policy toward Asia in the Cold War Years: The Transformation of the "Liberal International Order" and "Japan-U.S. Cooperation"*] (Koyo Shobo, 2019); *Reisn to "Amerika no Seiki": Ajia ni okeru "Hi-koshiki Teikoku" no Chitsujo Keisei* [*The Cold War and the "American Century": An Informal Empire's Order-Making in Asia*] (Iwanami Shoten, 2016); and *Amerika no Sekai Senryaku* [*U.S. Global Strategy*] (Chuokoron-Shinsha, 2008). Most recently, he has published "Informal empire and the Cold War" (*The Journal of Imperial and Commonwealth History*, Vol. 49, No. 3, June 2021).

Dane Kennedy is the Elmer Louis Kayser Professor Emeritus of History and International Affairs at George Washington University in Washington, DC. He is the author of eight books on various aspects of British imperial and world history, most recently *The Imperial History Wars: Debating the British Empire* (Bloomsbury, 2018) and *Decolonization: A Very Short Introduction* (Oxford University Press, 2016). He also has edited three books, including *How Empire Shaped Us* (ed. with Antoinette Burton) (Bloomsbury, 2016). He has served as Director of the National History Center (2014–20) and President of the North American Conference of British Studies (2011–13).

Mark Metzler is Professor of History and International Studies at the University of Washington in Seattle and Visiting Professor at Waseda University in Tokyo. His books include *Capital as Will and Imagination: Schumpeter's Guide to the Postwar Japanese Miracle* (Cornell University Press, 2013) and, with Simon Bytheway, *Central Banks and Gold: How Tokyo, London, and New York Shaped the Modern World* (Cornell University Press, 2016). Concerning the late twentieth century, he has also written "Toward a financial history of Japan's long stagnation, 1990–2003" (*Journal of Asian Studies*, May 2008) and "Japan: the arc of industrialization" (*New Cambridge History of Japan*, 2023).

Kazushi Minami is Associate Professor at the Osaka School of International Public Policy, Osaka University, Japan. His first book, *People's Diplomacy: How Americans and Chinese Transformed US-China Relations*, is under contract with Cornell University Press. His articles have appeared in *Cold War History, Diplomatic History*, and the *Journal of Women's History*. He is currently at work on his second book project, which examines the role of oil in postwar international relations of East Asia.

David S. Painter taught International History at Georgetown University for thirty-one years before retiring at the end of 2020. His publications include *Oil and the American Century: The Political Economy of U.S. Foreign Oil Policy, 1941–1954* (Johns Hopkins University Press, 1986); *The Cold War: An International History* (Routledge, 1999); *Origins of the Cold War: An International History* (co-edited with Melvyn P. Leffler) (Routledge, 1994, 2005); *The Struggle for Iran: Oil, Autocracy, and the Cold War, 1951–54* (co-authored with Gregory Brew) (University of North Carolina Press, 2023); and articles on oil and international affairs, US policy toward the Third World, and the Cold War.

Shigeru Sato is Professor of History of Tax and Social Policy at the Tohoku Gakuin University, Sendai, Japan. His major publications include *Yuragu Chuukansou to Fukushikokka* [*The Wavering Middle Class and the Welfare States*] (ed. with Masayuki Takahashi, Susumu Nishioka, and Yasushi Kondo) (Minerva Shobou, 2023); *Zaiseishakaigaku to ha Nanika* [*Fiscal Science for Analyzing Real Society*] (ed. with Eisaku Ide, Shintaro Kurachi, Masato Furuichi, Ryo Muramatsu, and Seiichiro Mozumi) (Yuhikaku Publishing Co., Ltd., 2022); and *Sozei Teikou no Zaiseigaku* [*Public Finance of the Tax Resistance*] (with Furuichi Masato) (Iwanami Shoten, 2014). He was awarded the Susumu Sato Prize from the Japan Institute of Local Public Finance in May 2014.

Ikuto Yamaguchi is a Professor in the Department of History, Nara University, Japan. He has contributed chapters to "The development and activities of the Economic Commission for Asia and the Far East (ECAFE)" in *The Transformation of the International Order of Asia: Decolonization, the Cold War, and the Colombo Plan* (Routledge, 2015); "Anglo-American 'economic' special relationship" in *Igirisu to Amerika: Sekaichitsujyo wo Kizuita Yonhyaku-nen [The History of Anglo-American Relationship: Four Hundred Years that Made the World Order]* (Keiso-shobou, 2016); and "ECAFE and Asian industrialization strategies" in *Reisen-Henyouki no Kokusai-Kaihatu-Enjo to Ajia [The International Development Aid and Asia under the Transformation of Cold War Order in the 1960s]* (Minerva Shobou, 2017).

Index

Printed in the USA
CPSIA information can be obtained
at www.ICGtesting.com
LVHW011620260424
778545LV00003B/327

9 781350 413801